Unveiling Ter
Fundamentalism, a̶n̶d̶ ̶S̶p̶
Abuse

By Bill Whitehouse

Published 2009
Printed in the
United States

Cover Design by: Dave Wickersham
Interior design by: Interrogative Imperati ve Institute
Published by: Bilquees Press

Table of Contents

A Fate Worse Than Death

Let us begin with an observation. Under many circumstances, there seem to be, at least, two sets of, seemingly, antagonistic forces at work in human consciousness. One set of such forces is given expression through our struggle to discover the truth of things, while the other set of opposing forces is a manifestation of a tendency to hide, distort, or rebel against whatever the truth may be.

Deciding which is which in any given instance is not always an easy or problem-free task. Consequently, various kinds of methodologies are sought and/or developed in order to deal with the problem of trying to differentiate that which is true from that which is not true.

There are philosophical, scientific, theological, mathematical, psychological, mythological, sociological, political, economic and mystical methods for engaging the challenge of determining the truth. We tend to derive paradigms of meaning through the exercise of these methodologies, and these frameworks organize, shape, color, generate, and orient our interpretations and understandings of where we feel truth and falsehood are to be located within the realm of experience.

In addition to the aforementioned two, broad, kinds of force, there also is a third set of forces at work in consciousness. This involves a tendency toward dissociation – which is neither a function of truth nor falsehood, but is, instead, an attractor-like basin which constantly pulls at us like a maelstrom via the currents from certain facets of the horizons of our awareness.

Dissociation is an experience consisting of a pervasive sense of having lost essential contact with: meaning, purpose, direction, belonging, acceptance, identity, and reality. The presence of dissociation gives rise to intense, often overpowering and debilitating, feelings of anxiety, fear, depersonalization, de-realization, alienation, emptiness, disconnection, cynicism, doubt, depression, sadness, hopelessness, and anomie.

The foregoing needs to be distinguished, to some extent, from many of the traditional, psychiatric modes of referring to the phenomenon of dissociation in which so-called dissociative disorders tend, in a sense, to be considered synonymous with the experience of dissociation. I would like to differentiate between, on the one hand, the trauma of a dissociative experience -- as outlined in the preceding paragraph -- and the pathological coping strategies and defense mechanisms which may arise in response to the trauma of dissociation.

From this perspective, the so-called dissociative disorders are an individual's maladaptive responses to the continued presence of the intense pain of dissociative phenomenology. Dissociative disorders are the problems which arise — such as multiple personality disorder, fugue states, and the like — in reaction to the presence of dissociative trauma, but there is a difference between the trauma (over which the person may have little control) and the disorder which arises in relation to that trauma -- a disorder whose characteristics may reflect choices (such as they are) as well as individual vulnerabilities and/or inclinations of the person who develops such disorders. These disorders entail life problems for the individual because of their debilitating quality, but the existence of such problems seems to be a better proposition for an individual than the intense pain of the dissociative trauma which leads to the formation of symptoms inherent in a given disorder.

We seek meaning in our everyday lives and in relation to the big questions of existence because, among other things, if we don't, we tend to drift into the gravitational pull of dissociation. In fact, the experience of dissociation is so painful (and we all have had encounters with this condition) that, in many cases we may not care whether the meanings through which we run our lives are true, or not ... just as long as the howling, vicious dogs of dissociation are kept at bay.

Philosophy, science, technology, hobbies, games, careers, television, athletics, politics, social relationships, shopping, war, religion, therapy, and addictions are among the ways we use to, on the one hand, avoid listening to the call of dissociation, by, on the other hand, seeking to invest our lives with meaning, irrespective of whether such meaning-structures may, or may not, have relevance to the truth in some ultimate sense. Truth may have priority in the scheme of things, but living in accordance with falsehood, whatever the associated problems may be, beats having to deal with the extreme unpleasantness and debilitation of dissociative states.

Whenever the promise of meaning enters our lives, we are induced to cross an emotional/physiological boundary which brings, — to varying degrees -- feelings of direction, purpose, identity, value, pleasure, happiness, belief, and motivation in conjunction with whatever the nature of such meaning may be. The more essential we feel such a sense of meaning to be, the more intense tend to be the emotions which are experienced in conjunction with such meaning.

In some instances (but not all) the rise of an interest in mystical pursuits (which may be scientifically explored through transpersonal psychology) may occur in individuals who currently are struggling, or have been struggling for quite some time, with the currents of dissociation. For such people, the usual array of meanings associated with society, family, career, education, activities, as well as relationships have lost their attractiveness or appeal, and, at the very least, are seen as being unable to provide answers to the great questions of life – such as: Who am I? Why am I here? What is the purpose of life? How do I find the truth(s) about being? To what should I commit my time, energy, and resources?

If such people are strong, they may have tried a variety of different things in a search to distance themselves from the intensely uncomfortable feelings of dissociation. Yet, in one way or another, if what has been tried has not been successful in assuaging the demons of dissociation, then they may be left with a taste of disappointment and a sense of promise having gone astray as they continue to try to manage the rest of their lives as best they can amidst the undertow of dissociation.

Some people refer to this quest in terms of a 'holy longing' -- a desire for direct experience of the sacred realms and the Divine. One feels within oneself a deep thirst and hunger for an ineffable 'something' – something beyond the ordinary doors of experience and perception ... something more essential and satisfyingly meaningful ... something life-defining.

Quite a few individuals spend their whole lives in pursuit of this elusive, mystical will-o-the-wisp. When the quest gets bogged down in this or that way, they wonder if, perhaps, mysticism is all just a figment of the imagination.

Then, it happens. They meet up, somehow, with a person or group which seems to offer an antidote to the poisons of dissociative trauma, and it is important to understand just how central and important such an event is in the life of an individual.

Unfortunately, all of us are a lot closer to dissociative dissolution than we may care to admit. We busily fill up the hours of our life with all manner of activity. Much of this activity is senseless. Moreover, there often is a frenetic quality to a great deal of our behavior in which issues of education, career, work, home, politics, hobbies, and leisure time become the basic sources of meaning-giving in our lives ... after all, if we don't derive essential meaning from such activities, then really, who are we, and what is life actually about, and what should be our true purpose?

For most of us -- some sooner than others -- the capacity of normal life to supply us with the kind of meaningfulness into which we can sink our essence or soul begins to suffer from the law of diminishing returns. The more this sense of dissolution takes place, the more the threat of the pain of dissociative trauma looms on the horizon.

Some people, when they face this Rubicon of life, retreat into ever more frantic commitment to the surface features of life -- such as career, politics, family, home, and community activities. Other individuals, however, cannot go back and need something deeper in their lives to provide them with a sense of essential meaning, purpose, and identity, and so they cross into a battle with the unknown.

With respect to the latter group of people, there tends to be a sense of urgency about their search. Part of this urgency comes from a vague sense of the enormity of the task in front of them and the concomitant realization that they cannot do what they need to do without some expert help ... someone to guide them through the unknown territory on the far shore.

Another part of the aforementioned urgency arises from the ominous threat of dissociative trauma nipping at their soul. They have sailed into the unknown, and they don't know if they will find anything on the other side ... something which will help defend them against the maelstrom of dissociation which could suck them down into a bottomless abyss arising from a loss of meaning, identity, purpose, peace, and stability with respect to lived existence.

Yet, when someone who, supposedly, is a spiritual guide or teacher enters their lives, an apparently viable solution to the impending threat of dissociative trauma appears to take concrete, accessible form. When such an alleged guide appears to be charismatic, interesting, warm, friendly, compassionate, entertaining, wise, calm, and in control of her or his life, then this all seems like manna from heaven.

They experience -- and it makes no difference, at the time, whether such experiences are rooted in truth or falsehood -- a deep, powerful,

8

intense sense of apparent (possibly real) love, acceptance, purpose, direction, honesty, compassion, kindness, generosity, identity, integrity, commitment, happiness, and community at the hands of a 'teacher' or those who are influenced by such a 'teacher'. Among other things that are going on emotionally and psychologically, enkephalins and endorphins begin to flow in such substantial quantities that one may feel an encompassing sense of joy, ecstasy, happiness, well-being, peace, and security.

One feels one has arrived at one's metaphysical, cosmic home. Furthermore, everything which is happening is framed in a way that suggests that what is going on is an expression of the presence of spiritual or mystical truth.

Such a framing may be accurate, as far as it goes, or it may be false. However, in the beginning, the individual has no way of knowing for sure what is going on except that the demons of dissociation have dissipated, and the presence of a dynamic paradigm of meaning has entered one's life.

In the imagery of the <u>Velveteen Rabbit</u> by Margery Williams, one feels that the presence of love, and associated qualities, has, finally, made one 'real', whole, alive, aware, and integrated. Whether this is really so, remains to be seen, but considerable time, experience, inquiry, and reflection will be necessary before one has enough information to be able to arrive at a reasonable assessment of the situation ... especially if certain facts are being actively kept from one's awareness, as is generally the case with respect to fraudulent spiritual guides.

There are people who claim that they could tell, instantaneously -- or within a very short period of time -- whether, or not, a given individual is an authentic, sincere teacher. There may be some people who are sufficiently gifted to do this, but there are, I believe, far fewer people who actually are capable of this than there are individuals who are making claims in this regard on their own behalf ... and, in the present context, I would eliminate from consideration those individuals who reject all such possibilities simply because they are inveterate cynics and skeptics concerning everything spiritual and/or mystical, and, therefore, are in no position to make a fair and knowing discernment about these sorts of matters since their perceptions are colored and shaped by the constant presence of cynicism and skepticism.

In the beginning, Hazrat Ahmad al-Alawi – a Sufi saint of the 20th century about whom Martin Lings wrote -- did not know the difference between someone who was a snake-charmer and someone who was a spiritual sage. Similarly, Hazrat al-Ghazali and Jalal-uddin Rumi each took time to find their respective ways to the truth of things with respect to mysticism.

For every rule of thumb one can come up with as a line of demarcation for discerning true teachers from false ones, there are exceptions to such a rule ... both on the side of legitimacy as well as in relation to spiritual charlatans. In instances where the quality of spiritual counterfeiting is poor, many of us may be able to gauge that some sort of fraudulent activity is going on, but when the quality of counterfeiting is high, distinguishing between the real and the false is very problematic.

Consequently, becoming entangled in a false modality of mysticism is not all that a difficult thing to do ... some people's opinion to the contrary notwithstanding. More importantly, once one's life has become immersed in such a group – one with the 'right' sort of dynamic 'guide'-- there are many emotional, psychological, and social forces which are capable of deepening such entanglement in very complex, subtle, and problematic ways.

For example, if one is faced with the prospect -- whether through personal choice or the decision of the group/teacher -- of leaving a given teacher or group, then an individual is very much aware that waiting for one on the other side of the boundary (which marks the boundary separating those who are within the group and those who are without) is the abyss of dissociation. Under such circumstances, the threat of the terrors of dissociation are even more ominous because of an intense sense of relative deprivation which is experienced in being disconnected from a way of life through which one previously derived the sum total of one's orientation to: God, meaning, purpose, identity, truth, reality, community, commitment, trust, love, self, direction, acceptance, peace, happiness, the world, and the life to come, as compared to the painful offerings of dissociation ... anxiety, fear, alienation, meaninglessness, purposelessness, depersonalization, de-realization, depression, sadness, grief, and so on which are beckoning to one due to one's departure from the aforementioned group.

When I first began to explore the dynamic character of the

10

relationship between various kinds of meaningfulness and the threat of dissociation, one of the images which came to mind was the following:

Meaningfulness) | (Dissociation

The line in the middle constitutes the potentially neutral ground between dissociation and meaningfulness. This middle area gives expression to the activities through which we seek to determine the way to meaning, objectivity, and 'truth'. It is the area within which we struggle for understanding and knowledge about how best to proceed.

When the methodological and hermeneutical activity of this middle area is successful, it helps to serve as a defense against the threat of being pulled into one, or another, state of dissociation. When such activity is not productive, then we struggle to resist the slide toward dissociative states involving anxiety, alienation, anomie, overwhelming stress, fear, loss of identity, and so on, which, in turn, may open us up to more pathological states such as P.T.S.D, an anxiety or dissociative disorder, or some other problematic condition.

With respect to the foregoing diagram, it is important to understand that meaningfulness and/or altered states do not necessarily equate with the truth of things. Rather, we may seek meaning and altered states in order to protect ourselves against being consumed by the ravages of one species, or another, of dissociation.

Furthermore, the phenomenology of going across the boundary into the realm of meaningfulness and/or altered states is experienced as being very pleasurable, if not given to ecstasy. In addition, this boundary crossing is also felt to be tremendously liberating ... as if one were 'born again' or had come to see 'reality' for the first time.

Once one has undergone such a boundary transition, one seeks to maintain it or re-invoke it because this realm -- when it is intensely felt (as often is the case in many experiences of conversion or initiation into a new spiritual tradition) -- brings one into a state of awareness which tends to dissolve a variety of concerns or worries. One feels like one is in a dream-like state which is both very real and, yet, somehow removed from the rest of life.

Similarly -- but in an opposite, antagonistic manner -- the phenomenology of traversing the boundary into the realm of dissociation is experienced as being extremely painful and debilitating. In many ways, the emotional, existential, and spiritual pain, together with

11

the dysfunctional life, which arise through conditions of dissociation -- such as alienation, anomie, de-realization, depersonalization, stress, confusion, uncertainty, loss of identity, purposelessness, and anxiety -- is so intense that for many individuals, dissociation is a 'fate worse than death'. Moreover, many people prefer the problems of becoming pathological – in the form of a maladaptive coping strategy -- to the presence of dissociative pain simply because in such pathology there is a certain buffering quality against the felt presence of dissociation.

In phenomenological terms, when an individual travels from within the arc of meaningfulness noted in the previous diagram back across the boundary toward the center portion and, possibly, toward dissociation, this process is felt to be quite disorienting, difficult, stressful, and emotionally painful. Alternatively, when one journeys from within the arc of dissociation toward either the center portion of the diagram or toward the boundary-arc of meaningfulness, this process is experienced as being very positive, liberating, and happy.

Given the choice between having meaning, even if possibly false, and being engulfed in a dissociative condition, not everyone will opt for the latter possibility -- even though the latter option might appear to be closer to the current truth of things than is the former. Given such difficult choices, one may wish to linger over the decision and not rush to judgment.

In view of the bleak nature of the alternatives facing one, an individual might desperately try to reconcile seemingly disparate experiences, events, or pieces of information in a manner that favors perpetuating meaning (even if false) over the possibility of sliding into dissociation. Confronted with such extremes of emotional consequences, a person might be forgiven if she or he wished to extend a few degrees of freedom to the inexplicable and, as a result, give the current framework of meaning -- problematic though it may be -- the benefit of a doubt, rather than plunge into the cold, dark waters of dissociation ... even though the latter action may be the step which is most courageous, honest, sincere, and truthful.

In the face of such diametrically opposite considerations, one lives in the interstitial shadows of ambiguity, uncertainty, doubt, ignorance, the unknown ... a harbinger of things to come if one should move further across the emotional and psychological boundary which marks departure from the teacher and/or group. This is an extremely painful position to be in, and the motivational forces are extremely strong in relation to inducing one to not only refrain from crossing the aforementioned boundary, but, as well, to get rid of the doubts and suspicions one is entertaining, for occupying a state of emotional limbo is almost as bad -- but not really -- as entering into the state of dissociation on the other side of said boundary.

In most cases, unless a person can be motivated to trust the reasonableness of moving into dissociation -- and the move is very counter-intuitive for most of us -- then there is a strong likelihood that a person will stay with a paradigm of meaning which, though flawed in substantial ways, seems to be more emotionally satisfying than does the prospect of dissociation ... especially if an individual sees no readily available hope for finding a worthwhile exit from the condition of dissociation once the current source of meaningfulness is left behind. Furthermore, the threat of continued dissociation is one of the primary reasons why some individuals -- even after they manage to escape from a environment of thought control and spiritual abuse -- will tend to seek out further abusive relationships, just to get another fix of the emotional and psychological 'Baba juice' (see the next paragraph) that often is associated with the crossing-over of the boundary which separates meaningfulness from dissociation ... the same boundary which, when re-crossed in the opposite direction (i.e., from meaning to dissociation), causes withdrawal-like symptoms due to the debilitating character of the dissociative symptoms that are encountered by an individual.

'Baba' means spiritual father, and the phrase 'Baba juice' is a term I have coined to allude to the trance-like state of ecstasy, liberation, contentment, and sense of well-being which occurs in some people when they are in the presence of a fraudulent spiritual guide. It is a very pleasant altered state of consciousness to be in but it is not a spiritually constructive condition ... in fact, quite the opposite.

Patterns of attitude formation, motivational networks, and habits tend to be rooted in what operant learning theorists refer to as a variable, intermittent schedule of reward contingencies. That is, something of a rewarding nature occurs in conjunction with a certain kind of activity, but, in subsequent life experiences, such rewards may not occur, except occasionally (if at all) but one continues on with such activity in the hope that a hoped-for reward will be forthcoming.

13

Once established, such learning linkages are very difficult to break. The gambler who rolls the dice one more time, the addict who seeks to recreate the first high, the promiscuous lover in search of the chemistry of that initial encounter of intimacy that came through the gaze or touch of another person, the seeker who longs for the return of an earlier feeling of ecstasy, well-being, peace, innocence, purpose, and meaning that occurred in relation with the meeting of a given 'teacher' – these are all potential examples of the principle of a variable, intermittent reinforcement contingency in action.

Although, ultimately, the only thing which can extricate someone from such forces is Grace' of one kind or another, nonetheless, if one looks at the dynamics of the phenomenon from a lesser perspective, then oftentimes, the only way to break free of the gravitational pull of such a set of circumstances (that is, the presence of variable, intermittent schedules of reinforcement, together with the desire to retain a sense of meaning, even if false, over the threat of impending dissociative states) is through the experience of traumatic events. In other words, if something happens between an individual and the teacher and/or religious/spiritual group with which that person is associating that violates -- in no unmistakable way -- the trust which ties that individual to the teacher/group, then the trauma of that betrayal of trust may supply enough impetus to help an individual to cross the boundary into a dissociative condition and accept the reality of the latter state rather than continue on with a meaning system which has become spiritually bankrupt.

The process of traversing the border that demarcates previous meaning (false though it might have been) and present dissociation is marked by a profound sadness and depression which tends to occur when a person begins to disengage from a teacher and/or group and is an expression of the individual's sense of having been disconnected from the feeling of being 'real' and in touch with the truth ... if only in a passing, indirect, and limited fashion.

At times, the pain which is felt in this condition of essential, dissociative betrayal is so intense that a person may become vulnerable to being induced to re-crossing the boundary back into what is perceived as the framework of meaning which, previously, was associated with the alleged spiritual guide or group. Oftentimes, one will see an individual bounce back and forth across this boundary line before some final

14

context of relative stability is achieved on one side, or the other, of the boundary line which separates continued association with the teacher and/or group from emotional and psychological disengagement.

The techniques which are used by fraudulent spiritual teachers and/or groups to induce people to not cross the boundary line that demarcates being initiated into a framework of such pseudo-meaning (as opposed to the real and essential meaningfulness of truth) from a condition of dissociative vulnerability are numerous. These include: Ericksonian-like hypnosis; trance inductions or other forms of altered states of consciousness; love-bombing; isolation; sleep deprivation; neuro-linguistic programming; various forms of variable, intermittent schedules of reinforcement; re-framing; misdirection; disinformation; prolonged conditions of ambiguity or tension; disruption of normal forms of social support; as well as the use of one's dependence on processes of consensual validation to undermine one's sense of reality.

The foregoing are but a few of the techniques that are employed to open up unsuspecting people to the 'joys' of being released from a condition of dissociation, The term "joys" is a collective way of referring to the administering of the 'Baba-juice' which takes place when one is given a new paradigm of meaning in an apparently extremely attractive package by someone: who claims to be an authentic spiritual guide (but who is not, in truth, genuine); who seems to be the best friend one could ever have hoped for; and who appears to be an immense 'blessing' which has come to one which is so great that, heretofore, one could never have imagined it possible for such a person to be in one's life.

The above characterizes one's experiences until one learns otherwise. However, coming to know the ins and outs of this 'otherwise' may be quite a few years down the road when, once again, one stares into the abyss of dissociation ... an abyss which has been made deeper, darker, and more hostile by the fact that one seemed to be so close to the truth only to find one has been kept far from the truth of many things -- including the actual nature of the teacher and, most importantly, one's own relationship with one's essential potential since a fraudulent guide cannot help one realize that about which such charlatans are fundamentally ignorant, though they pretend otherwise, and, for a time, one may have trusted that such people were telling the truth.

15

For lack of a better phrase, the foregoing approach to the issue of spiritual abuse is known as the mirror image theory. It bears this name because of the character of the dynamics that occur at the boundary marker of demarcation between meaning and dissociation.

As one goes from relative dissociation into meaning, there is a gaining of a sense of freedom, release, peace, security, purpose, identity, acceptance, belonging, commitment, and so on which was not present in the condition of dissociation. As previously indicated, this is experienced as being joyful, happy, ecstatic, unburdening.

However, as one crosses back across the boundary in the opposite direction -- that is, from meaning back to relative dissociation -- one experiences the pain of losing a sense of freedom, release, peace, security, purpose, identity, acceptance, belonging and commitment. Instead, one feels shame, anxiety, guilt, depression, grief, sadness, depersonalization, de-realization, loss of identity, purpose, motivation, and the like. In other words, one's feelings and condition in this situation of dissociation are the mirror image of, or a direct reversal of, what was experienced as one crossed over into the so-called meaning side of the boundary marker.

When an individual comes to understand the nature of the spiritual abuse which has been perpetrated upon him or her, there is a certain, new realization which occurs ... however inarticulate and vague this sort of realization may be. In this awareness, there is a sense that by having permitted oneself to be induced to cross the boundary from dissociation, or threatened dissociation, to the promised land of meaningfulness in the form of a relation with a certain alleged teacher or guide or group, one has made a maladaptive choice in coping strategy vis-à-vis the issue of dissociative trauma. Moreover, from a certain perspective, one's situation is worse than it was prior to one's encounter with the fraudulent teacher ... one has gone from the frying pan into the fire.

Prior to the appearance of the so-called teacher, there was a certain innocence, and, perhaps, naiveté, to one's search for meaningfulness. Once betrayed, however, in an essential way, one feels cast adrift in the middle of nowhere with nothing to defend one against the breaking storm of dissociation.

One is left with a feeling that there is no safe harbor to protect one and no direction which one can trust. These are intense, destabilizing, and debilitating emotions which were not there prior to the advent of

16

the so-called teacher.

Any program of counseling or therapy which does not take into account the profoundly intense dynamics of this boundary crossing phenomena described in this essay (and what is entailed going in either direction) will have a difficult time helping a person to develop survival strategies with which to cope with the condition of dissociation. Moreover, failure to take such boundary dynamics into account may do considerable spiritual damage to the affected individual by leaving unaddressed the essential dimension of the grief which is at the heart of the re-entry process involving the condition of dissociation.

Although the mirror image theory which has been outlined above has been applied to a context of spiritual abuse, the potential relevancy of this framework does not end there. In whatever set of circumstances the issue of abuse arises -- spousal, sexual, political, educational, or spiritual -- the dynamics of the mirror image phenomenon are present, and if one wishes to gain insight into the nature of such abuse one should look at the way the threat of dissociation plays off against the struggle for meaning -- even of a pathological kind -- in the structuring of relationships.

Finally, from the perspective of this mirror image theory, there is a potential vulnerability in all of us with respect to the possibility of being induced to flee from the threat of dissociative trauma and into the embrace of paradigms of meaning. On the surface, such frameworks of meaning may appear to be a God-send, but, in reality they may turn out to be just another expression of the sort of problems which arise when we are trying to elude the undertow of the maelstrom of dissociation which haunts consciousness, and, as a result, we do not clearly see the nature of the alternative we are selecting as our way of responding to the presence of dissociative pain in our lives.

Under the right set of circumstances, almost all of us are vulnerable to committing such a mistake in judgment ... and not necessarily because of any personal failing within us, or due to stupidity, or insincerity, or any other defect of character. Rather, we are all vulnerable to such a possibility, because of the very nature of being human − a nature which is constantly being stalked by the very real threat of dissociative trauma, and with respect to which, we are constantly under pressure to discover viable ways of dodging such an existential bullet.

2.) <u>The Construction of Reality</u>

Cardinal Law -- lately of the archdiocese of Boston but, now, having been forced to resign in disgrace from that position -- is a sign, for all of us. He knew about the molestation and sexual improprieties going on, and, yet, for decades, he continued to put parishioners in harm's way, without, apparently, even trying to take effective steps to bring the tragedy to an end ... both in relation to the abused as well as with respect to the abusers. He just kept moving the perpetrators around without telling people about the evil which was being parachuted into their communities and without appropriate safeguards being put into place to ensure that parish children would not be placed in harm's way.

Even in those cases where someone has had the courage to speak up and seek to address such situations –whether administratively, legally, or in other ways -- there are many obstacles to overcome, along with an array of daunting biases with which to struggle. For example, there have been a variety of instances reported where some parishioners were angry that action was being taken against this or that abusive priest because, well, it was upsetting to those parishioners. Apparently, the entire matter was quite inconvenient for the latter individuals because of the way the exposé brought doubt, uncertainty and anxiety into their lives, as well as the manner in which it disrupted the life of the parish.

In addition, the issue was just so embarrassing for everyone. The situation undermined the peace of mind of these parishioners. Wasn't anyone concerned about the opportunity that such a public washing of dirty linen gave to those seeking to point accusing fingers at Catholics?

Consequently, oftentimes, anger, resentment, hostility, and vilification, would be directed toward those who had been abused. Surely, the latter individuals were lying, and/or seeking publicity, and/or were trouble-makers, and/or wanted to make money, and/or were angry about their own misery or lack of worldly success and were merely trying to shift responsibility for their own short-comings to others, and/or such people were crazy, and/or were alcoholics, drug addicts, people of low moral character, sexual degenerates, and/or social activists agitating to advance their own dubious agenda, and/or people who, for some irrational reason, harbored resentments with respect to hard-working, spiritual men, or against religion, or toward God.

The abused should have kept their mouth shut. They should have gone about things quietly. They should have thought about the ramifications for others instead of being so damn self-centered and self-absorbed. They should have turned the other cheek. They should have remembered the beam in their own eye rather than whine about the mote in the eyes of others. They should have followed the advice about letting him who is without sin cast the first stone. They should have abided by the decision of those who are in authority and who know much more about spirituality than the abused. They should have left it to God and just got on with their lives.

One of the most gut-wrenching, emotionally draining, and spiritually depressing dimensions of circumstances involving spiritual abuse – of whatever variety – is that almost everyone has a vested interest which they wish to protect and, for such reasons, they really don't want to hear what an abused person might have to say. Whenever abused people try to bring their abuse to the attention of others -- even family and friends -- the people who have been abused tend to be met with all manner of: disbelief, anger, hostility, fear, hatred, resentment, suspicion, ridicule, character attacks, shunning, attempts to censor or discredit, as well as campaigns of threats, intimidation, and more.

In the process, the abused get exposed to more abuse. As a result, the abused feel even more alienated, depressed, rejected, and alone than they do already.

Many people want silence to be maintained about such issues, because they don't want to be put in a position where they have to choose and make a moral stand which conflicts with what they perceive to be their vested interests in the matter. Before the abused person came along and began blabbing, those in whom the abused person tried to confide (and, initially, such people often are members of the same group), had – or, so the latter supposed – purpose, peace, meaning, identity, community, knowledge, position, status, understanding, happiness, stability, methodology, faith, certitude, trust, a guide, and so on.

These people don't want anything upsetting their spiritual and existential applecart. If one were to listen, with care and consideration, to the events and issues that an abused person is trying to relate, then one might have to begin questioning the validity and truth of everything of importance in one's life. After all, if the integrity of a teacher, priest, minister, educator, or politician is being called into serious question, one may no longer be certain with respect to how to go about distinguishing between truth and falsehood – given that the spiritual compass one has relied on, for some time, is none other than the very person or persons whose virtue and moral character are being called into question.

20

Someone once e-mailed a certain internet Sufi discussion group and made an announcement about the existence of a Sufi Spiritual Abuse Recovery Assistance Group which had been created and was accessible to anyone who might feel the need of interacting with other individuals in order to learn more about such issues. The notice concerning the aforementioned spiritual abuse group was made in the other Sufi group, but there was an editorial comment attached to the posting.

In effect, the added comment went something like the following: if you have a question, go to your spiritual guide; if you have a problem, go to your spiritual guide; if you have doubts, go to your spiritual guide; if your faith feels vulnerable, go to your spiritual guide. The person who added this editorial comment to the notice about a spiritual abuse group just doesn't get it.

How can one go the spiritual guide if that person is at the very epicenter of all one's questions, problems, doubts, and uncertainties? To be sure, while pursuing a spiritual path, all seekers are likely to encounter the whisperings and the machinations of the ego. Such forces will seek to undermine the resolve of anyone who steps onto the mystical path, and one of the techniques used by such forces in order to accomplish this is by going to work on weakening an initiate's relationship with the spiritual guide through the raising of certain kinds of doubts, questions, and so on in relation to the teacher.

However, the sexual exploitation of a spiritual seeker by an alleged spiritual guide is not an instance of such whisperings and machinations. Furthermore, the use of lies, deceit, duplicity, manipulation, force, fear, intimidation, and authoritarian impositions in order to control how people think, feel, and behave is not a function of such whisperings and manipulation either.

Yet, so-called spiritual guides who are well-versed in various techniques of undue influence are so clever and subtle in the way they spin their webs that one is often left wondering whether one is actually witnessing what one feels one is witnessing. Even veteran politicians of the most corrupt kind would have a great deal to learn about how to spin and re-frame things in order to be able to keep people off-balance and puzzled about the actual nature of what is going on.

Because of the foregoing possibilities, abused people who are disclosing their experiences are often seeking consensual validation from other people who are involved in the same group situation. They want to be told that what is going on is not in their imagination, or that what is going on shouldn't be going on, and that the tales one is being told by the alleged spiritual guide are just a means of misdirection to take attention away from the actual character of the abusive behavior.

Yet, when an abused begins to speak out, people often do not listen. Damn the abused for opening his or her mouth and raising such terrible issues. Damn the abused for caring and wanting to warn people about someone – the teacher – who is actively harming those who are staking their whole lives on the veracity and alleged spirituality of such an individual. Damn the abused for making one feel so vulnerable and confused. Damn the abused for inducing one to question one's own motives and the intention of the so-called guide. Damn the abused for throwing into doubt one's assumed place in Paradise. Damn the abused for waking one from spiritual slumber. Damn the abused for undermining one's sense of being among the spiritual elite and chosen. Damn the abused for introducing factual evidence which indicates that people are being conned, swindled, cheated, lied to, manipulated, misinformed, and turned into obedient servants of evil. Damn the abused for making people feel like fools because they have turned over the keys to their hearts, minds, finances, talents, time, resources, and lives to a spiritual fraud. Damn the abused for raising the possibility that one has been wasting x-years of one's life.

The process which one goes through when one attempts to warn people about a spiritually abusive individual who professes to be a spiritual teacher is a very instructive one. It has taught me a great deal about myself and other people ... people whom I thought were my friends and people whom I thought cared about me or even loved me ... people whom I have lived with ... people whom I believed trusted me ... people who have known me for years and who have never known me to lie and who have sought out my assistance and counsel in many matters across the years ... people whom I would never have believed would have been capable of lying, manipulation, and deceit with respect to their interaction with me ... people who were willing to abandon relationships -- which had seen us sail many stormy seas together – without losing a moment's sleep over it ... people who were willing to believe lies about me simply because someone they trusted (but shouldn't have) told them that the lies were true (just as Joseph Goebbels, the Nazi Minister of Propaganda, had taught his staff to do) and without them giving any consideration to such trifling details such as the

22

truth of the matter concerning me, or the giving of evidence, or verification of such allegations.

Many of us are largely unaware of just how powerful some of the psychological and social forces are which manifest themselves in group dynamics or in the context of a teacher-student relationship. Or, perhaps, a more accurate way of saying this is that many of us have some awareness of these sort of forces but believe the latter are not all that powerful or apply to others, for the most part, and not us.

When someone carries the label of spiritual teacher, or guide, or leader, many people automatically will consider whatever such individuals say as being: without question; authoritative; true; sincere; based on acquired knowledge of a deep kind; expressions of Divine wisdom, and so on. This is so even though we may not be able to verify one thing the alleged teacher or leader says.

Degrees of freedom are automatically awarded to such individuals by many individuals such that whatever theses so-called spiritual guides or leaders say and do is assumed to be a manifestation of mystical, professional, secret, spiritual insight and understanding that has been gifted to them across many years of ascetic practices or work ... even though we may have never seen them perform any of these austerities and even though we are not privy to the precise nature of their relationship with Divinity. These same degrees of freedom are not likely to be extended to someone we meet on the street or even someone who is a friend if either of the latter were to begin espousing this or that kind of spiritual treatise.

There is a phenomenon in social psychology which is known as the 'halo effect'. This effect gives expression to the tendency within many of us that when we find people to be physically attractive, quite a few of tend to be willing to assign other positive qualities to those people as well ... irrespective of what the truth of the matter may be. Similarly, if we consider people to be physically unattractive, then many of us often are inclined to assign other negative qualities to those people quite independently of the realities of such situations.

When someone is called a spiritual teacher -- and the person is charming, charismatic, interesting, fun to be with, or plays a musical instrument, and the like – the very fact of the 'teacher-label' – together with whatever quality is displayed by the teacher which we, personally, find to be appealing and attractive in that teacher – then, these two factors are enough, quite frequently, to induce many people to assume (without verification) that such a person has many other positive qualities as well. In other words, we are dealing with a slight variation on the 'halo effect' outlined above.

No one really knows why there is this tendency in human beings. I'm only concerned, at the moment, with the fact that such a phenomenon does exist.

The presence of the 'halo effect' tends to induce us to lower our defenses and render us more receptive to whatever an alleged spiritual guide, minister, or leader has to say, and this tends to make us more vulnerable to whatever sorts of influence might be manifested through such an individual.

There is a reason why advertising often features sexually attractive men and women. Both sex appeal, as well as attractiveness, help generate a powerful halo effect which can shape how people think and feel about products and issues – there are also other themes involving modeling and learning theory that are applicable here, but, for the moment, the focus is on the way the presence of the 'halo effect' can affect our judgment and perceptions of reality.

To go in a slightly different but not unconnected direction, Henry Kissinger once said words to the effect that the greatest aphrodisiac was power. What greater power could there be than to be in the presence of a 'friend of God' or a person of immense political power? To be close to such an individual is heady stuff. Furthermore, to have such an individual know our name and to take an apparent interest in us and our lives and to be willing to help one, is often quite intoxicating and exhilarating.

This is another kind of halo effect at work. If one is in close proximity to a 'friend' of God, then perhaps, one is chosen and special just like this alleged Divine emissary is. One basks in the glow of juxtaposition, and one feels (or hopes or anticipates) that some of the assumed qualities of God's agent may belong -- in some lesser fashion of course, to oneself -- as well ... even though there may be little, or no, evidence to support the reality of such beliefs.

Quite a few years ago, Robert Rosenthal wrote about a phenomenon which he dubbed the 'Pygmalion Effect'. To make a long study short, he found he could alter the degree of academic success among randomly selected students merely by getting teachers to believe that such students possessed certain kinds of intellectual potential. By altering the expectations of teachers, he was able to show that these altered

24

expectations led to significantly better academic performance in those students who had been randomly selected and labeled as students who were ready for academic success as compared with other children for whom such expectations had not been indicated to the teachers. Teachers began to pay more attention to the 'designated' students and extend assistance to them ... assistance which previously was not being extended to those students. The teachers began to be more receptive to what these individuals said and did ... now 'seeing' intelligence and ability where, before, the teachers had 'seen' not much of anything.

If reality is 'framed' in certain ways (whether by a clever psychologist, experimenter, sales person, politician, leader, or an alleged spiritual guide), we tend to develop beliefs and expectations in accordance with the nature of the framing process. In school settings, this can lead to academic success or failure among students (because there is also a 'negative' Pygmalion Effect with which all too many students are familiar) according to the expectations that teachers have of such students ... and in spiritual circles, as well, the 'Pygmalion effect' can lead to our having various expectations about the spiritual abilities and qualities of an alleged teacher, once someone -- whether the teacher, a friend, a book, or a follower -- introduces the idea that such an individual is a spiritual guide, teacher, guru, among the elect, or whatever.

None of this necessarily has anything to do with the actual ability or quality of this alleged spiritual guide, leader, politician, or the like. Everything may be just a function of our expectations and how these expectations alter our perception of reality as well as how we interpret the nature of our interaction with others ... in this case, a so-called spiritual guide.

We meet someone who is called a spiritual guide, and immediately, many of us may begin to see, imagine, feel, think, and believe things which may have little to do with the on-going reality. We may read into events and construct our world view according to the manner in which our expectations create certain images in our minds and hearts. We may filter reality through such expectations and often tend to disregard whatever experiential evidence there is which is inconsistent with those sorts of expectation.

A fraudulent spiritual teacher might do various things to cultivate our expectations as well. One such individual whom I have met used to repeatedly say: "I never lie", or, "I never use people", or, "I am always sincere", or, "I never interfere in marriages", and, consequently, when people around him encountered evidence which contradicted what he claimed, and because they believed him to be a spiritual teacher -- which, thereby, afforded the so-called 'guide' quite a few degrees of latitude of good will -- they re-framed or reinterpreted the evidence to make it consistent with the mantra which he kept repeating ... well, after all, since by his own account, this 'man of God' never lies, or never uses people, and is always sincere, then 'obviously', what is going on must be something else – something which, because of the mysterious nature of mysticism, we just don't understand. In this way, many false spiritual guides are able to hide in plain sight, because we, ourselves, help to maintain that individual's camouflage.

Solomon Asch, a social psychologist, devised an experiment in 1951 which examined the way individual perception might be affected by other people. In simplified form, the study posed a task which, ostensibly, required subjects to judge which of three lines on one card matched a single line on another card.

Subjects were placed in a group setting, and unknown to the subject, the other people in the group were all confederates of the experimenter. Each person in the group was required to make a 'judgment' about which of three lines on card placed near the right side of the person was equal in length to a single line appearing on a card placed near the person's left side.

One of the variables studied was the effect which a subject's placement in the group of confederates had upon a subject's response. In other words, the researchers wanted to know if a subject's judgment, with respect to the assigned perceptual task, would vary with where in the group sequence a subject was asked to respond to that task.

When confederates selected a pairing which was clearly in error (that is, the line selected from among the three on one card did not match the single line on the other card, and the error was very obvious), the experimenters found that about a third of the subjects went along with the erroneous judgment of the confederates when the subjects were required to respond last in an experimental group. Furthermore, the more confederates there were in such a group who were asked to give a judgment before the subject gave his or her response, the more pronounced the influence of the group was on the judgment of a subject in cases where the confederates were clearly wrong in their 'judgments'.

The explanations which some of the subjects gave – when debriefed after the experiment as to why they went along with the erroneous group judgment -- are very instructive. Some of the subjects, when confronted with a group judgment that differed from their own, assumed that the group's judgment must be correct and their own perceptions must be wrong.

Some other subjects knew that the group was wrong in its judgment, but, nevertheless, they went along with the group because they didn't wish to be considered different from the group. Still other subjects claimed that they saw the mismatched pair as being equivalent despite the obvious difference in length.

Now, someone may look at the Asch experiment and say: "Big deal – so what if a few people were dumb enough to permit their judgment and behavior to be affected by what others in a group said or did. Surely, to discover that a third of the subjects tested were susceptible to being manipulated is not all that significant."

The Asch experiment was intentionally designed in a very simple way. It focused on a perceptual task where there could be little doubt that the judgment of the other people in the group (the confederates) was erroneous, and, yet nonetheless, a certain percentage of subjects went along with that incorrect judgment, and some of the subjects even swore up and down that they 'saw' the two lines as being equal when such was, very clearly, not the case.

What if we were to take a context which did not involve a simple, visual stimulus ... a situation where the issues were more complex, iffy, ambiguous, muddled, and open to a variety of interpretations? Isn't it likely that the percentage of people whose judgments might be affected by what others in a group said and did might rise significantly -- especially if those other 'confederates' were all saying very similar things to one another?

One tends to feel very uncomfortable when one goes in a direction which is not consonant with the position of a group of individuals with whom one is friendly or associating. This tends to create stress, anxiety, alienation, and anomie in the one who is in opposition to the group norms.

We are creatures of consensual validation. We often seek out the opinion of others to shore up our own confidence about what we see, hear, feel, believe, think, and do. Furthermore, in the absence of agreement about such matters, we tend to get nervous and uncomfortable, filled with existential angst about our status, vis-à-vis reality and the truth.

If one translates the foregoing considerations into spiritual group dynamics, one is likely to experience a great deal of dissonance when one tries to tell others that one believes the alleged teacher is perpetrating various kinds of spiritual abuse. More often than not, one will be met with considerable disbelief and anger toward oneself on the part of those in whom one confides or with whom one seeks to engage in discussion. More often than not, the abused person is perceived to be the problem, not the so-called teacher, and because of experiments like Asch's, one begins to understand that there are powerful forces at work... forces which can make an abused person wonder if the whole thing is just in her or his mind ... just a figment of their paranoid imagination ... and forces which can cause others who are listening to one's 'story' to shift, sometimes very rapidly, between believing and not believing what is being said.

Elizabeth Loftus, who is a professor of psychology as well as associated with the Law School, at the University of Washington, has been studying the relationship among imagination, memory, perception, and belief for a number of years. Her work in the area of false memory syndrome, together with the many problems surrounding the reliability of eye-witness testimony has shed a great deal of light on these processes.

Among the many things which Professor Loftus has demonstrated is how many of us have a tendency, under different circumstances, to construct reality based on the kinds of information or misinformation we are given by others ... information which frames the way we remember and perceive events. This distortion of remembered events, or the generation of false autobiographical beliefs (that is, beliefs which are not actually reflective of our past experience), or the confabulation (the interjection of imagined happenings to create a seemingly consistent story line concerning some event we have experienced) are all psychological processes that occur, from time to time, under a variety of settings, in many, if not most, of us. We may not even be aware that such processes are happening as we do it or as we are asked questions about our past or about on-going events.

The moral of the foregoing points is not that our understanding of reality or our grasp of the truth are total fabrications. At the same time, in the light of the sort of phenomena being studied by Professor Loftus, we should not be so quick to suppose that our understanding is accurately reflective of the truth of things either. There are many forces and factors which can alter and influence how we experience and interpret the events of life.

In very important ways, we construct worlds within our consciousness and project these onto the reality of things, treating the former as if they were the latter, and conflating the two. Disentangling the two is not an easy or straightforward process.

When someone claims to be a spiritual master, this claim may, or may not, be true. But, it is a claim which should not be accepted at face value because there are just too many ways in which we are vulnerable to having our perceptions, beliefs, understandings, and judgments concerning the nature of reality or truth altered and influenced in distorted, misleading, false directions.

Yet, many people -- unaware of the foregoing possibilities -- may insist that they 'know' that a given person is an authentic teacher, not realizing how their (i.e., the 'seekers') understandings have been shaped, colored, and framed by the use of a variety of psychological techniques and social forces. Under such circumstances, many of these people are unwilling to even consider or look at evidence which might contradict their constructed versions of reality concerning questions about the actual authenticity of a given, alleged spiritual guide or the legitimacy of a specific spiritual path. Moreover, many of these individuals may become quite hostile and mean when anyone approaches them with such evidence.

Attitudes and beliefs, once formed, are very resistant to change. We would like to claim that we are rational beings who are willing to examine evidence objectively through the use of logic and impartial, methodical analysis, but, unfortunately, when push comes to shove and we are faced with a choice of having, on the one hand, to change our attitudes and beliefs or, on the other hand, needing to reject evidence, many of us would prefer to ignore, hide, and re-frame evidence than we would be inclined to alter our precious attitudes and beliefs.

Back in the 1960s, Stanley Milgram, who was at Yale at the time, did a series of studies concerning obedience and compliance. The results are rather sobering and disturbing.

A newspaper ad is run in a New Haven newspaper which offers $4.50 in exchange for an hour's time of anyone who signed up for the experiment. The ad indicated the study is about memory and learning.

The people who respond to the ad are just average human beings who like the idea of participating in an interesting investigation at a prestigious university. These individuals are introduced to a person who is dressed in a white coat and looks like a scientist or academician and appears to be very serious about the project.

In addition, the people who have responded to the ad are introduced to a friendly, affable, fellow participant in the study. The individual conducting the project indicates that the study is designed to focus on the possible effects which punishment has in relation to learning.

One of the participants is to be a teacher, and one of the two individuals is to be a student. Lots are drawn in order to assign the student and teacher roles.

Once these roles have been assigned, the two participants are taken into a second room by the individual conducting the study. The person who has been identified as the student, through the drawing of lots, is strapped into a chair.

An electrode, to which a conductive gel has been applied, is attached to the student's arm. The person running the experiment explains that the electrode is connected to a generator in the other room which, when certain switches are thrown, is capable of delivering an electric shock to the student.

The purpose of the electric shocks is to punish the student for incorrect responses to the test items which are presented to the would-be learner. Naturally, the question is raised about whether, or not, the shocks are capable of doing any permanent damage. The participants are told that although the shocks can be quite painful, no tissue damage will occur.

The 'student' is left in one room strapped to a chair, and the 'teacher' is taken into an adjoining room containing the shock generator. The machine has a console with 30 switches and each of the toggles is labeled with a different voltage ... running from 15 volts up to 450 volts.

Furthermore, each of the switches also has a label associated with it that indicates the degree of severity for that given level of shock/punishment. These labels range from mild to dangerous, and the 29th and 30th switches have an XXX label next to them.

The learning task is described as a paired association task in which the teacher recites a word, and the student must give an appropriate word of association for the original word. Shocks are to be administered by the teacher whenever the learner gives an incorrect response, and, moreover, for each incorrect response on the part of the student, the learner is not only given a shock, but afterwards, the level of shock is increased by 15 volts which is to be delivered by throwing another, 'higher-level' switch among the graduated set of 30 switches whenever the next incorrect response is given for a subsequent word pair.

Before the experiment begins, the 'teacher' is given a 15 volt shock in order to both test the machine -- to be sure that it is functioning properly-- as well as to give the teacher a taste of what the punishment feels like at the very lowest level of shock. The shock is sufficient to make the arm of the 'teacher' tingle.

Once the experiment begins, the first several word pairings go easily and without any need of punishment. Eventually, however, a mistake is made by the learner, and a shock is administered.

In due time, the student is making quite a few errors. With each mistake, the level of voltage applied to the learner becomes higher and higher.

When the voltage of the shock reaches 75 volts, the teacher can hear an audible grunt from the student through the wall which separates the teacher from the learner. Similar sounds are heard when shocks of 90 and 105 volts are administered during subsequent punishment for incorrect responses.

When the level of shock reaches 120 volts, the student indicates clearly that the punishment is becoming very painful. When the shock reaches 150 volts, the learner yells out that he or she wants to be released and doesn't want to continue on with the experiment. The nature of such protests and exclamations of pain become more intense as the level of voltage is increased.

If a teacher should express reservations or anxieties about what is going on or about what she or he is hearing, the experimenter will simply indicate to the teacher that: the study needs to be completed, or that the learner is being paid for his or her participation, or that the teacher must continue and cannot stop. These instructions are given in a detached manner.

As the shocks proceed past 150 volts, the remonstrations of the learner become more and more agonizing. At a certain point, the learner yells the pain is unbearable.

When the 20th switch is reached (300 volts), frantic pounding is heard

31

on the wall behind which the learner is strapped in, and the student begs to be freed from the chair and to be let out of the room. After the 22nd switch has been thrown (330 volts), there are no further sounds emanating from the room in which the learner is situated.

The teacher is informed that silence on the part of the learner is to be interpreted as an incorrect response. With each lack of response to the next word pair, a shock is delivered and, as well, the level of shock continues to be increased by 15 volts, in anticipation of the next incorrect answer – or silence -- by the learner. Once the 30th switch has been thrown, the experiment is over.

Now, before continuing on, I should point out that, in fact, no shocks were ever administered to the 'dim-witted' learners. In fact, the learner was a confederate in the experiment who was playing a role, and everything had been pre-arranged so that the only actual subjects in the experiment were the people who had responded to the newspaper advertisement and became the 'teacher'.

Independently of the experimental set-up, psychologists and university students were asked to estimate the level of shock at which they -- if they had been assigned the role of teacher -- would discontinue participating in the experiment. On average, the psychologists who were polled said that if they had been the teacher, they would have dropped out when the level of shock reached 120 volts. The university students who were asked the same question indicated that, on average, they would have stopped at 135 volts.

150 volts is the point at which the learners invariably began to complain about the pain they feel from the shocks being administered. No one among either the psychologists or the university students who were polled indicated that they would have tossed all 30 switches.

When asked to predict what other 'teachers' might have done in such an experiment, the university students suggested that, on average, only 1/10th of one per cent of the teachers would go through all 30 levels of shock. The psychologists predicted that 4/10ths of one per cent of the subjects would run through the full complement of switches.

No one was prepared for what actually took place. Over 60 per cent of the subjects in the experiment – the ones who were the 'teachers' – went through the full complement of 30 switches.

Many of these subjects were in obvious emotional distress and agony as they did so. Many of them struggled with the moral issue of what was going on ...

32

that is, having to choose between whether to harm another human being or to continue to comply with the directives of the experimenter.

Many of the subjects stopped numerous times, only to be prodded back into action again by the detached, emotionless urging of the experimenter that the study needed to be completed or that the subject really had no choice but to go on as instructed. Many of the subjects broke down in tears or exhibited signs of anxiety, frustration, trembling, intense conflict, uncontrollable laughter, and indecision, but in the end, over 60 per cent of these 'average' people kept upping the level of what they believed were extremely painful shocks until those individuals ran out of switches to throw.

The same experiment was run in a number of other countries. The number of subjects in these other countries who threw all 30 switches never went below 60 per cent. Furthermore, in some countries, this percentage was even higher than in the United States ... reaching 85 per cent of the participants in one country.

In some of the other variants on this experiment, the researchers wanted to study what effect, if any, the teacher's proximity to the learner might have in relation to how far a subject would be willing to comply with the experimenter's wishes. In some of these instances, the researchers required the 'teacher' to hold down the hand of the 'learner' on the plate which, supposedly, was delivering shocks. The experimenters found that such a requirement did not appreciably affect the percentage of people who, if necessary, were prepared to see the experiment through across all 30 switches.

In all of the different variants of the experiment, the subjects were asked, after the experiment had been completed, to indicate – on a scale of 1 to 14 (with 14 being the most severe) – how painful they believed the shocks were. Most of them responded with '14', so they were aware of the pain that was being caused.

One of the reasons for going into such detail in relation to Milgram's research is to help illustrate a certain dimension of the forces which are at work in many of us when it comes to our willingness to comply and be obedient to someone whom we consider to be an expert, or knowledgeable, or whom we perceive to be in authority ... even when we have serious misgivings about what we are being told or about what we see going on. All too many people are prepared to behave in callous, hurtful, irrational ways as long as there is someone to whom they can defer – like a spiritual guide or political leader – telling one that it is all right to proceed, even though people (including the seeker) may be damaged in the

33

process. Moreover, for many of us, when our vested interests are being threatened, then truth, morality, integrity, decency, and justice frequently become the first casualties.

The subjects in the Milgram experiment were told that although the shocks which might be delivered to a learner could be very painful, no serious or permanent tissue damage would result. Presumably, this assurance may have played a role in helping to comfort or buffer the subjects such that although they believed the shocks which were being administered were painful, nevertheless, no permanent damage would result.

In view of this possibility, perhaps, it should not be surprising if 'seekers', who are troubled by what is going on within a supposedly mystical/spiritual group, often tend to find comfort in the words of an alleged spiritual guide who says that what he or she (that is, the so-called guide) is doing is necessary for the spiritual good of the people in the group ... or that even though while -- on a mundane, worldly level -- that which 'appears' to be going on may seem deceitful or a lie or manipulative or duplicitous or authoritarian or exploitive or controlling that, nonetheless, the alleged spiritual guide knows what she or he is doing, and, therefore, no permanent damage will result – only good will ensue.

In light of the Milgram studies, one should not be surprised when average, non-psychotic individuals are willing to participate in 'Divine trickery' which is designed, so the false teacher says, to help separate seekers from their normal modes of consciousness and problematic ways of understanding and engaging Divinity. After all, when people are induced to believe that spiritual reality doesn't have to operate in accordance with the requirements of rational considerations, then almost anything becomes possible for, and permissible to, someone if we believe that such a person is a spiritual being ... a friend of God ... someone who possesses insight into the mysteries of being.

Fraudulent teachers take a truth -- namely, that there is, most definitely, a difference between the rational and the trans-rational (which is not irrational but transcends normal modes of rational thought and logic) -- and they exploit that truth, twisting it and altering the nature of its reality to accommodate their own distorted purposes. To be sure, rational thought will never, on its own find the way to Revelation or to the spiritual station of a Prophet, or to the mystical understanding of a Rumi, Hafiz, or Ibn al-'Arabi, but this does not entitle someone to take license with the truth by trying to say that anything and everything one wishes to claim about what is, and is not, permissible on the mystical path, thereby, becomes true.

Yet, how is a would-be seeker to know this? If an alleged spiritual guide comes along and — like the authority-figure in the Milgram studies (i.e., the person in the white frock coat with the clip board who is, supposedly, the one conducting the experiment) — says, "hey look ... everything, despite appearances, is quite okay" ... well, shouldn't we leave such things to the experts, the academics, the people in charge, the authorities. Surely, they know what they are doing, and who are we -- the great unwashed and ignorant dregs of humanity -- to suggest otherwise?

The Inquisition, the Salem Witch Trials, Nazi Germany, Senator Joe McCarthy, Stalin's Russia, Mai Lai, Pol Pot's reign of terror, Jonestown, Sabra & Shatila, the Waco tragedy, Srebrenica, the first and second Iraq wars, the decades-long debacle of the Catholic Church, along with many other examples of abuse don't 'just' happen. They occur because they are linked to mechanisms, phenomena, effects, processes, and influences within human beings ... mechanisms and influences to which all of us may become vulnerable under the right set of circumstances.

Less one suppose that intelligence has anything to do with how a person might respond in the 'right' setting, one would do well to consider an experiment conducted by Philip Zimbardo at Stanford University during the summer of 1971. The results are, again, very instructive, if rather disquieting.

The experiment was intended to run for two weeks. Students were randomly divided up into two groups — guards and prisoners.

Within a few days the experiment had to be shut down because the guards were exhibiting considerable sadistic behavior, and a number of the prisoners were becoming deeply depressed and showing extensive symptoms of stress and anxiety.

There are at least two features of interest in this experiment — that is, aside from the obvious ... namely, the willingness of supposedly intelligent students to become sadistic toward fellow students even while being observed. The first point of interest revolves about the relatively short period of time which was needed for sadistic behavior to surface, and, secondly, the experiment had to be shut down by the professor rather than by those who were being abused but were trying to comply with the requirements of what they perceived to be the professor's expectations concerning the study.

| Construction of Reality |

Or, consider a study conducted by D.L. Rosenhahn, a professor of law and psychology at Stanford University. In the January 1973 issue of the journal, *Science*, an article of his was published, entitled: "On Being Sane in Insane Places".

Essentially, Rosenhahn had a number of his students go to 12 hospitals, across five different states, along both coasts of America. Eleven of these hospitals were public, and, as a result, they were funded through state, federal, or university funding, while one of the hospitals was privately run.

The task of these students was to see if they could gain admission as psychiatric patients by presenting only one symptom -- hearing voices that were rather unclear with respect to what was being said. All other information which these 'pseudo-patients' gave was to be truthful.

After being admitted, the abnormal symptoms would cease, and the pseudo-patients would seek to be released – which did not always happen ... at least, not right away. The resulting experiences of these pseudo-patients revealed a great deal about the institutional depersonalization which occurs during confinement with patients as well as about the difficulty of doctors to be able to distinguish between sane and insane people -- whether during admission or for purposes of release.

After the first part of the foregoing study had been completed, there were several hospitals that learned about the project and indicated that they were highly doubtful that such pseudo-patients could escape their diagnostic detection. The staff members at these hospitals were informed by Professor Rosenhahn that at some point – over a given, three month period – there would be a number of pseudo-patients sent to them, and the challenge would be to identify these latter individuals from among all the other people who came to them for diagnosis.

At such hospitals the staff members were asked to rate the potential patients who were being considered for admission as to the likelihood of being a pseudo-patient. By study's end, there were 193 patients who were rated by the staff members of the participating hospitals.

One percent of these patients (41) were considered, with a high level of confidence, to be pseudo-patients by at least one staff member of a given hospital. 12% of the 193 patients (23) were suspected of being pseudo-patients by at least one psychiatrist, and 10% of the sample (19) were judged to be possible pseudo-patients by both a staff member and a psychiatrist.

Actually, Professor Rosenhahn had pulled another fast one. During the three month period in which the study was conducted, no pseudo-patients were sent to either of the two hospitals that had accepted the challenge, and, therefore, there were a fairly large number of false-positives which had been committed during diagnosis by the staff and psychiatrists at those hospitals.

There are a number of lessons to be learned from the Rosenhahn study. Perhaps, one of the most important of these lessons – at least, in the present context – is how the expectations of professionals were capable of being manipulated to induce them to see something which was not true and, yet, believe they knew what was going on – all that was necessary was for the right kind of 'framing' of a situation to take place.

The placebo effect is a well-documented phenomenon. If people are led to believe -- or to have the expectation -- that a pill with no active ingredients is capable of producing certain kinds of effects, precisely those effects will take place in many people.

Consequently, if people are led to believe that a so-called spiritual guide has special sorts of knowledge, quality, ability, and so on, then many people will experience altered states of consciousness as a function of this expectation. The actual reality of an alleged teacher's spiritual status may, up to a point, be irrelevant to what is transpiring in an individual's life.

Between 1927 and 1932 a research project was conducted at the Hawthorne works of the Western Electric Company in Chicago. While there are many controversial methodological and interpretive issues swirling about these studies, in essence, the investigation attempted to examine the relationship between changes in working conditions and productivity.

A variety of physical and psychological factors were altered to see what impact such changes would have on worker productivity. Oddly enough, they found that regardless of whatever changes were introduced productivity increases ensued.

Harvard Business School professor George Elton Mayo – together with several associates, F.J. Roethlisberger and William J. Dickson – concluded, in part, that one way to explain or interpret the observed increases in productivity that took place – no matter what physical and psychological variables were introduced – was to suppose that what the workers were primarily responding to was the attention being paid to them and that they were trying to respond positively to this attention.

There is an old adage that a change is as good as a

vacation. Apparently, there is some indication in the Hawthorne Effect that merely by showing interest in people, the latter individuals may have experienced enhanced levels of: motivation, sense of importance, self-esteem, well-being, morale, and so on.

People who accept initiation through even a false teacher will often remark about all the great changes which they believe are entering their lives as a result of the 'blessing' of being associated with a given, alleged teacher. In many of these cases, a combination of suggestibility, placebo effect, together with variations on the Hawthorne, Halo, and Pygmalion Effects are structuring an individual's experience and reality.

There is a certain amount of corroborating data with respect to the Hawthorne Effect. However, the data comes from psychotherapy rather than management studies.

Many researchers have found that the success rates of various kinds of therapy are almost indistinguishable from one another. As long as these treatment methods contain elements of warmth, acceptance, personal contact, positive regard, support, encouragement, and so on, patients seem to do equally well and make various degrees of improvement with one kind of theoretical treatment just as much as with some other theoretical approach. On the other hand, there is the very disturbing bit of evidence -- for therapists -- that two-thirds of many classes of psychotic individuals experience spontaneous remission, for a time, irrespective of whether anything is done or not.

Similarly, many problems which people experience tend to sort themselves quite independently of the presence of a spiritual guide.

Of course, fraudulent teachers are very adept at re-framing such realities and taking credit for the positive things, while using on-going problems in the individual as case exhibits for the seeker's need to apply herself or himself all that much harder to a given mystical discipline.

Moreover, there has been evidence collected which suggests that patients tend to have dreams that reflect the theoretical predilections of their therapists. Therefore, should we be surprised when a seeker begins to have dreams which reflect the teachings of a fraudulent teacher?

The foregoing discussion is not meant to imply that there is no such thing as real mysticism or authentic guides or legitimate spiritual experiences. Rather, the intention is quite different since, in truth, I do accept the idea that there are hidden dimensions to life and that there are methods which enhance one's chances to be opened to these possibilities -- possibilities which are rooted in the essential identity of human beings as well as the purpose of life.

In general, there are only two kinds of mistakes a researcher can commit. A scientist may accept a hypothesis as true, when, in fact, it is false, or an investigator may consider a hypothesis to be false which, in reality, is true.

Seekers after mystical truth are, in effect, researchers. They are trying to test various hypotheses and determine what is, or is not, true.

Is a given spiritual or mystical path authentic? Is a given experience a function of imagination or an instance of an actual mystical state? Does a certain dream mean this, or that, or something else? Am I making spiritual progress? Will such and such a practice be spiritually beneficial or harmful? Am I wasting my time? With whom should I associate for best spiritual results? How should I balance the different facets of my life? What is the moral thing to do? Will I achieve Paradise and/or spiritual Self-realization? How will I know whether what I am experiencing is real or illusory or satanically inspired?

People who have invested heavily in one individual – for example, an alleged spiritual guide -- with respect to all their hopes, dreams, expectations, commitments, beliefs, values, purposes, and meanings concerning their (the seekers) spiritual future and welfare, then such heavily invested individuals often tend to be extremely resistant to any information which indicates there is considerable evidence to lend credence to the possibility that a so-called teacher is nothing more than a clever charlatan, and, therefore, the trust of the former individuals has not been well placed. There are many reasons for this, but part of the answer for such behavior is a function of a phenomenon known as cognitive dissonance.

Back in 1956, Leon Festinger -- along with Henry W. Riecken and Stanley Schachter -- wrote about a small cult that (long before the X-Files was even a gleam in the eye of Chris Carter) followed the teachings of Mrs. Marian Keech, a housewife, who believed or made claims to the effect, that she was in touch with aliens and was receiving messages from them via automatic writing. Apparently, the messages described a coming world-cataclysm from which people who obeyed the instructions coming to Mrs. Keech from the aliens might be saved.

Many, if not most, of the followers of Mrs. Keech sold, or gave away, their possessions and left the previous life which they had been living. They had put all their trust in one thing – the alien messages -- and were waiting for the appointed date.

When the predicted date of the cataclysm came and went, but nothing happened, the researchers were interested in what would happen to the cult. The people conducting the study discovered something rather curious.

Contrary to what one might expect, instead of turning their backs on the teachings, the commitment of many of the followers in the group became even more fervent than before the date of the failed 'prophecy'. And, of course, a relevant question to ask is: why should this sort of behavior take place under these kinds of circumstance -- namely, in the face of evidence that a key part of one's belief system has been falsified?

Cognitive dissonance is the study of the dynamics among attitudes/beliefs, experiential data, and behavior -- especially in those cases when there is dissonance, or disharmony, among these three components. Will attitudes/beliefs change, will behavior change, or will experience be re-framed in order to accommodate either the structure of one's attitudes/beliefs and/or the nature of one's behavior?

In many contexts involving groups which have formed around spiritual frauds, merely exposing members of that group to compelling evidence that there is something seriously amiss in, say, the moral conduct of the teacher, will not necessarily be enough to alter either the attitudes/beliefs or behaviors of those members. There are a lot of reasons for why this is so, and one has to look to the personal history, vulnerabilities, emotional character, personality, needs, and motivations of such individuals to gain insight into the particular mechanisms at work in a given person.

In almost all cases, however, one should try to follow the vested interests of these people. In other words, one has to try to understand what such people believe they stand to lose if they accept, as true, what is being said in the way of contradictory evidence concerning the authenticity of their spiritual guide.

Some people believe that salvation itself is at stake. Others may believe that Paradise/Heaven is being placed at risk ... or they see opportunities slipping away -- such as realizing the purpose of life ... or they feel threatened that they may become alienated from the truth ... or they fear becoming the vassal of Satanic forces should they leave their teacher (indeed, they perceive the presentation of evidence as one of the overtures of Satan) ... or they fear a loss of access to essential identity ... or they do not wish to forego the ego gratification and/or power and/or perks they receive as someone who has been appointed a 'teacher' by a given fraudulent spiritual guide.

Whenever one is talking about issues and forces as powerful, fundamental, and essential as the foregoing possibilities, it becomes understandable that for some people, the idea of changing either attitudes/beliefs or behaviors to accommodate available evidence is more antithetical to their interests than is re-framing the evidence and labeling the information as lies, or fabrications, or character assassination, or the workings of Satan, or the delusions of a disenchanted, former follower, or the result of some personal defect of the individual who is introducing, or trying to, the evidence.

Some of these 'true-believers' are even proud — arrogantly so — of their own willingness to completely ignore truth, reality, evidence, proof, and common sense while maintaining an unwavering commitment to the idea that their spiritual guide is authentic ... even when the evidence says otherwise. They equate dogmatism, authoritarian rigidity, foolishness, ignorance, and a closed heart or mind with the light of faith and are too self-absorbed to understand the differences.

Many spiritual charlatans are able to maintain their cover of alleged mystical acumen by keeping their distance from people. They limit access to themselves, not for legitimate reasons, but in order that people do not have the opportunity to discover that the emperor is, in fact, not wearing any mantel of spiritual authenticity.

I spent nearly 17 years with my first spiritual guide. During this period of time, I interacted with him a great deal ... often on an almost daily basis. I went on several extended journeys with him to a number of foreign countries.

I was able to observe his conduct across a wide variety of circumstances, problems, pressures, and issues. He was a man of complete integrity and elegance -- spiritually, academically, and socially -- as well as a friend and guide.

Pretty much everything I have learned that I consider to be of any value to my life arose through the time I spent with my spiritual guide ... from the things I learned by observing him live life. This was the essential pillar of my spiritual training, and whatever practices I have done in the way of prayers, fasting, seclusions, chants, contemplation, and so on, were rooted in the aforementioned spiritual edifice of the integrity of my spiritual guide's lived life.

Comparatively speaking, I spent very little time with a second person who, for an extended period time, I considered to be an authentic spiritual guide. Perhaps, all told, I may have spent 4 or 5 months – in sporadic, intermittent fashion – out of 10 years in close proximity to this second individual.

Moreover, many of these circumstances were of limited difficulty, consisting of talks or discussions, either of an individual nature or among a group of people. Much of my interaction with him was via phone or e-mail.

I have since come to learn that there were a number of things which were staged whenever I would visit this man. In other words, he behaved differently in my presence than he did in the presence of others, and when I came to learn of some of these differences, I knew things were being hidden from me and that my interaction with him was something of a managed stage play where everyone but me knew the nature of the production which was going on.

I came to know of my first – and, as far as I know, only – guide's spiritual character by direct exposure to his conduct. I came to learn of the second person's character – or lack thereof – by direct exposure to his conduct, especially after the artificial aspects of the relationship had been removed through ensuing events.

Both of the foregoing individuals spoke very well– although each in his own way -- about mysticism. Based on what was said, both individuals appeared to be very factually knowledgeable about spiritual matters, but the factor which separated the wheat from the chaff was the quality of conduct.

In this respect, one person (the first spiritual guide) had been nothing but pure joy, while the other individual (the second person mentioned above) had become a living nightmare who spewed evil wherever he went. For me, it took time to realize what this second individual was all about because of the many techniques he used to re-frame events which were going on, and because of a certain number of degrees of freedom he was granted by me based on an assumption -- a false one -- that he was an authentic spiritual guide.

Understanding what I do now, I can see how he

exploited vulnerabilities and the good-will which I had been willing to extend to him based on a variety of assumptions. Understanding what I do now, I have come to recognize the techniques of re-framing, misdirection, compliance, manipulation, misinformation, disinformation, deceit and duplicity he employed to keep me ignorant of what he was actually up to.

People who choose to stay with this sort of man and refuse to look at, or consider, the evidence which has accumulated concerning the spiritually fraudulent character of that individual, are protecting vested interests of their carnal souls. As indicated previously, what these interests are vary from individual to individual, and, such interests can be fairly complicated in structure.

Having tried to apprize a variety of individuals about the dangers of their situation concerning the individual in question, I have been vociferously rebuffed by a number of them. I do have a certain degree of appreciation with respect to the nature of the dynamics which are in play in such rebuffs ... and some of these processes, effects, phenomena, and forces have been outlined in the foregoing discussion.

3.) The Guru Papers

Approximately 15 years ago, a book entitled: The Guru Papers, by Joel Kramer & Diana Alstad, made quite a splash in many circles. The subtitle of the work was: 'Masks of Authoritarian Power'.

The following comments serve as something of an extended mini-review of the foregoing work. In this review, a substantial amount of time is given to providing readers with a fair and accurate overview of the perspective of the two authors, but toward the end of this essay, a certain amount of critical analysis concerning their work is provided, so please be patient.

One of the essential themes of the Kramer-Alstad study was that all Guru-devotee or teacher-seeker relationships are inherently, unavoidably, irrevocably, problematically, and without exception, authoritarian in nature. Although the authors knew most about the way things worked in Yogic and Buddhist systems, the two writers were quite clear that they believed no spiritual, mystical tradition was free from the destructive presence of authoritarian practices and influences.

Furthermore, these two authors argued that no one should suppose the central difficulty in such teacher-seeker relationships could be attributed to the personal failings of a few rotten apples in the barrel -- that is, Kramer and Alstad maintained that even if one could remove from consideration all those teachers who had given in to the dark side of themselves and, as a result, became abusers and exploiters of their followers, nevertheless, the remaining spiritual guides – no matter how good, decent, well-intended, and knowledgeable they might be – would still be ensconced in a system which was inextricably authoritarian. In other words, the problem was institutional or systemic and not a function of wayward and rogue 'teachers'. Even when the individual apples were good, the barrel in which they existed and operated was rotten with the insidious presence of authoritarian practices.

Early in The Guru Papers, the two authors made a distinction between, on the one hand, issues of authority, as well as hierarchy, and, on the other hand, authoritarian practices which are often confused and conflated with the former two principles. According to Kramer and Alstad, every society or social order requires the use of authority and hierarchy to be able to function properly, but when authoritarian influences seep into either the uses of authority or hierarchy, then, according to the authors, the seeds of eventual social disintegration are being sown.

While Kramer and Alstad are interested in a wide variety of social contexts which tend to become entangled with authoritarian abuses, the two researchers

45

key in on spiritual, religious, and mystical contexts because such traditional settings offer, in their opinion, an unusually fruitful opportunity to explore the way the absolutist nature of the Guru-seeker relationship is rooted, supposedly, in demands for total obedience and surrender, and, consequently, provides a window, as it were, onto the manner in which the exercise of authoritarian power leads to not only the control of physical contingencies, but to the shaping, structuring, coloring, and orienting of mental, emotional, motivational, and behavioral processes, as well.

According to the perspective of the authors of The Guru Papers, spiritual ideologies are used in authoritarian systems to, among other things, justify and render plausible, or reasonable, the exercise of authoritarian control. When one accepts a spiritual system, one, knowingly or unknowingly, commits oneself to submitting to whatever yoke of authoritarian power the system deems to be appropriate in order to enable the spiritual institution, in question, to operate smoothly, efficiently, and effectively as a means of – so the promise goes – helping individuals to become: realized, enlightened, fully human, awakened, saved, sanctified, or whatever other spiritual ideals are being promulgated by that spiritual system as being the goal(s) or purpose(s) of life.

Kramer and Alstad claim to have no quarrel with the idea of spirituality, per se. Rather, their stated concern is with processes which seek to justify, defend, enhance, promote, and/or mask the exercise of authoritarian control by creating gateway figures – i.e., teachers, gurus, masters -- who, allegedly, are the only ones who can safely and effectively guide one to the spiritual treasures on the other side of the spiritual gate – even when that gate resides within us – and do so by requiring followers to refrain from challenging, in any way, the guide's directives, interpretations, pronouncements, practices, demands, expectations, or understandings.

The two authors believe the vast majority of historical, traditional, social systems are saturated with the uses, and subsequent destructive effects, of authoritarian power. They feel the omnipresence of such practices and influences has undermined our individual and collective capacity for self-trust, and this, in turn, has shackled our creative potential for developing new social and institutional arrangements concerning constructive uses of authority and hierarchy that are capable of solving the many dilemmas with which we are confronted.

The creators of The Guru Papers are in search of a new paradigm – one that will attract commitment through consensus rather than the coercive

46

force inherent in authoritarian demands for mental, social, spiritual, emotional and physical obedience, submission, or conformity. The authors are seeking a paradigm shift that will give emphasis to helping people to learn how to trust and value their own experiences rather than succumbing to a rote-learning process of indoctrination fraught with unexamined assumptions, as well as a submissive compulsion to blindly follow antiquated, problematic value and methodological systems.

Of particular interest to Kramer and Alstad are the techniques used by authoritarian systems to inculcate a set of moral values which are internalized and used to control people. According to the authors, such techniques are even more important than the exercise of physical control, for the latter is quite limited in scope and cannot be used on a continuous basis without either, sooner or later, leading to social upheaval and significant challenges through some form of countervailing physical force, or simply leading to the fragmentation of society as the pressure of physical force generates ruptures in the social fabric that are unpredictable and, often, irreparable.

When authoritarian processes are used to shape how people think, believe, feel, speak, and act, then the world-view, paradigm, or framework through which reality is engaged and understood becomes the medium of control. The most dangerous shackles are the ones which are invisible to us because we do not see them for what they are -- namely, authoritarian demands for obedience which have been internalized and re-framed as unchallengeable moral certitudes that are justified by an ideology one has been induced not to question or critically reflect upon.

Moreover, from the perspective of Kramer and Alstad, one of the primary functions of encouraging the idea of moral certainty in people is that the latter instills in the minds of such individuals a self-righteous attitude that justifies perpetrating all manner of cruelty, hatred, anger, and oppression toward the 'miscreants' who have not, yet, submitted to such 'truths' and, therefore, serves as the ideological warrant for telling other people – by force, if necessary – how to live their lives, what goals to seek, which authorities to believe or trust, who to be and why. The sort of certitude which is indifferent to facts, evidence, critical analysis, contrary experience, unbiased evaluation, methodological rigor, unexplained anomalies, unanswered questions, and soulful reflection is impervious to anything other than its own interests, likes, dislikes, prejudices, goals, assumptions, and limitations.

Such rigidity and dogmatic impenetrability is used as the first line of

47

defense against any challenges to the moral justification for perpetrating a system which is, essentially, operated through authoritarian processes that, ultimately, demand total obedience and submission to the purveyors of the oppressive practices which have been used to indoctrinate people to accept such a moral, emotional, mental, and spiritual cul-de-sac or dead end in the first place. The system is circular, and, therefore, self-perpetuating as long as the underlying authoritarian practices enjoy the privileges of eminent domain that are assumed to be absolute, and, therefore, unchallengeable by virtue of the moral certitude which, supposedly, lies at the heart of the assumption which is vouchsafing those privileges and which, consequently, underwrites the justification for doing things in an authoritarian fashion.

According to the authors of The Guru Papers, morality is the mortar which cements the bricks of society together, and in order to avoid the appearance of requiring people to abide by arbitrarily derived rules of conduct, morality was embedded in religious systems that were, in turn, backed by claims to the ultimate authority of absolute truths which were Divine in nature. Thus, morality, religion, spirituality, goodness, justice, meaning, purpose, community, and identity all took their lead from a set of divinely given absolute principles.

Kramer and Alstad contend that central to the aforementioned set of principles was a 'renunciate' orientation to life. This renunciate philosophy or theology required individuals to sacrifice self-interest in the name of the 'higher good' as defined by a given religious framework and as interpreted by those who came to be the guardians of that system -- namely, the spiritual guides, clerics, officials, and so on, who, supposedly, were most knowledgeable about what Divinity wanted from humankind.

The two authors further argued that forgiveness, guilt, reward, shame, and punishment were among the primary tools used to induce people to adopt the renunciate perspective and eschew self-interest. In fact, the guardians of these spiritual frameworks pointed out that real self-interest was synonymous with adhering to a renunciate way of life -- that, in effect, there was no essential antagonism between the two.

Issues of death, life, loss, pain, purpose, meaning, difficulty, uncertainty, and the unknown were dealt with through the fixed symbols, myths, rituals, and mysteries of absolute truth. However, Kramer and Alstad maintain that the price for pushing back the apparent chaos of life-events in this fashion was a way of being which became anachronistic due to its inability to flexibly, reasonably, creatively, and effectively respond to the challenges and problems generated

48

through on-going history.

Under the relentless pressure of history, the authors contend that many of the myths, symbols, and rituals have been disconnected from their original sources, and, consequently, there has been a wide-spread loss of an essential sense of meaning, purpose, identity, and community which has led to considerable moral decay as people no longer see the relevance of abiding by renunciate theologies which do not seem to serve either collective or individual well-being. This state of affairs has, in the view of Kramer and Alstad, led to the rise of various forms of fundamentalism which seek to, ever more tightly, cling to traditional – or, what are believed to be traditional – values, methods, beliefs, and practices in an attempt to revive, through an exercise of sheer intensity of will-power, what seems to have been lost ... as if the mere urgency and direness of human desperation could turn back the calendar to a simpler, seemingly more innocent and spiritually advantageous time.

From the perspective of The Guru Papers, fundamentalists are experiencing a loss of control over their lives. They feel powerless in the face of modern forms of science, technology, culture, communication, government, education, and economics which have leveraged power i n ways that bring traditional modes of spiritual life under constant attack, generating many doubts and questions in the process, and, as well, create an onslaught of moral problems for traditionally minded and hearted individuals.

Kramer and Alstad believe that what is needed at this juncture of history is "an ethics for survival". In their opinion, renunciate systems focus on rewards and punishments in a world-to-come context that looks upon existence from a self-serving paradigm which favors authoritarian means as a way of serving such ends and, therefore, largely use tactics of fear and self-righteous anger to force people to submit to a system which does very little to solve the problems and eliminate the injustices of the present world.

The authors contend that renunciate systems of morality are inherently judgmental and use fear and force to impose this perspective on people. In other words, individuals become so imbued with the fear of bringing down upon themselves the wrath of God or of being denied the fruits of Heaven -- at least, according to the teachings of the guardians of the faith – that the commonality of people often become paralyzed with indecision ... not wishing to do anything which will jeopardize their standing in eternity and, in the process, help to perpetuate an authoritarian approach to life that spreads destructive seeds everywhere it blows.

49

Kramer and Alstad believe that the spirit of the authoritarian mind-set is nowhere more apparent than in mystical systems that are based on a teacher-seeker relationship in which a seeker blindly concedes authority to another person who claims to be a spiritual guide, and, in the process of such a concession, a number of untested and unproven assumptions are made concerning the character, understanding, and authenticity of the so-called teacher. Such a seeker is operating on presuppositions such as: the 'teacher' is morally superior to the seeker, and, as well, enjoys a far greater degree of spiritual knowledge, self-realization, insight, potential, and closeness to Divinity, than the seeker does — all of which supposedly enables the 'teacher' to understand what is best for another individual.

In the opinion of Kramer and Alstad, the foregoing sort of presuppositions lend themselves to the creation of different forms of dualism, and among the most important of these is the: sacred and non-sacred dichotomy. In the context of the teacher-seeker relationship, whatever the teacher is, says, thinks, feels, does, indicates, and suggests is sacred, and whatever is not in consonance with these dimensions of the teacher is non-sacred.

The task of the seeker becomes one of absorbing or of activating this sense of sacredness within herself or himself and, in addition, eliminating the non-sacred. The task of the teacher is to assist the seeker to do this.

As such, the teacher becomes the role model through which this is to be accomplished. However, the authors of The Guru Papers feel that much of what is passed off as sacred in such mystical circles is little more than vested interests, self-aggrandizement, cultural constructions, and individual preferences on the part of the 'teacher'.

When the 'teacher' becomes the unchallengeable arbiter of truth and 'seekers' adopt renunciate methodologies and moralities that encourage the latter to sacrifice their own capacity for experience, reflection, analysis, questioning, exploration, trust, identity, and realization at the altar of a teacher, then, in the opinion of Kramer and Alstad, one has an authoritarian recipe for spiritual disaster which is likely to produce little more than people who are dogmatic, rigid, static, self-righteous, judgmental, elitist, as well as incapable of either thinking for themselves or trusting their inner selves.

The Guru Papers approaches the issues of authoritarian power through the spectacles of a broadly evolutionary, progressive, humanistic, rationalistic, dialectical point of view. Although I believe the authors have some good insights to offer with respect to a number of the problems which

50

exist in many teacher-seeker relationships (both on the side of the guide, as well as on the side of the seeker), nonetheless, their overall analysis appears to suffer from many inadequacies, lacunae, presumptions, unanswered questions, and problems -- not the least of which is the entirely arbitrary nature of their conception of dialectical analysis, rationalistic methodology, and moral valuation, in addition to the constant vagueness in their book which dogs such key issues as: authority, hierarchy, self, trust, spirituality, creativity, evolution, truth, abstraction, purpose, identity, enlightenment, love and knowledge.

The Guru Papers is more than 370 pages long and, perhaps, at least that many pages might be necessary to demonstrate that the authors have not proven their central thesis that the nature of the teacher-seeker relationship is necessarily – that is, inherently -- authoritarian. I am – as I believe many people would be – quite prepared to concede that, all too frequently, such relationships are riddled with authoritarian practices and influences, but claiming that such practices and influences are systemic and unavoidable in these sorts of relationship, is quite another matter. In my view, the authors certainly have not proven their central thesis beyond a reasonable doubt, and, moreover, I do not believe they even have met a far less stringent burden of proof which requires them to have demonstrated that their thesis, on the basis of a preponderance of evidence, is likely true – in other words, that the teacher-seeker relationship is necessarily authoritarian in nature.

There are a number of comments which could be made in defense of the foregoing critical pronouncements concerning The Guru Papers. But, rather than occupy the reader's time with the long version of such comments, I only will note a few possibilities.

To begin with, demanding or expecting that Being should be reducible to rationalistic methodologies -- as Kramer and Alstad tend to do – is not only arbitrary and not amenable to proof, but it is, essentially, authoritarian in scope and principle. Moreover, such a position presupposes there is a consensus of opinion about what constitutes the rational or the logical, when, in truth, none exists.

This is not to say there is no such thing as logic or rational methodology, but, rather, it is a reflection of the fact that there are a variety of modalities of rational and logical processes about which much critical discussion has taken place. Differences in philosophy, science, theology, law, literature, culture, linguistics, education, and mysticism all testify to the fact that there is an on-going search for the logical, the rational, and the

51

commonsensical in everyday life.

Point-counterpoint-point-counterpoint … is the rhythm of intellectual life. The tapestry woven by various rational techniques produces an intriguing but chaotic set of antagonistic motifs in our individual and collective minds.

Where is the truth in all of this? What is its significance? How do we use it to identify the real?

Furthermore, there are forms of understanding with which we are all familiar which resist, if not defy, rational, logical analysis in many ways. There is an intelligence to seeing, hearing, feeling, being, and consciousness, which does not seem reducible to any discernible scheme of rational, logical discourse. Maybe, in the future this may all change, but, right now, reason and logic have not been able to fathom the mysteries which envelop our existence and through which we engage such existence.

The very nature of the mystical way is that it is said to be ineffable. Yes, all kinds of people have written whole libraries about the contexts surrounding the ineffable, but the unspoken and unspeakable remain what they are – secrets which, to whatever extent they can be grasped, are best engaged through trans-rational venues such as the heart, spirit, and Self.

One can agree with Kramer and Alstad that one should not pursue the mystical way naively, blindly, unquestioningly, mechanically, and without rational reflection. However, there are many times on the spiritual path when rational analysis will not provide one with definitive, certain, unchallengeable answers -- not unless we wish to make reason an authoritarian force within us that is absolute and which cannot be questioned as to its reliability, validity, potential, and limitations.

There are many aspects of life, many experiences, for which reason has not even the foggiest of plausible explanations for how they are possible. Consciousness, creativity, talent, language, logic, intelligence, and rationality are just a few of these unknown facts of life.

Many rationalists would like to reduce faith down to belief but balk when they realize that, from such a perspective, having faith in rationality becomes little more than an exercise in generating a belief system about the nature of thought. Faith is far more complex than mere belief, and, as a result, faith leads into unchartered territories, where the sextant of rationalism and the known charts of logic do not always help one find one's way in the darkness of existence.

We live in the midst of uncertainty, ignorance, ambiguity, possibility, antagonistic forces, and need. As a result, we are vulnerable.

We require someone to show us how to supplement and complement rational tools with other modalities of knowing and understanding. We need someone to initiate us into a process of being able to have a constructive dialectic between reason and the trans-rational.

Kramer and Alstad are smart, talented, articulate, serious explorers. Yet, I know they don't know how to do the foregoing. This is obvious – both from what they say as well as from what they don't say.

The authors tell me to trust myself, but they don't provide any solid clues about the nature of the self that I am supposed to trust. More importantly, they aren't very clear about why I should trust this mysterious 'self' to which they allude in their book.

What is this 'self' rooted in? The truth? Reality in some sense of this word? How do we know this? How can we be certain of this? Is this 'self' absolute and unchallengeable? Where did this 'self' come from? What is its purpose, or does it have any? Is this self a 'rational' self? A transpersonal 'self'? Is this 'self' solipsistic and the creator of reality? If so, how does it accomplish this? What values should this 'self' live or judge by? How are these values derived? Why should one trust the method of derivation? What is the significance of experience? Are they arbitrary or do they have a meaning, and, if so, what is that meaning, and how do we discover the nature of such meaning? What methods should be used? What happens when this 'self' comes into conflict or disagreement with other 'selves'? How should disputes be resolved? Why? How does one address all of the foregoing without slipping into authoritarian practices?

The authors of The Guru Papers have a theory about all of the foregoing, but that is all it is -- an untested, unproven, problematic, ambiguous, vague, incomplete theory. It is a world-view, a paradigm, a philosophical framework – a framework which cannot offer me one, incontestable, definitive smoking-gun of a reason why one should adopt their perspective ... other than, of course, the obvious fact that there seem to be problems everywhere else in the arena of rational discourse, and, so, why not try 'our' (i.e., their) way of doing things.

Beyond the foregoing issues, I think that Kramer and Alstad have made a mistake in reasoning that is quite similar to one which Freud, among many others, made. More specifically, one is on shaky ground when one tries to construct a model of healthy relationships based on an exploration of pathology.

In other words, the authors of The Guru Papers go into great deal of detail

53

about teacher-seeker relationships which have gone wrong, together with the difficulties that arise out of such dysfunctional relationships — both for individuals and society. One can agree with a great deal which they have to say in this respect.

Nevertheless, they are using an inductive variation of extrapolation which implies that because some — or even many — teacher-seeker relationships are diseased, then, all such relationships must be diseased and, moreover, that all teacher-seeker relationships must necessarily manifest the same debilitating set of processes from which there is no escape. However, if what they were saying were actually true, then the relationship which any reader has with their book must be inherently dysfunctional and, consequently, doomed to failure because the general format of this sort of relationship is that of someone who is imparting a version of reality/truth to someone who is interested in seeking after the nature of reality/truth — that is, loosely construed, a teacher-seeker relationship.

The authors might counter with something along the following lines. Precisely because we do not commit any of the mistakes present in problematic guru-devotee relationships, we have provided a healthy, constructive opportunity to explore issues, ideas, problems, and so on which is free from authoritarian influences and practices. The presumptuousness of such a riposte — if it were to happen — is in the belief that a spiritual guide could not accomplish what the authors have been able to pull off — or, so, the latter may believe.

Kramer and Alstad want to help a reader develop a sense of trust in the reader's inner self. They wish to do this without force, compulsion, trickery, deceit, duplicity, insincerity, manipulation, exploitation, dishonesty. They wish to achieve this through a reciprocity with, and respect for, the integrity and self-determining sovereignty of the other person.

The authors would like to have truth, facts, evidence, experience, and rigorous methodology decide such matters, rather than bias, prejudice, dogma, unexamined assumptions, conformity, and blind acceptance. Kramer and Alstad would like individuals to become free, autonomous, independent thinkers and doers who are interested in the welfare of all of creation even as those individuals strive to realize their own essential potential and unique identity.

The two writers would like people to reconcile and harmonize oppositions within themselves, as well as across all social relationships, by extending and expanding the notion of the sacred to include the whole of Being, and not just be restricted to the next-world and/or arbitrarily selected 'holy' people. The authors of The Guru Papers would like to establish modes of justice, decency, morality, and discernment which are not arrogant, narrow, self-serving, exclusionary attempts at justifying and perpetuating authoritarian systems of power.

Kramer and Alstad might be surprised to discover that there actually are spiritual, mystical guides who speak in the same sort of terms, goals, purposes, priorities intentions, and methods as do these authors. An authentic teacher – of whatever kind – is interested in only one thing ... assisting an individual to discover the truth about life, identity, capacity, justice, service, knowledge, community, love, self, integrity, freedom, realization, wisdom, as well as the nature of one's relationship with Being and the many levels and dimensions of manifested Creation.

An authentic teacher – spiritual or otherwise – does not want a student to become the teacher. Such teachers want a person to become herself or himself ... to realize his or her potential ... to come to know one's place in the scheme of things and to be freely committed to being all that one's capacity permits one to be.

An authentic teacher assists an individual to learn how, when, why, and where to trust herself or himself under different circumstances. Authentic teachers induce seekers to submit to the truth and to be satisfied with nothing less than the truth.

Over the last 40 years, or so, there have been two people in my life with whom I have had a teacher-seeker relationship. One of these was authentic, healthy, and constructive, while the other was not, but I learned from both sets of relationship.

If the sequence of life events had been reversed so that I had to endure the dysfunctional relationship first, I don't know how I might have responded to subsequent events –- including meeting up with someone who actually was an authentic spiritual guide. However, by the Grace of God, I didn't encounter the problematic relationship first, but instead I had a non-pathological relationship as my introduction to the mystical path. Many others have not been so fortunate.

I know from my own personal experience that Kramer and Alstad's thesis concerning the alleged inherent, authoritarian nature of all teacher-seeker relationships is wrong. My first – and, so far, only authentic – guide was the exact antithesis of an authoritarian. He never asked – directly or indirectly – for me to submit myself to him, or to conform to his ways of doing things, or to blindly and unquestioningly accept any of the things which he said or did. He was extremely humble and never even hinted at being superior to others. He permitted all manner of questions and was very generous in the time, resources, and efforts which he devoted to providing insights, principles, explanations, and teachings concerning various facets of spirituality – both exoteric and esoteric. In fact, his way of doing things was, ultimately, by the Grace of God, my salvation in dealing with the very problematic ramifications of the spiritually dysfunctional 'teacher' with whom I later came into contact after my mystical guide passed away in the late 1980s.

The line of demarcation which differentiates between spiritual authenticity and a spiritual fraud can be very tricky to discern. Even when, on the surface, everything appears to be 'kosher', nevertheless, if someone is described as a bona fide spiritual guide who does things in a constructive, well-intentioned, non-authoritarian manner, and, yet, such a person has not been authorized by Divinity, then, such an individual is a spiritual fraud and cannot serve as the channel of transmission for the spiritual assistance which is necessary to traverse the mystical path, and, as a result, is placing people in harm's way – both now, and, potentially, in the future – even though, on the surface everything seems to be done with appropriate spiritual etiquette and with due diligence for the welfare of associated practitioners.

When minions of Satan appear in the manifested form of a Charlie Manson, Jim Jones, and so on, the decision seems clear cut – although even here there were sincere people who were exploited. When the minions of Satan appear in the guise of a kindly, friendly, intelligent, charming, engaging, concerned, knowledgeable, passionate, committed teacher who claims spiritual authenticity where none exists, then one has a real problem on one's hand, because one is in the presence of the kind of spiritual quicksand in which the process of extrication may not be all that easy.

Among the chief reasons for such difficulty is that one often does not even realize one is dealing with a spiritual imposter. Indeed, beware of the arrogance which whispers to one's heart 'you could not make such an error', for it is happening every day among sincere people all over the world, and it is happening because we live in treacherous times where authentic spiritual light is very difficult to find and the forces of chaos, disinformation, and darkness are very prominent -- many of these forces call themselves spiritual guides or political leaders and many people believe them.

The authentic teachers of mysticism often indicate that no one comes to Self-realization except through encountering both the compassionate and

56

rigorous attributes of Divinity. I don't know what other, if any, rigorous, Divine attributes I will have to experience in my life as I continue my quest to learn how to serve the purpose of my existence, but there is no doubt in my mind, heart, and soul that a ten year period of my life -- the ones spent with a spiritual fraud – has been very spiritually rigorous in character, for the relationship with the mystical imposter has entailed a great variety of difficulties ... difficulties which Divinity permitted, for there is no reality other than God, and difficulties which I am very thankful have, God willing, come to an end.

4.) <u>Narcissistic Spirituality</u>

There have been various facets of the issue of spiritual abuse which ... been explored in preceding essays. One dimension of this topic that has been touched upon somewhat – although not in great detail – revolves around the nature of the perpetrator of spiritual abuse. What makes such a person tick? What are the motivations underlying his or her behavior? What is the nature of the pathology?

There are a number of proposals which might be offered in response to such questions. Some spiritual frauds are merely run-of-the-mill con artists who, through one means or another, have come to the realization that operating spiritual scams constitutes a fruitful realm with almost unlimited horizons of potential for an enterprising individual.

Other charlatans may see the realm of spirituality as a fertile medium through which to identify individuals who are vulnerable to being sexually exploited. Or, perhaps, a person's struggle with his or her nafs or carnal soul went awry, and a desire for fame and/or power began to take control of things, and spiritual seekers merely became a means to satisfy such a person's corrupted ends.

Some individuals may have started out on the Path with appropriate intentions, but, somewhere along the journey, took a detour into the darker, shadowy side of human potential, and not only became lost, but decided to entangle other people, as well. Historically, for example, there are a number of movements and groups which began with someone who had been associated, in some fashion, with the Sufi tradition, who had certain experiences, and, then, as a result of that person's own interpretation of such events, invented a philosophy, theology, or mystical path which, in turn, was offered and introduced to other people.

Some spiritually abusive people may be sociopathic. History, circumstances, and personal inclination come together in unhappy alliance and manifest themselves in the form of a wolf who preys on and/or devours her or his flock over a period of time.

I have known, to varying degrees, different people who probably fit into one, or another, of the foregoing, categories. However, when I began to reflect on my own personal situation vis–à–vis the spiritual fraud with whom I became entangled, none of the possibilities listed in the previous paragraphs seemed to really resonate with my experiences or the experiences of others who were spiritually abused by this individual.

Why did he do what he did? What was really going on?

After giving considerable thought and attention to this matter over a period of 8-9 months during 2002, there are some tentative conclusions which have begun to surface which feel right -- at least to me. Therefore, I thought I would share these reflections with others and let the chips fall where they may.

From one perspective, evil might be construed as anything that deviates, on one level or another, from the truth, and, therefore, in this sense, we all contribute to the introduction of evil into the world through the way in which we resist, rebel against, distort, hide, ignore, obstruct, and seek to undermine truth by means of our behaviors -- both individually and collectively. This sort of evil arises due to human weakness, short-sightedness, ignorance, error, selfishness, and the like.

There is another form of evil, however, which is more malevolent and pernicious. It exists for the sole purpose of leading people astray from the truth and commits acts intentionally with that goal in mind.

This kind of evil is very cunning, clever, perceptive, and duplicitous. It is always looking for ways to bring misery into the lives of people ... not primarily for whatever sexual gratification, money, fame, or power which may be the collateral gain from such ventures but in order to use the generation of misery as a means to leverage people away from seeking the truth.

There is, within most human beings, a longing for the truth. Some refer to this himma, or aspiration, as a holy longing – a deep, abiding, intense longing to come in contact with essential, ultimate Reality in an intimate, knowing way.

Human beings have come up with many ways to try to assuage this holy longing. Philosophy, psychology, theology, mythology, science, religion, and mysticism have all arisen in conjunction with this holy longing. Different people have pursued diverse roads in the hope of finding the legendary 'holy grail', 'philosopher's stone', 'alchemical elixir', 'golden fleece' occult secrets, the 'theory of everything', a universal set of equations, and altered states of consciousness which would open the doors of perception into the sanctum sanctorum, the holy of holies, of Being. There exists a force, or set of forces, however, which is (are) actively dedicated to corrupting the aforementioned holy longing. This is the malignant form of evil alluded to earlier.

Some people, such as Scott Peck, refer to this reality through phrases such as "people of the lie". Others use the term Satan or Iblis. Some individuals talk in terms of a force of dissolution and chaos which flows through existence, tugging at the fabric of being, seeking to unravel life so that acting upon the holy longing becomes difficult, problematic, bogged down, compromised, co-opted, or re-framed in unethical and unjust directions.

The term or name which is used to give expression to this dimension of existence is relatively unimportant, and different perspectives will be inclined to use that term or name which is most compatible with the world-view which is inherent in that perspective. What is important are the themes underlying, swirling about, and being given expression through those forces and phenomena which seek to obstruct or rebel against the seeking of truth.

Many people who have been touched by such evil abandon the holy longing altogether, and when this occurs, this mode of evil has achieved its purpose. Among other things, the impact of this kind of evil on their lives renders such people incapable of ever trusting anyone sufficiently to seek the kind of help and co-operation which seems vital to achieving progress with respect to struggling toward realizing one's holy longing.

The man who, for ten years (during the 1990s and shortly after the turn of the century) I referred to as my shaykh or spiritual guide was, and is, a manifestation of the more malignant manner of evil which has been outlined above. He enjoys -- indeed, revels -- in trying to lead people astray from the truth, and he often accomplished this in very clever, elaborate, and 'artful' ways (this is called: 'giving the Devil his due').

There is something about his manner which just makes you want to trust, believe, and accept what he says. The lies are so effortlessly delivered, in such a soft, gentle, re-assuring, peaceful, 'sincere', low-key manner.

Moreover, the lies always are delivered in a context steeped in a forked-tongue spirituality which is constructed in such a fashion that the truth is used to camouflage the lies. Consequently, truth becomes like a Trojan horse which hides the army of lies hiding within.

Because the charlatan in question is so knowledgeable about the theory of tasawwuf, or Sufi mystical science, and because he is so charismatic, entertaining and articulate, in several languages, with respect to the manner through which he weaves his lies into the truth, one rarely feels the poison enter one's system. He is a master of misdirection.

The wonder of it is that he can keep all of his lies straight. Yet, even when he slips, he is a marvel to behold and very inventive in the way he uses additional untruths to spin the original lie into the territory of plausible deniability and ambiguity.

I have scoured DSM-IV (Diagnostic and Statistical Manual For

Psychological Disorders), looking for possible matches between its many categories of disturbance and the behavior of my 'once-upon-a-time' shaykh. Although I am convinced that he serves the dark purposes of the sort of intentional evil which seeks to corrupt the holy longing inherent in human beings, nonetheless, I was interested in seeing whether there might be some less traditional, more modern way of thinking about such behavior – something which might appeal to the sensibilities of current research.

The only category in DSM-IV which resonated, to some degree, with my experiences, along with those of several other individuals with whom I have conversed about this man, was that of Narcissistic Personality Disorder. Consequently, in the remainder of this essay I would like to explore a variety of possibilities in this regard and, hopefully, make a few useful contributions along the way.

Perhaps the best way to begin this foray into psychological issues is to state that, in general, there has not been an extensive amount of study in relation to the nature and etiology of Narcissistic Personality Disorder. Opinions are fractured along a number of different fault lines -- some theorists favor an approach rooted in the impact which problematic genetic programming has upon personality and development; other researchers opt for perspectives that are immersed in issues of anomic societies, faulty parenting, dysfunctional families of one kind or another, maladaptive coping strategies, and so on.

There is no consensus among the experts. Moreover, there is precious little data to substantiate one model of Narcissistic Personality Disorder over another.

However, the existence of such a theoretical lack of settledness merely represents conceptual opportunity in another guise. Thus, into this breach I boldly go where no one may have gone before ... and, perhaps, with good reason – let us see.

There are a number of characteristics which need to show up in behavior in order, in any given case, to be able to arrive at a possible diagnosis of Narcissistic Personality Disorder. For example, individuals suffering from this malady tend to be deeply convinced that they are special, unique, rare people who only can be understood and appreciated by others (whether professionals, institutions, or 'gifted' people) who also are high-status and special in a similar or related way.

Such individuals have a constant, excessive need for either positive attention, praise, deference, and admiration from other people, or, alternatively, a need to be infamous, feared, or a source of notoriety of some kind. In either case –

whether that which is forthcoming from others is in the form of adulation or some kind of fear or condemnation – these emotions constitute what is known as 'narcissistic supply', and the narcissistic personality is constantly seeking to receive such a flow of emotion from others.

This sort of an individual has a very palpable sense of entitlement. In other words, this sort of person strongly feels she or he should be given priority, special treatment, or favored status in almost all things, and fully expects, if not demands, that everyone else should be inordinately sensitive to their need for obedience and compliance in relation to this sense of entitlement.

Although, on the surface, there may be remnants of a facade of compassion and empathy for other people, in truth, this facade is purely for show ... as one ploy, among many, to invite people to satisfy the "guide's" need for a constant flow of narcissistic supply. In truth, a narcissistic personality lacks any real empathy or feeling for others and is constantly exploiting them in order to derive further fixes of narcissistic supply of one kind or another.

A person with this disorder often is arrogant and boastful concerning herself or himself, while being equally disdainful of others. Furthermore, such people tend to fly into extreme rages and angry tirades if their search for narcissistic supply either goes unfulfilled or is challenged, resisted, frustrated or ignored in some fashion.

On the one hand, a narcissistic personality may believe -- in a deep fashion -- that the manner in which others feel about that person merely reflects the way in which such an individual feels about herself or himself. Ironically, however, the same individual may be intensely envious of others who may be receiving the sort of attention and adulation which that individual feels ought to be directed to her or him.

Not every person who suffers from this disorder may do so to the same degree. In some people, the foregoing symptoms may be sporadic, transient, relatively mild, or only arise in certain circumstances to which the person is currently reacting and, then, disappear when the nature of events changes. In other individuals, the full array of symptoms may be present in an intense, permanent fashion, and such individuals are extremely resistant to palliative treatment.

All of the foregoing qualities or properties of a Narcissistic Personality Disorder have been observed in the so-called 'shaykh', or spiritual guide, to whom I have been alluding in the earlier comments. What makes his case somewhat intriguing -- if one puts aside, for a moment, the horror of the damage he is inflicting on people -- are the many techniques he has for re-framing and misdirecting attention away from such characteristics.

This man feels entitled, big time, to be served by others, and, in fact, fully expects this to be done but uses other 'veterans' of the group to train people with respect to proper 'adab', or spiritual etiquette, in this regard rather than give people the impression, through his own actions, that he does expect from others what he claims not to expect. He says he is here to serve, but, the reality of the matter is that everyone occupies their time serving him and providing different means for satisfying his constant thirst and hunger in relation to different forms of narcissistic supply.

He constantly needs to be at the center of attention, as well as the focus of praise, admiration, and awe so that he has a steady flow of narcissistic supply to keep him going. Although he frequently speaks in a vocabulary of kindness, compassion, love, and empathy, nonetheless, if one is sufficiently 'fortunate' (there are two edges to this sort of fortune), to peak behind the Wizard's curtain, one begins to see that the man is virtually devoid of any real love, empathy, compassion, or caring for others -- everything is always, ultimately, sooner or later, about him and that to which he feels entitled.

He is firmly convinced that he is extremely unique, special, and a rare species of being. He tells (and only recently have I come to learn of such 'tales') select people he is the Qutb, spiritual pole, of the times, or that he is the king of a little country near Iran who has been forced into exile, or that there is a white light coming from his forehead which, in the past, only has been manifested in a select few spiritual luminaries, or that he has performed a fast for six months, during which he had neither food nor water (there are such fasts that have been observed by some of God's servants and such people are 'fed' by God and even have been known to gain weight during such fasts), or that he has been elevated to an extremely rare spiritual station in an august company of saints and awliya (friends) of God, or that he has been granted the authority to make qutbs (spiritual poles) and special saints of certain people -- although, naturally, of a lesser sort than, and under the auspices of, his own exalted status as the supreme qutb of the age, or that he has taken an 'oath of poverty', yet, roams about with big wads of money in his wallet and stashed in his closet.

Often times he never seems to tell the same story twice to different people. The story version which is selected appears to be the one which is most likely to elicit the greatest amount of narcissistic supply from a given individual or which is most likely to induce obedience, compliance and submission in another person with respect to this so-called 'teacher's program of entitlement and special status. And, naturally, these stories are 'secrets' which need to be kept and are only being told to such and such a person because of the latter's elect status in the cosmic scheme of things.

He masks his arrogance and haughtiness in the disguise of an outward cloak of humility and gratitude concerning the many Divine favors which have been bestowed upon him – favors which he talks about in terms that, superficially, appear to be directed at praising God but which, in truth, are merely opportunities for him to talk about himself. Yet, he also is quite disdainful of other 'shaykhs' or run-of-the-mill Muslims – constantly telling people how he is not like 'those' Muslims, while simultaneously saying that he does not speak ill of others ... unless, of course, the establishment of truth requires that certain unpleasant realities be discussed ... sometimes in considerable detail.

He relates how his shaykh permitted him (with a knowing wink, nod and smile) to be the 'bad boy' of the mystical realms, and thereby, disclose many of the 'secrets' which, heretofore, had been kept hidden behind closely guarded doors. He speaks of the permissions which he has been given by the spiritual hierarchy that have not been vouchsafed to other, less fortunate individuals.

Superficially, he credits his teacher for being the conduit of Divine gifts which have been bestowed on him and for all that this alleged shaykh has spiritually achieved. However, if one watches carefully -- and the movements are very deft and subtle -- beneath this sincere surface is an undertow of self-praise and self-adulation.

He manipulates and exploits people in order to arrange ways to maximize his potential for realizing his constant search for high quality narcissistic supply. He confers favors, or encourages others to grant services, so that people who are the recipients of such 'kindnesses' will feel indebted to him and, consequently, be a ready source of narcissistic supply for him and not because such people might actually be in need or in difficulty.

He claims to never compel anyone to do anything, but he has a myriad of gambits which induce people to do what he wants – even as such people believe their decisions are their own and arrived at freely. He prides himself on never interfering in people's lives but is constantly engaged in precisely that.

When his agenda is threatened or frustrated in some fashion, he goes into angry tirades, and then explains that he doesn't enjoy such outbursts but, sometimes, they are necessary for people's spiritual progress and growth. He is not upset with such individuals and he forgives them for their mistakes, but, occasionally, people need a good kick in the rear end to get them headed in the 'right' direction.

He favors those who serve as his mirror – people who will reflect back to him his own, high opinion of himself. He is envious of anyone who steals his thunder or who might be a rival to the affections of others, and, consequently, begins to scheme for ways to undermine and compromise such threats to the security of his narcissistic supply.

He isolates, ostracizes, and distances himself (and those in his inner circle) from anyone who is not compliant with his wishes. Although he maintains that people are free to make their own choices, nevertheless, those who take him at his word soon find themselves on the outside looking in, even as he denies that such is the case or that the individual is just imagining these sorts of scenarios or harboring unfounded resentments toward others.

He uses the technique of triangulation to near perfection. More specifically, others are prompted by him to pressure, influence, induce, cajole, persuade, or make suggestions to certain third-party 'targets' in order to render the latter more compliant and obedient, and, yet, tracing such pressure back to the original source -- namely, the so-called shaykh -- becomes very difficult because the mediating perpetrators have been told -- for reasons of a special, mystical nature – to remain silent about the reality of why what is going on is going on.

Consequently, the so-called shaykh can maneuver, manipulate, exploit, influence, and control people, while remaining in the shadows, seemingly innocent of any tawdry 'spiritual' machinations or intrigues. On the public stage he can assume the role of a shaykh complete with a bevy of counterfeit qualities to display in order to demonstrate his 'authenticity', but behind the scenes, the pathology of the 'Narcissistic Personality Disorder' is busily engaged.

According to the clinical literature, there are four broad categories of narcissism. On the one hand, an individual is said to be either 'Somatic' or 'Cerebral', and, on the other hand, such a person is described as being of either a 'Classic' or 'Inverted' type.

I will leave discussion of the latter two possibilities for another time since such a discussion will involve going into a considerable amount of detail about various psycho-dynamic theories of development – from: Freud and Jung, to: Horney, Sullivan, Kohut, and others. Therefore, I will concentrate, for the time being, on exploring, a little, the nature of Cerebral and Somatic types of Narcissistic Personality Disorder.

A Somatic Narcissist is someone who derives her or his narcissistic supply in relation to claimed beauty, impressive physique, and/or sexual attractiveness, potency, or prowess. A Cerebral Narcissist seeks her or his narcissistic supply through the acclaim of others concerning alleged intellectual achievement, talent, and genius.

I propose that a third category should be added to the foregoing – that is, Spiritual Narcissist. This is an individual who acquires the sought for narcissistic supply of adulation, praise, infamy, or the like, from others, in conjunction with claims concerning spiritual insight, knowledge, status, station, wisdom, and accomplishment.

A fundamental difference between, on the one hand, Cerebral and Somatic Narcissism, and, on the other hand, a Spiritual Narcissist is that the latter is a lot more difficult to detect under even the best of circumstances. For instance, if someone suffers from Narcissistic Personality Disorder of either a Cerebral or Somatic variety, but, is not particularly bright or attractive or sexually potent, then, the difference between claim and reality is readily divulged.

However, in the case of a spiritual narcissist, even if one is dealing with a fraud, differentiating between the speciousness of a claim and the reality of things may not be all that easy to accomplish simply because of the inherent complexity, ineffability, and difficult-to-prove nature of many of these claims. Such claims may, or may not, be true, but, more often than not, all one has to go on is the word of the individual, and if, for whatever reason, one extends the benefit of a doubt to such a person and presumes that truth is being spoken, then, that extended degree of freedom can be used to leverage a great many other beliefs, values, priorities, commitments, assumptions, sacrifices, and actions within a teacher-student context. Quite frequently, all a skilled spiritual narcissist needs is just enough room to place her or his foot in the doorway to a person's heart, and, before, long, that seeker will 'belong' -- and I don't use this term lightly or advisedly -- to the fraudulent spiritual guide.

The terribly insidious and seductive facet of spiritual narcissism is the ease with which all of the negative qualities or characteristics of a narcissist (e.g., self-serving entitlement, grandiosity, arrogance, boastfulness, envy, lack of empathy, demand or expectation of compliance, anger, and manipulative tendencies) can be re-framed in a much more appealing way. After all, 'if' one is a true mystic who has insight into the unseen, and 'if' one is an 'awliya', or friend,

67

of God, and 'if' one has been authorized by the mystical elect to assist people to the highest spiritual truths, and, thereby, realize the 'holy longing', then, all of the foregoing negative properties can be spun as necessary components in the Divine passion play which is designed to help people die to themselves by subduing their carnal soul.

For example, since submission is the goal of authentic mysticism, then, submitting to the alleged shaykh becomes – or, so, it is claimed – but a preliminary step in the journey toward complete submission to Divinity. Alternatively, since God works in mysterious ways to induce us to deepen our faith, and shaykhs do the same, then, consequently, sometimes the fraudulent shaykh is painted as an agent for Divine trickery which is, then, exploited to leverage our all -too-human vulnerabilities even as everything which is transpiring (problematic and troubling though it may be) is said to be for our own spiritual benefit and well-being.

In addition, sometimes God, on the surface, appears to be without empathy and compassion for the human condition, but such appearances are described as being illusory, and, in truth, God loves us deeply. Therefore, when the alleged shaykh appears indifferent to our sufferings and sacrifices, this can be framed as merely a reflection of how Divinity sometimes appears to us. Moreover, surely, 'if' God has showered blessings on an individual, what is wrong with – of course, in a humble, indirect manner – proclaiming such bestowals have been given expression through the locus of manifestation known as the 'shaykh' in order to engender love in the heart of the mureed (or follower/initiate) for the one who will guide them to Divinity?

What might easily be seen in a Cerebral or Somatic Narcissist for what it is - - namely, vanity, arrogance, and so on – becomes (to borrow a form of expression from Winston Churchill that has been, somewhat altered in the present rendering): an enigma wrapped in a riddle within a paradox of ambiguity in relation to spiritual narcissism. Are we being scammed or are we being told the truth? Will we lose if we reject such claims, or will be freed from spiritual treachery? Will we find our essential selves through such a person, or will we become alienated from our essential identity and Self?

The promise is great. But, verifiable answers are difficult to come by.

If we feel we are not making spiritual progress in conjunction with a given teacher, well, the problem lies with our lack of commitment to, and sincerity with, the mystical way. On the other hand, if a teacher informs us that we are making great spiritual advances even though this is not evident in the form of

68

altered states of consciousness or in other tangible ways, how are we to prove or disprove what is being said.

No matter what happens to an individual on the spiritual path, a clever spiritual narcissist can re-frame the situation in a way that keeps people enthralled with continuing to serve as an on-going source of narcissistic supply for such a fraudulent spiritual guide. 'Pleasant' events are re-framed as the beneficence of Divinity that is being channeled through the 'shaykh'. Difficult or unpleasant events can be re-framed as Divine trials, tests, and tribulations which are a necessary part of the Path and have nothing to do with the possibility that the shaykh is a spiritual narcissist and the problems one is encountering are a Divine prod to point one's holy longing in another, more 'constructive' direction.

When narcissistic supply (in the form of adulation, praise, and so on) is available in quantity, if not quality (or perceived to be by the one who is under the influence of Narcissistic Personality Disorder), this might be comparable to a manic-like state. On the other hand, if the quality or quantity of such narcissistic supply is perceived to be drying up (or actually is drying up), then this might be the side of the condition in which depression manifests itself.

During the manic phase, a narcissistic personality may be easy-going, affable, happy, generous, expansive, joyful, and ecstatic. During the depressed phase, such an individual may be pensive, silent, reflective, anxious, unhappy, cranky, angry, hyper-critical, down, withdrawn, given to rage, and so on.

Since the Sufi path is actually characterized by interspersed episodes of jazb (Divine attraction) and qabd (Divine contraction), confusing mania for jazb and depression for qabd might be quite easy to do among the followers of a person under the influence of Narcissistic Personality Disorder. After all, who among that individual's mureeds would have sufficient spiritual wherewithal to know otherwise? This is especially so if the fraudulent individual suffering from Narcissistic Personality Disorder re-frames the mania and depression in a manner that is consistent with the nature of mystical theory (i.e., as expansion and contraction).

Ironically, a narcissist will often come across to others as appearing to be someone – who on the surface, at least – is extremely earnest and sincere. Sometimes the intensity of this earnestness and sincerity may lead some individuals to wonder if the person is somehow disconnected from reality (or, at least, as it seems to be to the 'rest' of us), or, whether that person is simply unable to appraise the state of existence properly.

However, in the case of a spiritual narcissist, this very question or doubt can be turned back on itself. Instead of the narcissist being out of touch with reality, or being unable to properly judge the actual nature of events, the person harboring such questions and doubts becomes the source of the problem – that is, this latter individual is out of touch with the 'true' Reality and does not have the requisite spiritual insight to be able to properly assess the nature of Being.

At worst, the spiritual narcissist can maintain that she or he is only out of contact with physical/material reality and, furthermore, this may not necessarily be such a bad thing. The reconstruction of priorities concerning the levels of 'reality' serves the agenda of the narcissistic personality disordered individual and confronts the skeptic with a set of issues for which there is no readily identifiable answer with which everyone will agree and through which consensual validation can be achieved.

Once again, the complex, ineffable, hidden nature of the mystical path lends credence, plausible deniability and irresolvable ambiguity to the arsenal of tools through which a spiritual fraud can leverage people's understanding, beliefs, judgments and values. Potential weaknesses can be turned into formidable defenses in relation to a spiritual narcissist.

These aforementioned qualities of earnestness and apparent sincerity were, and are, two hallmark features of the individual whom, for ten years, I considered my shaykh. His sincerity and earnestness had an extremely attractive, charismatic quality to them.

The actor, Spencer Tracy once said that when a person can fake sincerity, then one really has it made as an actor. The spiritual fraud to who I am alluding had learned how to fake sincerity and earnestness to a degree that has to be witnessed in order to be (grudgingly) admired.

His ability -- the spiritual fraud, not Spencer Tracy -- to induce other people to provide him with an on-going narcissistic supply of adulation, praise, awe, compliance, obedience, entitlement, specialness, and so on, was very much rooted in his capacity to appear immensely sincere and earnest to others. Such sincerity and earnestness were used by him to re-frame certain issues, and misdirect his audience away from many other issues, as well as to get people to not only lower their natural defenses of doubt, skepticism, and mistrust, but to practically hand over the keys to the repository of all one's essential trust -- namely, the heart -- within a very short period of time.

Some people may find the foregoing analysis of a spiritually abusive individual somewhat comforting because it is couched in terms of a modern, psychological framework. Casting the situation in such a light may appear to offer some sort of intelligible explanation for why one person might spiritually abuse another individual.

From the perspective of a modified treatment of the DSM-IV rendering of Narcissistic Personality Disorder, we now can see that some people in spiritual/religious circles may suffer from such a malady and, thereby, we might have a somewhat better idea not only of some of the dynamics involved in this disorder but how the very properties of the disorder naturally lend themselves to assisting a person to become a chameleon within certain spiritual contexts. However, what remains unanswered is the why.

Why does someone develop this disorder? What is its etiology? Can it be avoided? Can it be cured?

I believe there are some 'lesser' forms of Narcissistic Personality Disorder which arise through the interplay of a conjunction of various components – some genetic, some social, some personal, some family dynamics, and one might explore the aforementioned issues of Classic and Inverted types of Narcissism to gain some insight into such issues. Nevertheless, I also believe there is a 'greater' modality of Narcissistic Personality Disorder which is possible, and this form of the pathology is deliberately chosen by an individual.

In spiritual terms -- at least in a largely Western sense -- the paradigm for such a deliberate choice is Iblis, or Satan. Because Iblis had an exceedingly high opinion of his place in the scheme of the universe, because he believed he was entitled, because he was arrogant and haughty, because he believed in his own sense of specialness and uniqueness, because he believed that the purpose of the universe was to serve as a source for his narcissistic supply of adulation, praise knowledge, and so on, because he was envious of human kind, because he went into a angry tirade when his narcissistic supply was threatened, because he was so convincing in his sincerity and earnestness concerning his love of God that he fooled himself, Iblis/Satan committed an essential error and fell from Grace.

This fall appears to be infinite and unforgivable in nature. And, given that according to the Qur'an there is one and only one sin which is, in the eyes of Divinity, totally unforgivable -- and that is shirk, or associating partners with God, or relegating to oneself some form of God-hood – then, presumably, in choosing to rebel against God by choosing the path of narcissism rather than servitude, Iblis/Satan committed the most egregious form of shirk.

Sadly, I have come to the conclusion that spiritual frauds like the person to whom I have been alluding throughout this essay bear a striking resemblance to Iblis/Satan in several respects. First, they have committed the basic error of all narcissists -- whether of the lesser or greater variety -- which is this: they choose to consider themselves as superior, unique, special, rare, entitled, worthy of adulation and praise, with a special dispensation to ignore, flaunt, or bend the principles upon which the universe works, and a concomitant right to exploit and manipulate others for their own ends (the ends of the latter, not the former).

Secondly, like Iblis/Satan, spiritual frauds do not repent for their wrong-doing, but instead, seek permission from God to lead others astray or to corrupt the holy longing which resides in the souls of all human beings. If a person who spiritually abuses others would sincerely repent, then, God willing, one could, in time, forgive such an individual for the incredibly destructive nature of their actions which they have imposed on people for self-serving and vainglorious purposes ... even if one might never again trust such a person to be the keeper of an outhouse, let alone a guide for the aspirations of holy longing.

Thirdly, like Iblis/Satan, charlatans use techniques of artfully-false sincerity and earnestness to seduce people and, if possible, corrupt them. Like Iblis/Satan, they disguise themselves in friendly, affable, kindly, sincere, empathetic, knowledgeable, compassionate, generous, charismatic, entertaining, enchanting packages which whisper to one amidst the shadows, ambiguities and interstitial zones of existence.

Fourthly, like Iblis/Satan, they don't really seem to care when adulation turns to infamy, as people begin to learn the true nature of their activities. As long as they can be the center of attention and the focus of people's preoccupation, then, for them, hatred is almost as good as adulation as far as the dynamics of narcissistic supply are concerned because the only principle which matters to them is that they are the object of people's attention, and if they can get someone to hate them for the rest of a person's life, they will be content since something of the spiritual narcissist's purpose has been achieved -- which is to lead people astray from the straight path where one must learn to overcome, move beyond and transform such emotions in spiritually constructive ways.

Finally, like Iblis/Satan, spiritual frauds, such as the one to whom I have been alluding throughout the preceding material, actually believe in God. They are not atheists or agnostics. They may -- as Iblis/Satan did and does -- even love God in their own way.

The horror of Iblis/Satan and such individuals is that they have deliberately chosen to place their agenda above Divine Purpose or, alternatively, to conflate their purposes with Divine Purpose. In fact, they wish to undermine the possibility of such a Purpose ever being realized and seek to take down with them as many people as will permit such spiritual charlatans to take permanent control of their lives. The even greater horror is that there are many such predatory dajjals (spiritual imposters) on the loose in the world these days ... among so-called Sufi shaykhs, among dogmatic and intolerant theologians, among government leaders, and among groups of terrorists -- may God protect us and save us all from such truly evil intentions.

Sometimes, by the Grace of God, the choices we make in this regard are successful. On other occasions, we are not so fortunate.

I have had two spiritual guides in my life, one was authentic, and one was not. If I were a baseball player, going 1 for 2 is a good batting average. On the other hand, if I were a goalie in ice-hockey, a .500 save percentage would relegate me, at best, to sitting on the sidelines in pick-up games.

Life is not a game. However, if it were, I'm not sure whether going 1 for 2 in the authentic guide department is okay or not ... I guess it beats going 0 for 2.

Only God knows why we do what we do, when we do it. However, irrespective of whatever choices are made, God's purpose is served.

May God guide us to the choices which, in the long run, will be best for our deen (spiritual way or method) -- whether these choices have, in the short run, pleasant or unpleasant consequences. May God encourage us to seek the truth in all matters. Ameen! Ameen! Ameen!

5.) <u>Fatwa</u>

A fatwa is a legal opinion concerning an interpretation of some dimension of shari'ah (sometimes referred to as Sacred Law) and is given by people who, supposedly, are competent to give such opinions. However, there is nothing binding upon Muslims with respect to the issuing of such an edict.

A fatwa is a legal brief. If one is persuaded by the structure of the argument and logic contained in this sort of document, then, one may use such a presentation to shape one's intention in conjunction with some spiritual problem, or other, with which one is attempting to resolve. If, alternatively, one is not persuaded by the arguments contained in such a brief, then, really, one can dismiss the document without prejudice.

In a book entitled <u>What is Right With Islam</u> by Imam Feisal Abdul Rauf, there is a fatwa which appears in an appendix. The heading for the fatwa is: "Fatwa Permitting U. S. Muslim Military Personnel to Participate in Afghanistan War Effort." This fatwa was not written by the author of the above mentioned book. Rather, it is the collective effort of five individuals who hail from Qatar, Egypt, and Syria. Notwithstanding the foregoing issue of authorship of the fatwa, the author of <u>What is Right With Islam</u> does mention in the main text of the book how he had recommended to *The New York Times* that it publish the fatwa. Furthermore, by not commenting on the fatwa and permitting the fatwa to stand as it is without critical or evaluative remarks, he has given his tacit endorsement to what is being said by the five framers of the aforementioned fatwa.

Ostensibly, the fatwa was generated in response to some inquiries by the "most senior chaplain of the American armed forces". Nothing was said about the circumstances under which the five authors of the fatwa were approached by the chaplain, or why these people, in particular, were consulted, or whether efforts had been made to obtain any other determination, dissenting or otherwise, in conjunction with the presenting problem.

A critical analysis of the fatwa in question is given below. This is not a counter-fatwa, but it does serve as a dissenting voice, and it encompasses a perspective which people might wish to consider when reflecting not only on the issue of whether Muslim armed services personnel should participate in wars against other Muslims, but, as well, the whole issue of what constitutes justifiable homicide in relation to people in general.

****

Early in the fatwa, one finds the following:

"All Muslims ought to be united against all those who terrorize the innocents, and those who permit killing of non-combatants without a justifiable reason."

The authors of the fatwa do not say what they mean by being "united", but one might offer the possibility that certain oppressive factions within the U.S. government – both present and past – certainly qualify as being among those to whom any person of decency would be opposed ... if in no other way than speaking out the truth in the face of tyranny.

Very serious and fundamental questions, for example, concerning legitimacy, justice, morality, and fairness could be raised about U. S. involvement in, to name but a few localities: Vietnam, Cambodia, Laos, Indonesia, the Philippines, Iran, Iraq, Africa, Palestine, and most of Latin America. If terrorizing of innocents and the killing of non-combatants without justifiable reason is the issue, then, one may want to expand one's frame of reference and think about state-sponsored terrorism in conjunction with more than just Afghanistan.

However, irrespective of who is terrorizing whom, none of this justifies killing and terrorizing innocent people during the process of tracking down criminals and apprehending them. Tens of thousands, if not hundreds of thousands, of innocents have been killed in, collectively, Afghanistan, Iraq, the Balkans, and the Sudan (when the pharmaceutical factory in Sudan was mistakenly bombed, by order of William Jefferson Clinton, as a suspected plant for producing weapons of mass destruction – which it was proven not to be -- the one source of pharmaceuticals for Sudan was lost and, as a result, tens of thousands of innocent people died from diseases and infections for which no pharmaceuticals were available to use in treatment) – by a self-serving, reprehensible U. S. government policy. There was no due process for any of these people to determine if there was justifiable reason as to why they should die. There was no due process to establish that such people were aiding, abetting, providing safety and comfort for, or helping to finance the perpetrators of any crimes.

Property has been destroyed in all of the foregoing instances. People have been terrorized. Innocents have been slain. International conventions have been broken. War crimes have been committed.

A rogue government has run amok on Earth. However, since this is all done behind a facade of words such as: freedom, humanitarian, liberation, justice, democracy, and rule of law, then everyone should understand that the unfortunates who have had to die, starve, become ill (through depleted uranium munitions, as well as the diseases which have been sprung loose through the systematic destruction of infrastructure), be uprooted into refugee status, and suffer – well, this is all for a good and noble cause: U. S. hegemony in which, like ancient Greece, only the real citizens (i.e., the perpetrators of crimes) get to consent to how they are to be governed ... everyone else is mere chattel or fodder or 'deserving' of exploitation and manipulation.

The fatwa continues with:

"We find it necessary to apprehend the true perpetrators of these crimes as well as those who aid and abet them through incitement, financing or other support. They must be brought to justice in an impartial court of law."

Of course, the U. S. government does not consider the World Court to be an impartial venue of law because the Court had the audacity to find the U. S. government guilty of violating Nicaraguan sovereignty, as well as conducting illegal blockades and systematically destroying the economy and people of that country. Nor, does the U. S. government consider the United Nations an impartial court of law because the United Nations has had the temerity to seek to place constraints on how or when or if the U. S. wields its considerable military might, not to mention that the U. S. government objects to being reminded that, for almost forty years, it has been stonewalling Resolution 242 which indicates, among other things, that no country – say Israel – has the right to hold onto territory gained through hostilities, or that the U. S. government wishes to ignore Resolution 687 which says, among other things, that once the matter in

Iraq is settled to the satisfaction of the UN Security Council -- something which is unlikely to happen because the U. S. will veto anything that is not in accordance with its plans for hegemony -- then, all weapons of mass destruction, including the nuclear weapons possessed by Israel, must be eliminated from the Middle East. The U. S. government finds such matters of international agreement inconvenient for its purposes of real politik, and, therefore, blames the failure of the UN on everyone but one of the real sources of difficulty which is undermining UN effectiveness -- namely, the United States government.

Now, some may wish to make the claim that the only impartial court of law is the vigilante system of the armed forces and the kangaroo courts known as military tribunals. Apparently, the only people who can be trusted are those who are infected with the same mental and spiritual disease which has been responsible for U. S. government lawlessness within the international community across many decades ... even though many truly independent people might see this as a conflict of interest with respect to basic issues of justice, fairness, and objectivity.

Really, what is the difference between what Osama and company are alleged to have done, or what the U. S. government has done, and is doing. Neither of these parties has bothered much with determining who the "true perpetrators" are. Neither of these parties has concerned themselves much with due process. Neither of these parties has given any evidence that they are concerned about whether or not the people who die, or those who are terrorized, or the property which is destroyed, or the individuals who suffer are, in fact, guilty of anything except being in the wrong place at the wrong time.

The Qur'an indicates: if even one innocent person is killed, it is as if the whole of humanity were killed. Osama – if he actually did have anything to do with 9/11 – stands condemned by the very book which he professes allegiance.

Moreover, the Prophet Muhammad (peace be upon him) indicated that one may not wage war on the elderly, women, children, non-combatants, and one may not seek to destroy the means of livelihood of a

78

people. And, yet, both principles of the "etiquette" of war were violated in relation both to the events of 9/11 as well as the events which unfolded subsequently to that date in relation to both Afghanistan and Iraq.

Returning to the text of the fatwa, the aforementioned legal brief seeks to address the whole problem of an individual having to differentiate the innocent from the "true perpetrators". Therefore, at a certain point, the fatwa offers a hadith of the Prophet which says:

"When two Muslims face each other in fighting and one kills the other, then both the killer and the killed are in the hell-fire. Someone said: we understand that the killer is in hell, why, then, the one who's being killed? The Prophet said: because he wanted to kill the other person."

The fatwa continues on with:

"The noble hadith mentioned above only refers to the situation where the Muslim is in charge of his affairs. He is capable of fighting or not fighting. This situation does not address the situation where a Muslim is a citizen of a state and a member of a regular army. In this case he has no choice but to follow orders."

I love the way people make things up on the fly. Unless a human being is mentally incompetent, one always is in charge of his or her affairs -- at least with respect to the choices one makes.

One choice a person has is to join, or not join, the military in the first place. One's country can be served in many ways, and being a patriot does not necessarily entail that one must kill others or destroy their property and infrastructure in order to have sincerity of commitment to the core values of the United States. Another choice one has is to choose a court martial over killing innocent people.

Alternatively, one might seek to become a conscientious objector. In other words, if, before the fact of enlistment, one were not aware of the extent to which innocent lives are terrorized and brutalized by modern warfare, then surely, when one becomes aware of this, one has a strong argument for disengaging from such activities -- an argument which is rooted in moral principle, and is not sullied by either cowardice nor a lack of love for, and patriotism toward, one's country.

Why the military would want to retain people for purposes of killing others when the hearts and souls of such people being retained are morally and spiritually not in synch with such actions, is a puzzle. Surely, the military must recognize that it takes courage to say "no" to the killing of innocents -- especially, when the military is likely to take harsh action simply because in this land of democratic freedoms, the military leadership (bold warriors that they are) feels threatened by an act of moral conscience. On the other hand, if everyone were to act in accordance with his or her moral conscience rather than submit to orders, perhaps the military might not have enough bodies to carry out the wishes of its masters in the government ... and this just won't do.

Being in charge of one's affairs does not mean one has control over the ramifications of one's choices, nor does it mean one will enjoy the consequences of one's choices. However, one always is in charge of the process of exercising one's God-given capacity to choose. This is both the strength and vulnerability of being human, and to suppose otherwise is rather shallow of the authors of the fatwa at issue.

I also would be curious as to what the reasoning is behind saying that the previous hadith, or saying of the Prophet, does not address the situation in which a Muslim is "a citizen of a state and a member of a regular army." Did the Prophet inform the authors of the fatwa that this was the case? How does one know what the scope of the Prophet's words and intentions are with respect to the cited hadith?

The fact of the matter is, we don't know. And, so, some jurists are inclined to create legal fictions in order to bridge their forays into the unknown.

In ecology there is something called: the 'precautionary principle'. This precept indicates that when one is faced with a situation in which the consequences of one's actions may lead either to foreseeable problems, or entail potential problems which our limited state of understanding is not capable of foreseeing but is capable of contemplating, then, it is better to err on the side of caution and wait until our ignorance becomes less and, as a result, we are better able to understand what is going on and what the consequences of our actions will be.

Thus, with respect to the aforementioned hadith, perhaps, it is better to err on the side of caution and entertain the possibility that the scope of the Prophet's words may actually have encompassed what the authors of the fatwa say it does not than to simply proceed, without any justification, and claim, as the authors of the fatwa do, that the hadith does not apply to Muslims who are citizens of a state and members of an army. The unsupported claim of a jurist (or even a number of them) does not take precedence over the guidance of the Prophet.

According to the authors of the fatwa, a Muslim who lives in a state where he or she is a member of a regular army:

"has no choice but to follow orders, otherwise his allegiance and his loyalty to his country could be in doubt. This would subject him to much harm since he would not enjoy the privileges of citizenship without performing its obligations."

Aside from the fact that, as the Bible reminds us, it is better to lose the world and all its attendant privileges and allurements than it is to lose one's soul, and aside from the fact that it is better to, possibly, spend a few years in prison than to live an eternity in hell, it is unfortunate that the ideas of loyalty, allegiance, and obligations should be limited – as the authors of the fatwa seem to indicate -- to doing what the purveyors of hegemony demand rather than to serving the principles and purposes for which the United States came into existence ... which certainly was not to embrace tyranny, injustice, immorality, and the destruction and terrorizing of innocent human beings.

We all have an absolute obligation to truth and justice. If anything, our loyalty and allegiance - - as citizens of the U. S. – are to the principles through which the United States was conceived and not to the grotesque, sordid soiled version to which the architects of hegemony wish to call citizens. There is no virtue in enjoying the privileges of citizenship which are predicated on the death, destruction and oppression of others who are innocent.

The harm to which one is exposed through blind taqlid (unquestioning adherence) to immoral, unjust, and ill-conceived orders is not loss of the enjoyment of the privileges of citizenship, but, rather, the harm is in the loss of one's way in life. At one point in 'A Man for All Seasons' Thomas Moore is cross-examining one of the people who have committed false witness against him and Thomas Moore asks the man what the medallion is which the individual wears around his neck. The man explains that it is emblematic of being the Chancellor of Wales, to which Thomas Moore responds with: "Whereas Holy Scripture tells us that it would not profit a man if he were to gain the whole world yet were to lose his soul ... but for Wales, Richard?" Should we really encourage people to exchange the integrity and spiritual well-being of the soul for this or that worldly trinket -- no matter what the hype or glitter surrounding that trinket may be?

According to the authors of the fatwa being discussed:

"The Muslim (soldier) must perform his duty in this fight despite the feeling of uneasiness of 'fighting without discriminating'. His intentions (niyya) must be to fight for enjoining of the truth and defeating falsehood. It's to prevent aggression on the innocents, or to apprehend the perpetrators and bring them to justice. It's not his concern what other consequences of the fighting that might result in his personal discomfort since he alone can neither control nor prevent it. Furthermore, all deeds are accounted (by God) according to the intentions."

This notion that "It's not his [the soldier's] concern what other consequences of the fighting that might result in his personal discomfort" resonates all too closely with a constant refrain of the people being prosecuted at the Nuremberg trials 'I was only following orders'. One of the principles arising out of those trials and which became a precedent within modern international law is this: one cannot use the excuse of following orders to justify participating in crimes against humanity.

Furthermore, one should take issue with the contention of the authors of the fatwa that one person "alone can neither control nor prevent" such events. Each person can control and prevent his or her own participation in whatever acts are repugnant to one's moral and spiritual commitments, and, as well, are in contravention of international law.

Unfortunately, the authors of the fatwa seem to be intent on instilling a sense of learned helplessness in people. They are saying that if one individual cannot prevent such things from happening, then, one should just permit oneself to be carried along by the flow of forces and not concern oneself about such matters -- as if such matters were not encompassed by one's spiritual and moral responsibility as a human being to seek the good and avoid the evil.

Furthermore, if I am a soldier and, therefore, I know how war works -- in theory, if not in practice -- then, I know that the way modern warfare is conducted will almost certainly lead to the killing of innocents, the destruction of the property of innocent people, and the terrorizing of innocent people. Given this knowledge, how does one form the intention that one will be fighting for truth and the defeating of falsehood when the very first casualty of war is, often, truth itself.

The plans for the invasion of Afghanistan had already been drawn up prior to 9/11, and 9/11 became a convenient justification or pretext for carrying out a plan which was in the works independently of 9/11. Afghanistan is today, as it has been for hundreds of years, a critical piece of the puzzle in the game of geo-politics.

For instance, because Iran cannot be trusted by the U. S. government to do the right thing for the hegemony of the latter, the 'best' -- although not the shortest -- route for the oil pipeline which has been on the drawing boards for quite some time is through Afghanistan and over to Pakistan. One of the objectives all along has been to gain control of the oil discoveries in the Caspian Sea region. The permanent military bases which are being built by the U. S. are all along the route of the proposed pipeline, and, in addition, such bases give the U. S. a ready set of staging areas to launch attacks on many places in that part of the world, which is also why the U. S. forces were being set up in, among other places, Uzbekistan. The quid pro quo of these arrangements is that Russia is given a free hand to do what it will with Chechnya and its resources -- where oppression, wholesale slaughter, and the violation of basic rights are permitted as long as they do not impact on the agenda of certain dimensions of U. S. government economic and foreign policy -- a policy which is steeped in the selfish, imperialistic, exploitive oils of hegemony with respect to the rest of the world.

How is one fighting for truth and the elimination of falsehood when one seeks to stop the Taliban but does nothing to stop the opium trade going on in Afghanistan which supplies 90% of the raw resources for the heroin which ends up on the streets of, among other places, the United States? And, ironically, the Taliban who are, for the most part, uncivilized and barbaric in their manner of rule were successful in stopping the flow of heroin into America from Afghanistan.

How is one fighting for truth and the elimination of falsehood when the vast majority of innocents outside of Kabul still live in terror and uncertainty, both because of, as well as, in spite of a U. S. military presence? How is one fighting for truth and the elimination of falsehood when the policy of the U. S. government is to protect its interests rather than the interests of the average citizen of Afghanistan, or to suppose that its interests and needs are one and the same with the needs and interests of most of the inhabitants of that country?

If God judges us according to our intentions, then, how does one expect to fare when one knows that – propaganda aside – one is, in many respects, not fighting for truth and the elimination of falsehood but, rather, one is fighting for the industrial-military complex's desire to control the world and its resources? Does one not have an obligation to seek for the truth with respect to what one is being told? Are there not numerous sources via the Internet, DVDs, books, magazines, and people like Chalmers Johnson, Noam Chomsky, Howard Zinn, Edward Herman, Robert McChesney, Nafeez Ahmad, Ralph Nader, Peter Monague, and others through whom to discover the evidence which discloses what is going on all around the world as well as within the United States?

Can we bury our minds and hearts in the toxic soil which is euphemistically called education in the United States and say: my intentions are pure and clear? Does God not see every little fleeting bit of evidence which we allow to slip through our consciousness unchallenged which suggests that the truth is something other than what we are being asked to digest as the "official" line on things?

Niyat, or intention, is not something which forms in a vacuum. It is

84

rooted in experience, and when the heart plays fast and loose with the truth of experience, then no matter what the superficial form of the intention may be, there is sub-text which flows in our heart of hearts and something of the truth registers with us ... and it is this which is our true intention rather than that which is given for public consumption, and it is this for which we will be held accountable.

The authors of the fatwa in question maintain:

"Muslim jurists have ruled that what a Muslim cannot control he cannot be held accountable for, as God (the Most High) says: "And keep your duty to God as much as you can" [64:16]. The Prophet (prayer and peace be upon him) said: "When I ask of you to do something, do it as much as you can."

One's duty to God does not consist in enabling the military-industrial complex to acquire hegemony over the world. One's duty to God does not consist in killing innocent people, destroying their property, or terrorizing non-combatants.

In addition, the Prophet hasn't asked one to do any of these things either. So, contrary to what the authors of the fatwa are suggesting, we are not obligated to do as much of these things as we can.

Moreover, one might ask the question: what does 'doing as much as one can' entail? Isn't it ironic that in a country which claims it is democratic and based upon principles of justice, fairness, truth, and liberty, one is not free to exercise one's conscience, in the matter of war, without running the risk of suffering considerable punitive damages. Yet, irrespective of whatever these damages may be, just as one is prepared to risk hardship in battle, one should be prepared to risk hardship in the cause of truth and justice.

This is what we can do. This is an essential part of what it means to be a human being.

The aforementioned fatwa says:

"even if fighting causes him discomfort spiritually or psychologically, this personal hardship must be endured for the greater public good, as the jurisprudence (fiqh) rule states."

And, how does one calculate the greater public good? What values does one use? What methods does one apply? What criteria are to be consulted?

According to the fatwa, "the Muslim here" -- that is, the one who is a soldier:

"is part of a whole, if he absconds, his departure will result in great harm, not only for him but for the Muslim community in his country -- and here there are many millions of them."

What is this "great harm" which will accrue to the soldier of conscience and his community? Very little is said in this regard, but mention is made that if a person does not sell his or her soul to the military-industrial complex, then it could be that the allegiance and loyalty of Muslims will come into doubt.

Allegiance and loyalty to what: To someone's warped way of dealing with the world? To someone's burning greed? To someone's indifference to the suffering of innocent people who are in the way of some geo-political objective? To someone's desire to proceed through life in an immoral, illegal way that violates the norms of decency which have been established by many countries and many billions of people?

Are the authors of the fatwa suggesting that in order not to have to deal with the unpleasantness of someone having doubts about where one's loyalties and allegiance lie, that one should betray the ideals of the Declaration of Independence and the Constitution -- not to mention, one's relationship with God and the truth? Is it really okay to destroy innocent people by the thousands, to destroy their property, to destroy their means of livelihood, so that Muslims in America won't have to deal with someone questioning their loyalty and allegiance? Is this the greater good?

The authors of the fatwa go on to say:

86

"The questioner [a Muslim military chaplain] inquires about the possibility of the Muslim military personnel in the American armed forces to serve in the back lines -- such as in the relief services sector and similar works. If such requests are granted by the authorities, without reservation or harm, to the soldiers, or to other American Muslim citizens, then, they should request that. Otherwise, if such a request raises doubts about their allegiance or loyalty, cast suspicions, present them with false accusations, harm their future careers, shed misgivings on their patriotism, or similar sentiments, then it is not permissible to ask for that."

Who and what is necessitating that it is not permissible to make such a request? Is it God? Is it the Prophet? Well, actually, it isn't. It is a group of five jurists who are saying this is impermissible. Moreover, they are saying it is impermissible on the basis of dubious interpretations of what the Qur'an and hadith have said.

And, why are they saying it is impermissible? Well, as everyone knows, the threat of harsh words, suspicions, doubts, false accusations, future careers, and the like are far more important than a few thousand lives over in Afghanistan. This is the calculus of the jurisprudence of the five people who have authored the fatwa in question.

Whether the lives of the innocent people in Afghanistan whose lives will be destroyed by a U. S. invasion are Muslim or not Muslim is immaterial. The Qur'an does not say: 'if anyone killed a Muslim human being - unless it be in punishment for murder or for spreading mischief on earth -- it would be as though he killed all of humanity'. The Qur'an states the prohibition against killing without qualification as far as the identity, race, ethnicity, gender, religion, or beliefs of the individual being killed are concerned.

The fatwa being examined here ends with:

"This is in accordance with the Islamic jurisprudence rules which state that necessities dictate exceptions, as well as the rule which says that one may endure a small harm to avoid a much greater harm."

The authors have stated things incorrectly by claiming that the principles of jurisprudence which they consider to be applicable actually demand what they are claiming.

First, the much greater harm in the issue before the authors of the fatwa is the killing of innocent people rather than not having to endure the suspicions, doubts and false accusations of others concerning one's loyalty, allegiance, duty, and patriotism which they have identified as the greater harm. In addition, the greater harm is in enabling Muslims to kill others -- whether those other human beings are Muslim or non-Muslim -- without just cause and due process and just because someone who has a hidden agenda says they should.

Secondly, the principle that "necessities dictate exceptions" presupposes that it is necessary to kill innocent human beings, and the authors of the fatwa have not established this, nor will they ever be able to establish this. The killing of innocent human beings is never necessary except in the schemes and machinations of those who lust after what does not belong to them and who have a pathological need to control the rest of the world.

6.) Openings

While I share some of the goals which are espoused in <u>What's Right With Islam</u> by Imam Feisal Abdul Rauf – namely, its ecumenical spirit, as well as its emphasis on such qualities as: peace, liberty, harmony, justice, democracy, plurality, and moral reciprocity – nevertheless, there seem to be a number of issues that are relevant to the realization of such goals, yet, which are not actually rigorously pursued in Imam Rauf's book, or if they are engaged, this seems to be done in ways that are of questionable persuasiveness, if not tenability.

The construction of a logical argument can be a complex, layered, nuanced process. Often times, this is the purpose of writing a book – to devote the time, space, and effort necessary to develop, in as persuasive a manner as possible (at least in principle) the essential features of a perspective together with the reasons, demonstrations, proofs, and so on that may assist other individuals to not only understand the world of discourse as one does, but, as well, to agree with what is being said.

Such arguments build on ideas both little and large. The dynamics of such ideas that are expressed through the inner structure of a work, form the woof and warp through which the horizon and foci of a discourse are woven. A lot of little things can matter as much as one large issue. Each informs, shapes, and colors the other. Consequently, the validity of each is often caught up with the logical character of the others.

The following analysis examines some of the little and large aspects of <u>What's Right With Islam.</u> This critical exploration is not exhaustive with respect to all which might have been discussed in conjunction with the aforementioned book, but I believe the reader will get the gist or drift of where I stand in relation to much of what is contained with Imam Rauf's book.

****

On page xviii of the Preface, one finds the following statement:

"The U. S. military victory over Saddam Hussein's regime in Iraq means that America is now responsible for shaping a new Iraq."

The foregoing assertion presumes much and evades even more. One can think of a lot of possibilities which might have been said – perhaps, should have been said -- in the foregoing observation rather than what was said. For example, one might have said: America is now morally responsible for re-building the infrastructure of Iraq at its (the U. S.'s) own expense; or, America is now morally responsible for paying indemnity to the tens of thousands of innocent families who lost loved ones as a result of the actions of the U. S. government but who had nothing to do with Saddam Hussein's regime; or, America is now legally and morally responsible for leaving Iraq and permitting Iraqis to shape their own destiny.

One has trouble understanding how a war which was predicated on lie after lie, and falsehood after falsehood, or which was conducted in violation of international law, and which was undertaken without legal authority to do so gives one any morally sanctioned responsibility to shape another country and people. Invading another country because one wishes to do so, or because it serves one's imperial designs or desire for hegemony, does not constitute legal authority. After all, if one may wage war simply because of unjustified desires, then, Nazi Germany had legal authority to invade Czechoslovakia and Poland, or the former Soviet Union had legal authority to invade Hungary, and so on.

Moreover, while Saddam Hussein and most of the rest of his pack of jokers may have been apprehended, any talk of victory in the foregoing quote is rather premature. A "victory" which entails, collectively, thousands of additional dead and in which it is not safe to walk the streets or go about life in a normal fashion is not like any victory I have ever heard of - - except, of course, that of a Pyrrhic victory which some might say is a euphemism for the fact that much more is at stake in Iraq than a PR banner hanging from the upper decks of an aircraft carrier somewhere off the coast of San Diego, far from the realities of what was transpiring in Iraq. A "victory" which stands a very good chance of, sooner or later, inducing Iraq to slide into a civil war is not much of a victory – except to those who want some sort of trophy to mount on the walls of their war room and who are not really all that concerned about what happens to the millions of innocents who have been placed in harm's way by the actions of the U. S. government.

Whatever the sins of Saddam Hussein may have been -- and they were many – there are three things which need to be kept in mind. First, almost

90

all of his sins were aided, abetted and subsidized by the United States government across a number of administrations, both Republican and Democrat. Secondly, it is an oxymoron to suppose one can generate democracy by fiat or through brutal oppression -- and this is as true for the United States as it was for Saddam Hussein. And, finally, the oil resources in Iraq do not belong to the West, or to Saddam Hussein, or to whomever else forms the government there, or to this or that corporation ... those resources belong to the Iraqi people -- all of them ... anything else is theft no matter what the contractual and legal euphemisms may read.

Imam Rauf goes on to liken what the U. S. military has done, and must do, in Iraq as falling under the rubric of a saying of Prophet Muhammad (peace be upon him) concerning the distinction between the lesser and greater jihad. According to Imam Rauf,

"America has now won the lesser jihad, that of toppling the Saddam regime."

Something can be a jihad only if it is in compliance with divinely established conditions of morality. There is nothing about the U. S. invasion of Iraq which is moral.

Even the pretext of liberating Iraq is an ethical farce because the forces within the Executive Branch, the Pentagon, and among the leading defense contractors who were architects of this tragedy never had any intention of really permitting the Iraqi people to have self-determination. As has happened so many times before in U. S. history when the U. S. wants a regime change somewhere (e.g., Noriega in Panama, Allende in Chile, Mossadegh in Iran), the central, motivating factor is that whomever is to be removed is someone who is refusing to comply with, or creating problems for, U. S. plans for economic and political hegemony in some given part of the world.

The U. S. government wants a tyrant in Iraq. But, they want their kind of tyrant -- someone who would be in harmony with U. S. interests, and the people of Iraq be dammed.

As long as Saddam served U. S. purposes (e.g., waging war against Iran), then, Saddam was 'the man' and he was given wide latitude to amuse

91

himself with the lives of the Iraqi people as he desired. When he stopped serving the purposes of U. S. hegemony and became too big a liability, the U. S. government (or, at least, certain elements within that government) began to plan for a regime change – not for the purpose of establishing democracy, but for the purpose of arranging for a new government which would be subservient to the interests of the cartel that is now, and has been for quite some time, running the U. S. government (Dwight Eisenhower knew very well what he was talking about when, nearly fifty years ago, he warned the people of the United States about the military-industrial complex which was undermining democracy in the United States.).

It is a travesty of all that the Prophet Muhammad (peace be upon him) taught and lived to try to claim that what the U. S. has done, and is doing, in Iraq is a lesser jihad, even remotely similar to anything in which the Prophet participated. Among other things, indiscriminate killing, injustice, wholesale destruction of a society's infrastructure and brutal oppression have no place in even a jihad of a lesser kind.

Imam Rauf goes on to say:

"Its (the U. S.'s) larger challenge lies ahead; winning the hearts and minds of Iraqis, and through them, the rest of the Muslim world. This waging of peace is now America's greater jihad."

The greater jihad is about purification of oneself. Before -- if ever -- one seeks to try to tell others how they ought to live their lives, one should put one's own house in order. Otherwise, at the very least, one is guilty of sheer hypocrisy.

If the U. S. government were really interested in waging peace, they never would have begun any of the wars -- not under Bush II, and not under Clinton, and not under Bush I. If the U. S. wants to win the hearts and minds of the Iraqis, then, it should stop killing them, oppressing them, destroying their means of livelihood, and interfering with their country.

The U. S. government is not capable of truly assisting other countries until it cleanses itself of its imperial ambitions. Until the U. S. government stops seeking to control the people of other countries (via corrupt, tyrannical governments) or refrains from exploiting those people and

92

cheating them (via dealings with corrupt, tyrannical governments), any mention of the 'greater jihad' in conjunction with U. S. policy is nothing but a charade which misdirects attention away from the actual, insidious activities of the U. S. government and its corporate buddies.

Just as the desire for anything beyond the struggle for truth sullies the idea of the greater jihad in relation to individuals, so too, the desire for anything beyond the struggle to live in accordance with truth taints the intentions of the U. S. government. One can't lust after the resources of another country and, simultaneously, claim that one is merely engaging in the greater jihad. One can't dream of exploiting another people and say, with any sincerity, that one's actions are those of the greater jihad.

The greater jihad for the U. S. government has nothing to do with winning the hearts of the Iraqi people or the rest of the Muslim world. The challenge facing the U. S. government is not waging peace in the world, but to purify its own political house and, thereby, liberate America from the stranglehold which bad government and large corporations have had on the American people.

If, God willing, the U. S. government is capable of accomplishing this process of self-purification, then, in many ways, world peace will follow naturally. After all, if the United States government (or the corporations it sponsors and subsidizes) is not marauding about and interfering in, oppressing, terrorizing, undermining, and destroying the lives of other peoples, then, many (although, regrettably, not all) of the causes of conflict in the world would disappear. Unfortunately, so far, the U. S. government has had neither the honesty nor the insight of an old Walt Kelly comic strip called "Pogo" in which one of the characters utters the line: "We have met the enemy, and they is us."

On page xxi of <u>What's Right With Islam</u>, Imam Rauf says:

"...continuing news of suicide bombers in Israel, and in Muslim countries such as Pakistan, Indonesia, and Iraq, and more recently in Saudi Arabia and Morocco, have further reinforced American stereotypes about and fear of Muslims.

"Fear breeds a number of things: hatred of anything associated with 'the enemy' -- from ethnic appearance to clothing and religion - and a circling-of-the-wagons mentality. This country veered uncritically to the right."

America did not just veer to the right. It was maneuvered in that direction. The generation of an atmosphere of fear has always been one of the main weapons of choice to use to whip the public into a state of compliancy with respect to the wishes of those who are in charge.

In the light of substantial historical evidence, such words and phrases as: "Remember the Maine", the U.S.S Lusitania, Pearl Harbor, the Gulf of Tonkin, the drug lord Noriega, the innocent college students at risk in Grenada, April Glaspie, the slaughter of the incubator babies in Kuwait, satellite photos allegedly showing Saddam about to attack Saudi Arabia, and weapons of mass destruction -- all of these incidents have been shown to carry suspect pedigrees concerning the validation of events being what they were portrayed to be by the U. S. government and its media outlets. In each of the foregoing cases, elements within the United States government have been implicated, either directly or indirectly, as helping to arrange for the perpetration of tragedies which enrage the people of the U. S. and help render the latter target group more supple for purposes of further government manipulation.

Similar evidence exists with respect to the 9/11 attacks. If one doubts this, then, you might want to read The War On Freedom by Nafeez Mossaddeq Ahmed in which considerable evidence is put forth about how and why the United States was attacked in 2001 by alleged remnants of al-Qaida. As the foregoing book points out, one of the scandals of the 9/11 Commission is that it never really explored important aspects of the relevant, available evidence. There were vast areas of essential data which were either ignored or glossed over by the Commission, and there were a number of fundamental questions which were never raised by it in any rigorous fashion, if at all.

Michael Moore's Fahrenheit 9/11 has a lot of fun with the seven to ten minutes of inaction when President Bush sat in a Florida classroom listening to children read about a pet goat rather than politely excusing himself and responding to the information he had been given about on-going events in the air. The fact of the matter is, however, news reports indicate President Bush knew about the hijackings before he ever went into the grade school classroom, and, so, the question which Michael Moore omitted is why didn't the President do anything about the situation <u>before</u> he went into the classroom?

With certain exceptions, only the President can give the order for commercial air planes to be shot down. Without a doubt, having to make a decision about whether to destroy innocent lives aboard those commercials flights rather than risk the potential of even greater loss of innocent lives on the ground would be a terrible burden for any human being.

However, if someone can give the order to attack Afghanistan with the understanding that innocent lives will be lost, and if someone can give the order to attack Iraq with the clear understanding that innocent lives will be lost, then, perhaps, someone should have been ready to make a decision that would have made subsequent decisions to attack Afghanistan and Iraq less easy than they appeared to be.

There may, or may not, be entirely reasonable answers for all of these questions. However, one won't know any of this one way or the other until all of this is given a rigorous public airing and critical scrutiny -- something the media has not done to date, nor, as far as I can see, has the 9/11 Commission properly addressed ... unless they did so behind closed doors and feel the U. S. public has no right to know about issues which directly affect our lives, our sense of security, or our confidence in the integrity of government.

The foregoing is not an effort to foment conspiracy theories. Rather, it is intended to induce people to question the version of events which is put forth by authority.

Time and time again, people in authority have proven themselves unworthy of the trust of the people. In fact, due to the sheer quantity of prevarications on the part of all too many government officials for all too many years, the general operating procedure of the public should be that anything the government says should be handled through HAZMAT protective gear until one can establish that the information is not toxic or hazardous to one's health.

Just because some government employee or elected official offers an "official" version of events, this doesn't mean the 'official version' is a true reflection of what actually happened. It may only mean that this sort of 'official version' is what such government figures want the public to believe in order to advance ulterior, illicit machinations of their own.

None of the foregoing is to suggest that the terrible things which were transpiring in Muslim countries were not taking place, or that there were no reasons for a prudent person to be fearful about how events were spinning out of control almost everywhere. However, such events were only part of what is going on, and there is much need for something akin to when Paul Harvey says: "And, now, the rest of the story", for much has been kept from the eyes, minds, and hearts of the American people by its own government officials ... not just with respect to 9/11 but with respect to several hundred years of history.

I agree with Imam Rauf when he says, in relation to the aforementioned reactionary 'move to the right' of America, that it was largely uncritical (at least among large sections of the public, much of the media, and most of the politicians). However, there were many forces in play which were designed to shield events from the probing, curious eye of critical reflection, and, therefore, it was not just happenstance that events were ushered toward the right in an uncritical fashion ... there was a conscious intentionality guiding this move rightward into a reactionary state of fear.

In conjunction with the foregoing, Imam Rauf raises the question:

"Was Samuel Huntington right? Were we witnessing a 'clash of civilizations' between the West and the rest - in this case between Western civilization and Islam?"

The short answer is 'no'.

What we were witnessing (which requires a much longer answer) were a series of staged events, or predictable reactions to staged events, that were designed to frame the understanding of the public in certain ways. The purpose of these attempts to frame people's perception of reality was to enable various parties to have a pretext of justification, and/or plausible deniability, with respect to seeking to organize the world according to an agenda of hegemony – and this is as true for the fundamentalist religious zealots as it is for the fundamentalist capitalistic and military zealots, both of whom seek to seduce their respective spheres of influence like a cat in heat.

According to Imam Rauf, the events of 9/11 changed him and his life.

"I went from refusing to get dragged into politics because I saw it as a no-win situation to being forced to explain myself and defend my faith."

Unlike the author of <u>What's Right With Islam</u>, I do not feel the need to explain myself or defend my faith. With respect to the latter matter, my faith is precisely that: 'my faith', and as such, it is not something which I have to defend to others.

Of course, Imam Rauf may have meant that he felt the need to defend Islam, but Islam does not need any defense. It is what it is, and God defends it very well -- which is why, among other things, there has been a long tradition of Prophets, some 125,000 individuals long, who have been sent to human beings in order to help people understand the nature of spirituality and why, as well, there have been a number of Books of Revelation which were issued down through the ages.

Furthermore, I do not feel the need to explain myself to anyone. I didn't fly those planes on September 11, 1991, I am not a member of al-Qaida nor do I support or endorse their activities, nor have I done anything to either subvert the Constitution of the United States, nor have I tried to exploit the peoples of other lands or interfere with their lives.

Several decades before 9/11 ever occurred, I chose not to participate in U. S. aggression against other peoples. I do not now countenance acts of aggression against the United States – whoever may be responsible for such acts.

The exercise of violence solves very few, if any, problems. In general, and with the possible exception of defending one's home or country against armed invasion, I tend to agree with the sentiments of Issac Asimov as expressed in his <u>Foundation</u> series when one of his characters says: "Violence is the last refuge of incompetence."

In addition, for more than thirty years, I have been actively engaged in striving for truth in matters of: spirituality, justice, equality, freedom, peace, and human rights, in conjunction with governments, universities, the media, Muslims, and non-Muslims.

Hostility and anger toward Muslims did not suddenly erupt on

97

September 1, 2001. I can remember in 1967 when I was working in the student center cafeteria at MIT.

The television was carrying news coverage of the 1967 war between Israel and some of its Arab neighbors. With each advance and victory of the Israeli army, there was much cheering and jubilation which took place in the room where the television was, and as well, there was much jeering and contempt toward the Arabs and Muslims.

I was not a Muslim at the time, and I was not partial to either side. However, I do remember that hostility, contempt, and anger which were present and directed toward Arabs and Muslims.

During half of the 1970s and for much of the 1980s, I experienced, first hand, as a recent convert to Islam, the deep-rooted suspicion, enmity, and ignorance that existed in many parts of the West with respect to Muslims and Islam. More specifically, as a member of a Muslim organization which published a report that was critical of the offensive and inaccurate material concerning Islam and the Prophet Muhammad (peace be upon him) which appeared in a number of school textbooks being used in the public school systems in the Province of Ontario, I went round and round the barn with all manner of alleged intellectuals, media types, and government officials about the many facets of prejudice.

During this period of time I received a remarkable education concerning the underbelly of Western 'civilization'. I discovered there were many so-called experts of Islamic Studies who preferred error to accuracy and who were quite indignant that anyone should object to the way in which their lack of understanding and personal animosities or special interests would be used to validate ignorance. I encountered representatives of the media who believed it was their God-given duty to perpetuate ignorance and bias concerning Muslims and Islam. I negotiated with government officials who did what such individuals often tend to do best: evade, procrastinate, stonewall, lie, and manipulate.

I remember an instance in which a group of people from a local mosque were lodging an official complaint with a business in the community. The group had asked me to be its spokesperson.

When we were ushered into the office of the manager of the business with which we were concerned, the manager looked at me, and, then, he looked at the others (who were from Pakistan, Africa, India, and the like), and, then, he looked back at me. He whispered to me -- because I was the closest to him: "I know what they are doing here, but what are you doing here." I pointed over to the group of people with whom I arrived and whispered back: "I'm one of them."

Alternatively, I also recall a number of instances when Muslims actively voiced their hostility toward me and resented my presence because my skin color and linguistic pedigree were not to their liking. So, prejudice and bias are not the exclusive preserves of non-Muslims.

In the early 1980's, Sheik Ahmad Zaki Yamani, the Minister of Oil for Saudi Arabia, came to Canada. My Sufi shaykh sought a meeting with Sheik Yamani in an attempt to get support from him with respect to some of the textbook bias work we were doing as well as in relation to a number of other matters.

My spiritual guide didn't think we had much of a chance of meeting with the extremely busy minister, but my shaykh thought: 'nothing ventured, nothing gained'. To his surprise, we received a call back from the person managing appointments for the oil Sheik and said we had been granted a five minute audience with the Oil Minister on such and such day.

When we went for our appointment, the RCMP and Canadian officials who were present (but outside the room where Sheik Yamani was receiving people) were quite curious about just who we were and why we were seeing the Saudi Oil Minister. What was scheduled for five minutes turned into a meeting that lasted more than an hour. Whatever curiosity the Canadian authorities had prior to our meeting with the Sheik was quadrupled, or more, by the time our meeting was through.

It turned out that the Oil Minister was, and is, a great lover of the Prophet Muhammad (peace be upon him). When he discovered that we also were lovers of the Prophet, all formalities, time constraints, and official distance which might have been between us disappeared.

While he served each of us (there were four of us) tea in a very humble and attentive way, he talked about his family, some of the miraculous things which had happened to him, and much more. He invited members of the group to visit with him in Saudi Arabia as his guests, all expenses paid. He gave each of us a personal gift of some kind.

As Saudi Oil Minister and one of the leading strategists of OPEC's 1973 price hike, he easily could have destroyed the West if he wanted to do so.

He was not interested in doing that — rather, he simply wanted international economic arrangements which would establish as much distributive justice as possible for all parties concerned -- Muslim and non-Muslim.

When the price hike came, people in the West were outraged with the OPEC countries. What right did OPEC have to do this?

These same people who were complaining would think nothing about mouthing the platitude of the law of supply and demand if they stood to benefit from the scarcity of a non-renewable resource. Moreover, these same people would lose absolutely no sleep over the hardships placed on nations through the economic restructuring pressures imposed by the World Bank or the International Monetary Fund as conditions for getting loans, and, yet, these same people would howl in outrage when the quality of their lives was adversely affected due to the pressures of economic restructuring caused by the action of others -- such as OPEC.

The events which ensued from 9/11 in relation to hostility toward, and hatred of, Muslims and Islam was more of the same of what has been going on for a long, long time. The only difference was that now Americans had been killed or were suffering, directly, or indirectly, as a result of the attacks, and, perhaps, for the very first time, Americans, as a people, had some visceral insight into how Muslims in other parts of the world have been feeling for several hundred years as imperial powers from the West killed, pillaged, plundered and raped their countries and peoples.

That people died in the World Trade Towers, the Pentagon, and in a field in Pennsylvania gives expression to a great injustice against those innocent individuals. But, the people of America should get a grip on themselves and garner a little historical perspective for such things have been happening with great regularity all over the world and our government is not innocent in such matters.

The fact that much of the American public is ignorant about these kinds of issues (and intentionally kept that way for the most part) does not mean that similar, if not worse, tragedies have not been occurring elsewhere in the world. If someone screams in pain and no one hears it or pays attention to it, the fact of the matter is that the person who screams still feels pain.

If anyone needs to explain themselves it is the U. S. government and all of those Muslim governments who have aided and abetted U. S. and Western imperial aims. If anyone needs to explain themselves it is the so-called

100

democratic countries which have bequeathed something other than democracy to its citizens. If there is anyone who needs to explain themselves, it is all the so-called Muslim leaders who have betrayed Islam and their compatriots by establishing something other than peaceful conditions in which a person's pursuit of Islam can prosper without compulsion and oppression. If there is something which is demanded of the present situation it is for a resolute intention among all human beings to seek, as much as possible, the truth of things and not be satisfied with the shoddy, self-serving "official" offerings of this or that government.

7.) A Study In Hypocrisy

I happened to catch part of an interview on a Sunday morning involving Wolf Blitzer of CNN and Senators Joe Lieberman of Connecticut and Chuck Hagel of Nebraska. The first question asked was about the controversy surrounding the publication of cartoon drawings depicting the Prophet Muhammad (peace be upon him) in a very demeaning and derogatory light.

The two Senators, each in his own inimitable style, said more or less the same thing. They defended freedom of the press and alluded to its importance to a strong viable democracy. In addition, they indicated such freedoms ought to be used responsibly with some intimation that, in this particular instance, the papers in Denmark, France, Germany, and Philadelphia (although none of these countries or the city was mentioned in the portion of the news program which I watched) may not have had their finest moment of journalistic responsibility. And, finally, they stated that while they understood and sympathized with the feelings of Muslims around the world who were outraged by the cartoon drawings, nevertheless, there could be no condoning the use of violence or the burning of property and embassies ... actions which were in evidence in many Muslim countries. The two Senators indicated that peaceful means, such as non-violent demonstrations, should have been used to protest the cartoons, not violence.

Further questions were asked by the host of the show in relation to how each of the guests believed that the cartoon incident might affect the 'War on Terror'. Platitudes were espoused by both of the participants about how such things surely can't help the war effort, but we must carry on doing the best we can under difficult circumstances ... or something to that effect.

I admired the courage of the two Senators who were willing to voice their opinions concerning such things as free speech, freedom of the press, democracy, responsibility, and non-violence. My heart resonates with much that was said, but, then, I began to wonder about certain things.

I wondered why such Senators would vote to give the President authority to use, in the days following September 11, 2001, whatever means are necessary to go after the terrorists who were responsible for the atrocities of that day which outraged all of America (and, indeed, people around the world) — when so many loved ones, family members, friends,

103

colleagues, firefighters, police, fellow citizens, and "illegal aliens" who were working at the Twin Towers that day who were lost ... I wondered why the Senators and their colleagues authorized the President to use whatever means are necessary rather than stand by their conveniently adopted principles of non-violence today (vis-à-vis the violence in the Muslim world over the offensive cartoons involving the Prophet Muhammad – peace be upon him) ... I wondered where their commitment to the principles of non-violence was when they set in motion the wanton destruction and murder of so many innocent Iraqis and Afghanis who, themselves, were victims of, respectively, Saddam Hussein's and the Taliban's oppression? Why didn't the two Senators, based upon their recently professed dedication to non-violence, counsel the President to merely go to Baghdad or Kabul and have peaceful protests in the streets there to show those people that we mean business and that we are incensed and deeply hurt over what we believe was done in New York, Washington, and a field in Pennsylvania?

Nope, the first response of the two good Senators (along with almost all of the other 'responsible' Senators and Representatives of the U. S. Congress) was to say let's go kill some people. We don't care whether, or not, the people we kill and maim are responsible for what went on in New York and Washington (which they weren't) ... let's go and kick some ass ... anybody's ass. Wow, those two Senators and the rest of Congress really showed the Muslim world what democracy is all about, didn't they? They really showed the Muslim world how when we do things on this side of the two ponds, we always go about business in a peaceful, honorable, non-violent manner.

Go into any bar or club in America and call the fathers, mothers, sisters, and sons of the people in attendance there all kinds of names and denigrate their loved ones, and we all know what will happen. Why the people in the bar would march right down to city hall, apply for a 'Parade Permit" and start demonstrating about the incident – because we are civilized in this country. We know how to treat people here ... and, naturally, this is why we are the leading exporter of arms in the world, and why we won't sign the convention against the proliferation of land-mines, and why we will not dismantle our nuclear weapons (even as we expect others to do so), and why we will not permit ourselves to be brought under the jurisdiction of the International Court of Justice, and why we believe we have the right

104

to consume 40% of the world's resources although we only constitute 5% of its people, and why our businesses believe they have the right to pollute the environment despite the overwhelming scientific evidence concerning global warming and its catastrophic results for everyone, and why we kill tens of thousands of people every year through homicides and drunks on the highways, and why we did use weapons of mass destruction in Hiroshima and Nagasaki, and why we have the highest per capita rate of incarceration in the world (people who are disproportionately those of color and among the poor), and why there are more than 48 million people without health coverage, and why there are tens of thousands of homeless people – many of them Vietnam veterans, and why we have millions of rich people who pay no taxes but, instead, have, quite patriotically, transferred this burden onto everyone else even as the former group reaps the benefits of those tax dollars. We know how to be civilized ... we are not like those rabble-rousing trouble-makers in other countries who destroy property and burn embassies over cartoons.

We are civilized because there were only ('merely'? 'just'?) unknown thousands of innocent Afghanis and Iraqis who have been killed. We are civilized because we have only used the chemical weapon white phosphorous just a little bit in Fallujah, and there are but a few hundred people – including women and children – who have had their flesh burned off down to the bone. We are civilized because there are merely 90-100 people who have died while in prison under our loving care in Afghanistan and Iraq, not to mention the many more who were tortured but did not die, and we are civilized because we made sure that the only people who would be penalized for such abuses were the powerless who were way down the chain of command. We are civilized because of the way we fail to look after the military veterans (and their children) who are suffering from the after-effects of Agent Orange, Depleted Uranium, and the Gulf-War Syndrome.

The two good, aforementioned Senators, being the skilled politicians they are, may say that they never authorized the President to kill just anybody. These deaths were just unfortunate side effects of the 'War on Terror' and the result of a mammoth failure of intelligence concerning who did (or did not do) what, when, and where.

But, then, I got to wondering along the following lines ... if -- as everyone now seems to agree (except, perhaps, Dick Cheney who – with

105

absolutely no substantive evidence except that which is tenuously and unacceptably based on the water-boarding torture of various individuals -- still wishes to insist there were meetings in Eastern Europe between al-Qaida and high officials of Saddam's administration and, as well, that there were al-Qaida terrorist cells which were active in Iraq prior to the second Gulf War) … if there is general agreement that Iraq had nothing to do with 9/11 and Iraq had no weapons of mass destruction, and that decisions were made on the basis of faulty Intel, then, why should anyone believe anything that either the intelligence community (doesn't the use of the word "community" give you a nice, warm feeling inside?) or the government says, or why should one trust any decisions which are being made on the basis of what they claim? After all, how do we know that the problems have been fixed or that we aren't continuing to base policy on the sort of Intel which is just as problematic as that which helped get us and the rest of the world in this mess to begin with?

Such skepticism seems especially warranted given that there is a great deal of evidence to indicate that prior to 9/11, the administration knew precisely who the perpetrators were, what the targets were, how the attacks were going to take place, and on which day. We are not talking about a mammoth failure of Intel but, rather, massive acts of treason by certain people who were entrusted with a fiduciary responsibility to the people of this country. The 9/11 Commission did nothing to expose the realities of such treason but merely became part of a process that ensured that Americans would have difficulty learning the actual facts of 9/11 because the Commission asked all the wrong questions, and it called upon all the wrong witnesses, and it made all the wrong choices for who was to be on the Commission and who would have the responsibility to ask the questions which needed to be asked but were not.

I further got to wondering how one can have a 'War on Terror' when no war has been declared by Congress. I guess, like Korea, this is just a police action in which one can get away with killing innocent (along with the not-so-innocent) people. However, calling things a 'Police Action on Terror' doesn't have quite the same patriotic ring to it.

Besides, unless we keep using the phrase "War on Terror", then the President and his supporters can't continue saying words to the effect that we are in a state of war, and, therefore, anyone who says anything against the war is being a traitor to the country and gives aid and comfort to the enemy. If we are only in a condition of an executive police action of sorts, then the rules governing a time of war do not exist, and people should be free to speak their minds without having to worry if the terror police (sometimes known as Homeland Security, FBI, NSA, and CIA) are going to come and 'disappear' you or throw you in jail without any civil liberties or send you off somewhere for a form of extreme rendition (which like "collateral damage" is another 1984-like term that has entered the lexicon as a euphemistic way of talking about terrorizing, torturing, and killing people without using such words).

However, even if we were in a time of war, one's duty is not to the President, or to Congress, or to the Supreme Court, but rather to the principles of truth, justice, freedom, and non-violence, without which democracy is not possible. One has a duty to speak the truth to power because, theoretically, this is a country of the people, not of the government, and when people in authority abuse their power, they have betrayed the people whom they claim to represent.

I have no wish to give aid and comfort to the enemy. This is why I will not support those insurgents in Iraq or Afghanistan or the West Bank who kill innocent people, or capture innocent (or otherwise) people and execute them without due process, or torture people for the sake of whatever cause they are espousing. But this is also why I will not support the American government as it continues to authorize the killing of innocent people, or captures innocent people and executes them without due process, or tortures people for the sake of the 'national interests' of companies like Halliburton who are given no-bid, open-ended, cost-plus contracts to have their way with the people of the world.

There may be those who believe that people, like myself, who mention such trivialities as the foregoing often seem to forget that we have been able to bring about a regime change which ousted an oppressive, murderous tyrant, Saddam Hussein, from power ... you know, the guy that America armed and to whom we sold chemical weapons and whom we supported even as we knew that he killed Shi'as and Kurds by the thousands, and the one we clandestinely supported in his internecine war with Iran. In fact, following Gulf War I, the American government, ever ready to help out its client-states and surrogates, even made it easy for Saddam to eliminate thousands of people in southern and northern Iraq ... people whom the American government induced to rebel against Saddam with promises of military support only to leave them high and dry in Saddam's killing fields.

Of course, there will be some who say that there is absolutely no comparison between what happened on 9/11 and the cartoons which were first published in Denmark. Nobody died in the latter case (except for the people who did which, to date, is entirely restricted to the protestors), but, altogether, nearly 3,000 people died on 9/11.

This just goes to show some of the cultural divide which exists, because when the Prophet Muhammad (peace be upon him) is used as an 'object' of derision, ridicule, slander, and contempt, then a part of the heart of every Muslim on the face of the planet is ripped apart. If it is wrong to rip apart the hearts of the families and friends of those who suffered through the losses of 9/11, then it is equally wrong to rip apart the hearts of those who will suffer as a result of the muck-raking (and I mean this in the most pejorative sense) journalism of papers in Denmark, France, Germany, Philadelphia, and elsewhere with respect to the character of the Prophet Muhammad (peace be upon him).

Perhaps, these journalists will use the Condoleezza Rice defense following 9/11 ... namely, that no one could have imagined that people would hijack planes and fly them into the World Trade Center or the Pentagon (even though the U.S. military actually ran exercises with precisely this set of contingencies prior to 9/11). In other words, the journalists could argue that they had no idea that their cartoons would lead to the kind of uproar which has taken place ... just as Salman Rushdie [someone who grew up among Muslims] disingenuously claimed that he had no idea that his Satanic Verses would cause such a stir. But if someone had suggested to these intellectually and morally-challenged individuals that let's have a competition and draw derogatory, sarcastic cartoons of Jesus (peace be upon him) or the holocaust, don't you think someone might have said: "Well, you know, we may want to tread a little carefully here, because it is conceivable that this or that Christian or Jew might get upset about things and take matters into their own hands like some Christians have done with the bombing of abortion clinics or the assassination of doctors, or like some of the Christians and Jews did with respect to the massacres of Sabra and Shatila or the Tomb of the Patriarchs?

Yes, in all likelihood, the foregoing sort of question, or a variation thereof, might have been raised in conjunction with cartoons that were

108

intended to denigrate the person of Jesus (peace be upon him) or the memory of the holocaust. But, apparently, the artistic and journalistic bright bulbs who sought to light up the rotunda of freedom around the world with the self-proclaimed brilliance of their insights and cleverness either were too ignorant of the cherished values of 150,000 of their fellow citizens in Denmark, not to mention the billion, or so, Muslims who inhabit the Earth, to raise such inconsequential issues, or did raise such questions, and, quite deliberately, didn't give a damn about the consequences.

Freedom of speech is not an absolute. One does not have a right to yell "Fire" in a crowded theater. One does not have a right to slander people. One does not have a right to commit perjury. One does not have the right to mislead and/or lie to the American people in the name of "national interests" or security.

Or, one can turn the above contention around and say, if one wishes, one does have a right to do such things, but, if one gets caught, then there are probably going to be some problematic consequences. The journalists in question with respect to the derogatory cartoons published in Denmark may (?) have had the right – at least, from a certain perspective – to publish what they did, but they also had a responsibility to foresee the consequences of their actions and not show such a reckless disregard for the virtual certainty of certain kinds of event following upon the exercise of their rights.

Those journalists may have had the right to publish what they did. However, they also are culpable for everything which ensued from printing what they did, including the deaths and the violence and the destruction of property.

They may not have committed the acts of violence directly. Nonetheless, they provided many of the ingredients necessary to help push things over the edge.

The foregoing is not intended to condone the violence by Muslims which transpired as this whole sorry affair picked up steam. Rather, it is to point out that the journalists should have been able to reasonably predict some of the ramifications of their actions, and because they chose not to exercise caution, those journalists are, in part, culpable and responsible for the violence that followed. In effect, they were inciting people to riot which is a criminal

109

offense in almost every country on the face of the Earth.

It is not just the rioters who were committing crimes. It is the people who have helped incite those people to riot who also have committed criminal acts.

Now, there will be some who will point out that the cartoons in question were originally published in September of 2005, but there were some people from the Muslim community in Denmark who took these cartoons around to various religious and government authorities in the Muslim world. As a result, there will be some who will wish to argue that it is these Muslims who are the instigators, not the original Danish journalists who were merely exercising their democratic right to freedom of the press.

In fact, we can embellish the foregoing scenario somewhat and indicate that there were people (so-called religious leaders) in the Muslim world who took the information about the cartoons and used it for their own political purposes which involved stirring up hatred, resentment, and violence against the freedom-loving West. Why, those rascals, doing such things ... things which we would never do over here -- groups like the 'Swiftboat Veterans for Truth" and the Committee to Re-elect Richard Nixon, the KKK, Pat Robertson, Rush Limbaugh, as well as so many other groups and individuals notwithstanding.

In fact, there are many people on 'Talk Radio', or among television's 'Talking Heads without Brains', who are doing precisely this with the events that have transpired in conjunction with the cartoon issue ... seeking to spin that information in a way that adds further fuel to the fire and creates further obstacles in the way of seeking peaceful modes of resolving the situation. They are stirring up hatred, resentment, and all manner of xenophobia toward Muslims.

For example, some intellectually and morally challenged individuals are saying that Syria and Iran are behind all of this violence and hatred which is being generated toward the freedom-loving and peace-loving peoples of the West. Let's go bomb them. Let's kill us some more innocent people. Let's keep the war on terror going against all these Muslims who don't think like we do.

Syria and Iran may or may not have had a hand in flaming the fires of discontent and chaos. But so does the West fan such flames because we will do anything but take a long look at ourselves, our militarism, our imperialism, our exploitation of the rest of the world, or the hundreds of thousands of innocents we have killed in the so-called name of freedom and peace.

We, in the West, are a bunch of rogue nations who are far more dangerous than Syria, Iran, or North Korea, because we have the potential to destroy and oppress so much more of the world than those three countries do, whatever their transgressions may, or may not, be ... in fact, in the case of the West, this is not a potential because we already are actively engaged in killing innocents in many parts of the world. We actually do have weapons of mass destruction, we actually do have chemical weapons, nerve gas, along with biological agents ... and we actually have used some of these weapons of mass destruction against other peoples.

In both Christianity and Islam there is a teaching – one which I fully believe is central to Judaism and all of the other great spiritual traditions of the world, as well – which says that when an individual kills one innocent person, it is as if that person slew all of humanity. The same is true with respect to oppression, injustice, terrorism and exploitation.

What is going on with the cartoon issue, as is also going on in relation to Afghanistan and Iraq, is not about freedom, peace, democracy, justice, or truth. It is about tyranny, hatred, disorder, injustice, deceit, terrorizing, and profits.

I am neither a Republican nor a Democrat. But, if I were, I would be ashamed of what I permitted my parties to do to help undermine the principles of democracy everywhere ... and especially in the United States.

I am not Danish, nor am I of French or German extraction, but, if I were, I would be ashamed that some people of my ancestry chose to denigrate the values and beliefs of fellow citizens whose only fault was that they were not of the same ethnicity, race, or religion as most of the others in those countries.

8.) <u>Nothing Beats a Good Game of Gulf</u>

The speaker was an attractive woman who appeared to be in her early thirties. The program I had been handed as I came into the room identified her as Rachel Donaldson. She was an assistant professor of moral and political philosophy at some college I had never heard of in Colorado.

Hardly any time passed before someone from the audience of about forty people accepted Professor Donaldson's invitation concerning questions. A man in the first row arose and said: "Professor Donaldson, maybe I missed something during your talk, but there seemed to be quite a few points made by you which sounded like you were trying to blame the United States for the first Gulf War. If memory serves me well, we were not the ones who invaded Kuwait. I'm wondering if you would elaborate on some of your views in this regard."

"Dr. Clarke," she began, "I believe the term I used with respect to the moral responsibilities of the United States in the Gulf War was 'complicity'. In fact, the idea of complicity could be applied with varying degrees of relevancy to all of the participants of that war.

"Let's be clear about something right up front. And, please, Dr. Clarke, bear with me a little on this.

"Approximately 15,000 and 25,000 Iraqi civilians died as a result of Coalition bombing of targets in Iraq in 1991. Since the end of that 43-day Gulf War, there have been hundreds of thousands of further deaths of Iraqi children.

"Many of these children have died from a variety of infectious diseases which have been epidemic in Iraq since the cessation of bombing. These diseases have arisen because of the unsanitary living conditions which have been created by the Allies' destruction of sewage systems, potable drinking water facilities, pumping stations, and power-generating capabilities.

"Malnutrition also has been a very important contributing factor in many of these post-war deaths. Due to a variety of reasons, including our continued application of sanctions against Iraq, food is both scarce and very expensive for the average Iraqi Many Iraqis are poor or unemployed or both and cannot afford the simple necessities of life."

She paused slightly and stared at the wall to her right, as if there were information there to be read off. When she found what she was looking for, she turned back to the audience.

"When the U. S. encouraged and promoted an uprising in southern Iraq following Desert Storm and, then abandoned those people to Iraq's still largely intact Republican Guard, a further 6,000, or more, people died. In addition, there were another 2,000 Kurds who were killed in an uprising in the north, again encouraged and abandoned by the Allies, which occurred at the same time as the uprising in the south.

"Furthermore, although the actual number of Iraqi military casualties probably will never be known because of the bulldozing tactics employed by the Allies, informed estimates indicate that anywhere from 75,000 to 110,000 Iraqi soldiers died during the war. There are further estimates of some 300,000 seriously wounded Iraqi soldiers who undoubtedly overburdened an already overtaxed and under-supplied Iraqi medical system.

"We need to add to the foregoing the 144 Americans who died during Desert Storm, as well as the roughly 300 Kuwait citizens who lost their lives. And, we must not forget the two Israelis and eight Palestinians who died in Israel and the occupied territories."

Professor Donaldson slowly began pacing back and forth, along a six-foot strip of the raised platform from which she was delivering her ideas. She spoke as she paced.

"In addition, let us consider the large scale displacement of people that went on just before, during, and just after the 43 days of war. For instance, about 400,000 people, mostly Egyptians, fled Iraq prior to the bombing. Another 1.5 million refugees left Kuwait, many of whom were foreign nationals working in Kuwait who, as a result of the displacement, lost jobs, homes, possessions and their savings.

"The Saudis deported about 700,000 Yemeni residents from Saudi Arabia simply because the Yemen government was not in favor of the Coalition's War Plan. In addition, the Kuwaitis forcibly, and with considerable abuse, deported some 150,000 Palestinians from Kuwait after the war.

"This forced exodus came as a result of two major reasons. On the

114

one hand, the Kuwaiti leaders objected to the way many Palestinians, both inside and outside Kuwait, were pleased with the Iraqi attempt, before the onset of Desert Storm, to link the solution of the Palestinian problem to a negotiated withdrawal of Iraq from Kuwait.

"Since the Kuwaitis had been among the biggest financial benefactors of the PLO prior to the Iraqi invasion of Kuwait, the Kuwaitis interpreted the Palestinian support of the linkage issue with a betrayal of, and ingratitude toward, Kuwait. Apparently, the Kuwaitis were prepared to help the Palestinians with a few dollars, but the Kuwaitis just were not interested in making the sort of sacrifices that might help solve the problem once and for all.

"The other reason for the forced exodus of Palestinians from Kuwait revolved around the fact that some Palestinians apparently collaborated with Iraq during the latter's occupation of Kuwait. However, there was no serious effort to determine who exactly was involved in these acts of collaboration. Furthermore, there was little if any remorse on the part of the Kuwaiti leaders for the repeated violation of human rights which accompanied the forcible expulsion of the Palestinians from Kuwait.

"Between March and April of 1991, there was a further displacement of roughly 2.5 million people. Most of these displaced people were Kurds from the north who as a result of the forced migration were reduced to living in sub-subsistence conditions along the borders of Iraq, Turkey and Iran."

Dr. Donaldson stopped pacing. She removed her glasses from her face with her right hand and began massaging her eyes with the thumb and first two fingers of her left hand. After a few seconds, she put her glasses back on.

"Finally," she said, "let us consider the tremendous environmental damage which has ensued from the Gulf War. To begin with, there are the obvious ramifications which come from the burning of oil tankers and terminals.

"The delicate marine ecology of the Gulf area has been seriously compromised. Phytoplankton, algae and sea grasses which are fundamental parts of the food chain have been affected. Consequently, the shrimp, fish and other aquatic forms of life that depend on these biological species for their continued existence are also threatened.

"While the oil fires were raging, calculations indicated that more than 100,000 tons of soot particles and some 50 tons of sulfur dioxide were being released into the atmosphere on a daily basis. Some of the projections for the dispersal distances of these chemicals suggest that 2000 kilometers, or more, is quite likely.

"These substances play a central role in the formation of acid rain. And, shortly after the war, there were reports from Turkey, Iran, Pakistan, and Russia concerning the destructive effects of these pollutants in their countries. Ground water, soil, and life forms are all being affected.

"Coalition bombing destroyed four nuclear research facilities and two nuclear reactors. Estimates indicate that there may have been 200-300 kilograms of radioactive waste materials, such as plutonium, strontium, cesium and iodine, being stored at these sites.

"Coalition military experts claim these facilities were bombed in such a way that there was no possibility of contamination or leakage being generated. However, given the general tenor of fabrications, disinformation and misleading statements concerning the effectiveness and accuracy of the so-called 'smart bombs' and given the fact that the military authorities are quite vague as to how their bombing techniques could guarantee there would be no contamination from, or leakage of, radioactive materials at the various nuclear sites, one has to take the assurances of the military experts with more than a grain of salt."

Dr. Donaldson was about to say something but checked herself, as if a further idea or piece of information suddenly had occurred to her. Her face brightened with the enthusiasm of someone who was intrigued with different facets of the topic being discussed, despite the depressing nature of the realities being explored.

"Incidentally, you may be interested to learn that in November 1990, several months before Desert Storm began in earnest, the International Atomic Energy Agency had inspected the nuclear research facilities in Iraq, including their Tammura-2 and IRT-5000 reactors. The Agency's investigation determined that the Iraqi nuclear facilities and reactors were being employed for peaceful research purposes.

"The International Atomic Energy Agency is the organization authorized by the United Nations to force compliance with the Nuclear Non-Proliferation Treaty. Consequently, the Agency has the task of ensuring that all nuclear research facilities and affiliated reactors are being used for exclusively peaceful purposes.

"In 1985, six years prior to Desert Storm, the IAEA passed a resolution which stipulated clearly that any armed attack on a nuclear facility being used for peaceful purposes was a violation of the Agency's statutes, as well as a violation of both International Law and the Charter of the United Nations Charter.

"This statute of the IAEA arose partly as a result of the Israeli bombing of Iraq's Osirak reactor facility in 1981. There were, however, other factors which shaped the IAEA statute, and, presumably one of these additional factors was to avoid situations where radioactive waste materials from peaceful facilities would be leaked, entirely unnecessarily, into the environment to cause serious contamination.

"Thus, the bombing of the Iraqi nuclear facilities represents an interesting paradox. On the one hand, we have the New World Order which had accrued to itself an alleged moral authority for waging the Gulf war.

"The New World Order allegedly was predicated on principles of peace, justice and respect for international law. Yet, in order to impose the New World Order, all three of its principles had to be violated in fundamental ways.

"Certainly, these violations were evident in the Coalition bombing of the Iraqi nuclear facilities, and there are many other aspects of the Gulf War which are further examples of such violations. These are precedents which do not augur well for the future."

Professor Donaldson ran both her hands through her hair several times. She tucked some of her relatively short cropped hair behind her ears, getting set for the next part of her response to Dr. Clarke's query.

"Last, but not least, on the ecological hit parade is the issue of the Iraqi chemical and biological weapons that were among the primary targets of the Coalition forces. The Iraqi facilities at, among other places, Samarra, Kamisiyah, Bayji, and Salman Pak were well-known to the military leaders of the Coalition forces.

"Those in command knew precisely what was being produced or stored or researched at each of the Iraqi facilities. Moreover, they did not come to this knowledge overnight. It had been with them for quite some time.

"There is something terribly ironic in this whole issue of chemical and biological weapons. The Coalition forces were extremely concerned about the possibility of the Iraqis releasing chemical and biological agents. In fact, the Coalition leaders were so worried about this possibility they informed the Iraqis that Baghdad would be hit with nuclear strikes if any chemical or biological weapons were used by the Iraqis.

"So what did these deep thinkers of the Coalition go and do? Why they went and released these toxic agents into the air, ground water and soil through their destruction of the Iraqi chemical and biological research, production and storage facilities."

As she said "deep thinkers", there was a derisive tone to the words. Her body language matched the tone of voice. Both conveyed a sense of not quite being able to comprehend how someone could act in a way that would bring to realization the very purpose such a person allegedly was committed to preventing.

"There is a growing body of evidence," she said, "which indicates that tens of thousands of American participants in the Gulf War are suffering from something called 'The Gulf War Syndrome'. This Syndrome exhibits a wide variety of debilitating neurological and physiological symptoms, along with a disturbingly high incidence of birth defects among their post-war children.

"The American authorities have been doing their best to deny the existence of any such disease. Yet, for more than twenty years these same authorities denied any culpability in the tragedy of the thousands of Vietnam veterans who had been exposed to, and suffered from, the toxic effects of Agent Orange which had been used extensively in Vietnam.

"The Gulf War Syndrome may be, in part, a function of the contamination resulting from the more than 25 Iraqi storage, production and research facilities destroyed by Coalition bombing. Or, the Gulf War syndrome might be the result of some of the experimental drugs being foisted on the Coalition forces as alleged protection against the possible release of Iraqi chemical and biological agents.

"Possibly, the Gulf War Syndrome is a function of being exposed to the depleted uranium used in the heavy artillery shells of Coalition forces. On the other hand, the Gulf War Syndrome may have something to do with breathing in all the toxic substances which were released by the burning oil tankers and terminals.

"The Gulf War Syndrome also may be a combination of all of the foregoing factors coming together in a destructive synergy. Sorting it all out may not be an easy puzzle to solve.

"The problem is, nobody with any power bothered to think it all through before the fact of implementing Desert Storm. Apparently, no one stopped to consider the possibility that the actions of the Coalition leaders and forces could generate something like the Gulf War Syndrome or the other destructive aspects of the war."

A mood of frustration, sorrow and anger seemed to descend on Professor Donaldson. She shook her head a few times before proceeding.

"The Coalition leaders were too preoccupied with their power and technological wizardry. Their moral arrogance, ignorance, carelessness, heedlessness, biases, presumptions, and hatreds would not permit them to consider the possibilities which were staring them in the face.

"Apparently, nobody sat down and said: 'We are about to kill hundreds of thousands of people, more than half of whom are innocent civilians, including hundreds of thousands of children. Is there some way in which this can be avoided?'

"Seemingly, nobody sat down and reflected: 'We are about to create some 5 million refugees, forcing many, if not most of them, into extremely marginal and tenuous subsistence conditions. Is there something we could do to avoid disrupting the lives of millions of innocent bystanders?'

119

"Presumably, nobody sat down and had the insight to realize we are about to set in motion forces that will substantially degrade the ecological viability of thousands of cubic miles of air, water, land and life forms. Is there any alternative plan which would permit us to avoid this?

"Unfortunately, nobody seems to have stopped to realize we are about to unnecessarily expose tens of thousands of American soldiers and their unborn children, as well as thousands of Iraqis and others, to toxic chemical, biological and radioactive agents. These agents will debilitate, deform and kill them. Can we find some solution to the problem which would avoid such a tragedy?

She turned and looked directly at Dr. Clarke. The words which followed were directed toward him, but the arguments conveyed by those words were directed toward the thinking of the leaders of the Coalition, along with the thinking of those who supported the perspective she was critiquing.

"Dr. Clarke, the power of life, death and destruction were entirely in the discretionary hands of the Coalition forces and their political leaders. It was their decision to unleash those forces. They could have refrained from doing so, but they didn't.

"From the very moment that Iraq invaded Kuwait, there were a large number of efforts of negotiation and diplomacy on the part of Jordan, the PLO, Algeria, France, and, even, Iraq to find a peaceful solution to the invasion. From the beginning, Kuwait and the Unite d States were impervious to all of these overtures.

"Hundreds of thousands of people lost their lives. Hundreds of thousands more people were wounded. Millions of lives were displaced. Incalculable damage was done to the environment. Billions of dollars which could have been used to solve the crisis in a peaceful and just manner were wasted on war."

In a dramatic gesture, Dr. Donaldson flung her arms out to her sides. Her whole body looked like it was posing a question.

"And, why did this all come about?" she asked, as her voice gave expression to what her body already was asking. Responding to her own question, she said: "All the destruction, death and horror came about

120

as a result of unresolved disputes over: (a) two islands by the name of Warba and Bubiyan which would have provided the Iraqis with access to the sea; (b) several miles of border clarification involving the Rumaila oil field, and (c) 10 billion dollars of debt incurred by Iraq from Kuwait while the former was, among other things, effectively serving and protecting western interests, especially those of Kuwait and Saudi Arabia, during the Iran/Iraq, eight-year war."

The tone of her voice became both incensed as well as imploring. "Wouldn't it have been quicker, cheaper, more peaceful, more effective, less destructive, and, therefore, ultimately, more just to say to the Iraqis: 'Here, take the islands, forget about the debt, and we'll readjust the border of the Rumaila oil field in a way that will be largely in your favor?' Wouldn't this have been something of a bargain when compared to the actual costs of death, destruction, disease, displacement, debt and ecological degradation which resulted from the war?"

Dr. Donaldson left her questions to hang suspended above the hearts of her audience, hoping they would act as a moral counterpart to the sword of Damocles. She quickly surveyed the audience, scratched her head, smoothed her hair in the spot just scratched, and shrugged.

"Perhaps, some of you may be thinking: how naive and impractical. Why give up two islands, an oil field and 10 billion dollars to a murdering dictator?

"Such people, I believe, are working on the assumption that property, possessions, and money are more important than ecology, people, and sharing. We all are far too preoccupied with trying to figure out how to kick people off the life raft of existence than we are concerned with finding ways to make room so that more people can be given safety on that raft.

"Suggestions which propose a sharing of resources and land among all the people of Earth are not what is impractical and naive. What is impractical and naive is the belief that we are ever going to solve our problems through greed, selfishness and hostility."

Professor Donaldson sighed slightly. She scanned the audience again. This time her sweep was slower, almost geared to make personal

121

contact with different individuals in the audience.

Eventually, she spoke again. "And, for those of you in the audience who feel all of the foregoing is 20-20 hindsight, there is one simple question I have for you. If we didn't know the extent of the death and destruction which we were going to cause in the Gulf War, then why did we go ahead and act in ignorance without careful consideration of the terrible consequences of our actions?"

Almost as soon as she had raised her question, she began shaking her head in a deliberate, but emphatic, manner. She stopped the movement, seemed to reflect for a few seconds and, then, shook her head in an emphatic manner a few more times.

"However, I do not believe we can escape behind a mea culpa of ignorance in relation to the ramifications of our decisions in the Gulf War. Politicians and military officials are very good at constructing computer models concerning the likely outcomes of different military strategies.

"The people who were in charge of the Coalition knew what they were doing. They knew the human, ecological, and infra-structural damage which they intended to inflict. In fact, it was their precise, technical knowledge of the devastating effects of their intended actions that was the motivation shaping all of their decisions for 43 terrible days.

"Personally speaking, I find this knowing willingness to inflict almost unimaginable pain, suffering, death and destruction on both the innocent and the not-so-innocent to be far more horrifying and worrisome than any such act done out of ill-considered blindness. However, whether we did what we did with cold calculation or with blind, unthinking foolishness, we have a terrible complicity in the tragedy of the Gulf War."

Dr. Donaldson began pacing again. Her hands were behind her back, and she was looking at the floor as she paced. She appeared to be getting ready for the next part of her reply to Dr. Clarke.

She stopped pacing and faced the audience again. "There is a tendency when commenting about international events to try to reduce things to a black and white, good-guy and bad-guy, scenario. As such,

122

we say that whoever happens to be designated as the current bad-guys by the ruling powers must be the cause of everything evil in the world.

"Alternatively, we tend to consider ourselves to be innocent, pure, and, entirely blameless for the evil that the bad-guys do. More often than not, we are in deep denial about the role we play in helping to set events in motion.

"We say the Iraqis could have, and should have, refrained from invading Kuwait. They had a choice, and they were wrong in the choice which they exercised.

"Moreover, we say that once in Kuwait, the Iraqis had the ability to withdraw from Kuwait. They did not, and, therefore, once again, they made the wrong choice."

She paused and looked into the eyes of different people in the audience. She did this for, maybe, ten seconds and continued on speaking.

"The Gulf War did not arise in a vacuum. There is a history behind it.

"The lives of countries and individuals consist of a chain of events. The links of these chains are not independent of one another. They have interlocking meaning.

"Conveniently, we forget about all the ways in which we helped to support Iraq militarily and economically after its invasion of Iran over unresolved issues of access to the sea and disputed borders ... issues eerily similar to those surrounding Iraq's invasion of Kuwait. We forget about how our Ambassador to Iraq told the Iraqis, just days before the invasion, that the United States has no opinion in the matter of Iraq's border disputes with Kuwait.

"We forget about how, in the years leading up to the Gulf crisis, we provided Iraq with billions of dollars in loans and credits with which they, with our knowledge, built up their military capabilities. We forget about the fact that we had precise intelligence reports concerning what Iraq was doing in its programs of research, production and storage of chemical and biological weapons, and, yet, we did nothing.

"We forget about the fact that we knew all about the oppression, murders, and human rights abuses taking place in Iraq, but,

123

nonetheless, we became Iraq's biggest trading partner just prior to the Gulf war. We chose to look the other way about all the terrible things which were going on in Iraq because American business could make a buck.

"We forget that in our great concern for the Kurdish people and the despicable way in which they were gassed, abused and forced to live in squalid conditions by the Iraqi military, we never did anything before the Gulf War to help the Kurds to establish a homeland or to alleviate their suffering. And, we didn't do this because it would have created tensions in our relations with Turkey and Iran, each of which was serving our interests in a variety of ways.

"We forget how the Coalition leaders were so confident of their moral position vis–à–vis Iraq that they felt compelled to call upon witnesses to lie during Congressional hearings and falsely accuse the Iraqi occupiers of having bayoneted and smashed the helpless bodies of babies in incubators in a hospital in Kuwait. This is all too reminiscent of the U. S. government's decision to lie to the American public about the fabricated Gulf of Tonkin incident which helped convince Americans about the wisdom of becoming more deeply mired in Vietnam.

"We allow ourselves to forget that as a result of Kuwait's greed to sell more and more oil at prices which were favorable to western vested interests, Kuwait's actions were pounding further nails into the coffin of Iraq's already war-torn economy, with devastating effects on the Iraqi people. We forget that more than two weeks prior to the threatened invasion, Iraq had tried to bring its concerns to the attention of Kuwait and other members of the Arab League. Promises were made, but nothing was done.

"Conveniently, we forget that the United States had rejected all discussion of sanctions, negotiations, and diplomacy as means of resolving the Iraq-Kuwait invasion crisis. We, like Iraq, had choices, and we, like them, consistently made wrong choices."

She let her words sink in. While she did this, she slowly ran the fingers of her right hand back and forth across her forehead, as if it helped her to concentrate.

Professor Donaldson discontinued the motion and began speaking:

124

"We made the wrong choices because we helped construct the international environment out of which the Iraqi invasion of Kuwait arose. We made the wrong choices because the invasion crisis could have been solved, even before it arose, with little, or no, cost in human life and ecological damage. We made the wrong choices because the invasion crisis could have been solved, even after it arose, with a little bit of compassion, imagination, creativity, understanding and flexibility on the part of the Coalition leaders."

Each sentence that began with: "we made the wrong choice", was followed by a dramatic pause. Apparently, she was trying to give emphasis not only to what had just been said, but to what was to follow, as well.

In a matter-of-fact tone of voice, she said: "The Iraqis were wrong to do what they did. We were wrong to do what we did. Consequently, we have complicity in the terrible sequence of events which transpired in the Gulf."

She became a little bit more animated and emphatic when she said: "In fact, in my opinion, we have greater complicity in the tragedy of the Gulf War than does Iraq. The greater moral responsibility in any conflict always rests with the one who is in the position to avoid the greater evil. And, quite frankly, the damage inflicted by Iraq in invading Kuwait pales in comparison to the totally unnecessary damage inflicted by the Coalition forces in responding to the wrongs of Iraq.

"The exercise of force carries with it a fiduciary responsibility with respect to all those who may be affected by the sphere of influence of such an exercise. The Coalition leaders violated, in virtually every conceivable way, their fiduciary responsibilities with respect to their exercise of force in the Gulf crisis. It was excessive, disproportionate, indiscriminate and unnecessary, and, in many ways, totally ineffective as far as the stated goals of securing peace, justice and respect for international law are concerned."

Professor Donaldson smiled, somewhat apologetically, both to Dr. Clarke and the rest of the audience, and said: I'm sorry for going on at such length. I hope I have satisfied your desire for an elaboration of my point of view."

125

Dr. Clarke stood again and said: "Thank you very much, Professor Donaldson, for your detailed response. You've given us all, I'm sure, a great deal to ponder on.

"Of course, I don't necessarily agree with everything which you have stated in your analysis of the Gulf war situation. Some of these points of difference would, perhaps, be better left for another occasion.

"However, if I might be permitted to touch on just one such issue, I would question the validity of your belief that the Coalition had any choice in the course of action to be pursued with respect to Iraq. Surely, Professor Donaldson, if Iraq had been allowed to swallow Kuwait whole without a lesson in table manners from the Coalition, everybody in the Gulf region would have been at risk of being next on the menu.

"Moreover, the greater Gulf area contains something like 40-60% of the known, world oil reserves. The civilized world simply could not afford to have a brutal and, quite possibly, psychopathic thug in control of such resources, wouldn't you agree, Professor?"

Professor Donaldson was thoughtful for about 15 seconds before starting to speak. "I would agree with you, Dr. Clarke, that the Iraqi people were oppressed by a brutal dictator who depended on violence in a fashion similar to the way an alcoholic depends on booze. I'm not sure I would agree with you on much of anything else you have said."

Before launching into her reply, Professor Donaldson was quiet for another twenty seconds. She looked at some of the walls of the room as well as the room's floor. Her eyes were traveling about the room, but her attention appeared to be focused on something within her.

She pulled out of her brief, reflective mode and started with: "Both during the time leading up to the Gulf war, as well in its aftermath, lots of analysts seemed to assume, almost automatically, that Iraq had nothing but grandiose delusions of grandeur driving it. These commentators all jumped on the bandwagon of a popular theory going around at the time which claimed that Iraq's intentions were to absorb all of the Gulf region into the greater glory of an expanding Iraqi empire which, subsequently, would proceed to bring the hated West to its knees.

"I'm not sure the evidence necessarily supports such a view. First

126

of all, look at the parallels between the conditions which started the Iran-Iraq war and the circumstances that initiated the Gulf war. I alluded to these parallels earlier.

"In both of the first two wars in the Gulf, Iraq invaded another country for very similar reasons. In each instance, Iraq desperately wanted access to the sea in order to supplement, if not replace, the more costly and cumbersome piping of oil through Turkey and Saudi Arabia. Moreover, in the circumstances leading up to both Gulf wars, there was a dispute over boundaries which carried significant economic ramifications for Iraq: the Shatt al-Arab boundary in the case of Iran and the Rumeila oilfield in the case of Kuwait.

"In both the Iran-Iraq War and the second Gulf war, Iraq was extremely upset with the problems that the country being invaded was creating for Iraq. In the first Gulf war, Iraq was angry with the social and political difficulties which the Iranian revolution was stirring up among the substantial Shi'a population of Iraq.

"In the second Gulf war, Iraq was angry with Kuwait for playing havoc with the Iraqi economy which had been run into the ground as a result of the Iran-Iraq war. Kuwait was dumping quantities of oil onto the world markets far in excess of the agreed-upon quotas and, as a result, driving down the price of oil at a time when Iraq needed money to rebuild its economy and country.

"In addition, Iraq felt Kuwait was not only trying to wage economic war against Iraq but that Kuwait seemed to have a very short memory, or little sense of gratitude, concerning the sacrifices which Iraq had made during the Iran-Iraq War. These sacrifices of Iraqi life, property and economy had considerable direct benefits for Kuwait and the whole Gulf region."

Having laid the foundations for what was to follow, Professor Donaldson gave the audience a short mental break, before developing her position further. When the mini-break ended, she asked a series of questions.

"If Iraq had a mind-set focused on conquering Kuwait, why did it bother to stop at the border for a number of days in order to give Kuwait an opportunity to reconsider its intransigence? Why was Iraq open to the negotiating efforts of a number of Arab intermediaries? Why was Iraq willing to attend a mini-summit in Jeddah in order to discuss the matter?

"If I were a brutal dictator with imperialistic designs on conquering the whole Middle East, I wouldn't think twice about running roughshod over whatever stood in my way. I certainly wouldn't hang around a disputed border region and give my intended prey, or anyone else, an opportunity to prevent, or interfere with, my plans to seize my intended targets."

She shifted gears and steered in a slightly different, but related, direction. "A number of people have suggested that Iraq was trying to extort or blackmail Kuwait into concessions. As such, the show of force along the border was intended to intimidate Kuwait and elicit the desired response from them.

"If the foregoing is the case, then the intention of Iraq would not appear to be one of conquering Kuwait and, subsequently, the rest of the Middle East. Rather, Iraq had a specific purpose: namely, to gain access to the sea; to have a favorable settlement to the boundary dispute issue; and, thirdly, to get Kuwait to either forgive Iraq's war debt or to stop driving the price of oil down or both.

"In other words, the available evidence suggests Iraq may have been playing the situation straight up, although rather brutally. Iraq was not merely going through the motions of massing on the Kuwait border. If Kuwait refused to deal with Iraq in a way in which Iraq felt was fair under the circumstances, then Iraq, by force, would take steps to convince Kuwait of the desperateness and urgency of Iraq's economic problems.

"In short, Iraq was not bluffing. It was fed up with the situation. Iraq was fully prepared to take action immediately if Kuwait did not respond with what Iraq considered to be signs of good faith concerning Iraq's specific complaints against Kuwait.

"I believe the evidence which has been cited previously is quite consistent with my somewhat less sinister interpretation of Iraqi intentions and actions in relation to Kuwait. But, let's explore a few other possibilities."

She spent a short time collecting and organizing her thoughts. When she was ready, she began exploring some of the considerations to which she had alluded.

"If I were a brutal dictator with aspirations to conquer other countries in the Middle East, and if I had several hundred thousand troops at my disposal, half of which were supposedly stationed along the Saudi border ... and I'll revisit this issue of alleged border massing shortly ... then after having secured Kuwait, I wouldn't have hesitated to move into Saudi Arabia and conquer it while the opportunity presented itself, especially since there would not have been anyone available to stop me.

"If I'm willing to run the risk of invoking the wrath of the world for my invasion of Kuwait, do I have anything more to lose, as far as world condemnation is concerned, by adding Saudi Arabia to my list? 'In for a penny, in for a pound', would be my motto if I were a brutal dictator intent on conquering and controlling the Gulf region."

As a sort of afterthought to what had been said previously, she declared: "Incidentally, in passing, one ought to remember that U. S. intelligence actually misled, in several respects, the Saudis concerning the alleged offensive posture of Iraqi forces. More specifically, among other things, the U. S. satellite photographs of Iraqi troop deployment along the Saudi border could only show possibilities. Those photos couldn't possibly have disclosed what the intentions of the Iraqis were concerning Saudi Arabia.

"The significance of the photos had to be interpreted in order to forge a link between troop deployment and Iraqi invasion intentions vis–à–vis Saudi Arabia. As it turns out, these interpretations of the satellite photos were wrong because Iraq never did invade Saudi Arabia.

"More ominously, the fact of the matter is that Russian satellite photos of the border area between Iraq and Saudi Arabia clearly indicated that contrary to U. S. claims there were no – I repeat no – troops massed at the border. Either the Russians doctored their pictures or U. S. intelligence doctored its pictures, and, quite frankly, the Russians had no pressing motive for indicating that there wasn't any border massing of Iraqi troops when, according to U. S. officials, there

129

was such massing. On the other hand, the U. S. administration did have a substantial interest in providing fudged intelligence.

"This misdirection by the United States played a key role in convincing the Saudis that an invasion of Saudi Arabia by Iraq was imminent. As a result, the Saudis acceded to U. S. pressure to begin deploying U. S. forces on Saudi soil.

"In any event, it is unfortunate that the Saudis didn't appear to ask themselves a few questions. For instance, if Iraq really were intent on invading Saudi Arabia, why didn't the Iraqi forces take the plunge when it could have done so with a minimum number of casualties? Why didn't the Iraqis go ahead and invade Saudi Arabia when its international public image would not have taken much more of a beating than already was the case for having invaded Kuwait?

"There are quite a few people, both within Saudi Arabia as well as outside of that country, who would not shed any tears if the ruling Saudi monarchy were to be removed from its throne of power. An Iraqi invasion of Saudi Arabia might have brought a surprising mixture of responses from the four corners of the Muslim world, with the reaction of people in the streets being, very possibly, markedly different than the official statements issuing from those countries.

"Furthermore, the United States' rapid deployment force would not have been able to adequately defend Saudi Arabia. It would have been up against a much larger Iraqi army with already established lines of communication and logistical support."

Professor Donaldson pursed her lips quickly, several times in succession. Her eyes were narrowed somewhat. Both of these physical features seemed to be external markers for an internal process of focus.

She arched her eyebrows, and her face appeared to have a quality which suggested she were considering various possibilities. Sharing these with her audience, she began: "One might reasonably anticipate that in the relatively few hours which a few divisions of the Iraqi army would have needed to travel the roughly 175 miles to the Dhahran oil field complex from the border, the Iraqis already would have pretty much secured the area and been chowing-down before the U. S. would have been able to evaluate, coordinate, plan and launch an offensive of any kind even capable of reaching Dhahran, let alone be able to accomplish anything of an effective nature.

"In point of fact, the United States required 119 hours of preparation before it was ready to get Desert Shield off the ground. Roughly 19 hours were needed by the U. S. in 1989 to prepare for its invasion of tiny Panama.

"Even using the latter, much shorter preparation time rather than the former, much longer prep time, the United States would have been in a difficult situation if Iraq had decided to invade Saudi Arabia. In my opinion, I believe the Iraqis were aware of this, and, therefor e, if they didn't invade Saudi Arabia when they had the golden opportunity to do so, this is because, contrary to popular public opinion in the West, they never had the intention of invading Saudi Arabia."

Quickly expanding on, as well as attempting to for tify, her ideas, she followed up on her earlier points: "If I were a brutal dictator really intent on conquering the Middle East and bringing the West to its knees, then, by quickly invading Kuwait and Saudi Arabia, I would have accomplished two objectives. First, I would have established, at least for a time, a stranglehold on a great deal of the world's oil reserves and, therefore, would have been in a position to deal with the rest of the world from strength. Secondly, by conquering Kuwait and, especially, Saudi Arabia, my tactical situation would have created tremendous problems for both the Arab world and the West to respond to militarily.

"Among other things, the Coalition forces would not have been permitted to do to Saudi Arabia what they did to Bagh dad and the rest of Iraq without encountering serious political, economic and social repercussions. Getting a conquering army out of Saudi Arabia would have presented a very different set of problems for Coalition leaders than getting such an army out of j ust Kuwait.

"On the other hand, although Iraq might have been capable of over-running both Kuwait and Saudi Arabia, and, therefore, in the short run, creating many problems for the world, I do not believe Iraq would have been able to hold those countries e ven against a Coalition of countries from just the Middle East. After all, consider for a moment the fact that Iraq had been unable to defeat Iran despite receiving the

131

support of the United States, the Soviet Union and most of the other countries of the Middle East. Consequently, if only Egypt, Syria and Iran, with, perhaps, help from Turkey and, maybe even, Israel, were to co-ordinate an attack against Iraq, I think Iraq would have had a very difficult time of retaining control of Kuwait and Saudi Arabia."

Dr. Donaldson had an expression on her face which seemed to indicate she was tired of such talk or, perhaps, that she had strayed too far afield. She made a sort of dismissive gesture with her hands, more to herself, possibly, than to anyone in the audience.

"If we leave such speculative scenarios aside, there are a number of other considerations which undermine the contention that Iraq was intent on either swallowing up a number of Middle East countries or on bringing the West to its knees. For example, since the first Gulf war, the fact is, Iraq had developed much closer and more cordial relationships with a number of countries, including the United States.

"America had given Iraq considerable help during the Iran-Iraq war, despite being rather duplicitous toward Iraq in the Iran-Contra fiasco. Furthermore, as I indicated earlier, the United States had become Iraq's number one trading partner just prior to the second Gulf war.

"The United States had made billions of dollars in loans and credits available to the Iraqis. America also had helped Iraq to rebuild its military capabilities.

"Iraq wanted to be treated with respect and fairness by the United States. For the most part, things were moving in this direction.

"Iraq did have serious differences with the U. S. over their respective policies concerning Israel and the Palestinians. Quite frankly, however, I don't believe the Iraqis would have considered it in their best interests to jeopardize their developing relationship with the United States by going on an imperialistic binge in the Middle East.

"I believe the second Gulf came about like most wars. A combination of deceit, misunderstanding, miscommunication, miscalculation, stubbornness, pride, posturing, stupidity, selfishness and blindness were exhibited by parties on all sides of the Gulf War issue.

"Iraq, despite all its faults, is not the enemy in the Gulf war. We

132

all are the enemy.

"We all collectively join in to create mess after mess in both international and domestic affairs. The second Gulf war is not an exception to this central truth of world events. It is, regrettably, a most horrendous exemplar of what I am maintaining.

"Let me make one last comment in wrapping up my answer to your follow-up question Dr. Clarke. Everyone is convinced that allowing the control of much of the world's oil supplies to fall into the hands of countries like Iraq or Iran would be disastrous. I wouldn't wish to take issue with such a contention.

"At the same time, I'm not convinced the interests of the vast majority of the people of the Earth are better served, ultimately, by having control of much of the world's oil supplies in the hands of the United States. The governmental, military and corporate institutions of the United States are not necessarily the benign force of goodness that their spin-doctors try to convince everyone is the case. In fact, one could easily say the same thing about the governmental, military and corporate institutions of almost every country on the face of the earth."

9.) Dark Side of the Moon

Having finished responding to one questioner, Professor Donaldson was refreshing herself with a drink of water before taking the next question. When she was done quenching her thirst, she pointed toward a person three, or four, rows in front of me who had raised her hand. Dr. Donaldson said: "Yes, Karen, you have a question?"

"Actually, Rachel," Karen said, "I wanted to hear something more about what you have to say with respect to some of these Muslim terrorist groups. A few of the comments in your talk briefly dealt with this issue, and I found your ideas somewhat intriguing.

"I've read quite a few reports recently which state that, tragedies such as the Oklahoma City bombing notwithstanding, the FBI consider Islamic groups to be the number one source of terrorist threats to America today. Moreover, there are many places internationally which seem to be suffering from the same kind of problem.

"I don't really have a specific question to ask you on this. Nonetheless, I would be interested in listening to whatever you have to say on this general issue."

Dr. Donaldson took a deep breath and exhaled somewhat forcibly through her mouth. She arched her eyebrows slightly. She studied the ceiling for a few seconds, lowered her head, and began to speak.

"I guess the first thing which should be addressed is people's tendency to look at the issue of terrorism in very superficial terms." As she finished her sentence, she looked at Karen, smiled and said: "Don't worry, Karen, you are not the sort of person I have in mind when I speak about superficial views of terrorism."

After a bit of scattered laughter had subsided, Professor Donaldson continued on. "The first part of my response, Karen, may not seem as if it has anything to do with your request, so I would ask for your indulgence and the patience of the rest of the people here. However, I believe, or hope, that before I am through, you will all see the relevance of the earlier portion of my comments to Karen's request concerning the issue of terrorism among certain Muslim groups."

Having, to a degree, prepared her audience for what was to follow, Professor Donaldson began."There are a lot of complex currents which run through both individuals and organizations. Historical,

135

psychological, political, economic, religious, cultural, educational and ecological factors all are woven together in subtle dynamics that create an endless array of patterns in the life of an individual or organization.

"These patterns are not static entities. They change in various ways over time and across circumstances.

"Nevertheless, there usually are enough similarities and constants from one situation to the next enabling us to recognize various character traits in individuals as well as in organizations. These traits serve as a kind of identifying signature through which we distinguish one group from another or one individual from another.

"On the other hand, despite the presence of certain identifiable, relatively constant traits, people and organizations do not necessarily act in the same manner on all occasions. In other words, they exhibit what is referred to as dispositional behavior.

"Dispositional behavior is the tendency of an individual or an organization to act in certain ways in some circumstances and, yet, still allow for the possibility of acting differently in similar circumstances on other occasions. A dispositional trait occurs often enough to serve as something of an identifiable or distinguishing feature, but such a tendency is mixed in with an array of other behavioral possibilities.

"Thus, to have a disposition toward violent behavior does not mean an individual or organization will be violent under all circumstances. What it means is that in the past an individual or organization has been violent on enough occasions to permit someone to make a judgment which establishes an association or linkage between the descriptive term "violent" and a given organization or individual."

Professor Donaldson took a quick sip of water from the glass sitting on the rostrum. As she was putting the glass back down, she remarked: "One problem with making judgments concerning people's dispositional behavior, however, is this. In making such judgments, people have very different ideas about how many occasions of, say, violence, need to be observed in order to claim that a linkage between the descriptive qualifier 'violent' and a given individual or organization is accurate or fair.

"One person will observe representatives of an organization act violently, in some way, on only one occasion. However, for whatever reasons, such an individual will feel justified in describing such an organization as 'violent'.

"Another person may see members of an organization exhibit a number of violent acts on various occasions. Yet, when the observed episodes of violent acts are considered in the context of a wide variety of other, non-violent acts carried out by members of the same organization, the observer in question may not judge either the organization or its representatives as being characteristically inclined to violent behavior."

She paused for a moment, removed her glasses, took out a handkerchief, moistened the glasses with her breath, and began cleaning them. While going about the process of wiping her glasses, she continued speaking.

"Another problem in making judgments about the dispositional behavior of individuals and organizations revolves around the criteria and values we use for deciding what is to count as a violent act. Suppose, for example, individual 'A' attempts, unsuccessfully, to punch person 'B', and, in the process, person 'B' defends himself or herself and hits individual 'A'.

"Some observers may be inclined to call the act of the first individual a violent one, irrespective of whether or not that person landed a blow. Alternatively, if person 'B' is perceived not to have initiated the fight, an observer may not count the act of person 'B' to be a violent one even though 'B' landed a blow.

"On the other hand, still other observers may count the acts of both 'A' and 'B' as violent events. For these people, the question of who started the whole thing, or who, if anyone, landed a blow, is irrelevant."

Satisfied with the condition of her glasses, Professor Donaldson placed them back on her head. She spent a few seconds adjusting them, still talking as she finished the task.

"Of course, an act does not necessarily have to be in the form of a physical blow to qualify or count as a violent act. For instance, some people may wish to count unkind or mean words as instances of violent behavior.

"In addition, emotional outbursts, acts of omission, betrayal, indifference, rejection and indoctrination all might count as instances of violent behavior under certain circumstances. Similarly, creating conditions which cause or perpetuate hunger, poverty, homelessness, injustice or illness could be judged by some people to be acts of violence.

"Alternatively, an individual might be considered to have done violence to the truth through acts of lying, disinformation, propaganda, and prejudice. Furthermore, requiring people to attend educational programs which do not necessarily serve the economic, political or spiritual needs of the students may, for some people, count as a form of violence.

"Some vegetarians may wish to charge meat-eaters with doing violence to animal life." Dr. Donaldson flashed a brief smile and said: "On the other hand, some vegetables may want to remind vegetarians of the violence the latter inflicts on the former."

There were some audible laughs in the audience. Perhaps, there were a few appreciative vegetables in attendance that I had failed to notice on the way to my seat. Dr. Donaldson let the noise subside.

"Another problem surrounding the issue of dispositional judgments concerning, say, violent behavior is the following. We often evaluate situations very differently depending whether we are talking about others or about ourselves.

"Frequently, we are quite prepared to label someone else's behavior as violent, while denying that the same kind of act done by ourselves is violent. We have a tendency to rationalize our acts and, as a result, we color them as reasonable or justifiable or appropriate.

"Generally, this process of sanitizing our acts means that either we do not count our acts as violent or we call them legitimate acts of violence. In the latter case, we often like to argue that such legitimate acts of violence should not be considered as being relevant to any assessment, by ourselves or others, of our dispositional tendency toward violence.

"This process of rationalization and denial which allows us to dissociate our self-image from some of the acts we perform can lead to very bizarre situations. A person can be quite abusive of others, even to the point of torturing such people, and, yet, believe himself or herself to be a decent, peaceful, compassionate, non-violent individual. All it takes is a little creative emotional book-keeping in relation to whether we label our acts as liabilities or assets.

"One trick which is used to cook these emotional ledgers is the following. We say to ourselves the other person's acts of violence reveal something essential about that person. Such acts, we say, are inherent features of that person's being ... like some species of original sin.

"Our own acts of violence, on the other hand, are judged to be nothing more than peripheral, temporary lapses. Momentary storms in an otherwise peaceful sea. We tend to always see ourselves as playing Abel to the other person's Cain."

Professor Donaldson started to lean on the rostrum but found it a little unstable. She straightened up and moved to the side of the rostrum.

"Not surprisingly," she declared, "we often do not extend to others the same liberties, privileges or degrees of freedom involving dispositional judgments which we generously extend to ourselves. Instead, we frequently label the explanations of others, concerning their behavior, to be expressions of denial or propaganda or mere excuses intended to help them avoid responsibility for the real nature of their acts.

"Judgments about who does violence to who can become quite problematic. For example, one person censors another and, in the judgment of the latter, the former is doing violence to the freedoms, rights or beliefs of the latter. On the other hand, from the perspective of the one whom is doing the censoring, the views of the one being censored do violence to fundamental values, principles or standards of the ones doing the censoring.

"Such differences of opinion concerning the perceived locus of violence about, in this case, the issue of censorship, often lead to other actions by the concerned parties. These further actions raise the same question of who does violence to whom, in, yet, another context. The process is called 'escalation'."

Moving back behind the rostrum, she said: "The act of labeling can itself be an expression of violence. When rumor, gossip, slander, libel, innuendo, and unfounded speculation destroy a person's life, violence has been done to such an individual.

"Consequently, when governments or the media refer to an individual or an organization as a terrorist group, there are a number of questions which need to be asked and explored. For instance, what behaviors are being counted as constituting acts of terrorism?"

Dr. Donaldson scrunched up her lips in a way that suggested she were considering something. "Suppose," she began, "an organization is trying to defend itself against oppression or attempting to confront some sort of social injustice and, as a result, uses violence as part of its response to such perceived wrongs. Does the display of violence necessarily mean such an organization deserves to be labeled as 'terrorist'?

"Revolutionaries, freedom fighters, underground resistance groups, and guerrillas all use violence. When does their use of such violence qualify as acts of terrorism? How do we differentiate between possible legitimate uses of violence and illegitimate expressions of violence?"

She took another drink of water. This time she continued to hold the glass in her hand while expanding on her previous comments.

"Why were the mujahidin's acts of resistance with respect to the Russian invasion of Afghanistan widely considered to be the acts of patriots, but the mujahidin of Palestine or Lebanon are said to be terrorists? They both employed extreme acts of violence. In both cases, innocent people, along with not-so-innocent people, lost their lives as a result of the actions of the mujahidin. What factors are influencing our dispositional judgments to treat similar acts of violence in comparable situations in quite different ways?

"Consider another, related case. There were individuals who journeyed from various Muslim countries to Afghanistan in order to lend support to the mujahidin. They were said to be freedom fighters.

"Yet, when these individuals returned home and fought against injustices, oppression and abuses of human rights similar to those in Afghanistan, they became terrorists. What led to this transformation in our judgments of their dispositional behavior with respect to the use of violence?"

Professor Donaldson gave her question a chance to percolate in the minds of the audience. She returned the glass to the rostrum and quickly swept her eyes across the faces in the room, sighing slightly.

"When Jewish resistance groups, such as Irgun, Lehi or Haganah, took the lives of innocent people or Jewish collaborators, they were said to be fighting a war of liberation against British occupation. When the PLO took the lives of innocent people or Palestinian collaborators while trying to fight a war of liberation against Israeli occupation, the PLO was said to be a terrorist group. Why are we treating similar cases in very different ways?

"Between 1948 and 1956, various Israeli military operations massacred a total of over 1000 Palestinian civilians. These deaths occurred at places like: Deir Yassin, Doueimah, Qibya, al-Bureig, Kafr Kassim and Khan Yunis.

"The PLO did not come into existence until 1968, more than twelve years after the acts of Israeli violence against Palestinians to which I've just alluded. However, between 1968 and 1981, various PLO military operations massacred a total of some 280 Israeli citizens. Yet, despite beginning quite a long time after the initial Israeli acts of violence against Palestinians and despite being less than one-third as deadly as the attacks of their Israeli counterparts, the Palestinians are the only ones who are considered terrorists.

"There seems to be considerable inconsistency in the way the same kinds of acts of violence are being labeled in situations which bear many resemblances to one another. Considerations of race, religion, ethnic origins, national aspirations, political affiliation, economic interests, and media biases all can skew this labeling process."

She ran her hands through her hair and pushed the bridge of her glasses back up her nose toward her forehead. She took her right hand and cupped it around the nape of her neck and just left it there for a short while as she talked, letting her elbow sort of hang in front of her.

"Governments, police forces, the military, security people and intelligence agencies all use violence, just as revolutionary and

141

resistance fighters do. Naturally, not all acts of aggression or violence qualify as terrorist acts. And, this is true for both those who are in power as well as those who are not in power.

"Acts designed to protect sovereignty, peace and tranquility may, or may not, constitute an act of terrorism, depending on circumstances. The problem is: one person's tranquility is quite frequently founded on the misery and oppression of others.

"When does, for example, a government's use of violence qualify as terrorist acts against its citizens? Is a government or police force entitled to do anything it likes simply because it is a legally constituted body?

"Were the deaths at Kent State, more than twenty years ago, regrettable consequences of a legal use of force or were those deaths the result of an act of terrorism? Was the violence used against Native peoples at Wounded Knee in South Dakota in 1973 part of a federally-sponsored campaign of terror against Native peoples, or was such violence merely an attempt to stop the illegal activities of a numb er of Native people?

"When a government, friendly to the United States, employs tactics of death squads, torture, disappearances, abuse of human rights, sham trials, censorship, and indoctrination in order to protect its vested interests, are these not acts of violence which are of a terrorist nature? Should they no longer be considered of a violent or terrorist nature simply because the vested interests being protected may be beneficial to our country?"

Having asked a number of questions, Dr. Donaldson was quiet for ten seconds or so, allowing her ideas to have a little more time to bounce around in the minds and hearts of the audience. She looked down at the floor and massaged her forehead. She raised her head.

"Let's consider a hypothetical Muslim group. This group, and the individuals belonging to it, will be assumed to be dispositionally inclined toward playing an activist role of some sort in their communities. In other words, the group and its members have a tendency to act in ways that are intended to help influence and shape what goes on around them socially, spiritually, politically, economically, educationally and/or

142

ecologically.

"To be an activist, does not necessarily entail that one will be inclined to use tactics of violence or terror to achieve one's aims. Some activists are inclined toward violence, and some activists are not inclined toward violence.

"Furthermore, even among those activists who may be inclined toward acts of violence, there is a spectrum of dispositional possibilities. Some activists may exhibit violence only in situation-specific circumstances, such as when they are provoked or attacked. Other activists may be prepared to inflict violence on others but only in accordance with certain values or principles concerning who is and who is not to be a target. Still other activists who may be inclined to violent behavior may be quite indiscriminate in their destructive activities and interested in terrorizing everyone in an attempt to gain their objectives.

"For purposes of discussion, let's consider our hypothetical Muslim group to be a collection of socially concerned citizens. What are some of the issues which have brought individuals to such a group?

"There are a number of recurrent themes that keep surfacing in Muslims groups with an activist disposition. To begin with, there tends to be a general disillusionment among the members of these groups concerning the ability of existing political, economic and social institutions to deal effectively with a wide variety of social justice issues such as poverty, homelessness, hunger and other inequities.

"In addition, not only are many of these groups disenchanted with the performance of various social institutions, they also tend to reject different kinds of 'isms'. Materialism, modernism, secularism, imperialism, racism, and colonialism all are seen as being sources of problematic, if not malevolent, influences in the world."

Professor Donaldson held up the first two fingers of her left hand and shook them a few times very gently. As she did this, she said: "Secondly, questions of identity, purpose, meaning and values are driving forces for the members of these groups. Moreover, people in these groups seek to derive their answers to these questions from an understanding of Islam.

143

"However, not all Muslims and not all Muslim groups have an identical understanding of what they believe Islam says about issues of identity, purpose, meaning and so on. A lot of inter- and intra-group conflict arises as a result of these kinds of interpretational difference concerning Islam.

"Up to a certain point, such groups, or, more accurately, the individuals within them, will agree completely on what Islam entails in the way of beliefs, values and practices. Yet, despite these commonalities, differences of interpretation, application, interests, priorities, commitment, goals and intentions arise.

"These differences have a significant impact on how various individuals or groups go about trying to resolve, among other things, issues of social justice. In fact, whether or not a given Muslim individual or group feels violence is justified in solving, for example, social justice issues will depend on how they interpret Islam.

"As is true in every religious tradition, there are many Muslims who tend to treat their understanding of their own religious tradition as the only correct understanding of things. Consequently, when, for example, their own interpretation of Islam seems to give them permission or license to commit acts of violence, they believe this means that God is giving them permission or license to do so. They are assuming their way of seeing things reflects Divine perception of those same things."

Professor Donaldson again held up her left hand at about face level. This time her hand was showing three fingers.

"Thirdly, many of the people in these Muslim groups seem to feel a deep sense of urgency about solving the problems of society. As a result, there often is a sort of revolutionary fervor about their attitudes, feelings and activities.

"Moreover, not only do many of the individuals in these groups tend to believe that social transformation must happen now, very frequently many of them tend to believe they have unique roles to play in helping to bring about such change. Therefore, such individuals often believe their vision, piety, commitment, talent, leadership and knowledge will help make the difference between success and failure in

144

the desired process of transformation.

"The belief that one's potential contribution has an important role to play in bringing about change tends to create a deep sense of responsibility in an individual. As a result, such people and groups often feel pressure to act and discharge their alleged duty to destiny."

Professor Donaldson held up her right hand in a closed position. One by one her fingers came up as she ran through a summary of what she had said previously.

"The disillusionment with the efficacy of social institutions, the alienation from many of the 'isms' which are currently influential, the belief in the correctness of one's understanding, the sense of urgency, the revolutionary fervor, and the deep sense of having a unique contribution to make to the group's cause -- all of these combine to form a very powerful motivational dynamic, both within the individual and the larger group. The force of this dynamic often tends to manifest itself as a belief that the group and its members are participating in a revival of, or a return to, the original, pure spirit of Islam.

"This conviction that one is an instrument of the original spirit of Islam may be exploited in a variety of ways by both an organization and the individuals in that group. In fact, on a fairly regular basis, one encounters a primary method which is utilized by these groups in an attempt to channel the powerful dynamics surrounding the belief that one is serving the original, true, pure spirit of Islam. This method involves linking the aforementioned dynamics to the belief that one is going to earn the undying gratitude of God for serving the true Islam.

"In short, these groups claim that paradise or heaven is just around the corner for anyone who sincerely commits herself or himself to the group's interpretation of the original spirit of Islam. Many people find this kind of offer something which they cannot refuse. Indeed, some Muslims are prepared to excuse a multitude of sins with respect to themselves and in relation to their groups, in order not to jeopardize their chances for the desired reward."

Professor Donaldson checked her wristwatch. "My time is just about up, so I'll try to wrap this up fairly quickly." She took another drink of water.

"Many Muslim groups talk about the 'true Islam' and the original spirit of Islam. However, mixed in with this talk, one also finds, quite frequently, a number of other motivational forces hiding beneath the outward talk.

"This scenario of wolf-like motivations attempting to benefit from being hidden by the innocence and purity of sheep's wool is not exclusive to Muslims. It plays itself out in every religious tradition.

"Some individuals are powerless and desire to be powerful. Some are alienated and want to have a sense of belonging. For each of these groups of people, Islam is not important except as a possible means of satisfying a variety of needs which are not necessarily of a spiritual nature.

"Some Muslim groups want to bask in the euphoria of restoring what they believe is the lost glory of Islam. What they don't seem to understand is that Islam can never lose any of its glory. In reality, the glory which such people seek is the pride, arrogance and conceit of self-glorification.

"Some of these groups and individuals are driven by national, ethnic, tribal, racial and/or religious aspirations and/or hatreds. They wish to exploit Islam and hijack its moral authority to serve their dark purposes.

"The true Islam, the original spirit of Islam, is completely preoccupied with, and absorbed in, qualities of love, compassion, charitableness, chivalry, justice, forgiveness, tolerance, kindness, gratitude, gentleness, humility, self-purification, patience, harmony and selflessness. Knowing Divinity, serving Divinity, trusting in Divinity, remembering Divinity, cherishing Divinity and loving Divinity are the woof and warp of the true Islam.

"Consequently, to speak of Islamic terrorism is a contradiction in terms. On the other hand, to speak of the terrorism of someone who refers to himself or herself as Muslim is not necessarily a contradiction in terms.

"So called Muslims who advocate the use of force and violence in order to impose their distorted interpretation of Islam onto others do a great violence to the spirit of Islam. This is so for four reasons.

146

"First, the use of force and violence to induce compliance from others in matters of religion is inconsistent with one of the central precepts of Islam. More specifically, there can be no compulsion used in bringing about the realization of the essential spiritual nature of human beings.

"The kind of submission which God seeks comes only through an individual's free will or unforced offering. To intimidate, extort, or terrorize people, in order to get them to adopt a Muslim's interpretation of things, completely violates the spiritual etiquette of Islam.

"Secondly, with respect to those who resort to the use of force, violence or terror in order to secure acquiescence from others on a variety of social issues, such people display a profound lack of trust in God. These sorts of individual do not have confidence in the capacity of the will of Divinity to effectively carry out Divine purposes independently of what people do or don't do.

"People who rely on violence and terror to achieve their allegedly spiritual objectives have a very inflated opinion of themselves. They seem to assume that if they did not use violence or terror, God would be helpless to realize Divine wishes. Such people have a pathetic and extremely warped understanding of the ways of Divinity.

"Thirdly, whoever employs force and violence as tools of persuasion reveals an enormous poverty of imagination, creativity, wisdom and spiritual artistry. Submission comes through the heart's attraction to the beauty, nobility and integrity of the example which reflects the light of Divinity. Force and violence will never generate such attraction.

"Someone once said: 'Violence is the last refuge of incompetence'. People who are inclined to terror and violence as instruments of spiritual evangelism are admitting incompetence.

"In effect, they are acknowledging they lack the personal resources of integrity, inventiveness and a generosity of spirit which are needed to exercise spiritual competence in finding artful, non-violent solutions to problems in the face of adversity. There is absolutely nothing resourceful about killing other people.

"Fourthly, and finally, anyone who uses force, violence and/or terror as part of their yellow-brick road to paradise is debasing the nature of the intention which should be behind all of a Muslim's actions. Everything should be done for the sake of God's satisfaction and pleasure.

"If one is committing acts of violence because one believes this will be one's ticket of admission to heaven, the intention underlying one's acts is the achievement of paradise, not the pleasure of God. God's pleasure merely becomes a means to one's own ends.

"In addition, if a group or individual actually believes that God finds either pleasure or satisfaction in acts of terror or misguided violence, then such people have an extremely distorted understanding of how to go about pleasing God. Unfortunately, such beliefs have been very prevalent throughout history, and not just amongst Mu slims."

10.) An Open Letter to the Muslim Community

As-Salaam-u-'alaykum! (Peace be upon you)

There are many issues which need to be addressed by the Muslim community. Without wishing to say I have any of the answers, there are a great many problems surrounding the hermeneutics (the theory of interpretation) of such concepts as ijma (consensus), qiyas (reasoning ... often through analogies), and ijtihad (a process of striving for the truth in problematic, complex circumstances), all of which have, in different ways, contributed to what appears to be the rather moribund state of modern understanding concerning various facets of shari'ah and tariqa (different ways of referring to the spiritual path) – that is, ways of seeking truth and justice.

I have no wish to reinvent the spiritual wheel, and I have no desire to deviate from the teachings of either the Qur'an or the sunnah (actions) of the Prophet Muhammad (peace be upon him). However, quite frankly, what many people take those teachings to encompass may be quite other than what the actual original intention underlying what is being said may be.

For example, many people confuse tafsir and ta'wil (these are two methodological approaches that seek to understand the guidance of the Qur'an). and even in the latter case (that is ta'wil), some suppose that ta'wil means interpretation. In reality, ta'wil alludes to the process of being brought back to first principles through Divine assistance ... something quite different than interpretation and of great significance since interpretation (or the veiling of Revelation through personal, rational predilections) of the Qur'an is forbidden – a prohibition which went largely unheeded both by the proponents of kalaam (theology) and philosophy, and we suffer today as a result of the distortions which have arisen through the varied forms of these 'disciplines'.

Many people believe the doors of ijtihad closed in the 11th-12th century and believe this is quite appropriate. I feel such a belief is both arrogant and dismissive of the fact that Divinity continues to be manifested -- even if not in the form of Revelation or a continuing Prophetic tradition -- but in the form of ijtihad and, therefore, should not necessarily be arbitrarily foreclosed on by human beings. Rather, ijtihad should be examined for traces of how Divine guidance exists in modes which, God willing, might serve to complement two basic sources of Divine assistance [i.e., Qur'an and the Sunnah (actions) of the Prophet] and,

149

thereby, be used by human beings to address problems of today in circumstances which are, in some ways, quite different from the time of the Prophet.

Some Christians are fond of the letters 'wwjd' – what would Jesus (peace be upon him) do. An Islamic counterpart would be 'wwmd' - what would Muhammad (peace be upon him) do, and the fact of the matter is, I am not convinced that a lot of Muslims (and I am not necessarily excluding myself here) understand the nature of the niyat and insight which go into giving expression to action ... not only with respect to themselves, but especially in relation to the Prophet. For a non-Prophet to try to figure out what a Prophet might do in a given set of circumstances is, I think, a rather risky business ... and, yet, many people suppose they understand where the Prophet is coming from when he says the things which are reported in the hadith, or they believe they understand how a Prophet would balance different considerations, or what weights to assign, or what priorities are to be given to various principles, or whether something which has been recorded was intended for the parties to whom it was said only, or to the generality of Muslims who lived at that time, or in some more universal fashion ...

All too many people make pronouncements based on their interpretation of things or someone else's interpretation of things, and, unfortunately, there often is not much dialogue going on about the hermeneutical problems which are entailed by the process of interpretation or the possibilities which might be encompassed by different modalities of ijtihad, or why the process of reasoning should be limited to qiyas (thinking by analogy), or even what the structural character of qiyas actually is -- since there are a wide variety of bases in which analogical reasoning can be rooted. Similarly, everyone supposes they understand the scope and character of aql (reason or intellect) ... which usually reduces down to the manner in which they, themselves, think ... much as we suppose that common sense is just another way of talking about what we believe reflects our own way of doing things.

Many Muslim thinkers have painted the Muslim community into an almost untenable position. Many of the rest of us have let them.

Perhaps, it is time for something new and different to be tried – but something which is fully reconcilable with the spirit of the Qur'an and

150

sunnah. Ijtihad (striving to understand the truth of a given situation) is the bridge here, but trying to find the right framework of ijtihad or an appropriate set of principles for this project is the challenge before us.

I don't want to revolutionize Islam -- because Islam is God-given and quite adequate to the needs of human beings as it is. What needs to be revolutionized are the ways in which Muslims understand the nature, principles, and essence of the many dimensions and levels encompassed by Islam.

One should not try to reduce Islam down to what this or that group of Muslims think or say. Presumably, this may be one of the reasons why the Prophet said: "My community will never agree in error" -- and I believe it is an error to seek to stifle the voice of ijtihad.

In saying this, I do not mean to say that every exercise of ijtihad is correct. There is a difference between permissible degrees of freedom and seeking to take license.

Although the Prophet warned against bi'dat – those innovative measures which transgressed sacred boundaries -- many Muslims have used this warning as a weapon to bludgeon anything with which they disagreed, and, then, they cite the hadiths concerning bi'dat in order to defend such attacks. However, most, if not all, of the hadiths concerning bi'dat tend to be of a general, ambiguous nature, and later Muslims have merely inserted their own theological antipathies into this ambiguity, claiming that what they mean is what the Prophet meant.

This is not only a specious mode of reasoning, it is, spiritually speaking, extremely dangerous to suppose one knows what the Prophet thought and meant on any given occasion. Only God and the Prophet know this, and unless God provides the sort of Divine assistance which gives insight into such matters, then, in reality, one is merely voicing an opinion -- which may, or may not, be well-formed.

When Hazrat 'Umar (may God be pleased with him) introduced the nightly, public observance of tarawih prayers during the month of fasting -- despite the fact the Prophet, with the exception of the first few nights, said these prayers in private -- Hazrat 'Umar (may God be pleased with him) described this as a good innovation. So, obviously, not all innovation should be confused with the kind of innovation or bi'dat against which the

151

Prophet sought to warn us.

Similarly, if all innovation is inappropriate, then why was the Prophet reported to have said: "If a person sets down in Islam a good custom (sunna hasana), which is put into practice, that person will have written for oneself the wage of those who put it into practice, while nothing will be diminished from the wages of those who put the custom into practice; and, if a person sets down in Islam a bad custom which put into practice, then this person will have written for one the load of those who put it into practice, while nothing will be diminished from the load of those who put the custom into practice." Ijtihad -- along with other uses of reason, discussion, and rigorous examination -- may be necessary to struggle toward being able to differentiate between good customs and problematic customs.

Clearly, the onus of moral responsibility is on anyone pursuing ijtihad, just as spiritual responsibility rests heavily upon any individual (s) who would initiate laying down a new custom in Islam. But, then, isn't this the nature of human existence -- to strive, in the face of uncertainty and ambiguity, toward a healthy, constructive faith, not only for oneself but the community as well?

Jihad is not primarily about risking oneself physically against an armed antagonist, but, rather, jihad -- and ijtihad is, as the root of the word suggests, a form of jihad -- is embedded in a willingness to struggle against ignorance, bias, hatred, prejudices, negative emotions, likes and dislikes ... all of the processes within us which impair and distort understanding of, and acting upon, the truth.

The Qur'an says: "O ye who believe, fight against those infidels close to you." (9: 123). There is no infidel closer to each of us than our own nafs or ego, and ijtihad is a process of struggling against the tendencies within the nafs to be kufr [that is, to be 'guided' by unbelief of one species or another) and, in the process, seek both to hide, as well as to hide from, the truth -- not only with respect to ourselves, but also in relation to others, Creation, and Divinity.

If the five pillars were all there is to deen (spiritual way), then why do the Qur'an and the Sunnah deal with so much more than those five pillars? If the so-called 'religious law' is all there were to deen, then, why are such matters restricted to just 500, or so, verses in the Qur'an? If the five pillars were all there is to deen, then why did the Prophet speak about iman, ahsan, tariqa, and haqiqa? If being Muslim exhausted the possibilities of Islam, then why did the Qur'an and the Prophet also speak about being Mu'min (a person of deep faith) and Mohsin (one who practices spiritual excellence)?

If the five pillars were all there is to deen, then why would the Prophet Muhammad (peace be upon him) be so pleased with Mu'adh ibn Jabal (may God be pleased with him) when the latter indicated, after being asked by the Prophet what his judicial envoy to Yeman would do if he could not find an answer to a legal question in either the Qur'an or the sunnah, that he (i.e., Mu'adh -- may God be pleased with him) would form his own opinion concerning such matters? Why would the Prophet say, upon hearing this response: "Praise be to God Who hath guided the envoy of His envoy to what pleases the envoy of God"?

All too frequently affairs in mosques and Muslim communities all around the world are controlled by the rule of pedigree rather than the principles of spiritual understanding. For example, if someone knows Arabic, then ipso facto, this aspect of pedigree is apparently supposed to make someone's opinion superior to that of someone who does not speak or read Arabic. Yet, nowhere in the Qur'an does one find anything to support such a presumption.

Rather, the criterion which is mentioned in the Qur'an as a means of differentiating among Muslims is the condition of taqwa (piety or God-consciousness). Taqwa is not dependent on one's linguistic skills but on the condition of one's heart, the purity of one's niyat, or intention, and the propriety and judiciousness, God willing, of one's actions.

Arabic will not necessarily help one penetrate to the meaning of the Qur'an. Indeed, among the many verses in the Qur'an which indicate this are the following: "Say: My Lord, increase me in knowledge." (20: 114), and: "We raise by grades (of Mercy) whom We will, and over every lord of knowledge, there is one more knowing. (12:76). Our need is for Divine Grace and support, not necessarily facility with the Arabic language.

To be sure, knowledge of Arabic might be one form of such Grace. Nevertheless, Arabic is not the Source of such Grace, but, rather, God is, and knowledge of Arabic may be, under the appropriate circumstances, just one manifestation of that Grace.

Knowledge of Arabic did not help the people of pre-Islamic Arabia. God

153

had to intervene before Divine assistance came in the form of an Arabic tongue - namely, the Prophet Muhammad (peace be upon him) to whom revelation was given. Moreover, since Arabic is a created thing, one cannot reduce the Qur'an, which is believed to be the uncreated word of God, down to created being. At best, Arabic is a locus of manifestation through which uncreated Divine guidance is given expression.

Obviously, knowledge of Arabic is not of any assistance to those who feel their facility with Arabic gives them the right to kill innocent people. In fact, these killers of innocents, place their own interpretation of things above the Qur'an. The Qur'an says:

"Whoever kills a human being for other than manslaughter or corruption in the earth, it shall be as if that person killed all of humankind, and whosoever saves the life of another human being, it shall be as if that person had saved the life of all humankind." (5:32)

Without feeling at all inclined to side with the perpetuation of Israeli atrocities against innocents in the occupied territories of Palestine, the fact of the matter is, despite knowledge of Arabic, the leaders and followers of Hamas and Hezbollah continue to kill innocent people in Israel – people about whom such leaders have no knowledge about whether, or not, those people are guilty of manslaughter or corruption in the earth. Furthermore, even if such people were guilty of corruption, I have seen no evidence which warrants that such life and death decisions have been arrogated by God to various Muslim organizations, and, surely, it is an exercise in self-serving hubris for the leaders of such organizations to claim they have been appointed by God to look after such matters.

There is no difference between, on the one hand, terrorists like Osama bin Laden and, on the other hand, those individuals who are either fraudulent Sufi shaykhs or who seek to force everyone to submit to their individual brand of exoteric, dogmatic theology. All of these categories of individual are spiritually abusive toward those who may be mesmerized by them because bin Laden, false mystical guides, and theological zealots are not necessarily interested in helping people toward the truth, but, rather, often seek to induce people to become committed to the self-

154

serving agendas of such spiritual narcissists. Each of these sorts of individual perpetrate spiritual terrorism in relation to their followers before they seek to do damage -- whether socially, economically, politically, physically, or spiritually -- to those who are 'considered other' and, therefore, treated as alien and inhuman by the self-appointed "leaders".

Moreover, alleged "leaders" such as bin Laden, or the 'shaykhs' who become idols to their mureeds, or the exoteric theologians who insist that their way is the only way to understand Islam induce their followers to suppose that the belief system being promulgated represents a 'ticket to heaven'. Yet, such "leaders" continue to avoid the fact that little, or none, of what they are doing -- as opposed to what they are giving lip-service to -- reflects either the teachings of the Qur'an or the teachings of the Prophet Muhammad (peace be upon him).

For example, the Qur'an says: "Say: Surely, my prayer and my service of sacrifice, my life and my death are all for God, the Lord of the worlds." (6:162). There is nothing in this about paradise or 70 virgins.

In fact, what the terrorist "leaders" are counseling the suicide bombers to do (and the same argument could, with slight modifications, be extended to mystical charlatans as well as many exoteric theologians) is an exercise in shirk, for the alleged "leaders" are waving the promise of Paradise and sexual favors before such individuals, and this is nothing less than associating partners with God since niyats (intentions) are being formed and actions are taken that are being done for other than the sake of God. Instead, under such circumstances, the focus is on the reward rather than the a willingness to offer service and, if necessary, sacrifice one's life and death for the Purpose or Himma of God, without any thought of compensation -- as the Qur'an indicates:

"Those who spend their wealth for increase in self-purification, and have in their minds no favor from anyone for which a reward is expected in return, but only the desire to seek for the Countenance of their Lord Most High." (92: 18-20)

If what such "leaders" are telling the followers were true, then why

155

don't we see these leaders doing precisely the deeds which they are — in a very exploitive manner — encouraging Arabic-speaking youth to do? Why do these "leaders" always use proxies to suffer the consequences of their (that is, the leaders') beliefs? If Paradise is the purpose of life — and I don't know anywhere in the Qur'an where it says that Paradise, per se, is the purpose of life — then why aren't these brave "leaders" assuming the roles of presumed martyrs rather than sending children and others to do such things? 'O ye of little faith'.

And, less anyone may misunderstand the foregoing I am not advocating that the "leaders" actually should, themselves, go around terrorizing or killing innocent people rather than using children to do this. Irrespective of whether young people are exploited to undertake such acts or so-called "leaders" actually walk the walk instead of just talk the talk, what is being done (the indiscriminate killing of innocent people) is wrong from any Islamic perspective one cares to examine.

Muhammad (peace be upon him) never killed anyone. However, he was always in the midst of the most dangerous part of any battle.

Jesus (peace be upon him) will not hide from the dajjal (the spiritual imposter associated with the 'End of Days'). Jesus (peace be upon him) will seek out and confront the imposter directly.

Obviously, people like bin Laden don't have much faith in the rightness and justness of their cause. They hide in the shadows and seek to get others to risk their lives ... apparently believing -- unlike Muhammad (peace be upon him) and Jesus (peace be upon him) – that God will not be with them if they should come out into the open and fight with integrity and nobility rather than through terrorizing the innocent from afar via proxy agents.

Imam Hussein and Imam Hassan (may God be pleased with them both) each knew, respectively, that he would be killed prior to the time of his death. Yet, this knowledge did not cause them to shy away from what had to be done, nor did such knowledge sway them to harm either innocent people or not-so-innocent individuals.

Indeed, as the Qur'an indicates: "You express your desire for death if you are truthful." (62:6) However, since the aforementioned, terrorist "leaders", such as bin Laden, only express the desire for the death of others

156

(whether this be their followers who are duped or the innocent victims of the carnage which such individuals let loose on the world), and do not express a desire for their own death, one might well question the truthfulness of what such so-called leaders pronounce to the world. But, since these people speak Arabic, well, I guess, we should all bow down to what they say -- rather than to Divinity -- because if it is spoken in Arabic, then it must be true.

I don't have a problem with people who speak, read, and write Arabic. I have a problem with people who try to argue that because they speak, read, and write Arabic that this facility, in and of itself, grants them some sort of superior understanding of Islam or the Qur'an or the life of the Prophet. If this were really true, the Muslim world would not be in such a mess, for the spiritual mess with which the Muslim community is faced has been created, in no small part, by Arabic-speaking people – whether these be national leaders, imams, the members of local mosque councils, mullahs, academics, theologians, or terrorists.

In fact, my experience of the last, nearly forty years as an aspiring Muslim and seeker of truth has shown me, again and again, that many -- although not all -- of the so-called leaders of various Muslim communities are practitioners of emotional, social, educational, and spiritual terror. In other words, all too frequently, such so-called "leaders" seek to terrorize anyone (and they utilize many techniques to accomplish this ... from: rumor mongering, to: campaigns of slander, outright lies, and character assassination) who does not agree with them and who is unwilling to be a servant of taqlid -- that is, blind following of a dogma – which they have dressed in the clothes of Islam for public consumption.

The time is long overdue for the Muslim community to reclaim Islam. However, the people from whom Islam needs to be reclaimed are not those in the West who seek to distort or undermine Islam through various kinds of media, educational, and intel-op mischief. Rather, the ones from whom Islam needs to be reclaimed -- and such knowledge is a birthright of every human being -- are those within the Muslim community who seek to exploit Islam and Muslims to serve the agendas of the nafs of the former "leaders" as well as those so-called leader's entanglements in dunya.

Islam is supposed to be a deen (a spiritual way) which is unmediated by any form of clerical intervention. Yet, everywhere one looks within the

Muslim community, there are imams, theologians, mullahs, official-sounding councils, educational institutions, media moguls, and politicians that are seeking to become the intermediary between individuals and Divinity.

Not only do we live in an age in which the door to ijtihad (a process directed toward seeking the truth of a matter) should not be closed, we live in times when this form of rigorous striving toward truth is more necessary than ever. The challenge before us is to learn how to use this process wisely -- in a constructive manner which gives expression to all facets of the Qur'an and the sunnah (actions) of the Prophet and not just selected portions which have been removed from the full spiritual ecology of Islam in order to subjugate and exploit the minds, hearts, and lives of the Muslim community -- both individually and collectively.

Each individual has the responsibility to strive to realize the truth according to her or his God-given capacity to do so. This responsibility cannot be contracted out.

The Prophet Muhammad (peace be upon him) is reported to have said:

"Islam began as something strange, and it will revert to being strange as it was in the beginning, so good tidings for the strangers." Someone asked: "Who are the strangers." The Prophet said: "The ones who break away from their people for the sake of Islam."

Islam may be reverting to something strange as it was in the beginning. The people from whom the strangers must break away are those who claim to understand Islam but, on the basis of their terrorist actions (both spiritual and physical), clearly do not.

However, the process of breaking away through, among other things, the exercise of ijtihad is not a child's game. We must all be sobered by the fact that the Prophet Muahmmad (peace be upon him) is reported to have said:

"There are 71 sects among Jews, and only one of them is correct. There are 72 sects among Christians, and only one of them is correct. There are 73 sects among Muslims, and one of them is correct."

158

Ijtihad is the process of seeking for the truth. It does not constitute a license to create or advocate one of the aforementioned 72 other sects.

Moreover, clearly the Prophet was indicating there are truth seekers amongst both the Christians and Jews, for he spoke about the 'true way' which could be found among all the different sects in both the Jewish and Christian spiritual traditions. Consequently, a person should seek out all those -- whether Muslim or non-Muslim -- who are sincere seekers of the truth.

In fact, did not the Prophet counsel us: "To seek knowledge, even unto China"? Furthermore, this was said at a time when one might suppose there were no people who had declared Shahadah (the attestation of acceptance of Islam as one's way of life) in any formal sense, and, yet, the Prophet was alluding to the existence of knowledge even there.

Knowledge, understanding and wisdom are not the preserve of Muslims. God gives to whomsoever Divinity pleases.

However the duties and obligations of a Muslim extend far beyond the Muslim community. The Prophet Muhammad (peace be upon him) is reported to have said:

"Assist any person who is oppressed – whether Muslim or non-Muslim."

In addition, the Prophet is reported to have said:

"If you love your Creator, then love your fellow human beings first."

Or:

"Creation is like God's family, for its sustenance is from God. Therefore, the most beloved unto God is the individual who does good to God's family."

And, finally,

"What actions are most excellent? To gladden the heart of a human being, to feed the hungry, to help the afflicted; to lighten the sorrow of the sorrowful, and to remove the wrongs of the injured."

There is no preference to be given to Muslims over non-Muslims in any of the foregoing. We must strive, through the process of ijtihad -- both individually and collectively, as well as in conjunction with both Muslim and non-Muslim -- to find constructive, creative solutions to the many problems with which humankind is confronted. Truly, we are all in this realm of Creation together, and we must sever the shackles of taqlid (blind obedience) which have been holding the Muslim community – and the rest of the world -- hostage for years.

No one except God, the Prophets appointed by God, and the authentic spiritual teachers designated by God have a right to provide me with guidance and counsel concerning the nature of what Islam is about. My duty, as it is the duty of every human being, is to rigorously explore the teachings of God, the Prophets, and the saints, in order to try to discover the nature of deen (a spiritual path to truth and justice) which is the God-given means of helping me to realize fitra – that is, one's innate, spiritual capacity.

I am willing to listen to, and discuss issues with, almost anyone in relation to the foregoing spiritual quest. But, I do not feel under any compulsion to accept what someone else says just because they may have been born into a Muslim family, or because they speak Arabic, or because they studied what they claim to be shari'ah in Mecca or Medina, or because they have a title such as imam (leader) or shaykh (spiritual guide).

I would be remiss in my spiritual duties to give any of these people a free, critically unexamined ride -- although there is an adab (spiritual etiquette) to this process of critical examination. Moreover, those people who claim to understand Islam would be lacking in humility to presume that things should be any way other than this.

Of course, one of the tactics which is used by "leaders" attempting to retain their power, influence, status, fame, jobs, and/or funding is to claim that the foregoing ideas are divisive and undermine the unity of the

Muslim community. I hate to be the one to break the news to these ill-informed, but often-calculating "leaders", but there is no unity in the Muslim community. This is part of the problem.

There is no consensus within the Muslim community on how to proceed, or what to do, in relation to any number of problems with which the Muslim community is confronted. The Muslim community does not speak with one voice. It speaks with 73 voices and the 72 false voices are attempting to drown out, if not confuse the process of striving for truth -- indeed, these 72 false voices all say, with respect to anything which differs from their point of view, that the unity of the Muslim community is being undermined and threatened by, for instance, the exercise of ijtihad.

As we approach closer and closer to the Latter Days (if we have not already entered them), I do not know -- prior to the second-coming of Jesus (peace be upon him) and his victory over the dajjal or anti-Christ -- if there is a part of the Divine purpose which will permit the Muslim community to attain any semblance of unity -- especially, since, for nearly 1400 years, successive Muslim communities have squandered countless opportunities to accomplish this very thing. However, the absence of such unity notwithstanding, every Muslim still has a responsibility to seek the truth -- indeed, the Prophet is reported to have said that:

"the seeking of knowledge is an ordinance obligatory upon every Muslim"

and just so we are clear about what kind of knowledge the Prophet is referring to, he also is reported to have said:

"Should the day come wherein I increase not in knowledge wherewith to draw nearer to God, let the dawn of that day be accursed",

and again:

"No person will be learned unless one puts one's knowledge into practice."

Consequently, for people to cry foul with respect to the issue of "Muslim unity" in order to stifle a sincere discussion about, and search for, the truth is a red-herring. Such ploys are nothing more than an attempt to control the discussion in a manner that is favorable to the perspective in which they have a vested interest and, unfortunately all too frequently, wish to impose on others (and this is done in nearly every Muslim country and community on the face of the earth and not just among the Taliban of Afghanistan) -- even though, according to the Qur'an, there is supposed to be no compulsion in matters of deen (the spiritual way).

Time is running out -- both individually and collectively. How we use the time which remains is of great importance. As the Prophet Muhammad (peace be upon him) is reported to have said:

"Every person who rises in the morning either does that which will be the means of one's redemption or one's spiritual ruin".

We should not be so arrogant as to suppose we know everything there is to know about such matters or that our way of understanding the Prophet's or the Quranic teachings is correct -- either wholly or in part.

We must continue to strive and struggle for the truth. Ijtihad -- when sincerely and rigorously pursued with equanimity and adab (spiritual etiquette) -- is one of these ways.

11.) The Two Commandments

According to Imam Rauf in his book <u>What's Right With Islam</u>, there are at least two core values which are shared by America and Islam. First, both accept the principle that one should love God with all one's soul, heart, strength, and mind. Secondly, each endorses the value of loving one's neighbor, as one loves oneself.

While on the level of ideals, there may be some truth to the foregoing contention, nevertheless, in practice, one might raise considerable doubt as to the degree to which either Americans or Muslims actually seek to live in accordance with such ideals. Neither Americans nor Muslim are, on the whole, what they once were or might have become.

There is a reason why the Prophet Muhammad (peace be upon him) indicated that if those who enjoyed the company of the Prophet were to leave out even one-tenth of what was obligatory upon them, they would face severe, spiritual consequences, but, nonetheless, there would come a time when if a people -- who had not seen the Prophet -- were to do even one-tenth of what was obligatory upon them, then such people would, nonetheless, achieve Paradise. Spiritually speaking, on average, people are getting worse, not better, and the ramifications of such spiritual illnesses are reflected in the events of the world, both locally and as a whole.

To be sure, one comes across instances of humanity among both Americans and Muslims who are bright beacons of spiritual expression and living embodiments of the aforementioned ideals, but, unfortunately, this does not occur with anywhere near the frequency of what may have been the case in the past. In fact, there is often considerable disagreement among people with respect to just what it means to, for example, love God with all one's soul, heart, strength and mind.

Moreover, one might also have reservations about being loved by someone else as they love themselves because, perhaps, one may not be enamored with the manner in which such people love themselves. One might feel more comfortable with having others do unto one as such people would have one do unto them.

Isn't: 'loving one's neighbor as one loves oneself' the same thing as: 'do unto others as one would have others do unto you'? Not necessarily.

Suppose I live my life in accordance with a particular theology, and let us further suppose that I really love this theology along with all that I believe it has done for my life. Now, if I follow the principle that I should love my neighbor as I love myself, then I am going to want my neighbor to love this theology that I am loving for myself ... and, thus, is born the evangelical spirit which is at the heart of a lot of problems in the world, both with respect to Americans and Muslims.

If, on the other hand, I adopt the principle that I should try to do unto others as I would have others do unto me, then my approach to things may be quite different. More specifically, since I would not necessarily like someone coming into my life trying to foist onto me what they love for themselves, I might be somewhat cautious about what I try to impose on such an individual, knowing that I am attempting to establish a precedent through my behavior which creates an invitation for the other person to interact with me as I am interacting with them -- namely, if I don't seek to proselytize in relation to you, please don't proselytize with respect to me.

So, whether, or not, I want someone to love me as they love themselves really depends on how they love themselves. There are quite a few ways of loving oneself on which I would just as soon take a pass.

However, I can think of no exceptions to the principle of reciprocity which is at the heart of the Golden Rule. "So in everything, do to others what you would have them do to you, for this sums up the Law and the Prophets." (Matthew 7:12)

If I do not wish to be oppressed and exploited by others, then I should not seek to oppress or exploit such individuals. If I wish to be treated with justice, then I should endeavor to do justice to others. If I do not wish to be hungry, then I should be willing to feed others. If I do not wish to be deprived of my livelihood, then I should try to not deprive others of their livelihood. If I do not wish to be killed or harmed, then I should strive not to kill or harm other people. If I wish to be forgiven for the injustices and unkindness which I have perpetrated against others, then I need to entertain the idea of working on forgiving those who have done injustice to me.

If I do not treat others as I would want to be treated, then it should come as no surprise to me if others should follow my lead and treat me as I have treated them. Extraordinary strength of character is required not to offer tit for tat, which, unfortunately, is the road most traveled by the majority of us. Life lived in accordance with the Golden Rule is clean, simple, and straightforward -- although doing so does require some integrity for which we must struggle. Life lived in accordance with the hypocrisy of wanting to be treated one way, but doing the opposite in relation to other people, tends to be a very messy affair which explains, perhaps, why the world is such a mess.

Thus, there are two kinds of reciprocity. One kind leads, God willing, to felicity, while the other form of reciprocity leads to nothing but difficulty and heartache.

The former kind is the more difficult path to pursue, but it leads, God willing, to ease. The latter form of reciprocity is born in the ease of giving expression to the natural inclinations of the unredeemed soul, but it ends, always, in difficulty -- unless God wishes otherwise.

According to Imam Rauf, Muslims tend to fulfill this second commandment -- that is, to love one's neighbor as one's self -- through a strong sense of valuing the community over individualism, as well as by means of seeking to instill a deep-rooted sense of feeling a responsibility toward others, including through charitable acts. There is a great deal of wealth in the Muslim world, and there is a great deal of poverty, and, so, a natural question to ask is this: if what Imam Rauf says is true, then why are the two aforementioned facts concerning the Muslim world simultaneously true?

Is one to conclude that the extent of poverty just overwhelms the capacity of rich Muslims who are being as generous as they can be? Or, does the answer to the foregoing question lie in another direction?

The Qur'an says:

"And, they ask thee (O Muhammad) what they ought to spend (in the way of God). Say: that which is left after meeting your needs." (Qur'an, 2:219)

165

But, how many Muslims -- rich or otherwise -- actually adhere to this teaching? More often than not, they seek the advice of some of the kissing cousins of the accountants for Enron, Worldcom, and others who are morally challenged, to help the wealthy make every luxury on which they spend money a "need" so that they will be free of any obligation to their fellow human beings, just as all too many very wealthy corporations often find ways not to have to pay any income tax.

There is a related idea in the Bible when Jesus (peace be upon him) says:

"It is easier for a camel to go through the eye of a needle than for a rich man to enter the kingdom of God." (Mark 10:25)

How many Christians believe that the Bible is the literal word of God, and, yet, hold on to their wealth as if the above words of Jesus (peace be upon him) had never been uttered?

Furthermore, to suppose, as Imam Rauf seems to indicate on page 2 of his book, that Islam favors community over the individual seems, at the very least, rather a questionable contention. Islam indicates that both community and individuals should strive to be in harmony with one another, but this is a matter of balance not of preferring one to the other, since both the community and individuals have responsibilities, one to the other.

In addition, the issue of charity is not a matter of favoring the community over the individual but of making sure that the community has the means of looking after, and helping, those individuals who are in need. Charity is an individual responsibility which, aside from being one of the pillars of deen, is also an expression of one individual's compassion for, and empathy with, other individuals. Helping others is an individual responsibility which has communal ramifications, and is not a statement about the priority of community over the individual.

Individualism which is an expression of nafs-i-ammarah (the

166

unredeemed, carnal soul) is not acceptable within Islam, but this has nothing to do with the priority of community over the individual. Instead, this is an acknowledgment of the damage to others which the unredeemed nafs can do.

Individualism that is an expression of the unique gifts which God has bequeathed upon a human being is one of the resources of a community and, as such, should be both protected and encouraged so that, God willing, its inherent potential might be realized for the benefit of all -- including the individual. All a person has to contribute is who, in essence, she or he is, and this is nothing other than our individuality which -- when that locus is properly purified, calibrated, and activated -- can serve as a locus of manifestation through which Divine Grace shines.

With respect to this potential of the individual, one has an obligation before God, and, as well, one owes a duty of care both to oneself and to others -- individually and collectively -- to struggle to fulfill one's most essential nature or fitra. To state the foregoing, however, is a very different proposition than to claim that the community has priority over, or should be valued more than, the individual, as Imam Rauf seems to be claiming is the case in the Muslim world -- in fact, to whatever extent this claim is the norm, it may constitute a distortion of the principles of Islam.

****

In <u>What's Right With Islam</u>, Imam Rauf states he believes that what Muslims do right is to observe the first commandment -- that is, through observance of the five pillars, Muslims, he feels, fulfill the requirements of loving God with all their soul, heart, mind, and strength. Aside from the problem of trying to determine just how observant Muslims are with respect to the five pillars -- and I think it is presumptuous and foolhardy to offer self-congratulations before the results of the Day of Judgment have been announced -- one might note, as well, that reducing the idea of 'loving God with all one's soul, heart, mind, and strength' down to the five pillars may also be problematic.

167

The term 'love' is used very loosely these days by all too many people. What is love?

Shaykh al-Shibli (may Allah be pleased with him) says that love:

"is like a cup of fire which blazes terribly; when it takes root in the senses and settles in the heart, it annihilates."

Hazrat Muin-ud-din Chishti (may Allah be pleased with him) concurs with the Shaykh when Khawaja Sahib says that:

"the heart of one devoted to God is a fire place of love; whatever comes into it is burnt and becomes annihilated."

Hazrat Ra'bia of Basra (may Allah be pleased with her) resonates with the same essential principle of love when she prays:

"Oh, Allah, if I worship Thee out of desire of Heaven, then, deny me Heaven, and if I worship Thee out of fear of Hell, then, throw me into Hell, but if I worship Thee for Thee and Thee alone, then, grant me Thy vision".

In addition, there is a tradition told among the Sufis which says:

"God indicates that the souls of humankind were loving Him, and, then, they were shown the world, and 9/10ths of humankind forget about God and became immersed in the world. Then, the remaining 1/10th who are still loving God were shown the delights of Paradise, and 9/10ths of these souls forgot about God and became preoccupied with Paradise. Of the 1/10th who are left, still loving God, difficulties are showered on them, and, as a result, 9/10ths of these individuals ran away from God. Of the 1/10th of 1/10th of 1/10th of the original population who still remain, God tells them that He will visit such tribulations upon them that they will be crushed, and these souls responded: "As long as it is from Thee Oh Lord."

All of the foregoing is rooted firmly in a Hadith Qudsi which says:

"Whoever seeks Me, finds Me; whoever finds Me, comes to know Me; whoever comes to know Me, loves Me; whoever loves Me, that person I slay; whomever I slay, I owe that person blood-money, and to whomever I owe blood-money, I am the recompense for that blood-money."

Clearly, the one who loves God is slain in the fire of annihilation, known as fana, in which nothing but the Reality of Divinity fills the awareness of the one who is immersed in this condition.

Some Sufis speak about nine stages of love. These are: compatibility, inclination, fellowship, passion, friendship, exclusive friendship, ardent affection, enslavement, and bewilderment.

For most of us, there is more than a little daylight between our spiritual condition as we engage the five pillars and the stage of bewilderment as an expression of the dynamics of love between Creator and created. One may aspire to love God with all one's soul, heart, mind, and strength, but the reality is that most of us fall far short of realizing this aspiration, and the sad fact is that one may not presume that all -- or even a majority of -- Muslims necessarily have such an aspiration.

Seeking to love God is somewhat like making New Year resolutions. It is often done with a sense of sacred commitment which tends to fizzle out in the midst of lived life when we come face to face with just how difficult our own carnal souls make the task to which we have so nobly offered our lives.

Trying to adhere to the five pillars of Islam is a good thing. But trying to accomplish this, and even, if God wishes, succeeding in doing so cannot necessarily be equated with the station of loving God with all one's soul, heart, mind, and strength.

There is a reason why God instructed the Prophet through the

Qur'an to tell the bedouins, who claimed they believed, to say, rather, that they submit, because belief had not, yet, entered their hearts. There is a reason why distinctions are drawn among: muslim, mo'min, and mohsin, or, islam, iman, and ihsan.

Imam Rauf states:

"By the seventeenth century, two extremely powerful ideas arose in Europe, ideas that paradoxically formed the core of its institutional support for the second commandment [i.e., to love one's neighbor as oneself -- my added note].

-- The notion that reasonable interest on a monetary loan does not amount to usury -- an idea that made possible a certain system of banking.

-- The invention of the corporation, especially that the corporation is a separate 'person' with owners protected from responsibility for any liability, such as unpaid debt or crime, incurred by the company. It is ironic that enormous good has come from the inventions of banking and the corporation ... But these two institutions combined with the emergence of modern liberal democracy to radically improve the fortunes of the Western world. ... Not being able to accept these ideas is one of the primary reasons the Muslim world lagged behind the West and Asian Pacific nations." (Page 3, What's Right With Islam.)

Earth calling Commander Tom! Earth Calling Commander Tom! Hello, is anyone there?

One would be hard-pressed to find a more perverse form of argument than to say that at the heart of western institutional support for the second commandment (i.e., loving one's neighbor as one love's oneself) is the invention of interest-based banking and the limited liability corporation. I can't think of anyone -- except perhaps a banker -- who would believe (without blushing with thorough embarrassment) that an act of loving oneself was to charge oneself interest and, therefore, charging interest to one's neighbors is the loving thing to do.

170

A bank will rarely, if ever, do anything in which there is not something in it for the bank. In fact, a bank will rarely do anything unless things are arranged in such a manner that no matter what happens to anyone else, the bank will come out of things a distinct winner.

This is sort of similar to the case with the 'House' in gambling establishments. The only difference is that banks call on the courts to settle all outstanding debts, rather than seeking the services of people with deformed noses pushed to one side of their faces and who go by names like "Lefty" and "The Animal".

I don't consider this an expression of love. It may be one way of doing business, but it isn't love.

To complicate matters a little, one should not forget compound interest. This is one aspect of things which really gets the saliva of bankers working overtime.

Think of it. Charging interest on interest and not having to do anything for this added bonus except to collect and, when necessary, sue and foreclose.

Of course, one might argue that banks show their love for their neighbors by permitting people to buy, for example, houses and, to make things easy for the customer, arranging for low payments over, say, a 25 year period. When one does the math -- and depending on the interests rates ... whether these are fixed or floating -- by the time someone gets done paying for the house, they have paid anywhere from 4 to 8 times what the market value of the house is worth.

And, let us not forget that one pays most (the vast majority) of the interest up front to the bank before one's payments begin to nibble away at the principle. So, if something should happen somewhere along the line to adversely affect one's capacity to earn an income which is capable of paying the mortgage payment, then even if one has paid interest amounting to more than the value of the house, the bank gets to foreclose, take control of the house and the property on which it is situated, and do the whole thing over again. Now, this is real love, ... and excuse me for a moment while I wipe a tear from my eye.

We should also remember with fondness and gratitude the

Savings and Loans banks who ended up losing billions of dollars and, in the best spirit of sharing, had American taxpayers foot the bill for the irresponsible speculations and business dealings bequeathed to us by these paragons of the commandment to love one's neighbor as oneself.

Moreover, one would be remiss if one were to not make at least a passing reference to all of the most recent 2008-2009 fiascoes involving banks and insurance companies which are 'too big to fail' ... banks and insurance companies and investment houses that just so loved the American people and desired nothing more than to be shown love by those people in the form of multi-billion bailouts. After all, the great unwashed masses are just too stupid to understand how becoming caught up in the derivatives market was all done for the benefit of the public and with such great risk to the banks. And what would the banks get in return for all of their risk-taking on behalf of the people, why nothing but billions of dollars in profits until, of course, margins were called and the bottom fell out and of the derivatives market, and, naturally, it only seems fair that the public should subsidize the losses which accrued as a result of these many manifestations of the bankers love for the community ... I mean, we are all in this together, aren't we?

In addition, let us not forget the World Bank and the International Monetary Fund. These institutions manifest what might be called 'tough love'. As a condition for giving loans, they require countries to restructure society in ways that are bad for most of the inhabitants of that country but which are quite profitable for the leaders, bankers, or foreign corporations within the countries to whom the money is loaned .

Among the requirements which are expected to be instituted by the country receiving such loans are: lower wages, provide no benefits to workers, cut social assistance programs, require poor peasants to pay for health care and education, degrade environmental standards, discourage, if not eliminate (both literally and figuratively) attempts to unionize, tear down the trade barriers which will enable foreign corporations to exploit the resources and people of the country on the cheap, while, simultaneously, destroying local, indigenous economies,

172

and, thereby, force mass migration of peasants to urban areas where they can live in slums and serve as a cheap pool of labor for the government and corporations. Our cups runneth over with the sweet wine of love being poured by the World Bank and the International Monetary Fund.

The people of the countries to whom these loans are given have little, or no, say in what their governments commit those people to. Like the limited liability corporations with which Imam Rauf is so enamored, governments can do almost anything they want with the money which is being loaned, and the common people are the ones who will be on the hook for the debt.

Governments, like many limited liability corporations, love to socialize costs while privatizing profits. The common people subsidize the lifestyle of the government officials by incurring debt which the former did not ask for but which was imposed on them by the thoughtfulness and benevolence of the latter officials who, as we all know, are the protectors and defenders of democracy and all that humankind holds sacred (it is hard to keep a straight face in relation to such a statement).

After government officials siphon off portions of the loan for their own, personal enrichment, and following the distribution of the appropriate bribes and inducements to an assortment of vested interests (such as land owners, rich business people, and other sectors of the country's plutocracy), and after the government spends money on beefing up national security by buying weapons from foreign corporations and paying advisors to teach the national military how to oppress the people of their own country who are likely to get a little testy over the re-structuring process which is about to be foisted on them, then what remains of the loans can be used to help subsidize foreign corporations to further rape the country. So much love is being bestowed on the rank and file people of these countries ... I just don't know how they stand it.

In the United States, 88% of the wealth of the country is owned by just 10 % of the people. Nearly 50% of the wealth of America is owned by 1 % of the people.

Interest charging banks and limited liability corporations (with a considerable helping hand from all three branches of government), have arranged things this way in the United States. The situation is even worse in many other countries.

A number of years ago, I taught a course in criminology for the law and security division of a community college. The textbook I used indicated that, year in and year out, limited liability corporations are responsible for more deaths and theft of money -- and by a substantial margin -- than all forms of street crime combined (including drugs).

I taught the course about thirty years ago. Things have only gotten worse.

All one has to do is mention a few words to help demonstrate the truth of this. For instance, for a starter, try: Enron, Union Carbide, any of the tobacco companies, Exxon, Halliburton, WorldCom, Bank of Credit and Commerce International (BCCI), Monsanto, and Arthur Andersen.

There are hundreds of corporations which could be added to this list. Among other things, these companies specialize in: stealing money from employees, placing employees and the general population in harm's way (either financially and/or environmentally), defrauding the public, and/or being recipients of all manner of corporate welfare handouts which are paid for by taxpayers.

Not every corporation is morally challenged. Many try to be good corporate neighbors, and some even succeed at this -- although, unfortunately, all too frequently this comes with certain costs attached to it in the way of tax concessions from the state and local municipalities or an unwritten agreement for various environmental regulatory laws not to be enforced.

Like Herr Doktor Frankenstein's infamous creation, the limited liability corporation has become something of a monster. This monster, however, unlike Frankenstein's creation, is not fictional ... it is all too real.

Given the natural inclination of human beings toward: greed, arrogance, pride, selfishness, cruelty, and oppression of others, and given this is the case with respect to a species of being who lives, on average, for 70+ years (at least in the United States), and given that human beings are said to have a potential for morality and a sense of justice, if not fairness, and despite this potential, nevertheless, all too many human beings give in to their natural inclinations, and, in so doing, wreak havoc on Earth, then what might we expect when we permit an "artificial person" to be invented which has: perpetual life; unlimited appetites for power, money, and property; an almost complete freedom from any mode of accountability, an absence of morality, and absolutely no sense of shame?

Furthermore, let us add one further ingredient into the laboratory flask. Let us create legal precedents (e.g., Dodge v. Ford, 1916) which make it mandatory for such artificial persons to serve only its prime directive – that is, to maximize returns on investments on 'pain' of legal remedies being applied to chastise any miscreant who does not permit the artificial person from fulfilling its purpose.

Whatever 'good' might have arisen from such an invention, the good has, for the most part, only accrued to the few (remember, 88% of all wealth in the U. S. is owned by only 10% of the people, and these figures are worse in many other countries), and this has come with huge costs being levied against society as a whole. War, degradation of the environment, unsafe working conditions, the exploitation of non-renewable resources, oppression, the corruption of democratic processes, the corporate biasing of media, loss of worker rights or protections, and the undermining of the judicial process are just a few of the costs which have been borne by the vast majority of people.

Why would the Muslim world want to accept such a creature into its midst? In fact, whenever and wherever such a creature has been accepted into the Muslim world, this has brought -- except for the few -- little but suffering, loss of liberty, oppression, and war.

As a Muslim, I believe one's apportioned allotment is assigned by God. One may have to struggle to realize one's portion, but whatever is destined for one, in the way of material/financial blessings, will come quite independently of interest-charging banks and limited liability corporations.

One of the choices which any human being has is the decision to seek what is destined for one through permissible or impermissible means ... through means which are moral and just, or immoral and

175

unjust. There is something inherently problematic about seeking to serve an entity which has no soul and feels no need to be ashamed before Divinity. There is something deeply disturbing about the idea that the reason why the Muslim world lags behind the West is because of its refusal to bow down before the corporate idol which has been fashioned from gold.

The Qur'an says:

"And surely We shall test you with some fear and hunger and loss of wealth and lives and crops; but give glad tidings to the steadfast - who say when misfortune strikes them: Surely, to Allah we belong and to Allah is our returning." (2:155-156)

The world of corporations and modern banking are two misfortunes which have struck the entire world ... Muslim and non-Muslim alike. The task facing us all in the midst of these misfortunes is to find ways of remaining steadfast with integrity.

There are better ways to distribute justice and material goods to humankind than through the artificial persons known as transnational corporations and banks. Real human beings have the potential for finding far better solutions to the problems besetting humankind than can artificial persons who are, for the most part, little more than sociopaths in many of their behaviors.

One cannot measure or evaluate the economic efficiency of a given process until one adds up all of the costs which are entailed by such a process. Corporations are engaged in a zero-sum game in which they win and everybody else loses -- not necessarily in the surface transactions of such an entity -- but this is so when one looks at all of the hidden costs of permitting corporations to do business as 'artificial people' who enjoy all the privileges and rights of non-artificial people -- and, actually, even more privileges -- but who have no dimension of moral sensibility, public accountability, or commitment to justice for everyone, then one begins to understand that the bottom line for a corporation and the bottom line for society, as a whole, add up in two entirely different ways.

Large corporations -- to the extent that they are 'successful'-- are efficient only when one narrows the focus to issues revolving about ROI (return on investment) and excludes from consideration almost every other dimension of the costly ramifications of the dynamics between corporations and the rest of society. In almost any way one cares to calculate things, the concept of the limited liability corporation has been antithetical to the establishment of real democracy, justice, liberty and the pursuit of happiness for the vast majority of people in any given society in which the idea of corporations as an artificial person has been permitted to take root.

One might come a lot closer to the truth of why the Muslim world has lagged behind the West economically if one takes a closer look at how the military-industrial complex of the West has managed to corrupt -- and, if it cannot corrupt, then to kill, overthrow, control, extort, hold hostage, or remove from office -- virtually every Muslim government for the past several hundred years. So-called Muslim leaders have, by and large, betrayed the generality of Muslims by engaging in illicit intercourse with the 'artificial persons' who have been whispering sweet nothings into the ears and numbered bank accounts of such so-called leaders.

Moreover, all too many imams, mullahs, theologians, Muslim journalists, educators, shaykhs, and qadis (legal judges) have betrayed the vast generality of Muslims by seeking to indoctrinate the latter through methods of spiritual abuse which have, by and large, closed off the populace to what Islam actually is. As a result, many Muslims no better understand the nature of the spiritual abuses which have been perpetrated against them than do the vast majority of Americans understand how limited liability corporations and banks have torn to shreds much of the fabric of democracy in the United States.

Indeed, there has been a massive failure of leadership both among Muslims and Americans which has led to the betrayal of essential principles and values in the United States and in the Muslim world alike. This is one of the experiential truths which Americans and Muslims share.

12.) Common Roots

In What's Right With Islam Imam Rauf says:

"There is little doubt today that the rise of religious fundamentalism represented the reaction of religion against the antireligious secular modernism that peaked in the mid-twentieth century." (page xx of Preface)

I'm not so sure the foregoing is correct. Essentially, fundamentalism is not an expression of spirituality but, rather, constitutes a desire for power that appears in the guise of a religious form. The power in question has to do with a desire to impose one's perspective on others quite irrespective of the presence of secular modernism ... although secular modernism can assume the role of a stage prop which can be used to incite the emotions of a target audience that fundamentalists seek to control in order to bring about the agenda of the latter.

This tendency to seek power and control over the lives of others existed within the Muslim community from a very early period ... just like it exists, as a potential, within all communities -- both religious and non-religious. Historically, Muslim theologians were often motivated by the desire for such power – that is, a desire to expand their sphere of influence by establishing and imposing the religious norms to which the theologians believed everyone should be subject. Similarly, Muslim jurists frequently were inclined toward such an agenda and, thereby, sought to enforce a certain conception of life upon everyone within the community, and, as well, many Muslim politicians were operating out of a similar sort of framework in which the ultimate goal was to rule over people rather than serve God even as the idea of the latter was used to hide a program of authoritarian control.

Whatever the actual sins of modernism, colonialism, imperialism, and capitalism may be – and these sins are many – the fact of the matter is that those in the Muslim community (theologians, jurists, political rulers) who were either jockeying for power or who were attempting to hold on to power used the very real sins of colonialism et al as a means of misdirecting attention away from their own sins (that is, those of the would-be Muslim "leaders") of wishing to control, exploit, and abuse Muslim peoples. Among fundamentalists, the issue was never – except superficially -- about defending Muslims from the Western hordes but was, rather, an attempt to make sure that the reins of oppression were held by so-called 'Muslims' rather than Westerners.

If one takes a look at the long list of fundamentalists from: the karijis [a sect that came into being during the Caliphacy of Hazrat 'Ali (may Allah be pleased with him) and who – that is, the kharijis – considered all Muslims who did not accept their interpretation of Islam to be infidels], down through: ibn Taymiyyah [1268-1328 who, among other things glorified the idea of jihad – which he construed in terms of armed conflict – to be superior to Islamic pillars such as fasting and the hajj or pilgrimage], Muhammad al-Wahhab [1703 – 1792 who was a founder of a radical, puritanical, dogmatic theology which calls for a return to medieval Islam], Muhammad Abdus Salam Faraj [1952- 1982 who argued that all of the problems existing in the Muslim world were the result of a failure by Muslims to consider jihad -- in the sense of armed, violent conflict -- to be a mandatory duty of every Muslim in relation to combating all non-Muslims as well as those who were 'insufficiently' Muslim], and such groups as the Taliban, al-Qaidah, Hamas, and Hezbollah (along with many other individuals and groups who have not been noted above), all of these groups and individuals have one thing in common – the desire to recreate the world in their own image, using force and compulsion wherever necessary. The common thread among the foregoing fundamentalists is very resonant with the motivation running through modernism, colonialism, imperialism, and capitalism – namely, a desire to impose one's 'will to power' upon innocent people, along with the presumption accompanying this 'will to power' – namely, that one has the right to manipulate and oppress the lives of others.

Rallying cries revolve around this or that cause (whether this be the panicked hysteria in the West concerning religious fundamentalism, or the frenzied mobs in the East focused on the evils of capitalism and imperialism), but these rallying cries are just techniques of manipulation used by both sides for purposes of creating and managing the fear of various communities. People who are afraid

180

constitute a formidable resource which has been mined for centuries by those who wish to exploit that resource to the advantage of the 'leaders' and to the disadvantage of the people who are sacrificed while fear is stoked to a burning rage all around the world.

To be sure, there are those in the Muslim world who are quite prepared to kill anyone who does not think as the former do. However, there also are people in the West who are quite prepared to kill all who stand in the way of capitalistic or 'democratic' hegemony – whether of an economical, political, and/or militaristic sort. The existence of such real threats is just a pretext that can serve to generate undue influence upon populations – both East and West – in order to induce those respective populations to act out of fear rather than insight, understanding, compassion, or wisdom.

Like actors in a gangster movie, the players on whatever side (West or East) were, and are, interested only in being able to impose their own will on other human beings. The conflict was not and is not a clash of cultures as Huntington tries to argue but, instead, a clash of mobsters and tyrants who were, and are, seeking to slice up the worldly pie in a manner that was, and is, advantageous to any given mobster organization – whether Muslim or non-Muslim.

Imam Rauf indicates that being "told that Islam is a religion of peace doesn't jive with images of Muslims" advocating violence against America, Christians, or Jews. On the other hand, being told that the West stands for democracy, freedom, and justice doesn't jive with images of Western corporations, governments, and militaries destroying lives, communities, and countries all over the world while they plunder resources of various peoples that have been usurped by oppressive tyrants in such communities and countries ... tyrants who often are created, funded, supported, armed, trained, and protected by the West.

All too many people in the West and East seem to forget that Jesus (peace be upon him) is reported to have raised a question about those who would find fault with the mote in the eye of one's neighbor while ignoring the beam in one's own eye. Framing the issues becomes very important in the war to control how people think and feel about any given situation. Attention is always directed away from the beam in one's own eye so that one self-righteously can point out the mote in the eye of the other as being the source of the world's problems.

Acting in inhuman ways becomes so much easier when people – with the help of the media, government officials, and religious figures -- can define a problem in terms of the barbaric and uncivilized acts of 'the Other' while completely ignoring the etiological role played by the many atrocities perpetrated against the Other prior to the onset of the Other's treacherous acts – atrocities which are largely or totally ignored by a given side's way of framing things in a self-serving, distorted, and self-righteous manner. The other side is always the causal agent for the existence of evil in the world, when, in truth, events are almost always due to a more complicated dynamic in which forces and factors from all sides converge and synergistically interact with one another to generate crisis, escalation, and tragedy.

Early in What's Right With Islam Imam Rauf speaks a little about the First Amendment of the U.S. Constitution, referring to that aspect of the amendment which addresses the issue of the relationship between church and state. He indicates how the founding fathers wished to ensure that religion would not be able to gain access to the corridors of power and, in the process, be imposed upon people. However, Imam Rauf indicates that later on, during the twentieth century, a more militant, anti-religious form of secularism began to hold sway within the institutions of governance, thereby violating what he believed to be the actual intent of the First Amendment authors which, according to Imam Rauf, was never meant to create an atheistic or agnostic society.

Trying to figure out the intent of the founding fathers is a tricky business. Legislatures, courts, jurists, educators, and commentators have been trying to do this for more than two hundred years.

There are, at least, several components to this hermeneutical task. First, there is the intent of the people who actually drafted the amendment, and, secondly, there is the intent of those who voted on the amendment.

Even if there are written records to document, to a degree, what the drafters of an amendment were thinking when a given amendment was proposed, there may not be a great deal of information which

182

details the thinking process of those who voted for or against such an amendment. Did the thinking of the latter coincide precisely with that of the drafters of an amendment, or did it differ, and, if so, in what way? How did they envision the amendment playing out in the actual course of events? What did they believe the constraints and degrees of freedom of such an amendment to be? What did they believe they were signing on to or rejecting?

Were all the people who voted on the amendment inclined toward religion, and, if so, in what way were they religious? Were they orthodox something or other? What did orthodoxy mean to them? Did they have a formal affiliation with religious institutions, or were they independent thinkers and doers when it came to religious observance? What role did they believe government should play in supporting and helping people to seek and, possibly, secure the purpose of life? What did they believe the purpose of life to be?

In order for someone, such as Imam Rauf, to make a statement about what the intention of the founding fathers was, or was not, with respect to the First Amendment, one would have to be able to answer all of the foregoing questions and quite a few more. Imam Rauf may, or may not, be correct in his opinion concerning the intent of the founding fathers, but this is an empirical question which requires evidence not just unsupported supposition.

More importantly, perhaps, there is an issue concerning the First Amendment which Imam Rauf – along with many others – does not seem to consider. If I understand his position, he feels there should be some sort of balance between the aspirations of the state and the aspirations of religion such that while the latter should never be permitted to dominate activities of state, nonetheless, the state should not oppose or undermine the attempts of religious people to give active expression to their individual faith.

One question which I have with respect to the foregoing is this: Why should the state be permitted to have any aspirations at all? Another question I have is the following: Why should the aspirations of the state be permitted to dominate people's lives and be imposed on them if one prevents religion from doing this very same thing?

If the First Amendment is intended, in part, as a safeguard

183

against the unwarranted intrusion of any given religious framework into the lives of the people, then why should one permit the intrusion of any given political framework into the lives of people? If the purpose of this aspect of the First Amendment is to ensure that people do not become unwilling victims of the imposed religious aspirations of others, then, why is there not a reciprocal protection against the imposed political, economic, and philosophical aspirations of others? Why are political and economic philosophies being given a free pass with respect to retaining the right to be imposed on unwilling recipients? If the idea of this facet of the First Amendment is to protect the people against being oppressed by a religion not of their own choosing, then why are the people not being protected against being oppressed by political philosophies, economic programs, and public policies not of their own choosing? Why is the presumption of governance being given to philosophy – whether this is political, economic, and/or social in nature?

Oppression is oppression whether it comes from religion or politics. If the majority were of a given religious denomination, we do not say: 'Well, the will of the majority should be enforced but, rather, one points to the First Amendment and indicates that no religion – irrespective of its majority status – may dominate state policy'.

In a sense, this portion of the First Amendment is directed toward protecting the rights of minorities against the imposition of religious beliefs. No such protections are afforded minorities against the imposition of unwanted political and philosophical beliefs.

I find this to be a curious asymmetry. Is one to suppose that politics and philosophy are somehow more objective or more neutral or less biased than religion is? Is one to assume that politics and philosophy are inherently more humane, just, and compassionate than any religion could be? Is one to automatically presume that politics and philosophy are better equipped to be less arbitrary, oppressive and authoritarian than religions are?

What and where is the evidence to support such presumption? Why is it okay to rule over people in the name of politics, economics, or philosophy, but not okay to rule over people in the name of religion?

Irrespective of what the founding fathers may, or may not, have thought about such matters, I agree with the idea that religion ought not to become entangled in the principles of governance in such a way that religion is imposed on the community being governed. At the same time, I also believe that politics, economics, and philosophy ought not to become entangled in the principles of governance in such a way that they are imposed on the community being governed.

If one agrees that the principles inherent in protecting people from having religion imposed on them are valuable safeguards against tyranny and oppression, then consistency requires that the same principles be applied to safeguard the public against the tyranny and oppression inherent in any political, philosophical, or economic system that is imposed on others without their consent. Moreover, if people do not wish to be consistent in the manner in which they seek to protect the community against tyranny and oppression, then one needs to inquire into the nature of the motivation underlying this inconsistency and preferential asymmetry.

Imam Rauf claims that:

"Muslims believe that America needs to reestablish the original understanding of the First Amendment, which balances the separation of church and state with freedom of religion by allowing all religions equal standing and by honoring the role of religion in building a good society. This balance is enormously important to Muslims."

Aside from the fact that I find it somewhat disconcerting to be told that Muslims believe 'such and such' when I am a Muslim, and I don't necessarily believe what Imam Rauf says I believe, and aside from the already mentioned idea that I'm not sure that what he claims the original intention or understanding of the First Amendment to be actually constitutes the original understanding of all parties who voted on that amendment, I also wonder about the meaning of the idea of 'balance' to which he alludes in his foregoing claim.

How does one maintain a separation of church and state in a balanced way? What are the criteria by which one evaluates the

185

conditions of balance? What methodologies are to be used in analyzing the idea of balance? What assumptions underlie such criteria and methodologies? How does one define the "good society"? What justifies such a definition?

For example, suppose a person's spiritual perspective holds that killing is wrong, as well as maintains that most wars are not about protecting the homeland but advancing the special interests of various corporations, power blocs, and ideological agendas, then 'collateral damage' is really a euphemism for cold-blooded murder and not just an 'unfortunate' side effect of that which is necessary (and necessity here is always framed by those who are seeking to advance their economic, political, material, and/or financial interests). How does one 'balance' such a perspective with the perspective of those who have no problem with taking innocent human lives if this will further their worldly goals? Why should the former be required to support (e.g., through taxes) the perpetration of that (i.e., murder and oppression) to which they do not subscribe, and why should they have to be subjected to the possibility of being charged with 'treasonous' behavior simply because they do not want to lend the kind of support that violates their sense of right and wrong?

There is no balance here. An almost automatic preference tends to be given to the war-mongers, as well as to those with vested material/financial interests and to those who have an ideological agenda which they wish to oppressively impose on people, both domestic and foreign, and the question is why are there no protections against such political, philosophical, and economic tyranny if a central purpose of the 1st amendment is to ensure that oppressive elements do not control governance and if one of the central purposes of the Bill of Rights is to protect, among other things, disempowered minorities against the tyranny of majority rule?

Religion is about meaning, purpose, identity, values, and potential. Philosophy and politics are about meaning, purpose, identity, values, and potential. How does one balance conflicting and sometimes diametrically opposed ways of setting about to answer questions concerning such themes?

If the founding fathers believed in such a balance, then what, precisely, did they mean by this? Did they really understand what they were advocating or voting on? Did they have it all worked out, or was it something of a rough idea whose structural character and horizons were lost in shadows of unasked questions and unknown contingencies?

If one were to bring the founding fathers together today and ask them about whether they truly believed in the idea of allowing all religions equal standing and whether, or not, the founding fathers wanted to honor the role of all religion in building a good society, how would they respond? Would they maintain that, for example, Islam, Hinduism, Buddhism, Taoism, as well as the spiritual ways of various Native peoples constituted authentic religious traditions and ought to be accorded equal standing and honored for the way in which they contributed to the building of a good society? And, if they truly believed all these things, then why – to raise but one issue -- were Native peoples treated in such abysmal, destructive, inhumane ways from the very beginning?

Imam Rauf goes on to say that:

"Muslims have yet to fully incorporate the institutional expressions of democratic capitalism ... into their various essential institutions: the rule of law (an independent judiciary), human rights, a stable currency, equal opportunity, free markets, social safety nets, and so forth. These principles, in my view, are among the most important institutional expressions of the second commandment that humanity has invented."

Aside from the problems I might have with Imam Rauf's tendency, from time to time, to make sweeping generalizations about what Muslims have, or have not, done across all geographical areas and historical periods, and aside from any questions which I might have about what it would mean to "fully incorporate" such institutional expressions of democratic capitalism or whether even the West has yet to accomplish this, I have a lot of difficulty with the mythology being spewed forth with respect to the alleged accomplishments of

187

'democratic capitalism'.

For instance, one could talk about the manner in which the judiciary has often been anything but independent as they (across all levels – from municipal, to county, state, and federal) frequently served the interests of power, capital and corporations against the interests of the poor and unempowered. As far as human rights are concerned, one might want to speak with Native peoples, Blacks, women and other minority groups who subsist along the margins of enjoying the full protections of human rights. Moreover, we don't have a stable currency, we have a floating value currency which has been set loose from any meaningful backing by actual material value (e.g., gold or silver), and the jury is still out as to how long the whole financial house of cards will survive before it falls apart, as has occurred on so many occasions throughout U.S. history. In the matter of 'equal opportunity', there are tens of millions of people in the United States who do not have equal opportunity with respect to education, jobs, housing, legal representation, medical care, or government access. In addition, the markets are not free but are distorted by such forces as: government subsidies, corporate welfare, a judiciary which lacks sufficient intelligence to understand that a corporation is not a person, an inequitable system of taxation, regulatory agencies which dance to the beat of lobbyists, and corrupt politicians who serve vested interests against the interests of the people they supposedly represent and against the interests of a truly free system of enterprise. Finally, it is difficult to get excited about a social safety net which has so many rips and tears that millions upon millions of people have fallen through the holes in that safety net.

Imam Rauf maintains that what America has done right is to create institutions which have perfected democratic capitalism. At any moment I expect Rod Serling to step out of the shadows and begin to talk about a man (namely Imam Rauf) who does not yet seem to understand that he has become trapped in the Twilight Zone as this inhabitant of a surreal realm addresses people as if his perceptions and beliefs defined the true nature of things even though what is being discussed by Imam Rauf is not perfected, is not really democratic, and constitutes a perverted, re-framed notion of what capitalism might have been if it had been guided by qualities of justice, morality, and spirituality rather than qualities of greed, inhumanity, and oppression.

Early in Chapter 1 of What's Right With Islam, Imam Rauf outlines how many of the earliest civilizations advocated acceptance of, or belief in, a variety of gods with each god being assigned a particular section of the universe over which to exercise authority. He goes on to indicate that the leaders of such civilizations – whether called a king, pharaoh, emperor, Caesar, czar, or potentate – were often considered god-like and that the rest of the population were born into one class or another -- ranging from: priestly, to: warrior, noblemen, farmer, merchant, financier, and the like – who performed roles within the greater society that allegedly served the greater good of a divinity, empire, and/or ruler.

Those who did not wish to accept the way things were set up and worked tended to be considered as traitors. Such individuals were usually ostracized, jailed, executed, or some combination of the three.

In many ways, things really haven't changed all that much. Corporations, nations, and so-called 'leaders' work out arrangements – either violently or peacefully – to divvy up the known universe into fiefdoms over which they exercise control. Now they go by the title of president, premier, prime minister, governor, or CEO.

These individuals often consider themselves to be god-like and frequently are treated as gods by their groupies, supporters, and underlings. The task of these leaders is to induce everyone else to serve what is referred to as the greater good, and almost invariably the 'greater good' is equivalent to whatever agenda the leaders are pushing at any given time ... an agenda which serves the needs of the 'leaders' and not necessarily the needs of the millions of people who, often unwittingly, assist the leaders to realize their agenda..

Nowadays, class is not necessarily a function of inherited roles such as farmer, merchant, religious cleric, warrior, and so on – although things sometimes do work out this way. Today, class is a function of money along with the power that accompanies such money, and, for the most part, people who begin wealthy stay wealthy, and those who begin poor remain poor.

The classes are fairly rigid in this sense with a limited number of exceptions to the general rule used to shore up the untenable argument that anyone can succeed in today's world. Yes, there are an abundance of rags to riches stories which are trotted out for purposes of propaganda, but, the reality of the matter is that there is only a very limited amount of vertical financial movement which is possible in today's world, and there is even less vertical movement when it comes to acquiring any meaningful sort of power within the structure of modern societies.

Moreover, as was true in the times of earlier civilizations, so too, today, those who are not in accord with the modern way of divvying up power, resources, and money are branded as traitors and, as a result, are ostracized, punished, jailed, executed, or some combination of the four. Some people like to think that substantial progress has been made when one compares early civilizations and present society, but, in all too many ways, nothing really has changed except names, dates, and titles.

According to Imam Rauf we are all free to think for ourselves and that the very idea of mind control is an anathema to any society which purports to be free. Even if one were to agree with Imam Rauf that we might be free to think for ourselves, individuals in this society are often not free to act on what they think (without facing severe sanctions such as loss of a job and/or career, financial hardship, ridicule by the media, or becoming a community outcast), and if one is not free within the sphere of activity, then one has to question the value of merely being able to think in a free manner that has little, or no, spillover into the realm of action.

However, putting aside for the moment the relationship between thinking and activity – which is a very complex, multifaceted problem within a pluralistic society – one might question how many people in this society are really free to even think for themselves. When one learns that five years after September 11, 2001, more than 40% of the people who listen to Fox News still believe there is a connection between Saddam Hussein and the tragedies of 9/11 and/or that Saddam Hussein and al-Qaida were co-conspirators in the events of 9/11 ... something which even President Bush finally admitted was not the case -- after much hemming, hawing, and many misleading statements by both him and Vice President Cheney on the matter -- then, really, how much of this 40% of the Fox listening audience can be thinking for themselves? When we live in an age when groups like 'the Swift-boat Veterans For Truth' or all too many talk radio hosts, along with media outlets that are financially dependent on corporate owners, sponsors, and advertisers, can, and do, muddy the waters with the express purpose of re-framing events in a distorted manner and, as a result, many recipients of these propaganda campaigns begin to treat distortion and bias as if they were fact ... when we exist within a environment of intentionally nurtured fear concerning non-existent entities such as 'weapons of mass destruction' that are used as a pretext for raining down upon other societies our actual weapons of mass destruction ... when we live at a time when we are not only urged, but expected to (with a potential for being penalized if we do not) accept the findings of a 9/11 Commission that did not have the time, money, security clearance, subpoena power, will, mandate, or integrity to actually get at the truth of 9/11 and was politically compromised from the very beginning by the very vested interests who were inherently opposed to a truly free and rigorous examination of an 'official story' that does not stand up to even casual critical examination ... when we grow up within a compulsory educational environment in which both American and world history are often air-brushed by teachers and textbooks with the cosmetics of mythology, rationalization, and self-serving biases ... then, really, how free are people to think for themselves?

There are many degrees of freedom through which to think about misinformation, disinformation, bias, error, falsehood, distortion, and delusion. However, if one does not understand that what one is thinking about is untrue, then all the freedom in the world is not necessarily going to help one in any constructive manner.

As Henry Ford is once reported to have said: "You can have any color of car you like as long as it's black." Similarly, all too many people would offer us the idea that we are free to think whatever we like as long as it conforms to the color of belief with which we are provided by those in politics, government, the media, the corporate world, and education who wish to control what we think about and the way in which we think about it.

Imam Rauf refers to the set of values – namely, liberty, equality, social justice, and fraternity ... which he believes to be at the core of monotheistic spiritual traditions such as Judaism, Christianity, and Islam – as the Abrahamic ethic. While in the light of current hostilities among Jews, Christians, and Muslims, it is understandable that Imam Rauf would wish to try to create a basis of common currency among the aforementioned monotheistic traditions by subsuming the above-noted set of values under the rubric of the Abrahamic ethic (millati ibrahim), I also think that this way of doing things carries dimensions of distortion and exclusion with it.

More specifically, the qualities of liberty, equality, social justice and fraternity were part of the message transmitted to humankind by all Prophets, starting with Adam (peace be upon him). The ethic to which this set of qualities gives expression, therefore, did not start with Abraham (peace be upon him) and, consequently, it is not an ethic which he invented or which started with him, but rather, this ethic consisted of principles dealing with morality and conduct that had been given by Divinity to human beings since the time that the latter first started to walk on the face of the Earth.

The fact of the matter is <u>until</u> Abraham (peace be upon him) received guidance from God, Abraham (peace be upon him) did not know what the truth of things was. As pointed out in the Qur'an, 6: 75-91, he had to go on a spiritual journey, and at one time or another during this quest he questioned whether the moon, stars, or the sun were appropriate objects of worship.

Because God guided Abraham (peace be upon him), the latter was able to navigate through the uncertainties entailed by his consideration of different objects as possible foci for his worship. Without this guidance, Abraham (peace be upon him) would have wandered into the same kinds of errors as did his father and the surrounding community.

Prophets and peoples were guided in this way before Abraham (peace be upon him). The guidance concerned not only the relationship between humankind and Divinity, but the guidance covered, as well, matters involving the relationship of human beings

192

one with another, and, thus, the core set of values encompassing liberty, equality, social justice, and fraternity existed long before the Prophetic mission of Abraham (peace be upon him).

Indeed, as the Qur'an indicates to Muhammad (peace be upon him):

"Verily, We have sent messengers before thee. Among them are some of whom We have told thee, and some of whom we did not tell thee. (40: 78)"

This was as true for Abraham (peace be upon him) as it was for Muhammad (peace be upon him) – there were communities which existed prior to both Abraham and Muhammad (peace be upon them both) that had been sent prophets, books of guidance, and spiritual assistance.

For example, Buddha is not mentioned in the Qur'an, nor is Krishna, nor are the great spiritual personalities of different indigenous peoples. However, perhaps these individuals were, nonetheless, sent by Divinity with guidance – guidance which included principles covering issues of liberty, equality, social justice and fraternity.

In fact, the so-called founding fathers borrowed a great many of 'their' ideas from the principles by which many Native peoples lived their lives. Representatives from the Native peoples were invited to, attended, and contributed a great many substantial and constructive ideas to a number of pre-Constitutional sessions called by the 'founding fathers'.

These contributions revolved around issues of liberty, equality, social justice, and fraternity. Many of these ideas were incorporated into the framework of the Constitution and, later, the Bill of Rights.

The Qur'an does make reference to the millati (ethic, way, principles, method) of Abraham in, for example, the verse:

"Who forsakes the millati of Abraham except the one who depreciates

193

himself." (2: 130)

Nonetheless, by and large, this millati is consistent with, and reflects, the essence of, the millati which had been taught to people via prophets who came before Abraham (peace be upon him). The millati of Abraham was taught to him just as it was taught to some of those who preceded him, and, so, in reality, the millati Abraham is really the millati of God.

Imam Rauf says:

"While it's true that India, China, and Japan are not generally monotheistic societies, increasingly they are implementing democratic systems of government – systems anchored in the concept of human equality and thus emanating from the Abrahamic ethic. This is the ethic which is embedded in human nature. (page 15)"

However, if what Imam Rauf claims – namely, that the ethic in question is embedded in human nature – is true, then movements toward liberty, equality, and social justice did not emanate from the Abrahamic ethic, but, rather, arose through the presence of Divine guidance in people's lives across time and geographical locales around the world quite independently of Prophet Abraham (peace be upon him).

There have been a lot of different spiritual traditions in India, China and Japan, and one wonders if Imam Rauf is not guilty of a certain amount of overgeneralization, if not distortion, when he claims that these are not generally monotheistic societies. First, one has the problem of trying to disentangle the original nature of a given spiritual tradition from the purely human theological hermeneutics that may have been layered over the original like a complex palimpsest. In other words, even if one were to agree that in some instances there was an absence of what we might recognize as monotheism in the spiritual traditions of such countries, nonetheless, this may be irrelevant to teachings concerning the Oneness of Being which might originally have been taught to human beings through

Divine emissaries who had been sent to such societies ... emissaries who are not necessarily mentioned in the Qur'an or the Bible but who are known, nonetheless, to Divinity.

In addition, one could put forth defensible positions that there are strains of Buddhism, Taoism, and the Vedanta – to name just three -- which are rigorously oriented to the idea that Reality is One ... even if terms such as God, Divinity, and theism are not used. These same traditions taught values involving freedom, equality, social justice, and fraternity – values which would resonate with what Imam Rauf considers to be the inherent nature of human beings in general and, therefore, are not necessarily derivative from – although quite consonant with -- what he refers to as the Abrahamic ethic.

Later on (page 33) in his book, Imam Rauf says that:

"Muslims thereby relate to humanity on three levels: to all humanity as humans, to all religious communities as common heirs of a divinely revealed religious tradition, and to Jews and Christians as direct recipients of the Abrahmaic ethic as such."

Aside from a failure of the foregoing statement to make a distinction between what Islam calls Muslims to do and what Muslims may actually do [and, unfortunately, not all Muslims do relate to other human beings as fellow members of humankind], in addition, contrary to what Imam Rauf claims not all Muslims relate "to all religious communities as common heirs to a divinely revealed religious tradition". In fact just a small number of pages prior (page 15) to the present quote (page 33), Imam Rauf made comments about how India, China, and Japan are not generally monotheistic societies, and, then indicated on page 32 that the Abrahamic ethic was rooted in a radical monotheism expressed in loving one God with all one's being. So, readers, quite understandably, may have a tendency to become somewhat confused about what Imam Rauf is really saying in this respect.

On page 34 of <u>What's Right With Islam</u>, under a section labeled: 'Hindus and Buddhists: Older Kids On The Block', Imam Rauf does cite the Quranic verses (4: 163-164) which stipulate that God has sent many messengers to humankind but Divinity has not disclosed the identities of those messengers to everyone. Based on these verses and a few other citations, Imam Rauf argues that "Hindus and Buddhists are descendants from religious teachings originally brought forth from prophets descended from Adam and Noah. (page 35)".

There is a Hadith in which the Prophet Muhammad (peace be upon him) is reported to have said that:

"There are 71 sects among Jews, and only one of them is correct. There are 73 sects among Christians, and only one of them is correct. There are 73 sects among Muslims, and only one of them is correct."

By interpolation, or extrapolation, one might argue that if Hinduism and Buddhism are derived from spiritual "teachings originally brought forth from prophets descended from Adam and Noah", then there are x-number of sects in Hinduism and Buddhism, and, perhaps, only one each is respectively correct.

Based on my reading, studies, and discussions with various Hindus and Buddhists, I believe there is a great deal of truth and wisdom inherent in the Hindu and Buddhist spiritual traditions. Nonetheless, I do not believe that by acknowledging this truth, one is, therefore, compelled to accept every iota of Hindu and Buddhist theology as necessarily being accurately reflective of the original spiritual teachings that were given to prophets in those societies anymore than one should feel obligated to accept every scrap of Muslim, Christian, or Jewish theology which exists as being necessarily accurately reflective of the actual spiritual teachings which were given to prophets in the latter societies.

So, while I am quite willing to recognize – as a general principle – that there are various elements, themes, and teachings within Hinduism and Buddhism which do arise out of, and deeply resonate with, original spiritual teachings which pre-dated the appearance of Hinduism and Buddhism, I am not really sure what Imam Rauf has in mind here because he spends almost no time delineating either of these latter two spiritual traditions. Perhaps, wishing to be something of a diplomat or politician, he is trying to be inclusive without really saying anything at all that might entail hermeneutical difficulties for his position.

However, several recurrent themes in Imam Rauf's book are the Oneness of God and the importance of monotheism to the Abrahmic ethic. Given that there are prominent strains of Hinduism which are inclined to polytheism, and there are prominent strains of Buddhism which are oriented around a non-theistic approach to spirituality, one is not quite sure what Imam Rauf is saying.

Is he playing to the majoritarian reading audience of Christians, Jews, and Muslims, with a few amorphous and ambiguous protective bon mots mentioned in passing with respect to several other religious traditions in order to create, at the very least, an appearance of inclusiveness and acceptance of other spiritual paths? Or, is he being somewhat disingenuous about how he words things? Or, is Imam Rauf just muddled in his thinking on these issues?

Furthermore, I find it interesting that there is no mention of traditions like Taoism or the spirituality of various indigenous peoples such as North American Native peoples, the Aborigines of Australia, or the Maori of New Zealand. To be sure, one cannot explore and discuss everything within a book of limited pages and many purposes, but when a reader is grappling with trying to understand what, precisely, Imam Rauf is saying or arguing, then a few more points of reference in this context than were supplied by him in his book might greatly facilitate matters.

To claim on behalf of Muslims that everyone of us accepts "all religious communities as common heirs to a divinely revealed religious tradition" is just not tenable empirically since there are many Muslims whom I know, or whom I have read about, who would not agree to what Imam Rauf stipulates as being the case in this respect. Moreover, such a claim is not tenable rationally since no one – whether they be Jewish, Christian, Muslim, Hind, Buddhist, Taoist, or from an indigenous spiritual tradition -- could reasonably expect anyone to accept anything and everything which bears the moniker of "religious".

197

Truth is what it is. Various religious traditions are attempts, some of which are much better than others, to merge horizons with at least certain aspects of that truth, and there are few, if any, who would maintain that any tradition which refers to itself as religious or spiritual necessarily succeeds, wholly or partially, in such efforts.

On page 16 of <u>What's Right With Islam</u>, Imam Rauf cites the following Quranic verse – namely:

"Be religious in accordance with your truest inclinations, the immutable nature (fitra) of God upon which He created people – there is no altering God's creation – that is right religiousness, but most people do not know. (30:30)"

Imam Rauf claims "that any person who listens to his or her heart or conscience would recognize that God is One, that humanity is one family, that humans should be free and should treat each other fairly and with justice."

Given, as I am quite sure that Imam Rauf would agree, that human beings are inclined to error without the support of Divine guidance and assistance, one may not be able to accept what he says in the foregoing without a certain amount of qualification. One of the lessons of history is that, for the most part, human beings all too frequently are not spiritually in accord with their truest inclinations or fitra since they do not recognize that God is One or that humanity constitutes one family or that human beings ought to be free and ought to treat one another with equitability.

Because the foregoing is very often the nature of human affairs, this is precisely why guidance is necessary and why Divine books and messengers are sent to humankind. If human beings could act in accordance with our truest inclinations or fitra on our own, then Divine guidance would not be necessary, but such does not appear to be the case.

Many people listen to what they believe is their heart or their conscience only to later discover – if they are fortunate -- that the real teachings of the heart, conscience, and fitra are something other than what they previously believed or thought. Not only is the art of listening to one's heart or being in accordance with one's fitra difficult to accomplish, but learning how to differentiate among the different forces – both destructive and constructive – which seek to undermine the proper functioning of the heart, conscience, or fitra -- entails an extremely difficult set of tasks.

In general terms we may all agree that qualities such as freedom, equality, social justice and fraternity are very important. However, both Divinity and the Devil are in the details of working out what any of these qualities actually mean amidst the many particularized problems and complexities of everyday existence.

Like the Peanuts character, Linus once said – "I love humanity! It's people I can't stand." Consequently, when one looks into one's heart and conscience, we may all see a tain constructed from general ideas (like Linus's humanity) concerning freedom, equality, social justice, and fraternity, but the particular images of freedom, equality, and so on that are reflected from the glass covering the tain (like Linus's actual people) may be very different from one individual to the next.

For example, I agree with Imam Rauf about the importance of each of the qualities which he mentions. Yet, nonetheless -- as I am pointing out in the present discussion, as well as other essays appearing elsewhere in this collection which critically engage What's Right With Islam -- my understanding of these qualities (along with a number of additional themes) seems to be quite different than his conception of what freedom, equality, social justice and fraternity may involve. Some of these differences are minor, but others appear to be much more substantial.

What does it mean to say: that God is One (e.g., there has been an on-going historical controversy between those who maintained that there is a 'oneness of witnessing' but rejected the position of those who advocated a 'oneness of Being', and vice versa), or that humanity is one family (is it a dysfunctional family, or a family beset by internecine struggles like Cain and Abel, or a family locked in unending machinations and manipulations like the brothers of Joseph – peace be upon him)? What degrees of freedom should be extended to any given individual and what degrees of constraint? What do we mean when we say that one should treat others fairly and with justice?

Imam Rauf seeks to draw a parallel between the "self-evident Truths" of the Declaration of Independence and the natural inclination of our minds and heart to acknowledge the truth of the Abrahamic ethic. Yet, initially, these truths of the framers of the Declaration of Independence that were allegedly so self-evident excluded women (unless they were property owners), blacks, slaves, the homeless, and Native peoples from having a rightful place among the men who were "created equal and endowed by their Creator with certain inalienable rights."

Apparently, like the central characters of Orwell's <u>Animal Farm</u>: 'All of us are equal, but some of us are more equal than others'. In any event, once again, the idea that all we have to do is look within our conscience and hearts to see the truth of things raises a lot of unanswered questions for a perspective like that which Iman Rauf is putting forth concerning the alleged self-evident nature of the truths about freedom, liberty, social justice, and fraternity.

Is Imam Rauf correct about things, or am I correct about things, or are both of us wrong, or are we partially right and partially wrong? God knows best, but what I do know is that the problem is not as simple as Imam Rauf seems to indicate – that is, we do not just look into our hearts or conscience and realize the nature of fitra. This requires considerable: spiritual guidance, Divine assistance, as well as struggle from ourselves. Indeed, if things were as Imam Rauf appears to suppose them to be, there would be no need for revelation, Prophets, or other forms of Divine assistance.

According to Imam Rauf "those that practice what their hearts tell them are practicing the right religion". The Qur'an refers to this as "deen Allah" (Qur'an, 3: 83), and Imam Rauf says that this 'deen' has been bequeathed to human faculties of reason and understanding. Moreover, Imam Rauf claims, on the one hand, that the primary component of this understanding is the recognition that God is One and, on the other hand, that both jinn and human beings have been created for no other purpose than to worship God – Who "desires no aid from" humans nor jinn (Qur'an 51: 57) – and that the nature of worship "involves the observance of His patterns which are knowable by reason (page 16)".

In the Qur'an one finds the following:

"The seven heavens and the earth and all that is therein praise God and there is nothing that does not glorify God in praise, but you understand not their manner of praise." (17: 44)

Apparently, reason is not enough since we all have it and, yet, there are patterns of praise and worship inherent in the nature of things – including humankind -- which we do not understand.

Abraham's father, who constructed and fashioned idols which gave expression to polytheism rather than monotheism, had reason, but he did not observe or understand or grasp the Divine patterns ... or, perhaps, he did observe such patterns but just interpreted them incorrectly. Might one suppose that Abraham's father looked into his heart or conscience and that reason told him that polytheism was the right way to go? Do we have any evidence to indicate that this was not the case?

Presumably, just looking into one's heart or conscience and working toward a reasoned understanding is not enough. Not all reasoning is necessarily correct. Not everything which we believe our hearts and conscience are telling us is necessarily an accurate reflection of what God ay be trying to disclose to us through the signs and patterns of nature, revelation, or prophetic missions. Something is missing from the equation.

In the Qur'an are the following two verses:

"And whoever is blind in this world will be blind in the Hereafter, and even further from the path." (17: 72),

and,

"It is not their eyes which are blind, but the hearts in their breast."
(22: 46)

Obviously, according to the Qur'an there are forces which can obscure the vision of the heart. If the vision of the heart is not clear, then various kinds of blindness plague human understanding and reason.

Spiritually speaking, the heart is a capacity with different dimensions, potentials and characteristics. One facet of the heart is known as the 'qalb' – an Arabic term meaning that which turns or fluctuates.

The qalb can be oriented toward the carnal soul, Iblis, and/or the multiplicity of emotional and rationalistic entanglements knows as 'dunya' or the 'world'. The qalb also can be oriented toward the ruh or spirit.

In fact, the qalb is a battleground of forces for both good and evil which determines one's degree of receptivity to spiritually destructive and constructive currents running through the heart. If one is attuned to spiritually destructive currents, then one will be beset with one kind or another of blindness with respect to correct understanding or reasoning. If, on the other hand, one is, by the Grace of God, receptive to spiritually constructive influences running through the heart, then one's understanding and reasoning are modulated in a way which assists one to 'see' and understand some element of truth and to be able to use this understanding to direct reasoning in an efficacious manner.

All of the foregoing can be summed up in a saying which has been attributed to the Prophet Muhammad (peace be upon him).

"There is an organ within the human being which, if it is problematic, then, the whole of one's being becomes problematic, but, if that organ is sound, then, the whole of being is sound, and that organ is the heart."

A little later on in Chapter 1 of <u>What's Right With Islam</u> Imam Rauf does indicate that there is a strong tendency within human nature to resist the primordial, spiritual capacity of fitra which God has bestowed upon humankind. He describes this inclination toward resistance as a form of 'forgetfulness' and indicates that this is not primarily a matter of forgetting what we know – that is, a lapse in memory – but, rather, constitutes a failure to apply what we know. In effect, we know better than we often do.

I tend to disagree somewhat with Imam Rauf in relation to the forgoing position. While I do accept the idea that human beings may not act in a way which is consistent with what we know to be right or moral, one has to address the issue of why such inconsistency between knowledge and action arises in the first place. I believe this inconsistency points toward a deeper problem.

Essentially, the problem of forgetting revolves around the issue of identity. We have forgotten who we are. We have forgotten our spiritual potential. We have forgotten our origins. We have forgotten why we have been brought into this world. We have forgotten our relationship with God. We have forgotten how to reconnect with that which we have forgotten.

Even when, by the Grace of God, we recognize something to be true and correct, we often do not act in consort with that understanding because we have forgotten that nothing is possible without Divine support and assistance. We have forgotten that – in the reported words of the Prophet –

"This life is but a tillage for the next life, therefore, do good deeds here that you may reap benefits there ... for striving is an ordinance of God, and whatever God has ordained can be attained only by striving."

In short, we have forgotten that effort and struggle is necessary to, among other things, acquire understanding and, then, in addition, convert such understanding into appropriate action.

In pre-eternity the Qur'an indicates that Allah addressed the

203

spirits with:

"Am I not your Lord? (Alastu bi rabbikum) And the spirits answered: "'Yes, we testify (Qarbala)'. " (7: 172).

When we were brought into this world, most of us forgot this conversation and the myriad ramifications of the central question and answer of that dialogue.

Furthermore, this inclination toward forgetfulness is not merely a passive phenomenon but can become a very rigorous tendency toward rebelling against anything which might lead to remembering our essential identity and its concomitant responsibilities. More specifically, not only do we have a carnal soul which incites us to forgetfulness, but, as the Qur'an indicates:

"If anyone forsakes the remembrance of the Most Gracious, We appoint a devil to be an intimate companion for that person and who will hinder that individual from the path. Yet, they think they are being guided in the right direction." (43: 36-37)

Therefore, the problem of forgetfulness goes beyond not acting in accordance with what we may know to be right, just, or moral. In fact, this latter kind of forgetfulness can be subsumed under the more essential form of forgetting outlined above – a more essential form of forgetfulness that explains why, among other things, a disparity between knowledge and action arises in the first place.

Imam Rauf goes on to state that:

"If there is anything in the Islamic view that approximates the Christian idea of original sin, in the sense of something that can be described as the universal human flaw, it is that humans forget." (page 23).

I believe this statement to be problematic in several ways.

First of all, the theological concept of original sin usually does not refer to some universal flaw in human beings but rather refers to what is inherited by every human being due to the mistakes of Adam (peace be upon him) and Eve (may Allah be pleased with her) when they disobeyed God in the Garden of Eden. This is the sin for which people are said – at least by many Christians – to be in need of baptism ... for which even Jesus (peace be upon him) was supposedly required to be baptized by John the Baptist (peace be upon him) ... although there are aspects of baptism, depending on which brand of Christian theology one is considering, that extend beyond just the need to be cleansed of original sin and which enter into a condition of complete spiritual renewal.

To speak in terms of a potential for rebellion against the truth (i.e., the nafs or carnal soul) is a very different idea than is the notion of original sin. Although, spiritually speaking, all human beings do inherit the capacity to rebel against truth, this capacity has to be acted upon through choice – that is, one has to choose to rebel in order for this aspect of human potential to be given expression. However, in the matter of original sin, one gets no choice in the matter – one inherits the stain of sin without ever exercising choice. This is diametrically opposed to the Islamic perspective in which all human beings are born innocent and sin-free and, then the intentions and choices of life determine whether, or not, we commit spiritual errors for which we are to be held accountable.

Imam Rauf develops a general framework for some of the problems which arose following the passing away of the Prophet Muhammad (peace be upon him) from this world. These included: the generating of written manuscripts that were faithful to the recited Qur'an; the emergence of practice of tafsir which was an exegetical practice that focused on delineating the circumstances surrounding the occurrence of any given instance of revelation in an attempt to gain insight into the meaning of such revelation relative to the nature of the historical and social context in which such revelations emerged; and, the development of fiqh, or theories of jurisprudence, as ways of organizing and regulating society.

The foregoing problems are presented against the backdrop of a challenge which Imam Rauf believes faces every faith tradition – namely, how to translate original teachings into a form that not only makes sense to a different set of historical and sociological circumstances but, as well, preserves the essential truths of the original teachings. Moreover, he points out that, generally speaking, the tendency down through history has been for divisions to arise within the community out of which a given expression of Divine guidance arose.

For instance, he mentions the rift which took place following the termination of the initial Earthly mission of Jesus (peace be upon him) between the Jewish and Christian communities even though Jesus is reported to have said that he does 'not come to reject what came before (i.e., Judaism) but to confirm it and add to it.' And, Imam Rauf also alludes to divisions within the Muslim community about issues of propriety surrounding the creation of a written Qur'an, the nature of tafsir, and the rise of various schools of religious jurisprudence in relation to Islam.

Imam Rauf proceeds to cite a verse of the Qur'an that he feels reflects on the foregoing situation of divisiveness:

"[God] ordained for you of religion that which He enjoined upon Noah, and We have revealed to you, and which We enjoined on Abraham and Moses and Jesus – to establish religion (deen) and to not be divided therein." (42: 13)

Imam Rauf then summarizes what he believes to be one of the teachings of the foregoing verse – namely, that "divisive attitudes and practices are signs of a non- or anti-monotheistic, anti-Abrahamic ethic." (page 29)

To state what would appear to be an obvious point, if all we have to do is look into our hearts and conscience in order to grasp the truth of the Abrahmaic ethic as Imam Rauf earlier argued, then how is the kind of divisiveness noted above possible? Even when there is agreement that it is the deen (or spiritual method and way) of Noah,

206

Abraham, Moses, Jesus, and Muhammad (peace be upon them all) which should be followed, differences emerge with respect to establishing the precise nature of that deen.

Moreover, prophets were consistently charged with introducing divisiveness into their respective communities by those who were opposed to them. So, how does one differentiate the establishing of truth -- which always encroaches on someone's vested interests and, therefore, is inherently divisive – from the sort of anti-monotheistic attitude and anti-Abrahamic ethic to which Imam Rauf alludes?

On page 31 of <u>What's Right With Islam</u>, Imam Rauf maintains that:

"What is right about any religion or societal structure is therefore the extent to which individuals and societies fully manifest the principles of the Abrahamic ethic".

Just prior to the foregoing conclusion, he lists a number of failings of the Muslim community in this respect after the Prophet Muhammad (peace be upon him) passed away – namely, the disappearance of the rule of law applied by an independent judiciary; the judgment that apostasy is the equivalent of treason; continuation of the practice of slavery despite the many Quranic verses that sought to eliminate that institution; and, the on-going oppression of women.

Today, many of these same failings noted with respect to the Muslim community following the passing away of the Prophet Muhammad (peace be upon him) exist in America. For instance, people on both the left and right indicate that the rule of law has been lost amidst a politicizing of the judiciary which has undermined the capacity of the latter to render decisions which are truly independent of political corruption, biases, and agendas. Furthermore, in the post-9/11 environment there are many people who believe that any criticism of a government which systematically oppresses not only its own citizens, but, as well, the populations of other countries on the basis of delusional, self-serving systems of grandiosity and imperialistic greed constitute not only an act of treason but also gives expression to apostasy with respect to the state religion known as the 'war on terror' – where terror is always a function of the atrocities and injustices which others commit and, by definition, never a function of the atrocities and injustices which we commit. In addition, America is filled with people who have become thoroughly enslaved by transnational corporations, money-changers (now known as banks, financial institutions, and the Federal Reserve) whom Jesus (peace be upon him) opposed, and politicians/business people who do not believe that workers ought to be paid fairly or who do not believe that the health and bodily well-being of workers ought to be protected in the workplace, or who do not believe that there is anything wrong with continuing to degrade the environment so that the powerful, wealthy friends of politicians can become more powerful and more wealthy. Finally, America's cup runneth over when it comes to the oppression of women through rape, sexual abuse, authoritarian husbands (as well as fathers and brothers), and the denial of equal opportunity in education, government, and the workplace to women.

How does one compare the extent to which America does not fully manifest the Abrahamic ethic with the extent to which Muslim countries do not fully manifest the Abrahamic ethic, when, in truth, both are failing in major ways? The fact that one country might have a hypothetical score of 30 relative to the hypothetical score of 20 for another country (with a perfect score being 100) is not something about which either country ought to take satisfaction.

Imam Rauf believes that:

"The challenge still facing human society today is how to worship God without dividing ourselves and how to institutionalize such a unified understanding. (page 32)"

Imam Rauf feels that the way to meet this challenge is through a radical monotheism that entails both loving God with all one's being, as well as, establishing a love for others that is equal to the love we have for ourselves and through this love ensure that all human beings enjoy liberty, equality, social justice, and fraternity.

I know of a couple in which the man continuously abused his wife for decades in all manner of ways. Yet, this man was convinced that he loved his wife and that no one would or could love that woman like he did in his own inimitable style.

The woman was not free. She had no semblance of equality of treatment. There was an almost complete absence of justice in the relationship, and there was little, real sense of mutuality and reciprocity which bonded the two.

However, despite the many abusive dimensions of the relationship, the man believed that everything which was done revolved around his supposed love for his wife, and the wife was pushed into such a deep dissociative condition through the presence of the husband's abuse that she came to believe that deep down, beneath all the abuse, was a loving, caring man who had genuine regard for her well-being. Such is the nature of many abusive relationships.

There are many politicians and government officials who act abusively and oppressively toward the citizens of a given country or state, and the politicians and government officials have deluded themselves into believing they are acting out of intentions such as love, compassion, justice, and fairness that supposedly promote the 'greater good' when, in truth, only the good of the relative few are being advanced and served by the agendas of the politicians and governments. There are many citizens who have been pushed so far into a dissociative condition by the presence of such abuse that they can be induced into believing that everything is being done for their (the citizen's) good.

For example, if you make people sufficiently afraid, and if you lie to them about the reasons why they should be afraid, and if you provide them with an identifiable source toward which to direct that fear, then, in the eye of this category 5 hurricane of fear, almost anything the government does to further oppress the citizens can be couched in terms of actions taken to save the citizens from being hurt by the alleged source of fear – a fear which in many, if not most, ways has been manufactured via fabrications and a distorted re-framing of historical and social circumstances. Abusive political relationships exhibit many of the characteristics, themes, and techniques of abusive

209

personal relationships like the husband and wife couple I used to know.

Similarly, just as we often delude ourselves into believing that we love others as we love ourselves, so, too, we often delude ourselves into believing that we love God with our whole being. All too many of us profess a love for God that is really rooted in a desire to have a comfortable material life on Earth, or rooted in a desire for Paradise, or rooted in a fear of Hell, or rooted in a sense of self-glorification related to the presumptuous belief that we are God's elite or chosen emissaries.

There is a story which arises out of the Sufi mystical tradition that runs along the following lines. God says: I created men and they were bound to Me, and they were coming to me when I showed them the world, 9/10ths of them became world-bound, and 1/10th remained with Me. When I told them about Paradise, 9/10ths of those who had remained with Me desired Paradise and only 1/10th remained with Me. When I poured My troubles and My pains upon those who stayed with Me, they cried for help and 9/10ths left and 1/10th remained with Me. And when I threatened those who remained with Me that I would heap upon them such troubles as would make the mountains crumble, they said: "As long as it comes from You it is alright with us".

This latter 1/10th of 1/10th of 1/10th of the original set of human beings are those who love God with their whole being. The Qur'an describes these kinds of individuals in the following way: "Those who spend their wealth for increase in self-purification and have in their minds no favor from anyone for which a reward is expected in return, but only the desire to seek for the Countenance of their Lord Most High." (92: 18-20) And, again: "Say: Surely, my prayer and my service of sacrifice, my life and my death are all for Allah, the Lord of the worlds." (6: 162)

Elsewhere the Qur'an states:

"They ask thee (O Muhammad) what they ought to spend in the way of God. Say: that which is left after meeting your needs." (2: 219)

210

Many people fulfill this Divine directive by expanding the nature of needs exponentially and reducing what is left over to be spent in the way of Allah proportionately. Their love for God is modulated and limited by the desires of the self and what is meant by loving God with one's whole being is re-framed to refer only to that portion of being which, on occasion, we might loan out in a temporary manner – and assuming, of course, that such a loan is largely free of difficulties and complications.

Contrary to what Imam Rauf asserts, many of us have not just forgotten to apply what we know, we have forgotten what it means to love God with our whole being. We have forgotten what it means to truly love another human being. We have forgotten the real meaning of liberty, freedom, social justice, and fraternity. We live in a state of spiritual amnesia from which we desperately need to recover.

On pages 35 and 36 of What's Right With Islam Imam Rauf outlines five principles which he believes are at the heart of all "globalized' religions – that is, those traditions which were brought to humankind worldwide through the locus of manifestation of authentic prophets and messengers of Divinity. The very first principle concerns the transcendent, singular, unique, unknowable nature of God.

However, God is not only transcendent, God is also immanent. By definition, we cannot know those dimensions of Divinity which are transcendent and unknowable except in a general, referential manner that does nothing more than acknowledge the existence of such realms in relation to the nature of Divinity. Nevertheless, there are facets of Divine Presence which are not unknowable and are capable of, to a degree, being understood according to one's God-given capacity to gain insight into such dimensions of Divinity together with a need for the Divine Grace that renders such realms accessible to our capacities for knowing them.

In addition, I'm not quite certain in what way saying that God is unknowable and transcendent – however true this may be – can be considered a primary, essential principle of 'globalized' religion. What does one do with such a statement? What practical ramifications does it have?

Once one says that God is unknowable and transcendent, then

211

that is the end of the matter. Everything else is merely ignorance.

Transcendence and unknowability, without a countervailing immanence, is a virtually useless piece of understanding. In fact, one can't even call the former knowledge since to contend that something is unknowable and transcendent means that the statement is entirely unverifiable ... this is the essential nature of being unknowable and transcendent.

The second 'globalized' principle cited by Imam Rauf alludes, somewhat elliptically, to the foregoing issue of immanence. More specifically, he states that "God as All-Being is relevant to His Creation." Through Creation, God provides us with our raison d'etre for being by means of the purpose, norms, and ethics toward which human beings are to aspire in the living of life. According to Imam Rauf, God is "the one through whom we learn to know right from wrong."

In concert with a point made previously in the current essay, if God is the One "through whom we learn right from wrong" then distinguishing between right and wrong is not merely a matter of looking into one's heart or conscience and reading off the message of fitra as Imam Rauf seemed to suggest earlier in the first chapter of his book. One has to be taught discernment by Divinity.

Moreover, even if one agrees that God is the One Who provides us with purpose, norms, and ethics, there is a great deal of disagreement about precisely what such purpose, norms and ethics entail. If, as Imam Rauf asserts – and I do not disagree with him on this point – that "God is the most important thing in our lives", questions still hover about the issue of what this all means. People can agree, in principle, that Divinity is relevant to our lives and still disagree about the nature of this relevancy or how one goes about realizing and integrating such relevancy into lived life.

Is the purpose of life to achieve Paradise and avoid Hell? Is the purpose of life to realize the full potential of fitra (our primordial spiritual capacity) quite independently of considerations of Heaven and Hell? Is the purpose of life to realize fitra so that we can come to know and observe, for the very first time in our lives, what worshiping Divinity is really all about in essence? Is the purpose of life to satisfy

212

the Hadith Qudsi which stated that 'God was a Hidden Treasure and loved to be known, so God brought forth Creation'? Is the purpose of life some combination of the foregoing, and, if so, what is the nature of the appropriate sort of combinatorial balance?

How does one go about accomplishing any of the foregoing purposes? What methods are to be used? What criteria are to be applied in evaluating how well, or poorly, one is doing with respect to the realization of any given purpose? How does one interact with others along the way who may be seeking quite different purposes and, yet, still believe that such purposes are divinely ordained? What does it mean to love one's neighbor in such a context?

The third principle of 'globalized' religion to be noted by Imam Rauf is that the nature of the aforementioned Divine relevance is knowable to humans through any of three modalities – taken separately or in combination. These are: (1) divination which is done through various modes of 'seeing' via appropriate states of consciousness and internal spiritual faculties; (2) science and history which consist of the collected knowledge that accumulates in relation to humankind and nature; (3) prophecy which is described as "direct revelation of the will of God through words for the ready use of human understanding."

Any divination which does not take place in a context that is fully modulated by a prophetic mission is problematic. As the Sufi master, Hazrat Junayd (may Allah be pleased with him), stated: This knowledge of ours [that is, Sufi knowledge] is delimited by the Qur'an and the sunnah (i.e., conduct of the Prophet).

Consequently, transpersonal or altered states of consciousness are not necessarily enough, in and of themselves, to ensure that what is being manifested in such states is necessarily an expression of authentic spiritual knowledge of some kind. This is true for the Islamic spiritual tradition, and, as well, I believe authentic spiritual guides from any spiritual tradition would agree that not everything which glitters in the way of divination is necessarily 'gold'. One needs to differentiate veridical spiritual experiences from those which may be generated through the ego, fantasy, Satanic suggestion, psychological problems, and delusional thinking.

213

Secondly, without wishing to dismiss or discount the value of rigorous, sound, insightful scholarship in the areas of science and history, the fact of the matter is that both science and history have been, and currently are, of limited value when it comes to uncovering the nature of Divinity's relevance to human beings. To be sure, there are many speculations rising out of the mists of quantum physics, evolution, astrophysics, and psychology concerning the origins, meaning, and purpose of life – but that's just what they are ... flights of speculation which, however interesting, intriguing and thought-provoking these may be, they cannot be proven to be true statements about the nature, purpose, and relevance of Divinity to humanity. In fact, many scientists would take umbrage with any attempt to try to forge a bridge between Divinity and humankind via science. To paraphrase Jesus (peace be upon him) 'render unto science the things which are science's and render unto Divinity the things which are God's.'

Of course, some would wish to argue that if there is no reality but God, then in part at least, the subject matter of science does engage Divinity whether scientists acknowledge this or not. From here it is just a skip, hop, and jump to saying that, in principle, science has the capacity to discover various facets of Divinity's relevance to humankind.

There is, however, an assumption implicit in the foregoing line of reasoning. This assumption is that the methods, techniques and processes of science are fully capable of penetrating into, illuminating, and grasping all dimensions of the relation of relevancy between Divinity and humankind.

The realm of the spirit and the nature of the Divine relevancy in human affairs may not necessarily be a function of physical, chemical, biological, material, or mathematical processes except in a very tangential or asymptotic sense. If this is so, then science is largely irrelevant to the issue of uncovering the nature of Divine relevancy to human purpose, meaning, norms, and ethics.

In any event, I have not seen any feasible experimental proofs for the aforementioned assumption. But, if it exists, the guy or gal who came up with the solution deserves at least a Nobel Prize for the discovery.

Finally, to try to argue, as Imam Rauf does, that prophecy "is the direct revelation of the will of God through words for the ready use of human understanding" is problematic in a number of ways. To begin with, I believe Imam Rauf's way of characterizing things with respect to the nature of prophecy is far too limited.

Some have said that prophecy consists of 46 parts. Prophecy is more than being a locus of manifestation of God's will through words ... however important this latter aspect may be.

There is a saying among the Sufis which states:

"Do not think that learning comes from discourse. It comes in 'keeping company'. "

Baraka, or Divine Grace, is also transmitted through Prophets, and it is, God willing, the presence of this baraka that underscores the importance of 'keeping company' with a prophet or any other species of Divine friend. In fact, one might say that the meaning of God's will as expressed through Divine words may not be properly understood unless that understanding comes about through support in the form of baraka that is transmitted, if God wishes, through a prophet or authorized vicegerent to those who are keeping company with God's appointed emissary.

Another problem inherent in Imam Rauf's way of describing things in conjunction with the medium of prophecy as one of three ways for generating knowledge concerning the nature of the relevancy of God to Creation is that the meanings and purposes of God's words are not always available for the "ready use of human understanding". There often are conditions surrounding the extent to which God's meanings and purposes will be disclosed through the revealed word.

The Qur'an states:

"If you have taqwa [my note - a reverential awareness in relation to God's presence], He will give you discrimination." (8:29)

215

The same kind of theme appears in 2: 282 of the Qur'an:

"Have taqwa, and God will teach you."

And, again,

"Say (Muhammad): I call to God upon insight. I and whoever follows after me."

Taqwa, discrimination, insight, and being taught by God are all necessary to engage the meanings of the Qur'an. I have heard my shaykh say on a number of occasions that if an individual approaches the Qur'an with the wrong kind of attitude, then the Qur'an closes itself to that individual even though such a person may continue to read the words, and part and parcel of the appropriate attitude is to have taqwa while engaging God's words.

Not everything in the Qur'an is necessarily for ready use by human understanding. As is indicated in the Qur'an:

"O Mankind! Surely you are ever toiling on towards your Lord, painfully toiling, but you shall meet Him ... you shall surely travel from stage to stage. (84: 6, 9)"

Part of this toiling is struggling to understand all that Divinity is saying to us through not only the words of revelation but the Divine mysteries which stand beneath, beyond, between, and all around those words.

Indeed, as the Prophet Muhammad (peace be upon him) is reported to have said:

"Truly, the Qur'an has an outward and an inward dimension, and the latter has its own inward dimension ... and so on up to seven dimensions."

216

Words may be the locus of manifestation through which revelation outwardly manifests itself in its most exoteric form, but the reality of revelation may extend into esoteric dimensions which transcend the limits of words:

"We raise by grades of (Mercy) whom We will, and over every lord of knowledge, there is one more knowing. (Qur'an 12: 76)"

The fourth principle of 'globalized religion' mentioned in What's Right With Islam revolves around the idea that human beings have the capacity to act in accordance with Divine imperatives. Because human beings have been granted free will, we can choose to act in a manner that is in concert with our knowledge of Divine imperatives and, thereby, do good while avoiding evil. "God has made nature subservient to us." (page 36)

Human beings also have a capacity to rebel against Divine imperatives. The Qur'an indicates:

"Truly, the soul commands unto evil." (12: 53)

In addition, the Qur'an states:

"Lo! We have placed all that is on the earth as an ornament thereof that We may try them – which of them is best in conduct." (18: 7)

As existentialist philosophers have long noted, one of the primary burdens of life is not only having to choose but to choose in a manner which may be characterized as being "authentic", as having moral integrity. One of the companions of the Prophet Muhammad (peace be upon him) gave expression to this essential challenge when he saw a leaf which had fallen from a tree and wished he could be that leaf so that he would not have to carry the burden of choice.

217

Contrary to what Imam Rauf argued earlier in the Chapter entitled "Common Roots", we do not just suffer from a kind of forgetfulness in which we fail -- due to a lapse in awareness or attention -- to act in accordance with what we know to be appropriate, just, right, or correct, but, as well, we also suffer from the nightmarish condition in which we often know what is right but choose to do otherwise despite what we know. We look Divinity straight in the face and brazenly choose to act in accordance with that within us which commands us to evil ... whether this be the soul, Iblis (Satan), the attraction of the 'ornaments' of creation (dunya), or the encouragement of other rebels who revel in their rebellion against Divinity's Himma or aspiration for humankind.

God has not made nature subservient to human beings. Rather, God has created both human beings and nature with a conditional potential for joining nature and human beings into a relationship of harmony and mutual benefit or disharmony and mutual destruction.

We have the capacity to know. We have the capacity to choose. We have the capacity to act in accordance with Divine preferences. However, we also have the capacity for ignorance, and we have the capacity for evil, and we have the capacity to flout or rebel against Divine preferences.

Nature does not become co-operative with humankind until that individual becomes a sincere servant of Divinity. This is when human beings realize their Divinely-given potential for being God's vicegerents on Earth ... vicegerents who have a fiduciary responsibility to the rest of Creation.

When our internal nature is made subservient to our free will, understanding and actions in relation to Divine preferences, then external nature also becomes consonant with – to the extent that this is possible -- the human being whose spiritual condition is in harmony with Divine wishes. When our internal nature has not been made subservient to Divine preferences through our choosing to exercise free will wisely, then not only is external nature not co-operative with human activity, but external nature actually rebels against human desires – and the environmental problems which have become rampant in every part of the world tends to bear witness to this truth.

One can only oppress nature for so long before its own form of insurgency begins. This is as true for internal nature as it is true for external nature, and the insurgency of our internal world is often manifested in the form of spiritual, physical, and psychological problems.

Imam Rauf believes that human beings know what the Divine preferences are. Even given the presence of Divine revelation in sacred books such as the Qur'an, the Gospel of Jesus (peace be upon him), the Torah of Moses (peace be upon him), and the Psalms of David (peace be upon him), I'm not so sure that human beings do know or understand what God's preferences for human beings are.

For example, a great deal of attention is given in the Muslim community to the five pillars of Islam – namely, (1) bearing witness that there is no god but God and that Muhammad is the Messenger of God; (2) saying prayers five times a day at the appointed times; (3) observing the requirements of fasting during the month of Ramazan; (4) giving zakat or charity based on a percentage of one's accumulated wealth, and (5) performing Hajj or pilgrimage to Mecca and surrounding areas at least once in one's life if one is financially and physically able to do so.

All of the foregoing pillars are important activities to keep in mind, and I have no wish to denigrate such practices. Indeed, I find that, by the Grace of Allah, such activities both help to order my life in constructive and valuable ways, as well as to spiritually strengthen me and, thereby, have enabled me to pursue horizons beyond just the five pillars.

The five pillars are part of the deen or method of spirituality, but there is much more to deen than the five pillars – and by this I do not mean to suggest that the rest of deen is about religious law as conceived of by theologians, legal scholars, and the five schools of Muslim jurisprudence. In fact, in many ways, I find Muslim law as traditionally conceived to be not only largely irrelevant to what I believe Divine preferences to be for human beings, but, as well, often constitutes a major set of obstacles in the way of ever realizing such Divine preferences.

219

The Qur'an discusses qualities such as patience, love, gratitude, sincerity, integrity, equality, equitability, righteousness, piety, humility, remembrance, insight, forbearance, forgiveness, harmony, balance, honesty, origins, the structure of human nature, nobility, courage, perseverance, striving, struggle, trust, dependence on Divinity, purifying the carnal soul, stations of the heart, human potential, Grace, wisdom, faith, purpose, models of excellence, identity, healing, reflection, character, ethics, opposition to oppressiveness, and much more. I do not find much consideration of these issues during discussions of Muslim law, and, yet, there is roughly 12 times as much exploration of the foregoing topics in the 6000-plus verses of the Qur'an than there is of the 500, or so, verses concerning issues such as inheritance, marriage, divorce, and other like matters that occupy most of the pages of Muslim legal theory.

Is it important to establish boundaries for matters such as marriage, divorce, and inheritance? Yes, it is, but so is learning to develop moral and spiritual character – qualities which not only transcend traditional approaches to the five pillars as well as Muslim systems of jurisprudence but qualities that actually serve to significantly enhance the quality of life of a community, state, or country.

The Prophet Muhammad (peace be upon him) is reported to have said:

"Shall I not inform you about a better act than fasting, charity, and prayer? ... making peace between one another. Enmity and malice tear up heavenly rewards by the root."

Here is something – namely, making peace -- which is described as being better than three of the pillars of Islam – and, yet, many Muslims tend to judge other Muslims on the basis of the latter's observance, or lack thereof, in relation to the five pillars rather than on the basis of a willingness of individuals to try to bring peace to troubled relationships and community.

Another statement which is attributed to the Prophet Muhammad (peace be upon him) is the following:

"God Almighty is the sustainer of people. Among them God loves best those who are of most benefit to others."

Another saying attributed to the Prophet Muhammad (peace be upon him) is the following:

"The Creation is as God's family, for its sustenance is from God. Therefore, the most beloved of God is the person who does good to God's family."

The Prophet is also reported to have asked and answered:

"Do you love your Creator? Then, love your fellow-beings first."

Declaring Shahadah (bearing witness to God's Oneness and the Prophetic mission of Muhammad – peace be upon him), prayer, fasting, and pilgrimage (four of the five pillars of Islam) may, if God wishes, help the individual, but they do not necessarily help the community or the rest of humankind. Naturally, if such activities enable an individual to become a better person then, indirectly, such personal observances may be of assistance to the community if those activities become catalytic agents for an individual to undertake various forms of community work – but this is not always the case.

Nevertheless, an injunction to strive to benefit other people is not, strictly speaking, one of the five pillars of Islam. To be sure, zakat or charity is a spiritual obligation which does carry direct benefit to the needy of society. However, not only is zakat described in the Qur'an as a way of purifying one's wealth and, therefore, is often pursued by human beings for its capacity to render benefit to the individual who is observing this practice rather than primarily for the manner in which it is intended to distribute wealth to those who are less fortunate, but the unfortunate fact of the matter is that many people

221

seek to satisfy only the minimum conditions of zakat and, as a result, do not seek to struggle with the question of whether, or not, there might be a lot more that could do with one's talents and resources in the way of charitable activity than is required by the letter of the law with respect to this pillar of Islam.

In short, all too many people may be content to observe only minimalist Islam with respect to the issue of charity rather than pursue the spirit of the principles inherent in zakat. Consequently, it is quite possible to comply with this pillar of Islam and still be largely disconnected from being committed to helping to alleviate the needs and problems which exist in a given community.

By emphasizing the five pillars of Islam, the impression is often given – by theologians, imams, mullahs, jurists, and Muslim legal scholars -- that these pillars constitute <u>the</u> deen of Islam. This is only partially true, and what is often entirely missing or de-emphasized in such a reductionistic approach to Islam is the significance of a development of the qualities of character which are every bit as important as – if not more so in certain respects -- the five pillars.

The Prophet Muhammad (peace be upon him) is reported to have said:

"I have been given all the Divine Names, and I have been sent to perfect good conduct."

Good conduct entails more than just the five pillars.

The Prophet was asked:

"Which part of faith is most excellent?" The Prophet was reported to have replied: "A beautiful character."

On another occasion, the Prophet is reported to have stated:

"The most perfect of the faithful in faith is the most beautiful of them character."

The Prophet is also reported to have said:

"Allah has 300 attributes, and he who acquires just one of these for his own character trait will inherit Paradise."

A beautiful character is more than observing the five pillars. A beautiful character is more than observing the five pillars with ihsan or spiritual excellence.

Furthermore, as the saying attributed to the Prophet noted in the last two lines of the paragraph immediately preceding the above paragraph suggests, there may be ways to Paradise, if God wishes, which are quite independent of the five pillars. Indeed, as Shakyh Abd al-Qadr (may Allah be pleased with him) intimated:

"I did not reach Allah by standing up at night, nor by fasting in the day, nor by studying knowledge. I reached Allah by generosity and humility and soundness of heart."

Does a beautiful character arise out of observance of the five pillars? Although this may be the case for some individuals, it is not necessarily the case for everyone.

The Prophet Muhammad is reported to have said:

"Many are there among you who fast and, yet, gain nothing from it except hunger and thirst, and there are many among you who pray throughout the night and, yet, gain nothing except wakefulness."

One might easily extrapolate this warning to the manner in which some people observe the other pillars of Islam.

For some, and, perhaps, for many, the lessons of: humility, gratitude, dependence, love, sincerity, perseverance, honesty, nobility equitability, generosity, integrity, courage, forbearance, forgiveness, and friendliness arise out of engaging the trials and tribulations of life which take place quite independently of the five pillars. The Qur'an indicates:

"Lo! Ritual worship preserves one from lewdness and iniquity, but, verily, remembrance of Allah is more important" (29: 45),

and remembrance of God's Presence according to the multiplicity of Names and Attributes of Divinity through which Divinity interacts with Creation is one of the primary ingredients in the formation of character amidst the trials of life ... trials that God has placed into our lives for just this purpose. Remembrance puts things in perspective.

As the Qur'an informs us:

"We have created life and death that We may try which of you is best in conduct. He is the Mighty, the Forgiving." (67: 2)

And, again, as indicated previously, conduct extends far beyond the five pillars and/or the legalistic prescriptions of this or that school of law.

All of the foregoing discussion about character or akhlaq and the ways in which character cannot necessarily be subsumed under, or neatly reduced, to the five pillars of Islam is intended to be juxtaposed next to Imam Rauf's belief that Muslims know what Divinity's preferences are for humankind. The questions which arise as a result of this sort of juxtaposition is especially pointed when all too many Muslim jurists, mullahs, imams, educators, and legal scholars use undue influence (in mosques, madrassas -- schools, Muslim gatherings, and the media) to re-frame the nature of those preferences and, in many ways, deflect attention away from and/or restrict the interpretation of such Divine preferences to purely legal matters as understood by traditional theories of Muslim law.

Imam Rauf might agree with many of the foregoing points. But, if he does, then this agreement sits in opposition, to some degree, with his contention that Muslims know what Divinity's preferences are for human kind.

Contrary to what Imam Rauf seems to suppose, I feel (based on those with whom I have interacted over some thirty-five years across four continents, as well as based on the books, articles, and lectures by a variety of Muslim authors upon which I have reflected) there seem to be a lot of Muslims who are confused about what the Divine preferences are for humankind. I also believe that a lot of this confusion is due to the misinformation and misunderstanding which is fed to them by so-called religious leaders in a pervasive pattern of spiritual abuse which is oppressively imposed from a very early age – both informally and formally.

The fifth and last principle to be listed by Imam Rauf as basic to any 'globalized' religion through which human beings come to understand the nature of Divine relevancy to humankind concerns the idea that human beings are both responsible and to be held accountable for what is done or not done while journeying through the life of this world. Unfortunately, at least in my opinion, he speaks about accountability in terms of reward and punishment.

I have difficulty reconciling Imam Rauf's earlier emphasis on loving "God with all our heart, mind, soul, and strength" (page 18) with the issue of reward and punishment. In fact, juxtaposing the two together seems something of an oxymoron.

Hazrat Abu Bakr Sadiq said:

"The sign of attachment with the Beloved is detachment from all else."

This "all else" includes matters pertaining to reward and punishment.

A Sufi saying which is appropriate here states:

"The Lover begs of the Beloved nothing but the Beloved. Accursed is the lover who begs of one's Beloved anything except the Beloved."

225

To speak of reward and punishment is really to introduce into any discussion of loving God with all one's being elements which pertain to other than a focus on the Beloved.

The Prophet Muhammad (peace be upon him) alluded to something of a similar nature when he is reported to have said:

"This world is prohibited to the people of the next world, and the next world is prohibited to the people of this world, and they are both forbidden to the people of Allah."

The people of God are those who, among other things, love Divinity independently of all considerations of reward and punishment.

'Ishq is an Arabic word which means ardent, intense love. The word is derived from the term 'ashiqa which refers to a plant that twines itself around another plant or small tree and deprives the latter of the sustenance necessary to develop leaves and fruit. Eventually, the deprived entity dries up, turns yellow, and dies.

Shaykh al-Shibli (may Allah be pleased with him) asks the question: "What is love?" and then answers the question.

"Love is like a cup of fire which blazes terribly ... when it takes root in the senses and settles in the heart, it annihilates."

Love is the 'ashika plant that crawls its way into our hearts and being and cuts one off from that which connects us, and sustains that connection, with the material world. Eventually, the one who is captivated by love dies to one self and to the world and passes away into the condition of fana when one's awareness is overwhelmed by the presence of the Beloved and is dead to everything else.

Love is the forging process which leads to spiritual transformation. The dross material of humanity is placed upon the anvil of life to be pounded by the hammer of experience.

The Divine Blacksmith tempers the dross material by alternately placing that material in spiritual conditions of fire (jalali) and water (jamali) before returning that material to the anvil for further pounding from life experience. And, in the end, if God wishes, the dross material is transformed into something of constructive use which has been purified and fortified to meet "the slings and arrows of outrageous fortune" with integrity and character.

None of the foregoing comments concerning love are meant to deny the realities of Heaven and Hell nor to deny those realities which revolve about the possibility of reward and punishment. However, this latter sort of vernacular really does not have much relevance to the topic of love.

In fact, we have arrived at something of a crossroads which underscores one of the fundamental differences between exoteric and esoteric approaches with respect to trying to understand the nature of Divine preferences for human beings. Exoteric approaches to spirituality (and included in this are most of the Muslim legal systems) tend to be rooted in a carrot and stick approach that emphasizes extrinsic techniques of motivation which work -- oftentimes in awkward, unnatural and oppressive ways -- on the human heart from the outside in, whereas esoteric approaches tend to be rooted in the most essential of intrinsic motivations – namely love -- in which spiritual desire and motivation flow from within in a way that is entirely consistent and synergistically resonant with, as well as nurturing to, our primordial spiritual capacity or fitra.

Paul said in 2 Corithinians 3: 6:

'The letter of the law killeth but the spirit giveth life.'

When I hear Muslims speak proudly about how they believe that Islam is the fastest growing religion in the world, I also think about how, in many ways, Islam is also the fastest dying religion in the world because soon after proclaiming the Shahadah that there is no god but God and Muhammad is the messenger of God, I see many of these newcomers initiated into a system of spiritual abuse in which idols are made of this or that theology or this and that Muslim legal system, as well as this or that traditional form of taqlid (blind obedience).

Taqlid is an Arabic word which is derived from a root that refers to a collar or restraint which is intended to control something – for example, an animal. All too many Muslims are rendered into beasts of burden whose imposed duty is to carry the theological and legal baggage of all too many imams, mullahs, jurists, legal scholars, Muslim leaders, and theologians ... beasts of burden who are threatened with the whip of hell-fire if they do not do as their idol-masters demand while simultaneously being seduced with come hither whisperings and endearments of a Paradise which often has been sadly and pathetically reduced to sexual pleasures even as God is forgotten.

Rather than attempting to delineate the essence of what has been taught by all authentic prophets worldwide and across history in the manner in which Imam Rauf has done on pages 35 and 36 of What's Right With Islam, I would offer the following alternative way of saying things. This way is, I believe, a way which is fully consonant with the spiritual teachings brought by the authentic emissaries of Divinity.

Life is rooted in self-awareness and the awareness of experience. Out of these several forms of awareness arise curiosity and questions concerning the significance of the contents of awareness. These questions revolve around issues of: identity, purpose, meaning, values, suffering, well-being, methods, and truth. In conjunction with these questions various kinds of intentions and choices emerge which begin to engage such themes according to personal predilections. All choices, no matter what they may be, entail struggle and striving. Out of these efforts various kinds of insight, interpretation, reflection, understanding, and judgment emanate in relation to the questions of life and the contents of consciousness. We act on or apply these understandings in emotional, psychological, worldly, or spiritual ways, and what we do will be evaluated ... by ourselves, by others, and by the nature of what is.

All of the foregoing is measured against the degree to which the process of life gives expression to or conforms to the truth, as well as the extent to which justice is done to that truth in relation to each and every facet of our awareness, experience, choice, struggling,

228

understanding, doing, and evaluating. Truth and justice are set by that which is independent of human construction, and it is the task of human existence to merge horizons with such truth and justice according to our capacity to do so. To the extent that one is successful in fully realizing one's capacity for truth and justice, then to this extent does one come to know, love, and worship the nature of Divine relevancy to humankind ... to this extent does one develop character ... to this extent does one come to know, if God wishes, the Hidden Treasure which Divinity loved to be known ... to this extent does one fulfill one's spiritual destiny.

Toward the latter part of Chapter One in What's Right With Islam, Imam Rauf titles the final section of that chapter in the following way: 'Jews and Christians: Siblings On The Block'. Imam Rauf cites a Quranic verse which informs Muslims that they should "not argue with the People of the Book except in the best way" (2: 62) When reading this verse, I am struck by the thought – as I am sure many Jews and Christians are struck by the thought – that suicide bombings probably don't capture the essence of what Divine guidance is getting at here.

A little further down the page Imam Rauf states with respect to the relationship among, on the one hand, Jews and Christians, and, on the other hand, Muslims the following:

"Disagreement between them certainly exists, but all disagreements are no more than family disputes".

While reading this I was struck by the idea – as I am sure many other Muslims are struck – that reducing Lebanon, Palestine, and Iraq to rubble while killing, maiming, and torturing tens of thousands of the inhabitants of these countries appears to be something more than a "family feud", "disagreement" or some other well-chosen euphemism. Imam Rauf must have attended the same school as did those who came up with the terms of "collateral damage" and "extreme rendition" as civilized ways of talking about murder, kidnapping, and torture.

Toward the bottom of page 37 of <u>What's Right With Islam</u> Imam Rauf says:

"The Quran did criticize the Jews for failure to uphold the Torah (5: 68-70) for excessive legalism and exaggerated authoritarianism by some of the rabbis (3: 50, 5: 66-68) and for nationalizing monothesism (2: 111)."

However, what Imam Rauf does not state is how Muslims should be criticized for failing to uphold the revealed scriptures which were given to them, or for the excessive legalism and exaggerated authoritarianism of various imams, mullahs, theologians, leaders, and jurists, or for the way in which Saudi Arabia, Afghanistan, Pakistan, Kuwait, Iran, and other Muslim localities have sought to nationalize Islamic monotheism ... and similar things could be said in criticism of Christians for committing precisely the same kinds of error.

On page 39 of <u>What's Right With Islam</u>, Imam Rauf indicates that the Qur'an praises Christians in various ways and declares Christians closest to Muslims because of "their warm practice of neighborly love." I'm sure that all the peoples in Central America, South America, the Middle East, Africa, Vietnam and the rest of Asia who have been oppressed and exploited by imperialistic, colonialistic, and capitalistic strains of Christianity across history – including today -- would fully concur with the foregoing.

Every spiritual, economic, political, and philosophical tradition is populated by both Cains and Ables. The Ables of the world – whether they be Muslim, Jewish, Christian, Buddhist, Hindu, Jain, Taoist, Aborigine, Maori, some form of indigenous spirituality from the Western Hemisphere, or humanists – they try to observe a "warm practice of neighborly love" to one another – even to the Cains ... whereas the Cains of the world – whether they be so-called Muslim, Jewish, Christian, humanist, and so on – tend not to observe a "warm practice of neighborly love" to anyone, including themselves.

According to Imam Rauf, we – Jews, Muslims, and Christians – are basically:

"All right as long as we believe in the one God, try to love God as best we can, and make our best effort in treating humanity humanely."

And, this is so he believes in spite of whatever mistakes we may have made in our understanding of Divinity and in our practical observance of such understanding.

The problem with the foregoing is that we continue to make mistakes with respect to the nature of Divinity, what it means to love God, or how to treat humanity humanely. Consequently, things are not all right, and events around the world are screaming this at the top of their lungs ... events for which Muslims, Jews, Christians, Hindus, Buddhists, the practitioners of many other spiritual traditions, and humanists bear the fullest of responsibility.

The Prophet Muhammad (peace be upon him) is reported to have asked the people with him:

"What actions are most excellent?" And, then, he is reported to have provided the following answer: "To gladden the heart of a human being; to feed the hungry; to help the afflicted; to lighten the sorrow of the sorrowful, and to remove the wrongs of the injured."

There is nothing in the foregoing saying which is restricted in its scope with respect to humankind. These actions are most excellent no matter who performs them and no matter in relation to whom they are performed.

13.) My Year Inside Radical Islam: A Critique

Several years ago I read the book <u>My Year Inside Radical Islam</u> by Daveed Gartenstein-Ross. While reading the book, a number of thoughts and emotions bubbled to the surface, among which were a certain sense of resonance with various facets of the author's experiences, as well as a sense of empathy for him because of his worries that he might be assassinated by some radicalized, fundamentalist, self-appointed, presumptuous 'agent' of an invented theology who believed that if anyone became Muslim, and then moved on to some other faith system, such an apostate must be killed. On the other hand, I also found myself in disagreement with a number of the author's ideas and some of his conclusions.

Once I finished the book, I had intended to write something, but the project kept being put on a back burner as other contingencies of life took on more immediate importance. However, now the original intention has been taken off the back burner and moved to a front burner where an analytical stew is being simmered in the form of the present essay.

Earlier, when I indicated that I felt a certain resonance with some of Mr. Gartenstein-Ross's experiences that had been described within the aforementioned book I did not mean to suggest I have spent time inside any sort of radical, fundamentalist Muslim group. Nonetheless, during various situations and circumstances, I have come in contact with such individuals along the path of my own spiritual journey, and I am familiar, to some extent, with the mind and heart-set of such people.

I always have felt very uncomfortable with those sorts of individuals, and there are many reasons for this sense of discomfort. For example, some of those people are quite ignorant about the nature of Islam, and when one couples such ignorance with an arrogance which is unwilling to entertain the possibility that maybe they don't know as much or understand as much about Islam as they suppose is the case, the result has truly frightening implications ... both for them as well as for others.

As problematic as this kind of ignorance and arrogance may be, what is even more worrisome is the inclination of such people to feel entitled to impose their views on other human beings ... whether these latter unfortunates are Muslim or non-Muslim. These self-proclaimed true-believers imagine themselves to be God's gift to humanity and, as such, they operate in accordance with a delusion which maintains that Divinity has assigned them the mission to cleanse humanity of its spiritual impurities.

I have met this kind of individual in the Muslim community. I have met such people in the Christian community. I have met similar people in the Jewish community. In addition, I have met such people in other communities as well. Apparently, ignorance, arrogance, and presumption know no community boundaries.

On the other hand, I also have met some wonderful, sincere, rigorous, compassionate, loving, considerate, kind, generous, and courageous seekers of truth in all of the foregoing communities. Such qualities are not the province of any one faith but are manifested in the lives of those who have been blessed with grace irrespective of the formal character of the spiritual path out of which they may operate.

It is a person's personal relationship with God or a person's personal relationship with the Reality which makes everything possible that matters ... not any theology. What matters is our heart and soul realized connection to the truth which lies at the center of our being and not the theological concepts and terms through which one wishes to label that truth.

In fact, more often than not, theology merely serves as a lens which introduces distortion into spiritual dynamics, and theology, more often than not, gives expression to a paradigm which filters out anything which is inconsistent with itself. In the end such paradigmatic filters frequently miss the truth as we become preoccupied with viewing life in terms of what we theologically project onto life rather than what Being has to reveal to us on its own terms ... if we would just be willing to listen to what it has to offer free from the chattering, accusations, and machinations of our ego-driven theologies.

Having said the foregoing by way of preface, the plan for the remainder of this essay is as follows: Since Daveed Gartenstein-Ross' book My Year Inside Radical Islam consists largely of a series of observations, reflections, insights, and reactions to what went on during his life in the period covered by the time-frame of the book, my plan is to do something similar. More specifically, within the framework of the present essay, I intend to put forth an array of observations, reflections, reactions, and, possibly, insights with respect to the time I spent inside of the aforementioned book ... some of these thoughts and feelings will be more developed than others.

****

By way of a very brief overview, the book entitled My Year Inside Radical Islam describes a journey which starts in Ashland, Oregon where Daveed Gartenstein-Ross grew up as the son of parents who were nominally Jewish yet who had become dissatisfied with various aspects of the Jewish faith and, as a result, went in search of a ecumenical approach to spiritual issues. Although, from time to time, a little more is said in the book about his relationship with his parents, most of My Year Inside Radical Islam provides an account of how he came into contact with Islam, followed by a detailed description of how he became involved with a group of fundamentalist Muslims, and, then an account of how and why he left Islam and made a decision to become Christian.

The purpose of this essay is not to find fault with Mr. Gartenstein-Ross's decision to become Christian. Such a decision is between God and him, and, quite frankly, I have absolutely no idea how God views such a decision.

Mr. Gartenstein-Ross made choices based on his circumstances, his understanding, and his needs at the time his decisions were made. During the present essay, I will have some things to say about various aspects of his understanding concerning different issues, but the rest is not my business.

****

On page 6 of My Year Inside Radical Islam Mr. Gartenstein-Ross mentions a book by a Christian author Josh McDowell and says:

"McDowell discussed at length C.S. Lewis' claim that there were three possible things Jesus could have been: a liar, a lunatic, or the Lord …. This is because Jesus claimed to be God in the New Testament."

As is the case with many theological meanderings, certain possibilities have been left out of the foregoing set of choices. For instance, maybe, Jesus (peace be upon him) is neither a liar, nor a lunatic, nor the Lord, but, instead, individuals – such as Lewis -- have interpreted the New Testament in accordance with the requirements of their own (i.e., Lewis') theology.

To the best of my knowledge, Jesus (peace be upon him) never claimed in the New Testament to be the Lord. What he is reported to have said in John 10, verse 30, is that:

"I and the Father are one."

However, almost every form of mysticism – not just Christianity -- touches upon this issue of oneness which seeks to reconcile our usual perceptions of multiplicity with the idea that, according to the mystics of just about every faith tradition, creation and Creator are joined together in a 'unity' in some sense which is difficult to delineate. What the nature of this unity involves is a mystery … except to those to whom the secret has been disclosed.

To say that creation is other than Divinity is to give expression to the idea that something apart from God exists, whereas to say that creation is the Creator reduces things down to some form of pantheism in which anyone or anything – not just Jesus [peace be upon him] -- may make the claim that 'I and the Father are one'.

The truth to which mystics allude is more complex and subtle than either some manner of dualism or some form of pantheism. In a sense all of creation is one with Divinity, but, simultaneously, Divinity transcends all of creation. Creation is dependent on Divinity, but Divinity – aside from the purposes inherent in creation – is quite

236

independent of creation.

When Jesus (peace be upon him) taught people to pray, he is reported to have begun with:

"Our Father in heaven hallowed be Thy name [John 6: verse 9].

Jesus (peace be upon him) did not say "Jesus' Father in heaven".

Rather, Jesus (peace be upon him) made it clear that, as creation, everyone had the same kind of connection with the One Who brought forth creation and, as such, God was the 'father' of all being, not just Jesus.

Furthermore, in Mathew 19:17, Mark 10:18, and Luke 18:19, Jesus (peace be upon him) is reported to have said variations upon the following teaching theme:

"Why callest me good? God alone is good."

A distinction is being made between God and creation. Whatever goodness we have – even that of Jesus (peace be upon him) or Moses (peace be upon him) or Muhammad (peace be upon him) -- is borrowed and derivative from Divinity.

Earlier in his book, Mr. Gartenstein-Ross echoes the foregoing when he says:

"I rejected the Christian idea that Jesus had been God; no matter how deep a person's spiritual insight, there's a fundamental difference between the Creator and his creation."

I agree with Mr. Gartenstein-Ross on this issue.

However, the point of the foregoing discussion is not meant to be a

237

critical exegesis of certain Christian beliefs as much as it is an attempt to point toward the fact that all of us stand in the middle of the vastness of mysterious Being and try, as best we can, to make sense out of what we encounter. Some of our attempts may be better than others, but it is not human beings who are the measure of truth, but, rather, it is truth which is the measure of human beings.

C.S. Lewis stood within the vastness of being and claimed that everything could be reduced down to one of three possibilities concerning the alleged claim of Jesus (peace be upon him) to be God, the Lord. Either Jesus (peace be upon him) was a liar, or he was a madman, or he was, indeed, God. Apparently, Lewis didn't consider it worthwhile to examine either the possibility that, perhaps, Jesus (peace be upon him) didn't mean what Lewis believed him to mean when Jesus (peace be upon him) said what he is reported to have said [i.e., that I and the Father are one], nor did Lewis appear to examine the possibility that, maybe, Jesus (peace be upon him) didn't claim what some people have attributed to him.

In this latter regard, there is a very interesting book by Bart D. Ehrman entitled: Misquoting Jesus. Ehrman began his spiritual explorations very much in lock-step with the sort of literalist fundamentalism which is taught at many Bible colleges in the United States, but as a result of some very rigorous exploration into the history of Biblical transcription and translation, Ehrman underwent tremendous transformations in his perspective concerning the nature of the New Testament.

Despite his findings, Bart Ehrman remains a very committed Christian. Nonetheless, Ehrman's aforementioned book takes the reader through a litany of hermeneutical problems concerning the reliability of, and inconsistencies among, the texts given expression through, among other things, the first four books of the New Testament.

I do not say the foregoing in order to try to cast doubt upon Christianity. Indeed, I do not believe such is the intent of Ehrman's book for, as indicated above, he remains, in his own way, a believer in, and follower of, Jesus (peace be upon him).

In any case, I am not the one who will sit in judgment of people either in this world or the next concerning their spiritual beliefs and actions. Rather, I, like others, am one of the ones who will be judged for my deeds and misdeeds ... my true beliefs and my false beliefs.

There are those, however, who would try to argue that by merely raising questions concerning the reliability or accuracy of certain textual sources – as Bart Ehrman does in his book <u>Misquoting Jesus</u> -- one is something of an apostate and, therefore, one is not deserving of the moniker: 'Christian'. Similar absurdities take place within both the Muslim and Jewish communities.

Indeed, there are many so-called religious leaders of all manner of theological persuasions who would have everyone believe that the truth comes directly from God's lips to their ears. Moreover, such spiritual luminaries would seek to imbue people with the working principle that to disobey such individuals is tantamount to disobeying God and, consequently, that the wrath of God will descend on all who would deviate from the 'teachings' of these self-appointed spokespeople of God.

Daveed Gartenstein-Ross writes in <u>My Year Inside Radical Islam</u> that it was the dogmatic force through which some Christian fundamentalists sought to impose on him their ideas about God and, in the process, seemed intent on creating a sense of inferiority in the author's own ideas concerning God and Jesus (peace be upon him) that actually moved the author a little further down the road toward becoming involved with the Muslim community. And, ironically, it was also this same kind of dogmatic intransigence on the part of the Muslim community with which he was involved that helped move him along a path away from that community and toward Christianity.

Mr. Gartenstein-Ross first encountered a Muslim and Islam while attending Wake Forest University in North Carolina. This Muslim encounter was in the form of al-Husein Madhany who was of South Asian ancestry and had been born in Kenya. Initially, the relationship between the two of them revolved around political issues concerning campus life as well as issues that overlapped with, but extended beyond, the horizons of the university.

Little by little, Mr. Gartenstein-Ross leaned about his friend's beliefs concerning Islam. According to the author, some of the things

239

he learned were that:

"The Qur'an is God's direct, literal word. I was also interested to learn that Muslims believe that the Old and New Testaments are earlier holy books inspired by God – but those books became corrupted over time and are no longer completely reliable." (page 18 of <u>My Year Inside Radical Islam</u>)

There are a few problems inherent in the foregoing 'learning'.

For example, what does it mean to say that the Qur'an is God's direct, literal word? It is literal in what sense or direct in what sense? In what sense can one say that the Qur'an is the word of God?

To be sure, on one level the Qur'an is manifested in the Arabic language. However, it would be a mistake to try to reduce the Qur'an down to merely language.

The Qur'an is infused with the baraka or Grace of God. Words may be the portals through which one encounters such Divine baraka, but the baraka is quite independent of the words, and, in fact, this is why some people can read the words of the Qur'an and, yet, derive no spiritual benefit because all they have engaged is language while remaining untouched by the Divine baraka associated with those words.

As far as the Qur'an being the literal word of God is concerned, I'm not really sure what this would mean. Of course, there are those who would wish to make their literalistic interpretations of the Qur'an be what they claim is meant by the literal word of God, but I also know from the reported words of the Prophet Muhammad (peace be upon him) that:

"The Qur'an has an outward and an inward dimension, and the latter has its own inward dimension, and so on, up to seven dimensions."

In addition, the Prophet Muhammad (peace be upon him) is reported to have said that:

240

"All of the Revealed Books are contained in the Qur'an. And the meaning of the Qur'an is contained within surah al-Fatiha [that is, the opening chapter of the Qur'an]. And, the meaning of surah al-Fatiha is contained in Bismillah ir-Rahaman ir-Raheem [that is, in the Name of Allah, the Compassionate, the Merciful], and the meaning of Bismillah ir-Rahman ir-Raheem is contained in Bismillah [that is, in the Name of], and the meaning of Bismillah is contained in the dot beneath bey [that is the Arabic letter with which Bismillah begins]."

So, what is meant by the literal word of God in all of this? There are literalist understandings of God's meaning, but God's meanings transcend all such understandings even if some -- but by no means all -- of those literal understandings may, within certain limits, give expression to part of the truth.

We may engage God's guidance through the language of the Qur'an. However, God willing, eventually understanding goes beyond mere words and gives expression to the light of God which illuminates faith, the heart, the spirit, and the entire soul of an individual.

Aside from the foregoing considerations, I would also take exception with the author of My Year Inside Radical Islam when he says in the excerpt quoted previously that "Muslims believe that the Old and New Testaments are earlier holy books inspired by God." To begin with, revelation and inspiration are two different phenomena.

God did not inspire Muhammad (peace be upon him) to write the Qur'an. Rather, the Qur'an was Divine guidance that descended upon the heart of the Prophet and which he was commanded to recite to others in the manner in which it had been revealed to the Prophet.

Artists are inspired. Song writers are inspired. Poets are inspired. And according to the nature of their God-given talents and life experience, they translate the divinely bestowed inspiration into a visible form ... such as paintings, songs, and poetry.

Revelation is Divine guidance which is disclosed to special individuals who are the recipients of such guidance and are known as a Rasul or one who proclaims to others the received revelation. These messengers do not transform the revelation as artists do with respect

241

to inspiration, but, rather, the task of a Rasul is to relate to others the linguistic form of the revelation precisely as it was bestowed upon such an individual.

Furthermore, while some Muslims may believe, as Mr. Gartenstein-Ross claims in the quote given earlier, that the Old and New Testaments are earlier Holy books inspired by God, this may be a very problematic, if not overly-simplistic, way of looking at such matters. What is referred to as the Bible is largely a human construction which contains remnants, here and there, of what had been revealed to earlier messengers.

The books of the Old Testament and the New Testament represent choices made by human beings concerning what they believed to be authentic spiritual scripture. Over the years, different books have been included in the Bible, and, as well, various books have been taken out of what is called the Bible because the latter books were considered, rightly or wrongly, to be apocryphal with respect to Divine guidance.

As my shaykh once said to me, with respect to the Book of Revelations, "There is truth there if one knows how to look." So, too, with certain other portions of the Bible, both in relation to the New and Old Testaments ... there is truth there if one knows how to look, but the corruptions which have entered into the historical process of translating, transcribing, interpreting, and compiling the various books of the Bible -- while excluding various other books that some claim to possess spiritual authority -- have made differentiating the true wheat from the false chaff a very difficult process.

To give but one example of the complexities which enter into such matters, consider the writings of St. Paul that are included in the New Testament. Whatever truths and spiritual inspiration may be contained in the letters of St. Paul, those letters are not revelation. Those letters are not the spiritual equivalent of the Divine revelation which was given to Jesus (peace be upon him), and St. Paul is not the spiritual equal of Jesus (peace be upon him).

St. Paul's letters give expression to his understanding of spiritual matters. There may be many truths contained in the text of his epistles, but while such truths might resonate with certain aspects of

242

the teachings of the Gospel of Jesus (peace be upon him), the teachings of St. Paul cannot necessarily be considered to be coextensive with the teachings of the revelation given to Jesus (peace be upon him).

Different strains of Christianity have developed their own style of hermeneutically engaging such theological issues. While there are many themes and principles on which such different strains of Christianity might agree, there are also many themes with which they have differed and over which blood has been spilled.

Similarly, there are many themes and principles upon which Muslims and Christians might agree, but, unfortunately, there also are some themes and principles over which differences have arisen. As a result, blood has been spilled in all directions.

People – whether Muslims, Christians, or Jews ... or anyone else for that matter – who believe they have the right to play God and not only serve as arbiters of truth but, as well, to serve as judge, jury and executioner on behalf of God with respect to the identity of such truth may not have as firm a grasp of the nature of Divine Guidance as they believe. Anybody who believes that God is in need of human beings to spill blood to serve Divine purposes may want to meditate a little more deeply and longer on Who and What God is and who and what human beings are.

All that has been said in conjunction with the foregoing comments concerning St. Paul and Jesus (peace be upon him) can also be applied to any number of Muslim theologians, philosophers, scientists, theoreticians, and leaders. Irrespective of whatever truths may, or may not, be contained in their writings, what such people wrote is not the Qur'an, and those people are not the spiritual equals of the Prophet Muhammad (peace be upon him) ... even though many of these same individuals would like to induce others to believe that the so-called "experts" – often self-appointed -- have somehow been authorized to speak for God and/or the Prophet Muhammad (peace be upon him).

Confusion has been let loose across the surface of the Earth. The lesser is conflated with the greater; the counterfeit mingles with the real, and that which is false is treated as being synonymous with that which is true.

243

On page 25 of <u>My Year Inside Radical Islam</u>, Mr. Gartenstein-Ross briefly discusses the part of Houston Smith's book <u>The World Religions</u> that examines Islam. One of the quotes drawn from the latter book has to do with Houston Smith's belief that the Qur'an "does not counsel turning the other cheek, or pacifism." Without appropriate qualifications, the quote from Professor Smith is not correct.

Throughout the Qur'an one is enjoined to have patience, to do righteousness, and not transgress beyond boundaries of propriety.

For example, in Surah 103, one finds the following:

"By the declining day, indeed human beings are in a state of loss except such as have faith and do righteous deeds, and join in the mutual teaching of the truth and of patience and constancy."

Moreover, in Surah 5, verse 8, God provides this guidance:

"O ye who believe! Be steadfast witnesses for Allah with respect to fair dealing and let not the hatred of others seduce you away from doing justice. Be just: that is nearest to Piety. Remain conscious of God, verily God is aware of all that you do."

Elsewhere in the Qur'an, one finds:

"The blame is only against those who oppress human beings with wrong-doing and insolently transgress beyond bounds through the land defying right and justice." [The Qur'an 42:42]

And, finally:

"[But whatever they may say or do] repel the evil [which they commit] with that which is better." (Qur'an, 23:96)

There are many other passages in the Qur'an beside the foregoing ones which speak about the importance of exhibiting patience in the face of adversity, doing justice, not transgressing proscribed boundaries of behaviour and approaching life through understanding and insight. In addition, the Prophet Muhammad (peace be upon him) is reported to have said:

"The right and the left are both ways of error, and the straight path is the middle way."

Sometimes pacifism is warranted, and sometimes it is not. Life is nuanced, subtle, complex, and apparently intended by God to be a considerable challenge to all who encounter it.

One principle – such as pacifism -- does not necessarily fit all situations. Rather, the guidance of the Qur'an gives expression to an array of spiritual principles which can be combined in different ways in order to resolve problems.

Consequently, to say as Houston Smith does in his book that the Qur'an "does not counsel turning the other cheek" is incomplete, and, as such, inaccurate. Sometimes turning one's cheek is the best recourse, and in such circumstances one should be governed by patience and restraint.

On other occasions, justice and equity may require one to defend against oppression in other ways, but these other ways do not necessarily entail using force or violence. For instance, the Prophet Muhammad (peace be upon him) is reported to have said that:

"One performs the best kind of jihad or spiritual struggle when one stands up and speaks out against injustice in the face of tyranny and oppression."

At one point in <u>My Year Inside Radical Islam</u>, Mr. Gartenstein-Ross talks about how he became Muslim. This occurred before coming in contact with a radicalized fundamentalist group in Ashland,

Oregon.

His Muslim friend from Wake Forest, al-Husein, had told the author about a Naqshbandi group in Italy [this is a reference to a group which, correctly or not, traces its spiritual lineage to a Sufi group known as the Naqshbandi silsilah]. Therefore, when Mr. Gartenstein-Ross was in Venice, he contacted the group.

While visiting with this group in Italy, certain events went on which led the author to inquire about becoming Muslim. The author was told by one of the members of the group that he would have to say the Shahadah, or declaration of faith, in public before two witnesses.

Actually, neither the public part nor the two witnesses issue is a necessary requirement for becoming Muslim. In the Qur'an it says:

"The one whose breast God has expanded unto Islam enjoys a light from one's Lord." (39:22)

Everything begins with baraka. Through baraka, intention becomes inclined toward declaring one's commit to the principle that there is no god but Allah – that is, the God – which is the literal meaning of al (the) lah (God).

Public declaration does not make one a Muslim. Two witnesses do not make one a Muslim.

God's Grace opens one's heart – or, at least, that part of the heart which is referred to as the 'breast' – to the possibility of Islam. One is called to Islam, and, then one has the choice of responding to the Divine overture or rejecting that invitation.

Some people argue that the formal ceremony conducted by the Prophet Muhammad (peace be upon him) at Hudaybiyah in which Muslims were asked to swear their allegiance to the Prophet constitutes the form on which the public declaration of faith is based. However, most, if not all of the individuals who took part in this ceremony already were Muslims, and, furthermore, as the Qur'an indicates:

"Those who swear allegiance to you [Muhammad] swear allegiance, in truth, to God. God's hand is above their hands. So whoever breaks one's oath breaks it only to the hurt of one's own soul."

Becoming Muslim is not a contract between the individual and the Muslim community. Becoming Muslim is an expression of the transition which has taken place with respect to an individual's relationship with God.

The transition has taken place in the privacy of one's heart. God is the witness to that transition. Indeed, God is the One Who has made such a transition possible.

I remember the process of my becoming Muslim. Through a complex set of circumstances, I had been introduced to the person who would, eventually, become my shaykh (the term "shaykh" is often used in conjunction with someone who has been properly authorized to serve as another individual's spiritual guide … although it should be noted that the word "shaykh" also may be used in other non-mystical contexts and, as such, tends to refer to someone who is accepted as a leader in some sense of this term).

Per the request of the shaykh, someone from the shaykh's circle had talked to me about the basic teachings of Islam. For two or three hours, I just sat and listened to what was being said.

At the time, what was important to me was what was being said, not who was saying it (whom I really didn't know) or how it was being said. For me, truth had entered into the chambers of my heart, and I was moved by what struck me as the truth which was flowing through whatever words were being spoken.

After the session, I was asked what I thought about things and whether I wanted to speak with the shaykh. I indicated that I had liked what I had heard, and, yes, I would like to meet the shaykh.

A meeting was arranged. As I recall, the first time I met my future shaykh was at his apartment where I was invited to eat with his family. After the meal and some discussion, a further meeting was arranged.

The next meeting took place at a local mosque. It was Christmas

247

Eve in the Christian world, and it was one of the nights of Ramadan in the Muslim world.

It was during the last ten days of the month of fasting, and some of the initiates of the shaykh were staying at the mosque during this ten-day period. I was introduced to one of them, and, then the shaykh took me to a space in the middle of the mosque and taught me how to say a dhikr or special chant.

At the time, I wasn't fasting, or saying prayers, or doing any of the other basic pillars of Islam, and, moreover, I had made no public declarations in front of witnesses. Yet, almost immediately upon beginning to say the dhikr, I underwent an opening of sorts.

After that evening, I began to spend more and more time with the shaykh and his circle. I attended the Thursday evening sessions and was invited to all of the spiritual anniversaries of the passing away of different great shaykhs within the Chishti Order of Sufis (one of the major spiritual lineages).

From time to time, there were people who were initiated into the Order, and these often were done during one of the celebrations. I began to feel that because I had not been initiated in any public way that I was not worthy of being a member of the Sufi circle, and, if truth be known, I probably wasn't worthy, but that is another story.

Eventually, after a year or so, my shaykh told me that I was to be initiated during our group's observance of the anniversary, or date of passing away from this world, of my shaykh's own spiritual guide. I told him about my concerns and fears that, perhaps, I was never going to be initiated.

He smiled and said: "I have always considered you part of the group. What is about to take place was just a formal way of acknowledging what already is the case".

****

Daveed Gartenstein-Ross's initial encounter with fundamentalists occurred in his hometown (Ashland) in Oregon. He had invited his friend, al-Hussein, to visit with him in Ashland and to meet his parents.

During this visit, Daveed and al-Husein discovered the existence of a mosque in the city. The two of them attended the Friday noon-day prayers.

The sermon or khutbah which is delivered prior to the actual ritual prayers was given by a Saudi who was living in northern California. This individual talked about the alleged duty of Muslims to immigrate to a country ruled by Muslims. More specifically, according to the speaker's perspective:

"The Holy Qur'an says: 'Verily, those who believed, and emigrated and strove hard and fought with their property and their lives in the cause of Allah, as well as those who give asylum and help – these are allies to one another. And to those who believed but did not emigrate, you owe no duty of protection to them until they emigrate.' So as Muslims we too must emigrate. We are living in the land ruled by the kufur [unbelievers]. This is not the way of Muhammad, he said."

Prior to hijra, or emigration, the Prophet lived for 13 years among the unbelievers. He emigrated to Yathrib, later known as Medina, because a plot to assassinate him had been uncovered by the Muslims and, therefore, staying in Mecca was no longer a viable option. In other words, the Prophet did not leave Mecca because it was a land ruled by unbelievers, but, instead, the Prophet left because he had run out of options with respect to being able to live safely in that city.

Initially, there were only two who emigrated to Yathrib – namely, Hazrat Abu Bakr Siddiq (may Allah be pleased with him) and the Prophet. All the other Muslim residents of Mecca stayed behind.

Gradually, over time, more Muslims from Mecca emigrated to Yathrib. However, there were other Muslims that were experiencing financial or life circumstances which prevented them from being able to emigrate.

The only permission which the Prophet had received from God to engage in fighting was for purely defensive purposes. To say that the Prophet was not under any obligation to protect the believers who remained behind in Mecca until they emigrated did not establish a precedent with respect to the need of Muslims to emigrate but, rather, was a reflection of the Divine permissions concerning rules of engagement with the non-believers which had been established by God.

If the believers in Mecca emigrated, then, those individuals could be defensively protected if the Muslims happened to be attacked. However, as long as the believers remained in Mecca, then, the Prophet did not have any Divine authorization and concomitant duty or obligation to attack Mecca in order to protect the believers who were continuing to live there.

According to Mr. Gartenstein-Ross, the Saudi speaker went on to say:

"Prophet Muhammad [upon him be blessings and peace] described the risks of living among the kufur. Our beloved Prophet said: "Anybody who meets, gathers together, lives, and stays with a Mushrik -- a polytheist or disbeliever in the oneness of Allah – and agrees to his ways and opinions and enjoys living with him, then he is like the Mushrik." So when you live among the kufur, and act like the kufur, and like to live with the kufur, then, brothers, you may become just like the kufur. If you do not take the duty of emigration seriously, your faith is in danger."

There are many problems with how the Saudi speaker is interpreting things in the foregoing quote. First of all, there is a difference between, on the one hand, outlining the nature of certain risks of living about people who are unbelievers and, on the other hand, trying to claim that such risks imply a duty to emigrate.

The Prophet never said that people have a duty to emigrate. He said that if people lived among unbelievers and came to agree with their opinions and their ways of living, then, obviously, one runs the risk of becoming like such people.

The Prophet lived with unbelievers for 13 years and, by the Grace of Allah, did not come to agree with their opinions about things or agree with their ways of living or enjoy living in their midst. Other Muslims, by God's Grace, were able to manage this as well.

Were there risks involved in such arrangements? Yes, there were, but Muslims did not become unbelievers merely by living among the unbelievers.

The Prophet was warning Muslims against opening themselves up to the opinions and ways of the unbelievers to such an extent that one not only came to agree with those ways of believing and doing things but enjoyed doing so. When one did this, then one's faith was at risk.

Warning people about risks to their faith is one thing. Saying that one has a duty to emigrate because of such risks is quite another thing … something foreign which is being added to, or projected onto, what the Prophet actually said.

The process of twisting the Qur'an and the sayings of the Prophet to lend support to ideas which were never being espoused by the Qur'an or the Prophet is a trademark tactic of the very sorts of people with whom Mr. Gartenstein-Ross began to become involved when he visited the mosque in Ashland, Oregon. Such teachings sow the seeds of ignorance and arrogance which have decimated the landscape of many Muslim and non-Muslim communities around the world – even in Saudi Arabia from which the person giving the Friday sermon came.

The irony of all this is that such would-be saviors of the Muslim community are actually among the very forces which place a sincere Muslim's faith at risk. If one emigrates toward such individuals and comes to agree with their opinions and their way of doing things and enjoys living with them, then one stands a very good chance of losing whatever legitimate faith one might have had.

To his credit, Daveed Gartenstein-Ross didn't necessarily accept the concepts being espoused by the Saudi speaker. However, Mr. Gartenstein-Ross also admitted that he had no reliable understanding of Islam through which to combat those ideas.

Initially, he was able to keep his distance from the undertow of such a theological maelstrom. However, in time, he found himself being pulled under by the currents emanating out from such a perspective.

I know just how seductive and powerful those currents can be for I have encountered them on a variety of occasions within the Muslim community. Fortunately, at the time of the encounters I had a Sufi shaykh who -- because of, by the Grace of God, his tremendous insight and understanding of Islam -- could explain to me in considerable detail the numerous logical, doctrinal, and historical defects contained within the structure of the theological arguments of such people. I was never left unsatisfied by the explanations I was given by my shaykh concerning such matters.

****

On pages 51-52 of <u>My Year Inside Radical Islam</u>, Daveed Gartenstein-Ross describes how the Muslim activities in Ashland, Oregon were being subsidized by a Saudi Arabian charitable institution known as al-Haramain Islamic Foundation. One of the proposed programs of the Muslim group in Ashland was called the 'Medina Project'.

According to the leader of the Ashland Muslim group, the idea at the heart of the Medina Project involved building an Islamic village in the United States. More specifically:

"The village would be run by sharia to the extent that U.S. laws allowed. While there wouldn't be any beheadings and amputations, the women would be veiled, pork would be banned, and so would alcohol."

Almost everywhere one hears 'sharia'ah, sharia'ah, shari'ah' from the lips of Muslim fundamentalists, mullahs, imams, theologians, and would-be revolutionaries. Yet, rather ironically, the Qur'an apparently mentions the term shari'ah just once.

In Surah 45, verse 18 one finds:

"O Prophet, We have put you on the Right Way (Shari'ah) concerning the religion, so follow it, and do not yield to the desires of ignorant people;"

All of the fundamentalists assume they know what the 'right way' is even as they engage one another in hostilities so that they may gain control and impose their own interpretations and theories concerning the precise nature of that 'right way'. Furthermore, such individuals also seem to assume they have God's permission to impose that way on just about anyone they like.

As far as the first assumption is concerned, everyone has the right to form his or her opinion – whether such opinions be correct or incorrect -- concerning what one believes the nature and purpose of one's relationship with God to be. However, as far as the second assumption is concerned – that is, the presumed right to impose their opinions on others -- I do not believe such individuals can point to any aspect of the Qur'an which indisputably demonstrates that God has arrogated to them the right to impose their opinions concerning spirituality or life upon others. In fact, even with respect to the Prophet, the Qur'an indicates:

"The guiding of them is not thy duty (O Muhammad), but Allah guideth whom He will." [Qur'an 2: 272).

The actual etymology of the verb 'shari'ah' is related to a process of traveling -- or being led -- toward, finding and drinking from, a place which contains water. So, the questions are: What is the nature of the path/way? What is the nature of leading? What is the nature of water? What is the nature of the drinking? Finally, do the answers to any of the foregoing questions provide evidence in support of the idea that shari'ah is meant to indicate a process that is to be imposed upon people in the sense of a code of law or conduct to which everyone must adhere and for which any wavering from that path should be met with the force of a body of social/public law that is considered to be the guardian and protector against such a 'way/path' being corrupted, undermined, compromised or not obeyed?

I find it strange that a term – namely, shari'ah -- which, as far as I can determine, is used only once in the Qur'an should have been propelled into the pre-eminent status it not only currently assumes in many discussions but which it has 'enjoyed' for hundreds of years in the Muslim community – at least within circles of jurisprudence, fatwa, qazis, muftis, imams, and books of fiqh (supposedly concerned with determining actions which are based on, and derived from, shari'ah).

Moreover, if one peruses the Qur'an in search of the 'right way', one finds a multiplicity of Arabic words (for example, deen, tariqa, sirat-ul mustaqueem, taqwa, and so on). Unfortunately, all of these terms are taken by many, if not most, fundamentalists and reduced down to just one way of thinking and understanding – that is, in a legalistic/legislative sense -- yet none of these terms should necessarily be construed in such a narrowly conceived, reductionistic fashion.

The Qur'an does not refer to itself as a book of jurisprudence but as a book of guidance, wisdom, and discernment. Yet, there has been a centuries-long attempt by all too many individuals to force-fit the Qur'an into becoming little more than a source document to serve the interests of jurisprudential and legalistic theologies.

If one wishes to use the term 'Divine Law' in conjunction with the Qur'an, one would be, I believe, closer to the truth of the matter if one were to think about the idea of law in terms which refer to 'the natural order of creation'. That is, Divine law refers to the nature of manifested existence and the principles (both spiritual and otherwise) which are operative within that natural order of things. This is consistent with another sense of the same Arabic root from which shari'ah comes which concerns the sort of lawgiver or legislator who has established the order of things and how those things operate in a given realm ... in the present case, creation.

For example the law of gravity does not say that one must obey gravity or that one has a duty or obligation to observe gravity. Rather, through experience, reflection, and the guidance of those who have some wisdom in such matters, one becomes aware of gravity's existence and properties. Moreover, one comes to understand that as one goes about one's life one may run into problems if one does not pay attention to the principle of gravity, and, in addition, one learns that there are consequences which follow upon a failure to observe such a principle – unless one can devise ways of defying (within certain limits) the presence of gravity through propellers, wings, rockets, jet engines, and the like.

Some people may like to look at what occurs when someone fails to pay close enough attention to the presence of gravity as some kind of 'punishment' for swaying from the path of reality. Nevertheless, once again, I feel it would be closer to the truth to say that actions – both spiritual and physical -- have consequences and, therefore, caveat emptor (let the buyer beware). In other words, there is a rigor to life – both spiritual and physical -- about which one pays heed, or not, to one's own benefit or risk.

Shari'ah is not about beheadings, amputations, lashings, corporal punishment, legal courts, banning alcohol, the length and shape of a beard, marriage, divorce, inheritance, dietary restrictions, dress codes, and the like. Shari'ah is about realizing the purpose of life by drawing upon the whole of the Qur'an as one struggles toward acquiring the Divine guidance that will assist one to fulfill one's spiritual capacity and recognize the nature of one's essential identity so that one will come to give expression to the process of ibadat, or worship, as God has intended.

To be sure, there are verses in the Qur'an which touch upon issues of punishment, alcohol, inheritance, diet, dress, marriage, apostasy, fighting, and so on. Yet, there are many, many more verses in the Qur'an (at a ratio of about 13 or 14 to 1) which explore issues of equity, fairness, balance, harmony, peace, forgiveness, patience, God-consciousness, remembrance, repentance, kindness, love, restraint, compassion, tolerance, insight, generosity, knowledge, wisdom, understanding, humility, purification of the heart, and honesty.

Why is it that the former legalisms have come to assume

dominance and pre-eminence over the development of spiritual character? Or, why do so many people seem to assume that punitive measures are the only road to spiritual purification? Or, why do so many people appear to automatically assume that the principles inherent in the development of spiritual character cannot or should not be applied to issues of jurisprudence?

There was a man who once came to the Prophet and confessed that he had broken the fast of Ramadan. The man wanted to know what would be necessary to set things right with respect to his mistake.

The Prophet informed the man that in such circumstances the Qur'an indicated one should fast for two consecutive months. Upon hearing this, the man replied by saying that if he could not even fast for one month, how would he be able to fast for two months?

The Prophet responded by saying that the Qur'an also indicated that one could also satisfy the conditions of the fast if one were to feed the poor. The man said that he had no money with which to feed the poor.

The Prophet called someone and told them to have food taken from the storehouse and brought to the Prophet. When this task had been completed, the Prophet gave the food to the man and said the man should distribute the food to the poor.

Upon receiving this instruction, the man commented that in the entire valley, there was no one poorer than he and his family. In reply, the Prophet said that the man should, then, take the food and feed his family, and that act would constitute expiation for the man's having broken the fast.

Among other things, Quranic principles of equity, compassion, generosity, and kindness were used by the Prophet in conjunction with the Quranic provisions concerning fasting to arrive at a manner of handling the situation which gave expression to shari'ah. Muslims as well as non-Muslims to whom I have recounted the foregoing hadith are moved by the obvious display of spiritual wisdom that is present in the interchange between the Prophet and the man who came to him seeking advice.

What is the moral, so to speak, of the story? The Qur'an is a book of spiritual principles, not a book of legal rules. Basic Quranic principles concerning fasting were taken by the Prophet and, then, were modulated in accordance with existing life contingencies and other principles of the Qur'an.

Shari'ah gives expression to an indefinitely large set of spiritual principles that can be combined together in different ways to assist individuals to realize life's purpose and a person's essential identity. However, one of the limiting factors in all of this, has to do with the depth of insight and understanding in the individual who is seeking to engage Quranic guidance in order to resolve any given issue or problem, and this is true both on an individual as well as a collective or social level.

As previously cited:

"O Prophet, We have put you on the Right Way (Shari'ah) concerning the religion, so follow it, and do not yield to the desires of ignorant people;" (Qur'an 45:18)

but, unfortunately, now that the Prophet is no longer with us physically, the desires of all too many ignorant people have come to dominate many communities. When such people do this only in relation to their own lives, then although such applied ignorance tends to lead to problematic ramifications, those problems are likely to be far, far fewer and more contained or isolated than when such ignorance seeks to legalistically and legislatively impose itself on everyone else.

When Muhammad (peace be upon him) was first called to the tasks of being God's rasul (messenger) and nabi (prophet), the society in and around Mecca was often crude, rude, lewd, and brutal. Infant girls were buried alive. Women were treated as third, fourth and fifth class citizens. Orphans were marginalized and neglected. Blood-feuds were the rule of the day. Punishment for transgressions was severe. Financial and material inequities pervaded and divided society. Slavery existed, and those who were unlucky enough to be slaves were

257

used and abused in any way that pleased their slave masters. Tribal alliances and antipathies structured society from top to bottom. Tribes or clans were not run in accordance with principles of justice but in accordance with the authoritarian rule of a leader or small group of such leaders who were only interested in protecting their vested interests. Excessive drinking of alcohol was rampant, as were the problems which arise out of such excesses. Public nudity in and around the Kaaba was not uncommon.

While there are some similarities between the social, economic, and historical conditions which prevailed during the pre-Islamic days of Meccan society and the conditions existing today, the times, circumstances, history, problems, and needs of the people during the life of the Prophet Muhammad (peace be upon him) were, in many ways, very, very different than what is the case today – and vice versa. If the Prophet were physically with us today, can anyone claim with certainty that she or he knows that the Prophet would approach the problems of today in exactly in the same way as he did during his lifetime more than 1400 years ago?

In ecology there is a guideline known as the 'Cautionary Principle'. In essence, this indicates that when one does not have demonstrative proof that some, say, industrial process will not harm people and/or the environment, then one should proceed with caution with respect to what degrees of freedom are granted to such an industrial process.

This principle also applies in the case of spiritual matters. If one cannot clearly demonstrate that, ultimately, a given application of a spiritual principle is not likely to have adverse consequences for the spiritual well-being of either individuals within that society or the group as a whole, then one should exercise considerable caution before applying such Quranic principles to the ecology of society.

Just as every medicine has a use and a value, this does not mean that using a given medicine without any consideration for the illness which needs to be remedied or the needs and condition of the patient will lead to successful results. So too, just because every spiritual principle in the Qur'an has a use and value, this does not mean that using any given Quranic principle without consideration for the illness which needs to be remedied or the needs and conditions of the individual or society to which it is being applied will necessarily lead to successful results.

Although there are ayats, or verses, in the Qur'an which are stated in specific, detailed form, this does not automatically mean that such verses must take precedence over all the other principles of guidance in the Qur'an. Patience, forgiveness, tolerance, love, humility, equitability, peace, compassion, remembrance, generosity, nobility, God-consciousness, and restraint are also specified in the Qur'an, and these latter spiritual principles are mentioned many more times and given far more emphasis than are the verses which fundamental legalists like to cite as being the principles which must govern public and private life.

The process of creating a public space within which individuals may pursue shari'ah according to their capacity and inclinations has been confused with the process of shari'ah which focuses on the development of character. In a sense, many Muslims have confused or conflated the frame (i.e., the process of creating a safe and stable social space) with the picture (i.e., the process of shari'ah, which is an individual and private activity rather than a public one).

Similarly, the punishments which are mentioned in the Qur'an are not shari'ah per se. Rather, such punishments were the specific guidance provided by Divinity to help society during the time of the Prophet to be able to establish a safe and stable space within which to pursue shari'ah – something that is entirely separate from, and not to be confused with, the process of structuring the public space that surrounds the activities of shari'ah.

However, there are different ways of creating the kind of public space within which people will be able to pursue shari'ah. As pointed out previously, the Qur'an God did provide some specific examples of how Muslims might go about creating the sort of safe and stable public space through which individuals could privately pursue, each in his or her own way, the development of character traits which is at the heart of the process of shari'ah. Nevertheless, God also provided many general spiritual principles in the Qur'an that also could be used to help create the kind of safe, stable public space through which

259

individuals could privately pursue the purpose of shari'ah.

When, God willing, character traits are developed and perfected, they possess the potential for having a constructive and positive influence on helping to maintain the peace and stability of the public sphere. When such traits become widespread, then, in effect, the process of pursuing shari'ah also becomes the means through which public space is constantly renewed in a safe and stable manner entirely without legalisms or legislative mandates.

One cannot legislate or make legal rules that force people to become loving human beings. However, once a person becomes a loving person, then the constructive impact such a person has upon the quality of public life is incalculable.

One cannot legislate or make legal rules or apply punishments which will cause people to pursue shari'ah. However, once shari'ah -- in the sense of an individual's development of character traits and purification of his or her nafs/ego takes place -- then legislation, rules, and punishments become largely peripheral issues.

Many fundamentalists want to return to the past in order to engage the Qur'an. The Qur'an doesn't exist in the past. It exists in the eternal now as always has been the case.

To filter the present through the times of the Prophet Muhammad (peace be upon him) is a fundamental [as well as a typical, fundamentalist] mistake. To demand that the Qur'an be engaged and understood through the filter of the circumstances, problems, and conditions of 1400 years ago is, I believe, to introduce substantial distortion into one's attempt to understand the nature of Quranic guidance.

All of the Qur'an is guidance. Nonetheless, not all of the guidance is necessarily intended for everyone.

For example, Alaf Lam Meem (Arabic letters which appear at the beginning of a number of surahs, or chapters, of the Qur'an) is guidance. Ha Meem (same as before) is guidance. Ta Ha and Ya Seen (same as before) are guidance. Yet, such guidance does not necessarily apply to anyone except those for whom God intended it.

People have made an assumption that injunctions in the Qur'an dealing with, say, punishment are incumbent for all peoples, circumstances, societies, and historical times, but these injunctions concerning punishment may not have been intended to apply to everyone any more than the series of Arabic letters at the beginning of certain surahs are necessarily intended for everyone. Rather, in each case, the guidance may be intended only for certain historical and social circumstances.

This distinction may be especially important when it comes to differentiating between the private sphere and the public sphere. Although there often is a public context in which the basic pillars and beliefs of Islam are embraced, the fact of the matter is that all of these pillars and beliefs are largely a matter of individual observance and responsibility.

This is also the case with respect to those aspects of character development extending beyond the basic pillars and beliefs. One may seek to practice love, kindness, generosity, forgiveness, tolerance, patience, and so on in relation to other people, but the development of such traits is a function of an individual's solitary struggle. One may observe the five daily prayers with other people, but each individual carries the responsibility of paying attention during prayers and applying as much of her or his spiritual capacity to the observance of prayers as one is individually able to do – nobody else can do this for a person.

Shari'ah is a matter of individual aspiration and not of public imposition. The Prophet is reported to have said:

"I have been given all the Names and have been sent to perfect good character."

He did not say that he has been sent to establish a good system of jurisprudence or corporal punishment.

The Prophet Muhammad (peace be upon him) is also reported to have said:

"Muslims are brothers and sisters in deen, and they must not oppress one another, nor abandon assisting each other, nor hold one another in contempt. The seat of righteousness is the heart. Therefore, that heart which is righteous does not hold a Muslim in contempt."

Yet, many of those with a fundamentalist inclination do seek to oppress others through the exercise of public power, and they do tend to harbor contempt for anyone who does not act or believe as such fundamentalists believe should be the case.

Moreover, the foregoing hadith indicates that the seat of righteousness is the heart. The hadith says nothing about the seat of righteousness being in government or the public sphere of power or a particular system of imposed punishment.

Through the Qur'an, Allah guided the people in the time of the Prophet in a way that they could understand and in a manner which fit in with their life styles, social conventions, history, ways of doing things, and sensibilities. In other words, during the time of the Prophet and under certain circumstances best understood by the Prophet, the process of beheading a person, or amputating a limb, or flogging an individual, or stoning a person were all expressions of following a portion of the guidance which had been given to the Prophet by God in order to establish order and security in an Arabian society that was used to dealing with certain aspects of life through the law of retribution and which is why God proscribed that sort of law for such a people so they would understand.

Nonetheless, through the Qur'an, God also provided guidance for people who would live in subsequent times which were different in many ways from those which existed during the life of the Prophet. Furthermore, these other dimensions of guidance were expressed in a manner that could be understood by, and which fit in with, the life-style, conventions, history, practices, and sensibilities of the people who would live in those later times.

This does not mean that people of subsequent generations were free to do whatever they liked. However, part of the beauty, generosity, and depth of the Qur'an is that it is filled with principles of guidance which are appropriate for all manner of circumstances and conditions, and, as such, the Qur'an has degrees of freedom contained within which are capable of assisting individuals in a variety of circumstances and situations – even if there are people today, unfortunately, who are unwilling to acknowledge these other dimensions of Quranic guidance.

Shari'ah has always remained what it is – the personal, private process of struggling to purify oneself, develop constructive character traits, realize spiritual capacity, and gain insight into the nature of one's essential relationship with God. The Qur'an says:

"I have not created human beings nor jinn except that they may worship Me [that is, Divinity]." (Qur'an 51:56-57),

and shari'ah, when properly pursued, is the key, God willing, to fulfilling the purpose for which human beings and jinn have been created – that is, ibadat or worship.

Is there a need for maintaining a safe and stable environment so that people may be free to pursue the real meaning of shari'ah in their own individual way? Yes, there is, but there also are alternative Quranic means of establishing and securing such an environment without necessarily having to resort to executions, amputations, floggings, stonings, oppressions, and so on. Moreover, we live in times when the latter sort of approach to establishing a public space that is conducive to spiritual pursuits is no longer appropriate, constructive, practical, or capable of encouraging spirituality.

Furthermore, all of the foregoing can be said without, for a moment, implying that what took place in the time of the Prophet Muhammad (peace be upon him) was in any way immoral, cruel, incorrect, uncivilized, or barbaric. God knew the people who lived in the time of the Prophet better than we do, and Divinity proscribed for those people what was necessary to help them create -- in their social, economic, historical, and spiritual circumstances -- a safe, secure, stable public sphere which could assist such individuals to begin to make the transition from what had been in pre-Islamic times to what might be through the degrees of freedom contained in the Divine guidance of the Qur'an.

In fact, the inclination of the Prophet was to discourage people coming to him and making their sins and transgressions public. The Prophet encouraged people to pursue repentance directly with God rather than having things mediated through public procedures.

Nevertheless, if people insisted on confessing their sins to the Prophet or insisted on making a public issue of such matters, then the Prophet was obligated to settle those matters in accordance with his duties as a Prophet of God and in accordance with the specific guidance given by Divinity for maintaining social order in those times. However, given that the Prophet is no longer physically present among us, there really is no one who currently exists who has the spiritual authority [despite the fact that many try to arrogate to themselves such authority] to carry out the same function as was performed by the Prophet in those earlier days, nor is there anyone currently available in the public sphere who has the depth of wisdom to verify that the specific rules contained in the Qur'an concerning, say, forms of punishment, are applicable to anyone beyond that portion of the community of the Prophet Muhammad (peace be upon him) that existed more than 1400 years ago.

In the days of the Prophet, when corporal forms of punishment came into play – and such was not the case all that frequently – those forms of punishment were understood as a way of having one's spiritual slate wiped clean with respect to what one would be held responsible for in the life to come. Today, those same forms of punishment have been stripped clean of what had been – at one time – their spiritual function and, instead, are frequently used as tools of oppression to control people and forcibly impose some invented theology upon a population which takes issue with the spiritual corruption, economic inequities, and social injustices being perpetrated by such governments as they try to hide behind the ruse of merely wishing to establish shari'ah as the law of the land, when, in point of fact, shari'ah was never intended to be a law which people were compelled to obey and has always been the right way for an individual to seek and realize God's purpose for that individual.

Earlier, the etymology of shari'ah had been noted as a path which leads one to water or the place where one drinks water. The nature of this water entails the sort of thirst-quenching experience which occurs when, God willing, an individual realizes her or his unique spiritual capacity and essential identity. This is the sort of water to which shari'ah leads a person, and this is why the Qur'an indicates that in such matters there is no compulsion (Qur'an 2:256), and this is why people make a mistake when they treat shari'ah as something which can be imposed on others.

On page 53-54 of Daveed Gartenstein-Ross's book <u>My Year Inside Radical Islam</u>, the author writes:

"I had known from the first time I encountered Ashland's Muslims and saw al-Husein debate with Sheikh Hassan that there was a name for the kind of Islam practiced by the community's leaders: Wahhabism. The Wahhabis are a Sunni sect founded by Muhammad ibn-Abdul Wahhab, an eighteenth-century theologian who lived in what is now Saudi Arabia. Abdul Wahhab was obsessed with returning Islam to the puritanical norms that he thought were practiced in Prophet Muhammad's time. He had a severe and strict interpretation of the faith.

"In accord with Abdul Wahhab's teachings, the Wahhabis have an absolutist vision for Islam that holds that the Qur'an and Prophet Muhammad's example (the Sunnah) are the only permissible guides for the laws of the state and the conduct of an individual. They resent Muslims whose norms differ from theirs ... the Sufis are also particularly despised. The Sufis ... tend to be more free-form in interpreting the Qur'an."

Starting with the last sentence first, the fact of the matter is that interpretation of the Qur'an – whether by Sufis or others – is not a part of shari'ah.

In Surah 3, verse 7, one finds:

"He [that is, God] it is Who hath revealed unto thee (Muhammad) the Scripture wherein are clear revelations -- They are the substance of the Book-- and others (which are) allegorical. But those in whose hearts is doubt pursue, forsooth, that which is allegorical seeking (to cause) dissension by seeking to explain it. None knoweth its explanation save Allah. And those who are of sound instruction say: We believe therein; the whole is from our Lord; but only men of understanding really heed."

Moreover, in another part of the Qur'an, Allah provides the following guidance:

"He granteth wisdom to whom He pleaseth; and he to whom wisdom is granted receiveth indeed a benefit overflowing; but none will grasp the message but men of understanding." (2:269)

Interpretation is not an expression of wisdom which God grants but is the antithesis of such wisdom. Interpretations are projected onto Divine guidance, whereas wisdom concerning that guidance is a gift of God.

Contrary to what Mr. Gartenstein-Ross claims, Sufis don't have a more 'free-form way' of interpreting the Qur'an. Rather, they try to refrain from interpreting the Qur'an and seek, instead, to struggle to be in a spiritual condition which, if God wishes, such an individual will receive wisdom from God concerning those Quranic verses which are not clear and straightforward.

Interpretations are invented explanations that are a function of ignorance and presumption. Wisdom is a received understanding which has been granted by God and is a function of, among other features, Divine grace/baraka and an individual's taqwa or God-consciousness.

According to the author of <u>My Year Inside Radical Islam</u> – and as previously noted:

"Abdul Wahhab was obsessed with returning Islam to the puritanical norms that he thought were practised in Prophet Muhammad's time. He had a severe and strict interpretation of the faith."

However, what was practiced by the Prophet Muhammad (peace be upon him) was not some form of puritanical doctrine but, rather, a way, or deen, or tariqa, or shari'ah, or sirat-ul-mustaqueen which helped individuals learn, God willing, how to become a person of understanding and wisdom concerning the nature and purpose of Quranic guidance. In contrast to what Abdul-Wahhab and others of fundamentalist leanings believe, this way of God was not meant to be imposed on anyone and, consequently, it could not become the law through which the state governed people.

As noted previously, the function of the state is different from the function of shari'ah. Sharia'ah is intended to govern the realm of private spiritual aspiration according to one's capacity as well as in accordance with Divinely granted understanding. The state is intended to create the sort of public space within which people would be able to freely and safely pursue shari'ah according to their understanding of things as long as that understanding did not spill over into compelling others to live in accordance with such a perspective.

The puritanical system to which Abdul-Wahhab wished to return people was a figment of his imagination. The puritanical system which he invented was the result of a revisionist history which Abdul-Wahhab constructed concerning the nature of Divine revelation and the life of the Prophet Muhammad (peace be upon him).

The severe and strict interpretation of faith which was held and promulgated by Abdul Wahhab was a projection of his own spiritual pathology onto both the Qur'an and the life of the Prophet Muhammad (peace be upon him). The system envisioned by Abdul Wahhab was not a process of returning Islam to its roots but a failure to understand the nature of those roots altogether and as such laid the foundations for a system of theological oppression which has, like a virulent pathogen, spread to many parts of the world.

The foregoing comments actually lead to an observation concerning the title of the book by Daveed Gartenstein-Ross. More specifically, <u>My Year Inside Radical Islam</u>, is something of a misnomer.

If a person spent a year with a group which counterfeited money and, then, wrote a book about his or her experiences during that period calling the memoir: <u>My Year Inside the Federal Treasury</u>, the people who read the book might object because they clearly understand that the counterfeiting outfit has nothing to do with the Federal Treasury Department except in relation to the counterfeiting group's attempt to pass off its product as a legitimate form of legal, monetary tender.

However, a similar sort of objection can be made with respect to the experiences of Mr. Gartenstein-Ross. He didn't really spend a year inside of radical Islam. Rather, he spent a year with a group of radical spiritual counterfeiters who did their best to try to convince Mr. Gartenstein-Ross that their product was the equivalent of Islam, which it wasn't.

To put forth such an observation concerning the problem with the title of Mr. Gartenstein-Ross' book doesn't undermine the importance of much of what the author has to say about the group in question since I would agree with many aspects of his critical commentary concerning the teachings of that group which are recounted in his book. I merely wish to place those critical observations in a proper context by saying that although the group in question may have been radical, and although that same group parasitically sought to usurp the name Islam and, in the process, the group attempted to create the impression that its radical philosophy was part and parcel of Islam, Mr. Gartenstein-Ross actually spent time inside a group of Muslim spiritual counterfeiters rather than having spent time inside an Islamic group.

On page 71 of his book, Daveed Gartenstein-Ross writes:

"When I was a campus activist at Wake Forest, I was always eager to speak against injustice, and often considered myself courageous when

I did. But my approach to Al-Haramain [i.e., the Muslim group in Ashland, Oregon] was the opposite. I recognized that disagreeing with prevailing religious sentiments could stigmatize me. My approach, starting with my first week on the job, was to avoid making waves, to try to understand where the others were coming from, and to emphasize our religious commonality rather than argue over differences."

Not wishing to create controversies or wanting to emphasize commonalities, rather than argue about differences or trying to understand someone else's perspective, are all important and commendable intentions. Nonetheless, I believe that the search for truth as well as Mr. Gartenstein-Ross's personal situation would have been better served if he had stuck with his tendency to speak out against injustice and give voice to the problems he saw rather than, due to a fear of being stigmatized, remain silent.

In a sense, Mr. Gartenstein-Ross became his own worst enemy with respect to being pulled into the spiritual quagmire represented by the Ashland group because, for a time, he seemed to have suspended the very tools with which God had equipped him – namely, an inherent dislike of injustice as well as a critical capacity for detecting when things don't make sense. In short, for a time, Mr. Gartenstein-Ross ceded his intellectual and moral authority to the group or leaders of the group in Ashland, when he would have been much better off if he listened to the counsel of his own heart ... which in many cases -- at least with respect to the things about which he wrote in his book -- was a better source of understanding concerning the nature of Islam than anything he was hearing from the Muslim group with which he was associating.

I say the foregoing not as someone who seeks to stand in judgment of Mr. Gartenstein-Ross but as someone who, so to speak, has been there and done that. There have been times in my own life when I should have listened to the counsel of my own heart but, instead, gave preference to the views and ideas of someone else out of a desire to not stir up controversy or disturb the peace and, in the process, ceded to someone else the very intellectual and moral authority for which God

269

had given me responsibility with respect to the exercise thereof.

The Prophet Muhammad (peace be upon him) is reported to have said that one should:

"Seek the guidance of your heart (istaftii qalbaka), whatever opinion others may give."

To be sure, there are some dangers associated with such counsel because one can easily mistake the musings of one's own ego or nafs for the guidance of one's heart. However, if one is sincere in seeking the truth, then, if God wishes, Divinity will help move the heart in the correct spiritual direction.

The question which arises here, of course, is how does one know one is being sincere? In relation to this issue, the Prophet Muhammad (peace be upon him) is reported to have said:

"All people are doomed to perish except those of action, and all people of action will perish except for the sincere, and the sincere are at great risk."

Why are the sincere at such risk? Because, among other things, there are many who are seeking to sway the sincere from the counsel of their heart – the very counsel to which the Prophet Muhammad peace be upon him) in the previously noted hadith is encouraging such sincere ones to listen to.

When one does not listen to the counsel or fatwa of one's heart, the vacuum which is created thereby becomes filled with the musings of whoever happens to be present and who is prepared, legitimately or illegitimately, to exploit another person's abdication of her or his spiritual responsibilities with respect to his or her own heart.

This is what happened to Mr. Gartenstein-Ross when he became inclined to remain silent amidst the radicalized propaganda, biases, and prejudices of the Ashland group. Through his own decision to remain relatively silent concerning the problems he encountered within the group, he unintentionally opened himself up to the malignant forces which would begin to work on him through the theological machinations of the Wahhabi-influenced group with which the author had, for a time, chosen to associate in Ashland, Oregon.

One of the first things the group tried to do was undermine Mr. Gartenstein-Ross' God-given right to try to ascertain, for himself, the truth with respect to an array of issues. For instance, at one point in his book, Mr. Gartenstein-Ross describes how, when working in the office of the Ashland group, he wrote an e-mail in response to a university student who was inquiring about the practice of infibulation, a process of genital mutilation which is forced upon women within various Muslim and non-Muslim communities in different parts of the world.

Very reasonably, Mr. Gartenstein-Ross wrote to the student and explained that one had to distinguish between the teachings of Islam and cultural practices which had nothing to do with such teachings but which, unfortunately, had been conflated with those teachings by people of mischief and those who had vested theological interests. The author clearly, and correctly, indicated to the student that the practice of infibulation has nothing to do with Islam.

One of the consequences which ensued from the e-mail was that the other members of the Ashland Muslim group were very upset with Mr. Gartenstein-Ross for having written such an e-mail. The author was told that he did not have the right to issue a fatwa, and there were numerous scholars in Saudi Arabia who were far more qualified than was Mr. Gartenstein-Ross and who were prepared to answer such complex questions of Islamic law.

Despite all too many facets of the Muslim community operating for some 1100-1200 years under the contrary delusion (since the rise of various schools of jurisprudence within the Muslim community), there is no such thing as Islamic law. While there are legal systems which have been generated by Muslims, and while, sometimes, these legal systems do seek to incorporate this or that understanding concerning what certain people believe Islam to be about, the result is not Islamic law but, rather, Muslim law.

A whole cacophony of religious scholars, imams, qazis, muftis,

271

and theologians have arrogated to themselves the right to make pronouncements – called fatwas -- which they believe to be binding on others. They have developed arcane, obscure, irrelevant, and deeply flawed methodologies for generating torturous explanations that attempt to justify such practices as female mutilation, or which seek to justify: why women should be completely covered, or why women should be deprived of the rights which the Qur'an clearly gives them, or why men should be beaten if they don't grow a beard, or why a women who is raped should be executed for fornication, or why honor killings are okay, or why not belonging to a given madhhab or school of jurisprudence is a heinous crime and renders one an unbeliever, and other similar iniquities.

The practice of infibulation or female mutilation is not a matter of complex Islamic law. It is a matter of a complex pathology.

There is nothing of a reliable nature in the Qur'an to support such a practice. There is nothing of a reliable nature in the sunnah of the Prophet Muhammad to support such a practice.

However, the fundamentalist mind-set seeks to induce one to believe that life is real only when one submits to the beliefs and teachings of certain acceptable – to the fundamentalists -- religious scholars. According to that mind-set, if one doesn't operate out of a given madhab's (school of jurisprudence) book of fiqh (application of law based on a given legal school's interpretation of the Qur'an, hadith, and subsequent legal commentary), then one is leading an invalid, haramic life.

For such a mind-set, validity is not a matter of whether a given understanding can be shown to conform to the guidance of the Qur'an. Rather, validity is purely a function of whether a given understanding conforms to a certain theological paradigm.

If one conforms, then one is a brother or sister. If one dissents, then one is likely to lose one's family affiliation and become branded as a kafir or unbeliever.

On page 94 of <u>My Year Inside Radical Islam</u>, one reads:

"As I was walking toward the red Tercel, a dark-haired woman who

272

looked to be in her late thirties greeted me. She wasn't wearing a hijab, the head scarf worn by Muslim women. I was surprised to see her. It took me a second to realize the reason for my surprise: it had been weeks since I'd had any real contact with a woman. And, to my dismay, I had begun to internalize the dress code of the Musalla. Her lack of hijab struck me as wrong."

What Mr. Gartenstein-Ross is describing when he talks about having begun to internalize the dress code of the Musalla or Muslim center in Ashland is, actually, an expression of Pavlovian classical conditioning. In some of the early experiments conducted by Pavlov, a dog would be presented with an unconditioned stimulus, such as food, and, the presentation of the food would automatically induce the dog to salivate, which was referred to as an unconditioned response. In the next stage of the experiment, a tone would be sounded at the same time as the food was presented, and when the tone and sight of the food were paired enough times, the sounding of the tone was enough to induce salivation in the dog even if no food was present.

The process through which the dress code was being internalized within Mr. Gartenstein-Ross is not exactly the same as the previously described experiment of Pavlov, but there are some important similarities. When most men who have grown up in North America meet a woman – such as the situation described by Mr. Gartenstein-Ross -- there is no inherent sense that there is anything wrong with the way such a woman is dressed as long as her clothes fall within certain broad parameters of aesthetics and decency.

In such a case, the unconditioned stimulus is the woman and her clothing. However, under normal circumstances, there is not necessarily any particular unconditioned response which is likely to be displayed by someone like Mr. Gartenstein-Ross in relation to such an encounter.

Yet, if one works and spends time within an environment like the fundamentalist-leaning group of Muslims in Ashland as Mr. Gartenstein-Ross did, then what happens is that every time a woman appears on the scene, certain behaviors, comments, or body language are given expression through the male hierarchy of the group. Having spent considerable time in such environments, I am well aware of the things that are said, or the behaviors which are encouraged and discouraged, or the kind of body language and facial expressions that are used to induce people – both men and women -- to conform to a specific way of doing things.

One of the chants of the fundamentalist mind-set is that women must be kept out of sight. Women should not participate in mosque activities – unless it is to cook food. Women should be herded into little rooms in the basement or to some other room away from the main focus of activity. Women should be dressed in a particular way. Women should observe hijab. Women need to be kept separate from men.

After enough pairings of the foregoing sort of theological perspective and the presence of women, then, in a relatively short period of time, the presence of a woman in and of herself -- unaccompanied by the presence of a fundamentalist-oriented commentator -- is enough to elicit the mind-set which has been conditioning the thoughts and feelings of someone who is in a position like that of Mr. Gartenstein-Ross. Consequently, a person who is in a position similar to that of Mr. Gartenstein-Ross begins to automatically disapprove of a given woman if she does not conform to the theological mind-set which is in place.

One does not think about what is going on. One merely feels what one has been conditioned to feel such that the unconditioned stimulus – the presence of a woman without hijab – is enough to elicit feelings of disapproval ... that is, the conditioned response.

Although both Muslim men and women are enjoined to be modest in their manner of dress, the Quranic verse which indicates that women should cover themselves does not stipulate that no part of a woman should be visible to the world. This extended notion of covering up is someone's interpretation of what God meant. If covering up is for the sake of modesty, and men are required to be modest in their dress, then why is it that women are required to be so much more modest and so much more covered up in this respect than men?

Why aren't men the ones who are stuffed into small rooms in the basement or up in the cramped quarters of the balconies? Why aren't men the ones who are kept away from the main center of activities within a mosque? Why aren't men the ones who are discouraged from taking part in mosque activities? Why aren't men the ones who are told that they cannot use the main entrance to enter the mosque? Why is it okay for a woman to listen to the sound of a male voice in the mosque, but for a man to listen to the sound of a woman's voice in a mosque somehow threatens to shake the foundations of all that is true and just?

In all too many mosques and Muslim centers, none of the foregoing questions are really open for discussion. Everyone – both men and women – has been conditioned to accept the status quo without engaging in any rigorous, critical exploration of whether such is the way things need to be or should be.

Almost everyone is on auto-pilot, operating in conjunction with classically conditioned responses. Reason, insight, critical inquiry, dialogue, rigorous examination, and wisdom concerning such issues are almost nowhere to be found.

As pointed out by Mr. Gartenstein-Ross, if one has objections to any of the foregoing, one is chastised and criticized for the weakness of one's faith, or one is given a book to read which is written by someone with the "right kind" of theological orientation, or one is recited a litany of obscure names residing in this or that Muslim country whom one is enjoined to treat as authoritative icons whose words are not to be disputed.

After all, those people are scholars. They are experts. They know Arabic.

Don't think! Don't reflect! Don't question! Just blindly accept what one is being told, and if one is not prepared to do this, then you, my friend, are likely to be accused of being an unbeliever ... or a minion of Satan.

In fundamentalist-leaning groups [and what is being said here applies as much to fundamentalist Christian and Jewish communities as it does to Muslim groups] there is tremendous pressure – both spoken and unspoken – that is imposed upon people – both men and women – to submit to the theology being promulgated by the group. One is encouraged to internalize the idea that obedience to what the theological leaders are saying is the only acceptable form of adab or spiritual etiquette.

If one objects to the idea of being required to show blind obedience to human beings, and, instead, one humbly expresses the opinion that 'I thought we were supposed to submit only to God", one is told that what these leaders are saying is precisely the same as what God is saying. From their perspective, what they are promulgating is what God meant even if what they claim God meant is not necessarily what God actually said in, say, the Qur'an.

According to the fundamentalist orientation, one should be ashamed for even considering the possibility that God might have meant something other than what the leaders are telling one is the case. Creating such controversy is described by those with vested theological interests as being tantamount to fitna or creating discord in the community.

Furthermore, one is "informed" by this same fundamentalist orientation to keep in mind that the Prophet Muhammad (peace be upon him) condemned the practice of fitna. But, while it is true that the Prophet is reported to have spoken against the practice of fitna – that is, the sowing of discord in the community – nevertheless, what, precisely, the Prophet meant by, or had in mind with respect to, the term of 'fitna' and what the fundamentalist mean when referring to such a term are not necessarily the same.

In other words, if you don't agree with them, then you are the source of fitna. To suggest that such people may be the source of fitna for introducing problematic ideas and understandings in the first place does not appear anywhere on their theological radar except as a hostile invader seeking to destroy Islam.

For the fundamentalist mind-set, the only way to achieve group and community harmony is if everyone submits to that theology. Thus, the fundamentalists have set up the game plan to be something of a fait accompli … keep one's mouth shut and do things a certain way or be labeled as an unbeliever and as one who creates fitna in the community.

The fundamentalist strategy often tends to consist of bullying, intimidation, indoctrination, control, and oppression. Sincere dialogue and rigorous exploration of the issues are not compatible with such a strategy as Mr. Gartenstein-Ross indicates was his experience on many occasions during the course of his interaction with the Muslim group in Ashland, Oregon.

There are several junctures in Mr. Gaertenstein-Ross' book when the issue of apostasy is, to a degree, discussed. This topic, of course, is of particular interest to the author of <u>My Year Inside of Radical Islam</u> because toward the end of his book he provides an account of how he left the Muslim community to become Christian.

Prior to the foregoing point, however, the issue of apostasy is explored within a period of time when Mr. Gartenstein-Ross still considered himself to be a Muslim. For example, on pages 153-154 of his book, Mr. Gartenstein-Ross relates the words of someone -- a fellow by the name of Abdul-Qaadir – for whom the author had respect on the basis of other conversations which they had engaged in previously.

Mr. Gartenstein-Ross wanted to know if such people (i.e., apostates) should be killed. His friend said:

"The reason a lot of people are uncomfortable with this is because they don't understand the notion of apostasy in Islam. ... They hear that you can be killed for leaving Islam, and their reaction is 'Huh?' What they're not considering is that religion and politics aren't separable in Islam the way they are in the West. When you take the Shahadah, you aren't just pledging your allegiance to Allah, you're aligning yourself with the Muslim state. Leaving Islam isn't just converting from one faith to another. It's more properly understood as treason."

Mr. Gartenstein-Ross reports that his response to the foregoing was: "That makes sense." Actually, the fact of the matter is that such a perspective makes no sense at all.

To say that religion and politics aren't separable in Islam is to propagate a myth. As the Qur'an points out, and as has previously been noted, when Muslims pledged their oath of allegiance to the Prophet at Hudaibiyah, not only was their oath given to Muhammad (peace be upon him) as the Prophet of God, but via revelation, God clarified the matter and said that the oath of allegiance given by Muslims was really to God for God's hand was above the hand of the Prophet.

There was no Muslim state at the time. There was a community in Yathrib whose people – both Muslim and non-Muslim – had, for the most part, agreed to accept the Prophet as leader of that community and who were prepared to accept his rulings in certain matters.

A constitution was established in order to formalize the nature of the relationship which had been agreed to between the Muslims in Yathrib and certain non-Muslim tribes. As such, this constitutional understanding did not bind the non-Muslim tribes to a Muslim state but, instead, outlined the duties and rights of the respective signatories and in this sense was more like a treaty among different peoples than a document which created a political state.

The Prophet Muhammad (peace be upon him) is reported to have said:

"Leave me alone so long as I leave you alone."

He did not encourage people to make requests that he lay down further spiritual precepts beyond what was given in the Qur'an, nor did he encourage them to question him minutely about deen for fear that people would burden themselves in such matters beyond what God had intended and beyond what they were able to do.

Certainly, the Prophet was not someone who busied himself with setting up a political, state apparatus. He did what was necessary in order to establish a judicious, safe, stable public sphere. However, this was done not for the purposes of politics or creating a state but, instead, was done in order to develop an atmosphere which was conducive to people pursuing shari'ah according to their individual capacities and inclinations.

When the Prophet Muhammad (peace be upon him) passed away, a convention was established in which certain people in the community gave oaths of allegiance to whomever was elected to be Caliph of the community. The taking of such an oath did not bind the individual to an Islamic state but was, rather, a contract between the leader and those who acceded to being led by such a person.

As Hazrat Abu Bakr Siddiq (may Allah be pleased with him) indicated upon becoming Caliph:

"Obey me as long as I obey Allah and His Prophet, when I disobey Him and His Prophet, then obey me not."

The issue of the relationship between a leader and those who came to be aligned with that leader through an oath was not a function of politics or membership in a state, but, rather, this was a matter of a person's understanding concerning the truth. When all parties involved in such an arrangement were on the same page with respect to their respective understanding of the nature of truth under a given set of circumstances, then all such parties worked together, and when there were differences entailed by their respective understandings of the truth, then allegiance no longer bound the two parties together.

Shortly after the Prophet passed away and prior to becoming Caliph, Hazrat Abu Bakr (may Allah be pleased with him) said:

"Listen to me, ye people. Those of you who worshipped Muhammad (peace be upon him) know that he is dead like any other mortal. But those of you who worship the God of Muhammad (peace be upon him) know that He is alive and would live forever."

Then he repeated a passage from the Qur'an:

"Muhammad is but a messenger, Messengers of God have passed away before him; What if he dies or is killed? Will you turn back upon your heels? And whosoever turns back upon his heels will by no

279

means do harm to Allah, and Allah will reward the thankful."

A Muslim's primary allegiance is to God. Messengers pass away, and Caliphs pass away, and leaders pass away, but Allah is ever-lasting, and, ultimately, it is one's relationship with God that is of essential importance – not one's relationship with a state or government ... Muslim or otherwise.

With respect to those who accept Islam and then turn away from it, the Qur'an says:

"Those who turn back to unbelief after the guidance has become clear are seduced by Shaitan who gives them false hopes." [47:25]

There is nothing in this ayat (verse) which alludes, either directly or indirectly, to the idea that such a person has committed treason with respect to the Muslim community. Moreover, there is a question concerning exactly what it means to "turn back to unbelief".

If someone becomes a Muslim and, then, due to various circumstances, leaves the Muslim community but still retains many of the same beliefs, values, and commitments, can one necessarily and categorically state that such a person has turned back to unbelief? If such a person believes in God, and the Prophets, and the life here-after, and the Day of Judgment, and the angels, and has respect and love for Prophet Muhammad (peace be upon him), and prays to God (but not necessarily in the prescribed format), and remembers God, and seeks to do good for the sake of God, and engages in charitable works, and is committed to fighting against injustice, and seeks, for the sake of God, to exercise qualities of patience, humility, honesty, love, compassion, kindness, forgiveness, and tolerance – can one say that such a person has turned back to unbelief? If one does not pray the five daily prayers or does not fast during the month of Ramazan or one does not go on Hajj even though one is physically and financially able to do so, but one believes in the oneness of God and gives zakat or charity, can one conclude that such a person has turned back to unbelief?

If someone comes to Islam accepting all the basic beliefs as well as observing the pillars of Islam, but because of spending time with certain Muslims who are authoritarian, dogmatic, oppressive, arrogant, intolerant, misogynistic, and ignorant, then decides that he or she does not want to turn into that kind of Muslim yet is led to believe, through the use of undue influence in a cult-like set of circumstances, that anything which does not reflect such oppressive, arrogant dogmatism is not the true Islam, and, as a result, such a person wishes not be considered a Muslim anymore, can this kind of individual really have been said to have returned to unbelief? Isn't it much closer to the truth to argue that leaving behind the ignorance of such a group is actually moving toward Islam and not away from it ... that leaving such a group is an act of belief in support of truth and a rejection of falsehood?

If a person gravitates toward Islam because she or he has been led to believe that the way of Divinity is about the sort of love, compassion, remembrance, piety, character, justice, kindness, tolerance, patience, friendship, and integrity which shatters the heart due to its breathtaking beauty and majesty, and, then one is, instead, shown through people's words and actions that some Muslims actually promote having contempt for others, judging others, talking behind their backs, maligning people, harboring enmity toward Muslims and non-Muslims alike, killing whomever disagrees with them, terrorizing humanity, being obsessed with harshly punishing others, oppressing people, and being intolerant toward one and all, why would anyone wish to stay mired in such a spiritual cesspool? Would not anyone with the least bit of understanding counsel such a person to leave the latter group of Muslims and return to her or his original understanding concerning Islam?

One begins to descend a very slippery slope when one starts to arrogate to oneself the right to decide who is, and who is not, a Muslim. A person treads on very dangerous spiritual ground when he or she assumes that God has appointed her or him to not only determine whose faith and deen constitutes the 'real Islam' but that God has, as well, authorized one to kill such individuals or punish them in any way.

281

Whatever might, or might not, have been the practices of the Prophet in relation to the issue of apostasy, this does not necessitate that such a practice must be observed in the present day. Just because the Prophet may have had, by the Grace of Allah, the spiritual wisdom and insight to make determinations in such matters, it does not, therefore, follow that anyone in today's world enjoys the same kind of spiritual wisdom and insight or that anyone in today's world has the same duties and responsibilities which accrue to a Prophet of God but which do not necessarily accrue to the rest of us.

According to some individuals, there is a reported hadith of the Prophet Muhammad in which he indicated that 'Whoever accepts Islam and then renounces that faith should be killed.' On the other hand, there also are reported hadiths which indicate that the Prophet told people to destroy their collections of hadith.

First of all, it is not clear what the Prophet meant – if he actually did say what he is reported to have said in this regard – when he allegedly indicated that anyone who commits apostasy should be killed. There are people who claim that they know what he meant, but I'm not quite sure why I should believe that such individuals actually know the mind and intentions of the Prophet.

Secondly, the Qur'an says:

"O believers! Obey Allah, obey the Rasool and those charged with authority among you. Should you have a dispute in anything, refer it to Allah and His Rasool, if you truly believe in Allah and the Last Day. This course of action will be better and more suitable." (Qur'an 4:59)

Now, if the Prophet ordered that collections of hadith were to be destroyed, I'm rather uneasy with the spiritual appropriateness of following something – namely, collections of hadith -- which has reached me in apparent contradiction to such guidance. This is especially so since the alleged saying concerning apostasy does not just require me to do something that affects only my own, individual life but, rather, is requiring me to do that which has serious ramifications for other human beings and their being able to continue to live.

The Qur'an indicates I may refer any such quandaries or disputes to Allah and His Rasool, and I have done this. The counsel of my heart which arises from this process of referral tells me something quite different than what the alleged hadith concerning apostasy indicates. Moreover, since the Prophet Muhammad (peace be upon him) is reported to have said, as previously indicated, that I should follow the counsel or fatwa of my heart no matter what others may say, then this too would seem to mitigate against following the – I repeat -- alleged hadith concerning apostasy.

Of course, there will be those who will point out that when the Prophet said one should listen to the fatwa of one's heart no matter what others may say, the Prophet was not suggesting that this gives people permission to act in contravention to spiritual principles. I tend to agree with such a perspective while simultaneously noting that there is both considerable ambiguity as well as quite a few degrees of freedom concerning the nature of what, precisely, is entailed by such principles.

In addition, although the previously noted ayat of the Qur'an does indicate that one also should obey those who are charged with authority among us, there are quite a few questions which arise with respect to the issue of precisely who it is that has been charged with such authority. There are many people who have usurped authority in illegitimate ways. There are many people who have arrogated to themselves the power to oppress the lives of others. Yet, I have a sense that those among us who actually have been charged by Divinity with true spiritual authority are few and far between.

Many people confuse power with authority. Just because God has granted one power, this does not mean that God also has granted one authority.

There are many pretenders who seek to use their power to leverage such authority or who use their power to act as a pseudo-substitute for such authority, but, in reality, I believe there are precious few people who have been charged with authentic authority. Furthermore, I am not at all convinced that such legitimate authority is necessarily given expression through the head of any specific political state or nation or that being charged with valid spiritual

283

authority necessarily entails membership in the circles of religious scholars, imams, muftis, jurists, mullahs, or theologians.

On pages 177-178 of <u>My Year Inside Radical Islam</u>, Daveed Gartenstein-Ross writes:

"... my spiritual needs are irrelevant if Allah exists. If Allah exists, none of our spiritual needs will be fulfilled if our relationship with Him is based on falsehood. If Allah exists, we don't forge a relationship with Him. Instead, He dictates a relationship with us. Salafism led me to comprehend this in a way that I never did before. The scientific methodology espoused by Bilal Philips and others like him was an effort to ensure that our understanding and actions accord with Allah's will.

"Salafis carefully interpret the Qu'ran and Sunna because they believe that the best way of interpreting Allah's will is going back to the earlier understanding of Islam. The earliest generation of Muslims is a pious example because if Muhammad were truly a prophet, those who were closest to him and experienced life under his rule would best understand the principles on which an ideal society should be built."

While one might agree that a person's spiritual needs might not be fulfilled if the individual's relationship with Divinity is based on falsehood rather than truth, this still leaves the problem of determining what is truth and what is falsehood. According to the quoted passage, those who are under the influence of the Salafi approach to things believe they are capable of differentiating truth and falsehood, but is this necessarily the case?

The Salafis claim to have a methodology which will bring one back to the earliest understanding of Islam ... the one which existed at the time of the Prophet and his Companions. The Salafis contend that the ones who were closest to the Prophet had the best understanding of the principles on which an ideal society should be built, and, therefore if one can understand what they understood, then, one will have what one needs to be able to build an ideal society.

Leaving aside the issue of whether, or not, the point of Divine guidance actually is to help people establish an ideal society, there are a few other potential problems with the Salafi perspective as outlined in the earlier quote. First of all, why should one be expected to permit one's relationship with God to be filtered through someone else's understanding (for example, that of the Salafis) of, in turn, another individual's understanding (for example, that of the Companions of the Prophet) of God's guidance?

Furthermore, what guarantee does one have that the manner in which Salafis go about interpreting the earliest sources is correct or leads to valid conclusions? Why should I suppose that the Salafis have correctly understood the intentions, meanings, and purposes of such earliest sources?

When someone says something, all one has to go on are the words. One does not have direct access to what is going on in the mind, heart, and soul of the person who utters such words, but, rather, one must try, as best one can, to try to deduce the condition of a person's mind, heart, and soul based on analyzing the words.

One may, or may not, also have a concrete context out of which words are spoken to assist one, somewhat, with deciphering what may have been meant by certain words in such a context. However, here again, one must not only deal with the problem of trying to determine whether, or not, one actually understands such a context in all of its historical, social, personal, and spiritual complexities, but as well, one still must deal with the problem of whether, or not, one accurately understands that context as the person making the statement understood such a context.

The truth of the matter is that most of us have difficulty trying to figure out what people mean when they speak in contexts going on today. Consequently, I have my doubts about how accurately someone will be able to render what was going on inside of the minds, hearts, and souls of people more than 1400 years ago.

Even if one were to agree with the idea that some of the people who lived in the time of the Prophet may have had the best and most intimate insight concerning the nature of Divine Revelation or the behavior of the Prophet, nevertheless, one must jump a huge historical and experiential chasm to be able to go on to claim with any degree of confidence that one understands things in precisely the way that people understood things some 1400 years ago. What is more, there is no way in which one can prove such claims.

The Salafi methodology and mode of approaching the problem of how does one differentiate truth from falsehood is unnecessarily circuitous, indirect, and complicated. God's guidance was meant to be engaged by individuals who depend on God's help to arrive at a correct understanding of revelation rather than seeking to have one's understanding of Divine guidance filtered through someone else's understanding of someone else's understanding.

Each individual has her or his own responsibility to struggle with the task and challenge of working toward ascertaining the nature and meaning of Divine guidance for himself or herself. My spiritual duty is to seek and to surrender to God's truth. My duty is not to seek and submit to someone else's version of that truth.

Unfortunately, shari'ah has been made a public issue when, in fact, it is a private matter. Shari'ah has been subordinated to a system of religious leadership and power struggles which demand obedience to the leadership and its perspective. Guidance is not a demand for obedience but is an attempt to draw one's attention to a path which leads toward, through, and by means of truth, justice, identity and purpose.

Spirituality has been "legalized" in the sense that the former has been reduced to being a function of legal dogmas and rules which are an oppressor of spirituality not the means of realizing and unleashing spirituality. Spirituality has been made a matter of obedience when, in truth, spirituality lies entirely at the opposite end of the spectrum from matters of obedience.

Spirituality is about honoring – through realizing and fulfilling – the amana or trust which has been bequeathed to us. Spirituality is not about ceding moral or intellectual authority to others. Spirituality is about what it means to be a servant of God who creatively serves the responsibilities of being God's khalifa, or vice-regent, on earth and, and as such, all of life becomes an expression of worship.

It is not possible to realize the amana or trust through obedience

286

to authority in and of itself. Mere obedience to authority removes the active and dynamic element of personal responsibility, commitment, and on-going intellectual and moral choice which is necessary for the struggle toward spirituality.

The Prophet Muhammad (peace be upon him) is reported to have said that: "the one who knows one's soul, knows one's Lord". One can't come to know one's soul by abdicating one's spiritual responsibilities and ceding them to another person's understanding of things – even if the latter understanding is correct.

The Qur'an gives expression to wisdom. Nonetheless, as the Prophet is reported to have indicated: "What good is the Qur'an without understanding?" Consequently, the understanding one must have is one's own understanding instead of mere obedience to another individual's way of understanding things.

All too often, obedience qua obedience entails a desire on the part of an individual to get out from beneath the felt existential burden of having to constantly and rigorously search for truth and justice. As a result, all too many people shy away from embracing the struggle which the Qur'an indicated that God intended life to be for human beings.

"And surely We shall test you with some fear and hunger and loss of wealth and lives and crops." (Qur'an, 2:155)

The struggle of life requires us to constantly seek that which is more true, just, and essential and to leave behind that which is less true, less just and less essential. The intention with which one pursues spirituality should not be to submit to and satisfy someone else's theological likes and dislikes but, instead, to seek the truth concerning oneself and one's relationship with Being and to do justice in accordance with that truth and in accordance with one's capacity for both truth and justice.

One must stand alone before God and affirm [through understanding and action] one's relationship with God – 'Am I not your Lord?' As the Prophet Muhammad (peace be upon him) is

287

reported to have said:

"Every one of you is a guardian, and every one of you shall be questioned about that which you are guarding."

The aforementioned affirmation is not out of obedience qua obedience. Instead, the indicated affirmation is an expression of one's recognition of the way things are with respect to the Divine order of creation and Allah's purpose for creation.

First comes understanding ... however limited this may be. Obedience without understanding is an empty form, and when the mind, heart, and soul have a proper insight into the nature of creation, then, intentions arise, God willing, which conform with the nature of truth and justice. This conformity between, on the one hand, intention, and, on the other hand, truth and justice is not obedience per se but, rather, the conformity constitutes action rooted in one's knowledge concerning the nature of one's being and its relation to Divinity.

Mr. Gartenstein-Ross lends credence to what is said above when his book described how he abdicated his own moral and intellectual authority and proceeded to cede them to the Salafi perspective. On page 154, he says:

"I didn't want to be racked by doubts and uncertainty. ... I wanted to live a life of conviction – like Abdul-Qaadir, like al-Husein [both imbued with the Salafi perspective]. I wanted a clear guide for telling right from wrong."

In exchange for what Mr. Gartenstein-Ross was led to believe would be a mental clarity free from doubts and uncertainty, all the author had to do was cede his intellectual, moral, and spiritual authority to the Salafi leaders. They would tell him what was true and what was false. He needn't worry about anything except submitting to what he was told.

As the author of <u>My Year Inside Radical Islam</u> wrote just prior to the above quotation:

"Now, when I heard a new fatwa or an unfamiliar point of Islamic law ... I no longer asked if it was moral. Rather, I asked whether this was a proper interpretation of the Qur'an and Sunna." (page 154)

The meaning of what constituted a "proper interpretation of the Qur'an and Sunna" would be provided by the Salafi leaders in their literature, audio recordings, DVDs, lectures, sermons, and everyday interactions.

If one bowed down to Salafi theology, then all doubts and uncertainty would disappear amidst the absolutist -- albeit rather arrogant, self-satisfied and unproven – pronouncements of the Salafi leadership. One didn't have to struggle with anything except the demand to submit to the theology being propagated by the Salafi brotherhood.

Mr. Gartenstein-Ross's original idea of seeking God and seeking to please God became lost amidst the theological musings of the Salafis. The author, by his own admission, became more preoccupied with not wanting "to be regarded as a heretic by my brothers and sisters in faith,"(page 154) and in the process he ceded his intellectual, moral, and spiritual authority to people who did not have his best spiritual interests at heart.

Later, in reference to himself, Mr. Gartenstein-Ross writes:

"When you became Muslim, you thought that the moderate interpretation was clearly right. You thought that extremists were either ignorant or manipulating the faith for their own gain. Your time at al-Haramain (the Ashland Muslim group) has made you question this. As your cherished vision of Islam collapsed, you're left feeling depressed, helpless, and confused."

The truth of the matter is that Mr. Gartenstein-Ross' cherished vision of Islam collapsed because he permitted spiritual vampires to come into his life and suck that vision from him. Of course, just as is the case in the movies, when Mr. Gartenstein-Ross decided to go to work at al-Haramain, he didn't realize he would be associating with such spiritual vampires, but, unfortunately, we don't always exercise due diligence under such circumstances and, as a result, we often have to scramble just to be able to stay sufficiently alive, in a spiritual sense, to be able to protect ourselves against those who would rob us of our God-given birthright to seek out, and live in accordance with, the truth.

Mr. Gartenstein-Ross' cherished vision of Islam collapsed because he ceded his intellectual, moral, and spiritual authority to others so that he wouldn't be "regarded as a heretic by his brothers and sisters." He permitted concerns about how others would perceive him – which is a worry of the ego and not a spiritual principle -- to cloud his judgment and to undermine his spirituality.

Mr. Gartenstein-Ross' cherished vision of Islam was ripped from his heart through a process of undue influence exercised on him by the people involved with the cult-like Ashland Muslim group that was associated with the allegedly charitable al-Haramain Foundation. Having been exposed to similar people and situations, I know the incredibly relentless, stifling, and oppressive pressure which can be placed on a person to induce him or her to submit to the theological propaganda being espoused by such fundamentalist-leaning self-proclaimed leaders.

Perhaps, the biggest difference between Mr. Gartenstein-Ross and myself is that, by God's Grace, I had someone whom I could trust to help me to resist permitting my understanding of, and love for, Islam to become corrupted. By his own admission (which was noted previously), Mr. Gartenstein-Ross had no one whom he could trust to help him protect his cherished view of Islam, and, consequently, he became "depressed, helpless, and confused" … just the sort of psychological and emotional condition which people of unscrupulous spiritual nature – such as the leaders of the Ashland Group -- love to take advantage of because a person who is drowning doesn't tend to consider what the cost may be when someone of questionable spiritual integrity throws one what seems to be a lifeline.

Mr. Gartenstein-Ross' experience was with a group that had a Salafi orientation. However, there are other fundamentalist-oriented groups within the Muslim community with whom he might have become entangled.

Moreover, although Mr. Gartenstein-Ross generally has good things to say about the Sufis throughout his book, the sad fact of the matter is that not all groups and teachers who refer to themselves as Sufi are necessarily authentic. We live in truly precarious spiritual times when spiritual counterfeiters are virtually everywhere and are busily engaged in trying to pass off what is ultimately worthless as legitimate spiritual tender.

Actually, on the one hand, given the obvious warmth that Mr. Gartenstein-Ross felt toward the Sufis, and given that it was his friend at Wake Forest who introduced him to Islam through ideas and teachings which were Sufi-oriented, and given that Mr. Gartenstein-Ross even took Shahadah with a Sufi group in Italy, one might ask the question of why the author of My Year Inside Radical Islam didn't communicate, in some way, with his Sufi connections in order to find a way of trying to counter what the Salafi group at the Ashland al-Haramain meeting place were doing as that group pulled the author deeper into the depths of the latter group's world view. On the other hand, the fact of the matter is that his friend at Wake Forest had himself come under the influence of a fundamentalist group and had largely distanced himself from the Sufi perspective. Furthermore, once these sort of fundamentalist groups are successful in creating a sense of vulnerability in a person such that the individual begins to have doubts about how to go about seeking spiritual truth, and, as a result, the individual begins to cede more and more of her or his intellectual, moral, and spiritual authority to the leaders of the fundamentalist group, then a person becomes less and less inclined to consider any source of understanding as being reliable except that which one is told is authentic by the fundamentalist group. In short, one begins to exist in an almost hermetically sealed environment in which seeking access to information and behaviors other than what the fundamentalist group are espousing doesn't tend to enter one's mind or heart.

In effect, one begins to self-censor one's own thoughts, feelings and behaviors in order to try to fit in with what is going on around one and to be accepted by the group. Moreover, whenever one says or does something which runs counter to the worldview of the fundamentalist group with which one is associating, one undergoes a new round of criticism, censorship, and indoctrination by the other group members ... which, in time, leads to further forms of self-censorship.

Little by little, one is emptied of oneself and replaced by the worldview of the group. The pressure applied to the individual is somewhat like what happens when a boa constrictor wraps its body around, say, a human being.

The person seeks to take in new air. However, at some point, the individual also has to exhale. When the individual does this, the boa constrictor wraps more tightly around the individual which, in turn, restricts the ability of the individual to take in new air with the next round of breathing.

This cyclical process of increasing constriction continues until the person is unable to take in any new air at all and/or the person's bones begin to break. What happens within fundamentalist groups as well as within inauthentic Sufi groups is similar to the interaction between a boa constrictor and its prey, except that in the case of such groups, it is the mind, heart, and soul of the individual which is broken, and as well, the individual becomes less and less willing – because of the group pressure which is being applied -- to take in new information and possibilities concerning the nature of truth and justice.

Toward the latter part of his book, Daveed Gartenstein-Ross describes some of the factors which played a role in his leaving what he believed to be Islam and converting to Christianity. Let us leave aside the issue that, perhaps, what Mr. Gartenstein-Ross left was not Islam but, instead, was someone's theological invention which the fundamentalist group in question referred to as Islam and, thereby, helped confuse people like Mr. Gartenstein-Ross who, while being very interested in learning about Islam, unfortunately, took up associating with the wrong people ... people who led him further away from Islam rather than deeper into it.

On pages 231 through 233 of <u>My Year Inside Radical Islam</u>, Mr. Gartenstein-Ross writes:

"In church the next Sunday, the sermon was about God's love. For months, I was sure that I couldn't possibly be worthy of God's love. … The sermon had an angle I didn't expect: that we weren't really worthy of God's love." Nobody deserves salvation," the preacher said. "We're all tarred with sin; we are all dead in our own sinfulness. None of us is worthy of standing before God on the Day of Judgment."

"Long pause. "But He loves us anyway. He loves us with a perfect divine love. The only way we can be worthy of standing before God is through the sacrifice of the perfect embodiment of humankind, the sacrifice of one without sin. That is why God gave us the ultimate sacrifice, the sacrifice of His only begotten son, the Lord Jesus Christ.

"This was the first time that I had considered that God might love me even though it was a love that I didn't deserve. The idea appealed to me deeply on an emotional level. But was it the truth?"

He goes on to write:

"I found that Islam and Christianity had two very different accounts of what became of Jesus. Christianity holds that Jesus was crucified, died, was buried, and rose from the dead. … Verse 4:157 [of the Qur'an] addressed the crucifixion: "That they said (in boast), 'We killed Christ Jesus, the son of Mary, the Messenger of Allah'; -- but they killed him not, nor crucified him, but so it was made to appear to them, and those who differ, therein are full of doubts." Which one was right?

"What principle could distinguish between the two accounts? I thought of the persecution that Jesus' disciples suffered because of their belief in the crucifixion and resurrection. They didn't die for a set of ideals – it was for a set of facts. Do people die for a set of facts that they know to be false?

"I felt that I was on to something. Slowly, with each layer that I

293

pulled back, I felt my ideas about God shifting."

I should start by saying that the point of the comments which are to follow has nothing to do with trying to establish who is right and who is wrong with respect to the life of Jesus (peace be upon him). We all have responsibility for the spiritual choices we make concerning beliefs and behaviors, and both Christians and Muslims believe that each of us will be held accountable for such choices on the Day of Judgment.

My focus is, instead, on a style of argument that is being used by Mr. Gartenstein-Ross. In fact, it is almost as if Mr. Gartenstein-Ross doesn't seem to understand that the manner in which he talks in his book about the kind of considerations which led to his conversion to Christianity tends to indicate that he appears to be committing many of the same kinds of mistakes he made with respect to his interaction with the Salafi-oriented group in Ashland, Oregon.

Other than referring to themselves, respectively, as Christian and Muslim, what is the difference between the Christian preacher to whom Mr. Gartenstein-Ross refers and the Salafi shaykhs or preachers whom he mentioned? They both are espousing their worldviews and seeking to influence the people who are listening to their respective sermons. They both believe themselves to be correct and to have a sound understanding about what the relationship is between God and creation.

According to the Christian preacher whom Mr. Gartenstein-Ross quotes, none of us is worthy of God's love. Well, maybe, but on what empirical evidence is such a claim based? How does one go about proving such a statement?

Isn't it conceivable that precisely because we are God's creation that such a fact, in and of itself, renders us worthy of Divine love not necessarily because of us, per se, but because human beings give expression, in part, to God's handiwork. Creation is worthy of God's love because creation comes from God. Why assume that God would create something which Divinity would find unworthy rather than create something which God loved and cherished?

Indeed, in the Qur'an one finds:

"Behold thy Lord said to the angels: "I will create a vicegerent on earth." They said "Wilt thou place there one who will make mischief therein and shed blood? Whilst we do celebrate Thy praises and glorify Thy holy (name)?" He said: "I know what ye know not." (Qur'an 2:30)

Allah has placed within each of us a potential for worthiness – a worthiness which was hidden from the understanding of the angels. Unworthiness is rooted only in the failure to nurture and develop the spiritual potential which God placed within us.

According to the Christian preacher cited by Mr. Gartenstein-Ross:

"We're all tarred with sin; we are all dead in our own sinfulness. None of us is worthy of standing before God on the Day of Judgment."

One might agree that we are all tarred in sin of one kind or another. Most of us are aware of our individual faults, the mistakes we make, and the people we hurt through our deeds and misdeeds. The empirical proof of such a claim is in our daily lives.

However, the further contention that "we are all dead in our own sinfulness" may be quite another matter. This is an expression of a theological position for which proof is much harder to come by, if one can demonstrate it at all.

One may believe that such is the case. Nevertheless, having such a belief and proving that such a belief is true is not necessarily one and the same thing even though many people do suppose that because they believe something, then somehow, merely having the belief means that the belief must be true.

Furthermore, when the Christian preacher mentioned by Mr. Gartenstein-Ross also claims that "None of us is worthy of standing before God on the Day of Judgment," such a statement tends to

295

generate a sense of dissonance with certain facets of both Christian and Islamic understandings. According to both religious traditions, the Day of Judgment is something which most of us will have to face irrespective of whether we are worthy or not and irrespective of whether we are ready or not. We don't get any choice in the matter.

The Christian preacher goes on to say:

"The only way we can be worthy of standing before God is through the sacrifice of the perfect embodiment of human kind, the sacrifice of one without sin. That is why God gave us the ultimate sacrifice, the sacrifice of His only begotten son, the Lord Jesus Christ."

First, the preacher says that none of is worthy to stand before God on the Day of Judgment, and, then it turns out that there is, after all, a way of being worthy of standing before God – namely, through Jesus (peace be upon him) who is described as being one that is without sin and who is the perfect embodiment of human kind.

I am willing to accept that Jesus (peace be upon him) is a perfect embodiment of human kind, and I am even willing to accept the idea that the life of Jesus (peace be upon him) was without sin. I also am willing to accept the idea that Jesus (peace be upon him) dedicated his whole life to God, and, in this sense sacrificed his life for the sake of God.

Nonetheless, saying all of the foregoing does not in any way require me to conclude that Jesus (peace be upon him) was the only perfect embodiment of human kind or that he was the only human being who was without sin or that he was the only person who willingly sacrificed his life for the sake of God. There may have been numerous examples of perfection, sinlessness, and sacrifice in the prophetic tradition.

So, if it is the case that what renders one worthy of standing before God on the Day of Judgment is because of the perfection, sinlessness, and sacrifice of a servant of God, then perhaps there are many individuals from among God's prophets and messengers whose quality of life renders their followers worthy of standing before God on the Day of Judgment. One cannot simply take Jesus (peace be upon him), remove him from the context of spiritual history, and conclude with any persuasiveness, that Jesus (peace be upon him) is the only one capable of making us worthy.

One also might raise a question about whether, or not, what renders someone worthy to stand before God on the Day of Judgment is a function of what someone else did quite independently of the choices we make as individuals. According to the theological perspective being espoused by the Christian preacher to whom Mr. Gartenstein-Ross alludes, the sacrifice of Jesus (peace be upon him) only renders us worthy of standing before God on the Day of Judgment if one believes in Jesus (peace be upon him) and the sacrifice that he is alleged to have made.

Therefore, the sacrifice of Jesus (peace be upon him), in and of itself, is not sufficient to render someone worthy of standing before God on the Day of Judgment. A person must make the decision to accept and believe in that sacrifice, and it is the making of such a choice that is said to be necessary if the sacrifice of Jesus (peace be upon him) is to be effective in the life of that person. According to such a theology, Jesus (peace be upon him) is purported to have done his part, but individuals must also do their part – that is, to accept and believe in Jesus (peace be upon him) in accordance with the dictates of the theology being espoused.

With respect to the foregoing, Mr. Gartenstein-Ross says:

"This was the first time that I had considered that God might love me even though it was a love that I didn't deserve. The idea appealed to me deeply on an emotional level."

The fact that an idea appeals to one on a deeply emotional level doesn't necessarily make such an idea true. There were many ideas described by Mr. Gartenstein-Ross in his book which allude to his being touched on a deeply emotional level ... ideas which had to do with certain aspects of Islam -- including its mystical, Sufi dimension -- and, ideas which were sufficiently intense and deep to induce him to

297

become a Muslim, and, yet, which, apparently, Mr. Gartenstein-Ross has decided to cast aside in favor of a certain kind of Christian theological argument. If both positions are rooted in something which touched him on a deeply emotional level, then, obviously, emotional considerations, in and of themselves, are not necessarily capable of settling the matter of what is true and what is not true.

Furthermore, there is certain ambiguity entailed by the perspective which Mr. Gartenstein-Ross is putting forth at this point. If the perfection, sinlessness, and sacrifice of Jesus (peace be upon him) only has efficacy if a person chooses to accept and believe in those dimensions of the life of Jesus (peace be upon him), then, clearly, there is something which renders one worthy of standing before God apart from, but related to, the issue of Jesus (peace be upon him) – namely, the choice or decision one makes concerning Jesus (peace be upon him).

In Islam one is required to make certain choices for which one will be held accountable on the Day of Judgment. In Christianity one is required to make certain choices for which one will be held accountable on the Day of Judgment.

Theologies have arisen among both Muslims and Christians concerning what the nature of such choices should be. There is nothing new in what Mr. Gartenstein-Ross is doing in conjunction with his move toward Christianity that he wasn't previously engaged in when a Muslim – that is, he is caught up in theology, and he is being influenced by what others are saying rather than thinking for himself or examining any of these issues in a critically rigorous manner.

Of course, Mr. Gartenstein-Ross believes there is a huge difference between the two theologies. He believes that the Christian theology is correct and that the Muslim theology is incorrect.

In support of his conclusions he says – as noted previously:

"What principle could distinguish between the two accounts? I thought of the persecution that Jesus' disciples suffered because of their belief in the crucifixion and resurrection. They didn't die for a set of ideals – it was for a set of facts. Do people die for a set of facts that they know to be false?"

This is not a very good argument. It is saturated with problems.

For example, he mentions how the disciples of Jesus (peace be upon him) suffered because of their willingness to believe the crucifixion and resurrection, but this, in and of itself, proves nothing except that they were committed to their beliefs. There were many Companions of the Prophet Muhammad (peace be upon him) who suffered, who were tortured, and who lost their lives because of their commitment to their belief in the Prophet and the Qur'an.

If willingness to endure suffering as a result of belief in something is the measure of truth, then, why make reference to only the disciples of Jesus (peace be upon him)? Should one not suppose that if one is to abide by the logic of the argument being put forth by Mr. Gartenstein-Ross at this point, then the fact that if a person suffers as a result of the beliefs she or he holds, this must be an indication that what that person believes is true?

Consider the following set of cases. One person believes in the existence of God and undergoes suffering as a result of that belief. Another person does not believe in the existence of God and undergoes suffering as a result of that belief.

Both of the aforementioned cases involve suffering. According to Mr. Gartenstein-Ross, the presence of willingness to suffer for what one believes is an indication that what is believed must be true, and, yet, what the believer in God holds and what the disbeliever in God holds cannot simultaneously be true.

At this juncture, Mr. Gartenstein-Ross asks what he appears to believe is a rhetorical question: "Do people die for a set of facts that they know to be false?" The implied answer is "No! People do not die for a set of facts that they know to be false, and, therefore, according to Mr. Gartenstein-Ross, one must conclude that the set of facts for which the disciples were willing to die were and are true.

However, while one might agree with Mr. Gartenstein-Ross that people are not likely to be willing to suffer or die for a set of facts which they <u>know</u> to be false, this is not the situation with which any of us really is confronted. We have beliefs, and one of those beliefs is that there is truth, and we hope that the other beliefs we have accurately reflect the nature of truth or reality, but, the fact of the matter is that in many cases we don't know whether, or not, the beliefs we hold are true.

People may not be willing to suffer or die for something which they know isn't true. Nonetheless, people often are willing to undergo suffering or to die for something which they <u>believe</u> to be true even if, ultimately, what they believe may turn out to be false.

The fact that certain people who claimed to be following Jesus (peace be upon him) were willing to suffer and die for what they believed with respect to the crucifixion and resurrection proves absolutely nothing about the truth of that in which they believed. The fact that certain people of a Salafi-orientation claim to be following the Qur'an and the Prophet Muhammad (peace be upon him) and are willing to suffer and die for what they believe in this respect proves absolutely nothing about the truth of that in which they believe.

When he was a Muslim, Mr. Gartenstein-Ross ceded his intellectual, moral, and spiritual authority to a group of fundamentalist Muslims who followed Salafi teachings. When he became a Christian, Mr. Gartenstein-Ross ceded his intellectual, moral, and spiritual authority to another set of theological teachings.

Mr. Gartenstein-Ross may feel that everything has changed with his rejection of Islam and his conversion to Christianity. And, of course, in certain ways this is true, but in an essential sense, nothing really has changed in his methodological approach to developing a spiritual world view.

In both cases he seems to have made choices on the basis of emotional considerations as well as on the basis of problematic theological thinking, rather than having made decisions due to any essential spiritual understanding. In both cases, he had a tendency to cede his intellectual, moral, and spiritual authority to other people rather than try to establish what the truth might be in terms that were rooted in his own spiritual capabilities.

When Mr. Gartenstein-Ross was inclined to ask lots of questions and engage in critical reflections concerning issues of morality, values, and justice, whether with respect to Christianity or Islam, then in my opinion, he came a lot closer to the truth of things, than when he was inclined to cede away his intellectual, moral, and spiritual authority to others. Moreover, this is so irrespective of whether one is talking about Christian or Muslim theology.

As Mr. Gartenstein-Ross said when he was at an existential point that was sort of in between Islam and Christianity:

"For months, I was sure that I couldn't possibly be worthy of God's love. How could I be? Here I was racked with doubts, unable to trust myself to do the right thing or to follow basic rules." (page 231)

Earlier in his book, Mr. Gartenstein-Ross said almost exactly the same thing as he hovered at a sort of spiritual fail-safe point at the edge of the Salafi sphere of influence – namely:

"I didn't want to be racked by doubts and uncertainty ... I wanted a clear guide for telling right from wrong." (page 154)

In the latter case, he permitted himself to be drawn into the Salafi theology. In the former case, he permitted himself to be drawn into the sphere of influence of Christian theology. In both cases he abdicated his spiritual responsibilities and ceded his intellectual, moral, and spiritual authority to someone else and permitted those people to establish the criteria for differentiating right from wrong and the true from the false.

Should one infer from the foregoing that I am saying that one should be the decider of truth? The answer to this question is: "No!"

God has given each of us spiritual sensibilities, faculties and capacities. These sensibilities, faculties, and capacities function best when we open ourselves up to be taught directly by God through the truth inherent in authentic revelation, through the truth which is manifested in the lives of the servants of Divinity, through the truth which is inherent in the nature of creation, as well as through the truth which is inherent in our unique spiritual capacity and essential identity.

The process of permitting oneself to be opened up to truth as it is manifested on different levels of being is a long, difficult struggle. During this process one must go through a great deal of purification with respect to the different aspects of the soul and, as well, one must undergo many spiritual transformations across states and stations in order, God willing, to acquire the character traits which tend to be reflective of a mind, heart, soul, and spirit which has committed itself to learning how to let God teach one to travel along the spiritual path.

In this spiritual quest, people who are spiritually knowledgeable can play very important catalytic and supportive roles in assisting one, God willing, to travel along the path. However, at every point along this journey, one has responsibility for properly exercising one's God-given intellectual, moral, and spiritual authority. When this authority is ceded to others, one is highly likely to encounter significant problems on the spiritual path.

I learned a great deal from the person I consider to be an authentic shaykh or spiritual guide. However, at no point did he ever ask me to cede away my intellectual, moral, or spiritual authority to him. Rather, he focused on helping me learn how to exercise such responsibilities in a way that would lead me toward realizing my own personal relationship with Divinity rather than toward a relationship which was being mediated through, and filtered by, someone else.

14.) The Phenomenology of Charisma

Twelve years ago (1997), Len Oakes, an Australian, wrote a book: Prophetic Charisma: The Psychology of Revolutionary Personalities. Building on the work of, among others, Max Weber and Heinz Kohut, as well as using insights gained through his experience with a cult-like group and leader, together with extensive psychological research involving testing, interviewing, and reading, Oakes sought to provide some degree of understanding and insight into the phenomenon of charisma.

While Oakes is to be commended for his attempt to bring light to an area which often exists in the shadows of our awareness, nevertheless, I feel his book is flawed in a number of essential ways. The following commentary constitutes some of my critical reflections upon Oakes' aforementioned book.

The first problem I have is the manner in which Oakes approaches the idea of a 'prophet'. In order to understand the nature of the problem surrounding Oakes' use of the term 'prophet', his theory will have to be delineated somewhat.

To begin with, and as the aforementioned title indicates, Oakes engagement of charisma is through a psychological study and not from a religious or spiritual perspective. Therefore, one can acknowledge and appreciate that the way in which he defines the idea of a 'prophet' will be in a manner which is compatible with the psychological thrust of his study.

Notwithstanding the above acknowledgment, there are always advantages and disadvantages surrounding any choice one makes for a working, or operational, definition of a given term. Consequently, one needs to determine if, how, and to what extent, Oakes's manner of defining key terms may introduce distortion and/or problems into his inquiry.

According to Oakes, a prophet is characterized as anyone who: (a) proclaims a mission containing not just a recipe for salvation, but a mission which does so in a way that seeks to revolutionize conventional values; (b) draws, gathers, or attracts individuals who become followers of such an individual and seek to implement the guidance provided by the person being referred to as a 'prophet'. Oakes tends to lump together a number of people, ranging, on the one hand, from: Jesus and Muhammad (peace be upon them both), to, on the other hand: various Swamis, ministers, alternative community leaders, and the like.

Despite whatever differences may exist among those individuals to whom the label 'prophet' is given, Oakes suggest that what all of these individuals share in common are qualities such as: (1) a capacity to inspire people; (2) a resistance to, and opposition toward, various forms of conventionality; (3) possessing a remarkable and compelling personality that tends to set them apart from most people; (4) a grandiose sense of self-confidence which is the source for a great deal of optimism and fearlessness with respect to propagating the mission of salvation; (5) a natural capacity for acting which well-serves a 'prophet's tendency to manipulate people; (6) great rhetorical skills; (7) self-contained, independent of others, not given to self-disclosure; (8) a capacity for social insight that seems to border on the preternatural. Using the foregoing definition, Oakes identifies individuals such as: Madame Blavatsky, Bagwan Shree Rajneesh, Prabhupada Bhaktivedanta (Hare Khrishna), L. Ron Hubbard, Joseph Smith, Sun Myung Moon, and Jim Jones as instances of modern day 'prophets'.

Depending on how one understood the idea of 'salvation' in the above definition of 'prophet, one could expand the boundaries of the set of individuals who constitute 'prophets'. For example, Adolph Hitler, who many Germans saw as the salvation of the German people, could, on the basis of the stated definition, be considered a 'prophet' because he attracted people who sought to follow his guidance concerning the nature of life and, as well, because some dimensions of such guidance sought to revolutionize certain realms of conventional values -- and, in fact, Oakes discusses Hitler along these lines at various junctures in the book on charisma.

Oakes also lists Fritz Perls and Werner Erhard as exemplars of modern prophets. Since the sort of 'salvation' which Perls and Erhard sought for their clients does not easily, if at all, lend itself to spirituality, religion, or mysticism, then if individuals like Perls and Erhard are to be considered 'prophets' in Oakes' sense of the word, one also, potentially, might be able to apply that same definition to a great many other people besides Perls and Erhard who gave expression to various artistic, literary, philosophical, scientific, psychological, social, economic, and political theories. Indeed, consistent with Oakes' definition of a prophet, there are many personalities across history who developed theories and paradigms that were intended, in one way or another, to serve as ways to salvation, and who, in the process, proposed an overthrow of conventional values, to one extent or another, as necessary realization of salvation, and, finally, who attracted people who were interested in learning how to live their lives in accordance with the teachings of the 'master'.

Oakes borrows a distinction, made by Heinz Kohut -- a psychoanalyst -- between 'messianic' and 'charismatic' personalities in order to try to frame Oakes' way of approaching issues such as 'prophets', charisma, and narcissism. Among other things, this distinction lends a certain degree of specificity to the discussion of prophets and helps address the issue of why people such as Perls, Freud, Hitler, and Erhard are part of the same group as a variety of individuals who are oriented in a largely religious/spiritual/mystical manner.

According to Oakes, messianic prophets: (1) tend to identify God as an 'external' source of inspiration; (2) often interact with Divinity in terms of a personal relationship which has an 'objective' nature; (3) usually teach by means of revelation; (4) seem to be motivated by a fantasy which construes one's individual existence to be part of the Godhead; (5) are psychologically oriented toward the external world and, as a result, able to perform reality checks; (6) frequently described as being very consistent with respect to behaviors or beliefs and, therefore, seen as stable over time; (7) are fairly modest with respect to making claims about themselves; (8) seek to do works of virtue and excellence in conjunction with the world, as well as to work for what is perceived to be the welfare of others; (9) apparently resigned to experiencing an eventual decline in influence and, as a result, often willing to make preparations for transition in leadership; (10) tend to generate new laws which foster a form of release that, ultimately, serves as a source of helping to constrain society; (11) give emphasis to doing 'God's work' which is at the heart of the messianic mission; (12) inclined to be other worldly and withdraw from the world's corrupting potential; (13) treat truth and duty to be the two highest forms of ethical expression.

On the other hand, for Oakes, <u>charismatic</u> prophets: (1) locate Divinity within rather than externally (as <u>messianic</u> prophets do); (2) filter their relationship with 'being' in terms of impersonal forces; (3) teach by example rather than through revelation; (4) are motivated by the fantasy that 'I and the Godhead' are one; (5) tend to be out of touch with external reality and, therefore, unable to run reality checks; (6) are perceived as being inconsistent with respect to both beliefs and behaviors which leads to considerable instability over time; (7) are fairly immodest and given to bouts of self-aggrandizement; (8) are not interested in the welfare of others, but, rather, are likely to be antisocial and self-serving; (9) often self-destruct or fall from grace through their behaviors; (10) are oriented toward rebellion, a certain lawlessness, and consider release/freedom to be good in and of themselves; (11) seek recognition rather than to be a vehicle of God's work; (12) use the corruption of the world as a justification for amorality and the opportunistic exploitation of circumstances; (13) consider love and freedom to be the highest forms of ethical expression.

For the most part, Oakes considers messianic and charismatic types of prophets to constitute groups that are, to a large extent, mutually exclusive categories. In other words, if one compares the thirteen points outlined above in conjunction with both types of 'prophets', then with respect to whatever quality or characteristic is said to describe one type of 'prophet', there tends to be an absence of any common ground shared by members of the two, respective groups and, actually, in relation to any of the aforementioned thirteen characteristics, members of the two groups tend to be proceeding in very different directions —sometimes in diametric opposition — with respect to each of the points. Oakes does indicate that elements of each type of prophet may be combined in different sorts of permutations so that some individuals may give expression to mixed combinations of both messianic and charismatic types. However, on the whole, Oakes seems to believe that in most cases one can identify a given 'prophet' as being either of a messianic kind or a charismatic kind.

Although, as noted above, Oakes alludes to the possibility that a given individual may give expression to qualities and characteristics from each of the two sets of characteristics, he doesn't pursue this possibility in any concrete manner. Consequently, one doesn't really know what he means by his allusion other than that he states it as a possibility.

One could imagine someone who teaches by example (a charismatic trait) as well as through revelation (a messianic characteristic). In addition, one could conceive of an individual who located Divinity both within (a charismatic tendency) and without (a messianic quality). One also can acknowledge the possibility of there being 'leaders' who did not focus on just love and freedom (a charismatic property) or on just truth and duty (a messianic feature) but on all of these qualities together ... that is, love, freedom, duty, and truth would be part of an integrated, harmonious whole which were in balance with one another.

On the other hand, one could not be both stable (a messianic trait) and unstable (a charismatic property). Moreover, one cannot seek to genuinely enhance the welfare of other people (a messianic characteristic) and, at the same time, be antisocial (a charismatic quality).

One cannot be both relatively humble (a messianic tendency) and engaged in self-aggrandizement (a charismatic inclination); nor can one both sincerely seek to be removed from the world's corruption (a messianic characteristic), as well as exploit that corruption to justify one's own descent into one's own amoral version of such corruption (a charismatic quality). One cannot be both attentive to the external world and, as a result, be capable of monitoring one's behavior in the light of that world (a messianic property), while, simultaneously, being out of touch with that external world and, therefore, unable to run various kinds of reality checks intended to constrain one's behavior (a charismatic property).

Furthermore, Oakes does not directly discuss the possibility of there being 'prophets' who were stable (messianic) but caught up in the throes of self-aggrandizement (charismatic), or 'prophets' who were interested in serving God (messianic) but wanted recognition for their efforts (charismatic). Oakes also does not speak about 'prophets' who might engage in reality checks (messianic) and, yet, also have a tendency to rebel, flaunt convention, and become entangled with legal skirmishes of one kind or another (charismatic) — in other words, a person might pay attention to the external world in order to better understand how to subvert it and manipulate it.

One could expand upon the nature and number of such permutations and combinations. Almost all, if not all, of the foregoing possibilities fall outside the horizons set by Oakes' exploration into the psychology of charisma.

One does not know how Oakes would respond to any of the foregoing possibilities other than to, perhaps, acknowledge them as issues which require further study. What one does know is that, in general, Oakes is inclined to place messianic prophets in a largely, if not wholly, spiritual-religious context, whereas so-called charismatic prophets tend to be perceived as individuals who do not necessarily participate in activities which can be described in religious, spiritual, or mystical terms.

Thus, individuals such as Hitler, Frued, Perls, and Erhard can be studied along side of overtly religious/spiritual figures such as Madame Blavatsky, Gurdjief Bhagwan Shree Rajneesh, Jim Jones, and Joseph Smith — to name but a few. This is because the characteristic which ties these individuals together is not spirituality, per se, but the quality of charisma which can be manifested in both religious as well as nonreligious contexts.

One wonders why Oakes chose to use the term 'prophet' -- as opposed to, say, 'leader' or some other comparable word — in order to refer to individuals who: proclaim a mission of salvation, seek to challenge or overthrow conventional values through that mission, and, in the process, try to induce people to participate in that mission by, among other things, applying the mission principles to their own lives through looking to the 'individual on a mission' as their guide or teacher concerning how one should go about

307

accomplishing this. One possibility is that Oakes wanted to concentrate on what he perceived to be the 'function' of a 'prophet', independently of religious and spiritual considerations.

Thus, if one removes the element of spirituality from the idea of a prophet and just looks at the behavior of such an individual, then according to Oakes, prophets are individuals who: (a) proclaim a mission; (b) couch the nature of that mission in terms of some kind of salvation; (c) often run into conflict with certain conventional values which exist at the time the mission is pursued; (d) seek to attract adherents to the mission, and (e) serve as a guide or teacher for those individuals who are trying to incorporate the mission's principles into their lives. If one separates the element of spirituality and religiosity from the 'functional behavior' of a prophet, then, individuals -- irrespective of whether they represented a religious or non-religious context -- might be considered to be observing 'prophetic' behavior if they satisfied the five conditions specified by Oakes which have been outlined above.

From a traditional, spiritual perspective, an individual does not proclaim himself or herself to be a 'prophet' or become a prophet by arbitrarily proclaiming that one has a mission. A Prophet is someone who has been appointed by Divinity to serve in a particular capacity for a given community.

Secondly, to reduce the task of a Prophet down to being a mission of salvation is problematic. To be sure, prophets do speak about the issue of salvation, but they also speak about: knowledge, truth, spiritual potential, identity, purpose, justice, death, and purity in ways which transcend mere salvation and re-orients one toward the possibility of additional realms of the sacred – sometimes referred to as the mystical dimension of spirituality.

Thirdly, to say that the intention of a Prophet is to clash with conventional values, or to rebel against such values, or to start a revolutionary movement which opposes such values, this also is problematic. A Prophet of God seeks to speak and behave in accordance with the truth – the reality of things – and while it may be the case that what is true does conflict with certain, conventional values, the purpose of giving voice to the truth is not to generate conflict, rebellion, or revolution.

Moreover, even if it were true that some conventional values were opposed by a given Prophet, one need not suppose that, therefore, all conventional values in a certain community would become the focus of opposition. Whether conventional values became objects of conflict, or which values might became objects of conflict, could depend on a variety of circumstances and, consequently, to maintain that a main feature of the 'prophetic' mission is to revolutionize conventional values is far too sweeping and ambiguous a claim.

Prophets, in a traditional spiritual sense, are sent to remind and warn people about a variety of things. They are sent to induce people to seek out the truth in all things. They are appointed in order to encourage people to be loving, thankful, sincere, honest, kind, forgiving, tolerant, modest, generous, considerate, friendly, respectful, aware, co-operative, hopeful, persevering, patient, peaceful, and to be inclined toward seeking repentance (with respect to both human beings and God) for the mistakes one has made. Prophets also are sent to discourage people from being: deceitful, exploitive, abusive, unjust, lacking in compassion, cruel, arrogant, hypocritical, dogmatic, intolerant, unloving, unfriendly, disputatious, immodest, thoughtless, insensitive, and so on.

There may be vested interests and various centers of power who become threatened, for one reason or another, by the activity of a Prophet, but the intent of a Prophet is not necessarily to wage war or rebel against those who have vested interests. Historically speaking, whenever and wherever possible, conciliation, harmony, peace, compromise, and negotiation are pursued by Prophets ... not confrontation and conflict.

Fourthly, a Prophet is not necessarily trying to attract followers. A Prophet is seeking to speak the truth as well as to offer guidance for anyone who is willing to engage that truth and guidance with a receptive heart and mind.

A Prophet is trying to assist people to realize the potential of their own relationship with the Truth/Reality. A Prophet is not trying to attract a following. The fact that a community of people may arise around that individual may only mean that they are a community with a common set of purposes rather than an amalgamation made up of a leader and his or her followers.

Of course, the foregoing points all raise the question of whether, or not, there is anyone who is actually appointed by Divinity to serve in a special, Divinely-ordained role of a Prophet. For the most part, Oakes tries to stay away from this issue and, therefore, restricts his discussion to what people claim to believe concerning their status as a 'prophet', quite independently of considerations of the truth or falsity of those claims.

However, Oakes does stray from a largely neutral stance when he says that messianic prophets tend to operate in accordance with the 'fantasy' that they are – in a yet to be explained (and possibly ineffable) sense – "part" of God, whereas

309

charismatic prophets are, according to Oakes, motivated by the 'fantasy' that they and the Godhead (or the psychic mother/father) are one – that they are 'God'. In other words, Oakes is making a statement about what he perceives to be the truth status of much of what a 'prophet' says when Oakes maintains that no matter whether one falls into the category of a messianic prophet or one is subsumed under the category of a charismatic prophet, both sets of individuals are motivated by a fantasy concerning their relationship with God.

One is free to believe whatever she or he likes about the truth or falsity concerning the existence of Divinity, or the 'authenticity' of a given spiritual claim about being a 'Prophet'. However, one cannot assume an aura of neutrality on such issues, while simultaneously trying to claim that, say, someone's understanding concerning the nature of his or her relationship with Divinity is necessarily rooted in fantasies of one kind or another.

To be sure, there are individuals who do suffer from delusions concerning their self-professed Divine nature or special status with God, and so on. Nevertheless, this does not automatically force one to conclude that anyone who makes such statements is delusional or under the influence of a fantasy or myth of some kind ... this remains to be determined on a case-by-case basis.

One cannot assume one's conclusions. Assumptions ought to be clearly identified as such, and there should be some thought given to how one's conclusions might be affected, adversely or otherwise, if the operational definition one is using – in this case, the idea of who and what a 'prophet is – turns out to be problematic, skewed, or incorrect.

Further evidence of the foregoing bias shows up in a variety of places in Oakes' book, but, perhaps, one of the clearest expressions of this slant comes in the conclusion when Oakes asks, and then answers, a question:

"But is the prophet really an enlightened spiritual being? If this question asks whether the prophet has personally experienced with the fullness of his being -- with his feelings and his relationships -- a spiritual reality, then, the answer appears to be no. Indeed, quite the opposite is true; it is the very shallowness of the prophet's feelings and relationships, his pervasive narcissism that prevents him from ever entering into a genuine relationship with another, or ever having anything other than pseudo feelings for others."

The foregoing statements may be quite accurate in their portrayal of the individuals whom Oakes actually studied in the field, and, as well, this sort of characterization may even be true of many of the religious, revolutionary, and charismatic personalities about whom Oakes learned during that phase of his research. In addition, Oakes is making an important point when he makes the quality of behavior a crucial, defining feature in determining whether, or not, someone should be considered to be a fully realized spiritual being.

Nonetheless, one hesitates to apply his conclusions across the board to any and all 'prophets'. Although Oakes does not say so directly, the implication of his foregoing perspective tend to extend to such spiritual luminaries as: Jesus, Moses, Muhammad, the Buddha, Krishna, David, Solomon, Joseph, Abraham, and a host of others (peace and blessings be upon them all) who are considered to be emissaries and prophets of Divinity.

To be sure, in the context of Oakes' study, the aforementioned remarks concerning whether, or not, prophets are spiritually realized human beings is primarily intended to refer to those individuals who fall into the category of 'charismatic prophet'. However, and as will be developed shortly, because Oakes' idea of charisma is, itself, problematic, a variety of difficulties arise in conjunction with his belief that, in general, 'prophets' are not really enlightened spiritual beings.

Part of the problem here is that some of the previously noted characteristics which, supposedly, differentiate between messianic and charismatic prophets raise some questions. For example, Oakes claims that one of the distinguishing features of a charismatic prophet is that such individuals tend to identify themselves with the Godhead, and, so, one might be puzzled about the idea of prophets not being spiritually realized human beings when one remembers that Jesus (peace be upon him) is reported to have said: "I and my Father are one" (this is a statement of tawhid/unity, not identity or incarnation).

Is Oakes prepared to claim that Jesus (peace be upon him) was not only an unrealized spiritual being but, as well, was, if one accepts Oakes' logic, a charismatic prophet who was narcissistic and incapable of forming genuine, sincere, loving relationships with other human beings? If so, where is the evidence for this, and, if not, then, perhaps, his theoretical framework will have to be modified accordingly.

Or, consider another possibility. According to Oakes, two of the characteristics of a charismatic prophet involve (a) locating Divinity within, rather than through external channels, and (b) filtering one's relationship with 'being' through a set of impersonal forces rather than through a personal relationship with a 'God'.

Presumably, on the basis of the foregoing, one might be required to place 'the Buddha' (peace be upon him) in the category of a 'charismatic prophet' since Buddhism is often portrayed, rightly or wrongly, as filtering one's relationship with Being through non-theistic forces of, to some extent, an impersonal nature. Yet, if one does this, is one forced to conclude that 'the Buddha' (peace be upon him) was a spiritually unrealized human being who was inclined to narcissism and only capable of having pseudo, shallow relationships with other individuals?

Similar questions arise in conjunction with some of the remarks made by Oakes concerning the Prophet Muhammad (peace be upon him). For example, Oakes indicates (page 182) that Muhammad (peace be upon him) was among a group of historical personalities who led successful movements and passed away with their integrity intact – i.e., no scandals. Oakes also identifies others who he judges to be like the Prophet Muhammad (peace be upon him) in this regard – e.g., Father Divine, Phineas Quimby, Prabhupada, Kathryn Kuhlman, and Ann Lee -- that is, 'prophets' who led successful, scandal-free movements.

These are individuals who did not self-destruct as is the tendency of many individuals who may fall into the category of 'charismatic prophets. Yet, at another juncture in his book (page 94), Oakes seeks to use Muhammad (peace be upon him) as an example of a historical prophet who, in Oakes' opinion, "played the part of a wounded innocent", by going into seclusion, in order to manipulate his wives into accepting his "dalliance with a slave girl".

Oakes does not provide any evidence to support his interpretation of the foregoing judgment. He states the foregoing as if it were an obvious fact and beyond question.

However, why should one accept such a judgment or interpretation? Why should one suppose that Muhammad (peace be upon him) was 'playing' the role of a 'wounded innocent'? Why should one suppose that he was trying to manipulate anyone? Why should one suppose that his relationship with the 'slave girl' was a mere "dalliance"?

Oakes is using a number of pejorative labels in reference to the Prophet. Where is the independent evidence which indicates that any of his ways of describing the situation are evidentially warranted rather than expressions of Oakes' arbitrary biases being imposed on something about which he has no genuine insight or understanding?

For Oakes, one of the defining features of charismatic prophets is their capacity for, and willingness to, manipulate others. Indeed, one of the features which, supposedly, permits us to differentiate 'messianic prophets' from 'charismatic prophets' is the amazing social insight possessed by members of the latter category -- a capacity which, according to Oakes, allows such individuals to, in a sense, know which buttons to push in order to maneuver people in a desired direction.

Consequently, as was the case with respect to the implications of Oakes' foregoing quote – for both Jesus (peace be upon him) and the Buddha (peace be upon him) -- concerning the lack of spiritual enlightenment in relation to 'prophets', once again, one is faced with an implication which paints Muhammad (peace be upon him) as someone who, according to the implications of Oakes' logic, may have been spiritually unenlightened, narcissistic, manipulative, and capable of only superficial, shallow relationships with others.

One of the arguments which some individuals have leveled against theoreticians like Freud is that he used his understanding of abnormal behavior and psycho-pathology to set the tone for what he considered to be healthy, normal psychological development. According to such critics, when one starts with a certain kind of sample set -- namely, people suffering from pathology – one may not be able to validly make the transition from: what that sample says about the nature of the people in such a sample, to: claims concerning the psychology of human nature in a population of people who do not suffer from such pathology.

Similarly, by using certain, arbitrarily decided-upon, behavioral and functional characteristics of individuals as the basis for labeling various individuals as 'prophets', one might wish to pause for a moment and ask whether the behavioral and functional characteristics being cited really are reflective of how an actual 'Prophet' might think, feel, act, or be motivated. Even if one wishes to argue that the latter considerations should not shape and orient a study in psychology, nevertheless, one still needs to take note of the lacunae which are, potentially, present when a researcher tries to do an end around, or ignore, the idea of 'authenticity' with respect to someone who claims to be, or is perceived to be, a prophet, and, as a result, employs arbitrarily chosen criteria to shape the operational definitions one uses to establish categories, differentiate individuals, and orient one's research.

If the definition of a 'prophet' does not necessarily reflect historical and/or traditional considerations, and if the sample being studied does not necessarily reflect historical and/or traditional 'realities' concerning the lives of Prophets, then at the very least, one should raise a caveat concerning the validity of applying the results of a given study -- like that of Oakes -- to a larger population containing some individuals who may actually be individuals who were appointed by Divinity to pursue goals, purposes, and activities which are in contradistinction to Oakes's operational definition of 'prophet' and who are neither necessarily delusional nor under the influence of one, or another, fantasy with respect to their relationship with Divinity.

What difference do the foregoing considerations make with respect to understanding the idea of 'prophetic charisma' or the psychology of revolutionary, religious personalities? As it turns out, perhaps a great many problematic ramifications may arise as a result of such considerations, and this might be most clearly described and explained through an examination of the way in which Oakes talks about two other themes -- charisma and narcissism -- within the context of a theory which claims to be directed toward helping us understand the nature of: 'prophetic charisma'.

I do not feel it would be distorting Oakes' position to say that, to a major extent, the phenomenon of charisma is, for him, an expression of, and rooted in, the phenomenon of narcissism. At least, this does seem to be the case as far as the idea of the psychology of religious personalities is concerned -- both with respect to 'prophets' as well as their followers.

Oakes indicates that someone can be referred to as charismatic when she or he is perceived to embody something referred to as "ultimate concerns". While this embodiment of ultimate concerns may be in relation to either oneself or others, however, the meaning of 'ultimate concern' tends to vary from person to person.

Nonetheless, when an individual has extraordinary needs in relation to whatever a given 'ultimate concern' may turn out to be for that person (and extraordinary needs are linked to the formation of a nuclear self early in life which is colored by, among other things, narcissistic forces), then according to Oakes, the perception of the embodiment of that ultimate concern in another human being gives expression to an extremely powerful magnetic force of attraction. This conjunction of 'ultimate concerns', 'extraordinary needs', and the 'embodiment' of such concerns in a person who, as a result, is perceived to be a vehicle for: accessing, being in proximity to, and/or realizing such ultimate concerns, is considered, by Oakes, to be at the heart of the phenomenon of charisma.

Although the foregoing description does not specifically limit charisma to spiritual contexts, nonetheless, Oakes does believe that charisma constitutes a spiritual power with a considerable potential to revolutionize society. Moreover, he believes charisma has the capacity to spiritualize the extraordinary needs and ultimate concerns of those who are seeking to have their needs and concerns fulfilled.

It is hard, at this point, to understand just what Oakes means by the idea that charisma can spiritualize ultimate concerns and extraordinary needs. If a given ultimate concern is not already spiritual in nature, or if an extraordinary need is not already rooted in spirituality of one kind or another, then how does charisma, per se, spiritualize either ultimate concerns or extraordinary needs? What does it mean to spiritualize something?

Furthermore, since Oakes has indicated that charisma is a function of the perception that someone embodies the ultimate concerns of oneself or others, and since he has indicated that charisma is a function of the perception that someone will serve as a means to the fulfillment of one's extraordinary needs, then one wonders about the precise dynamics of how either charisma, or its alleged spiritualizing dimension, works. After all, on the basis of the foregoing considerations, charisma seems to be something which is conferred on a given human being -- e.g., a prophet -- as a result of the perceived embodiment of one's ultimate concerns in, say, a 'prophet' due to the extraordinary needs of the one doing the perceiving.

If the foregoing characterization of things is correct, then charisma is not something which a 'prophet' possesses. Rather, charisma arises – and, sometimes, Oakes appears to suggest as much -- when the right alignment of 'prophet', 'ultimate concerns', 'extraordinary needs', and perception takes place. As such, charisma is a function of the dynamics of a certain kind of relationship between two, or more, people.

What a seeker brings to the equation are: ultimate concerns, extraordinary needs, and a perceptual mind-set which is actively or passively looking for something that resonates with those concerns and needs. What a 'prophet' brings to this dynamic are his or her own kind of extraordinary needs, together with a set of qualities which not only resonate, to some degree, with the concerns and needs of the seeker, but which, as well, are perceived to have something of a supernatural-like aura about them -- that is, there is something about the relationship which appears to be largely inexplicable, magical, mysterious, and resistant to any kind of easy explanation ... something which is experienced as seductive, alluring, magnetic, compelling, and somewhat mesmerizing.

One of the qualities which Oakes believes plays a significant role in the felt presence of charisma is the 'prophet's' talent for observation and an accompanying special ability to derive, from such observations, penetrating insights into the nature of on-going social dynamics as well as the extraordinary needs and ultimate concerns of individuals who engage the 'prophet'. Someone once remarked that one society's technology may appear like magic to another society which does not understand the principles through which such technology operates, and, similarly, when someone does not understand how a given person has arrived at her or his insight into one's extraordinary needs, ultimate concerns, or the surrounding social dynamics, then the individual with insight may be perceived as someone who has magical-like, supernatural-like capabilities and powers simply because one may not understand how such insight is possible.

Do some 'prophets' actually have psychic, occult, extrasensory, or non-ordinary powers of perception? Oakes does not believe so.

He believes everything is explicable through the manner in which ordinary abilities and talents may be developed to an amazing degree by individuals who have extraordinary needs. These needs are dependent for their fulfillment on the existence and use of such capabilities.

Oakes maintains (page 188) that a charismatic relationship begins with a seeker's surrender and trust. According to Oakes, only later does the seeker begin to project her or his own ultimate concerns onto the 'prophet' and through this projection become 'fused' with the person of the 'prophet' to such a degree that the 'seeker' interacts with the 'prophet' as if he or she were an expression of one's own inner, deeper, more essential 'self'.

If so, this leaves unanswered the question of why someone would trust or surrender to another individual without some sort of substantial motivation for doing so? Apparently, Oakes seems to be saying that trust and surrender arise prior to, and independently of, the establishing of a charismatic relationship which, according to Oakes, revolves around the dynamics of 'extraordinary needs', 'ultimate concerns', and the perceived embodiment of these qualities in the person of the 'prophet' – something which Oakes claims happens later in the relationship and, therefore, does not appear to be the initial reason why someone trusts and surrenders to the 'prophet'.

According to Oakes, charisma spiritualizes a relationship. Yet, somehow, trust and surrender -- which, presumably, are essential to any sort of spiritual relationship -- take place, on Oakes' account, before the main component of a charismatic relationship – namely, the perceived presence of the embodiment of ultimate concerns -- is established.

The foregoing sequence of events appears somewhat counterintuitive. A more likely explanation would seem to involve the possibility that the felt or perceived presence of charisma is what helps induce someone to trust and surrender to a 'prophet', and, if this is the case, then Oakes may be mistaken about when the projection of ultimate concerns on to a 'prophet' takes place.

Furthermore, one wonders if it is so much a matter of a 'seeker's' projection of ultimate concerns onto the 'prophet', as it may be a matter of such ultimate concerns actually being reflected in, or resonating with, some, or all, of the words and behaviors of the 'prophet'. In other words, is one to suppose that the perception of the embodiment of ultimate concerns in another human being is merely a delusion in which nothing of those ultimate concerns actually is present in what a 'prophet' says and does, or should one assume that, to varying degrees, something of a substantive nature concerning such ultimate concerns is actually touched upon by the teachings and actions of the 'prophet'?

To be sure, a seeker could be mistaken. For example, a seeker might believe that something of his or her ultimate concerns was present in what the 'prophet's said and did, only to discover, subsequently, that such was not the case or that whatever was present was being expressed in a fraudulent and manipulative manner. Or, a seeker initially might believe that a given 'prophet' could serve as a venue through which the seeker's extraordinary needs and ultimate concerns could be realized, only to, later on, come to the conclusion, rightly or wrongly, that the 'prophet' could not actually assist one to fulfill one's extraordinary needs or ultimate concerns. Alternatively, a seeker's first, cursory impression of a 'prophet' may have led the seeker to believe that the prophet and she or he shared a set of common concerns, values, and the like, only to realize, upon closer inspection, that the two, despite initial impressions, really aren't on the same page with respect to a variety of issues, concerns, goals, and values.

However, such mistakes are not necessarily delusional in character. They are beliefs that come to be, hopefully, constructively modified in the light of subsequent experience – something (that is, constructive modification) to which delusions are inherently resistant.

As such, it is not ultimate concerns, per se, that are being projected onto the prophet/leader/teacher. Instead, what is being projected is a hope concerning the potential value of what may ensue in relation to one's ultimate concerns by linking up with someone claiming to be a prophet/guide/leader.

Trust and surrender are offered in exchange for a promissory note, of sorts, about future considerations in conjunction with the fulfillment of extraordinary needs and ultimate concerns. The felt presence of charisma is perceived, rightly or wrongly, as an indicator that someone – namely, a prophet/leader/teacher – can satisfy the conditions of that promissory note. The felt presence of charisma, justifiably or unjustifiably, tends to create certain kinds of expectations concerning the fulfillment of ultimate concerns and extraordinary needs in the future.

Notwithstanding the foregoing considerations, one still is unclear about what charisma is or how the perceived presence of charisma has the capacity to induce or inspire trust, surrender, and expectations concerning one's ultimate concerns and extraordinary needs. One has a sense that, somehow, the perceived presence of charisma might have a 'spiritualizing effect in as much as trust and surrender, which are important components of spirituality, might be engendered, somehow, through the presence of something called 'charisma', and, yet, the manner in which this takes place – the dynamics of the spiritualizing process – remains elusive and puzzling.

Oakes believes that the secret of charisma lies in a narcissistic dimension of human development. More specifically, he believes that the alleged 'extraordinary needs' of both a 'prophet' and a seeker are entangled in the agenda of a 'nuclear self' which forms under certain conditions that, according to Oakes, are conducive to the emergence of narcissistic personality disorder in, at the very least, 'a charismatic prophet'.

Although at one point in his discussion of the phenomenon of narcissistic development Oakes voices a cautionary note concerning the question of how well can we know the mind and inner life of another human being, nevertheless, he soon leaves such caution behind when delineating Kohut's theory of narcissism and seeking to link that theory to the idea of charisma. Of course, generally speaking, it is often part and parcel of theoretical work to take some risks while venturing into uncharted conceptual territory, but some risks may be more viable than others.

Heinz Kohut developed his theory of narcissism while treating patients with narcissistic personality disorder. He sought to explain the origins of this disorder.

The patients being treated by Kohut tended to possess a grandiose sense of self-confidence, untouched by any sort of self-doubt. They often were very perceptive about people and social dynamics (sometimes uncannily so), could be quite persuasive, but also were given to blaming and accusing others of various failings and short-comings.

Such patients frequently were inclined toward exhibitionism and were given to voicing unrealistic, naïve fantasies concerning themselves and their place in the scheme of things. In addition, these individuals tended to demonstrate little evidence of possessing a conscience or experiencing any sort of guilt when involved in wrong doing. Moreover, their relationships with others usually were marked by an almost complete absence of empathy for people and, as well, appeared to be imbued with a belief that other people existed to serve the needs of the narcissist.

According to Freud, all of us go through a period of primary narcissism during infancy when we believe that everything not only revolves around us but that the world is, in a sense, a creation of our own. Furthermore, this period of narcissism is said to be characterized by a child's sense of oneness with the world -- meaning the mothering one -- which is posited to be a continuation of one's life in the womb when, supposedly, the boundaries between mother and child are completely dissolved.

During this period of felt-oneness, the child is said to bask in the nurturing glow of exaltation transmitted through the mother's gaze and treatment of the child. Through this sort of adoring interaction, the child feels worshiped and develops a sense of uninhibited, grandiose omnipotence which permeates the mind-set of the infant.

In the course of normal development, Freud indicates that primary narcissism becomes significantly attenuated and modulated as experience introduces a child to the pain of feeling alone in a world that, in many ways, appears indifferent to the desires of the child. Feelings of omnipotence are ravaged by the onslaught of a sense of helplessness.

With the waning of primary narcissism, the child no longer believes herself or himself to be the center of the universe. A Copernican–like revolution has shaken the foundations of the child's previously Ptolemaic existence.

The idea of 'primary narcissism' is a theoretical construct. Whether a fetus or an infant ever has a sense of oneness with the mother, or whether an infant ever operates out of a framework which is permeated with feelings of omnipotence and grandiosity, or whether an infant ever operates under the illusion/delusion that she or he is the creative and causal force behind the happenings of the universe, or whether the infant ever has a sense of being worshiped like a 'god', or whether an infant ever has the sense that he or she shares a state of perfection with a 'saintly' mothering one -- all of these are highly contentious, largely speculative considerations.

Instead, one might entertain the possibility that any deeply developed notion of primary narcissism in the Freudian sense might have a very difficult time becoming established in amidst the realities of this world. After all, almost from the first spank on the bottom which introduces us to this plane of existence, there is a great deal of human experience indicating: that we are not omnipotent; that however intimate one's relationship with the mothering one may be, there is felt separation in the sense that there are very real differences between how the mothering one behaves and how we might wish the mothering one to behave; that we cannot always make the nipple appear upon demand; that the discomfort of wet diapers or a colic-ridden system do not always disappear with the mere wish for this to be so; that we are not in control of how hot or cold we feel; that the ravages of colds, fevers and illness descend upon us without our permission; that an infant might have difficulty in believing that she or he rules over the universe when he or she can't even get her or his hands and fingers to go where he or she would like or accomplish what she or he would like.

The bundle of problematic desires, wishes, impulses, thoughts, and motivations within each of us which collectively are subsumed under the term "nafs" is a very different entity than the idea of primary narcissism. There is a considerable amount of metaphysical theory (e.g., oneness, omnipotence, and grandiosity, being worshiped, shared state of perfection), infusing the concept of primary narcissism which is absent from the notion of nafs that simply posits, based on observation and experience, that there are wishes, desires, thoughts, and motivations within us seeking expression and which tend to generate a sense of frustration or anger when the sought-for realizations are blocked, thwarted, or ignored in various ways.

Leaving aside such considerations for the moment, let's return to Kohut's theory of narcissism. According to Kohut, the mothering one filters the tendency of the world to intrude into the life of an infant, and, as a result, the mothering one has a role to play in helping to gradually initiate an infant into the realities of the world and away from the influence of the condition of primary narcissism.

Sometimes, however, Kohut maintains that something happens and the filtering process breaks down. There is some sort of traumatic tear in the process and, in one way or another, the child is deprived not only of the filtering assistance afforded by the mothering one but, as well, the child loses the process of gradual initiation into the realities of the world – realties which undermine and attack the child's sense of primary narcissism.

As a result, Kohut believes that some children, when faced with such a traumatic situation, seek to assume the responsibility of managing the filtering/initiation process by using the condition of primary narcissism as a coping strategy to try to filter and fend off the demands of the world. In such individuals, rather than the condition of primary narcissism becoming attenuated and modulated over time, this condition becomes strengthened and comes to dominant many aspects of that person's way of interacting with the world.

Although those individuals who become inclined to filer reality through the colored lenses of primary narcissism do learn, through trial and error (sometimes with great difficulty), how the world operates and how to negotiate many different kinds of problematic encounters with the world in a way that will help to avoid punishment while garnering various rewards, nonetheless, Kohut believes that, for the most part, such people are ensconced in a paradigm of reality which is self-serving, largely – if not completely – devoid of empathy for others, lacking in conscience, steeped in a sense of grandiosity concerning oneself, constantly seeking feedback from others which validates that sense of grandiosity and are often skilled in insightful social observation as well as the art of persuading and/or manipulating others to become tools for the acquisition of whatever is desired or sought -- especially positive feedback concerning one's fantasies and delusions about grandiosity (this is often referred to as 'narcissistic supply').

Anyone who opposes, seeks to constrain, or interferes with the paradigm of primary narcissism through which the world is perceived and engaged by someone in the throes of narcissistic personality disorder is likely to become the focal object of what Kohut refers to as 'narcissistic rage'. Such interlopers are resented, resisted, and riled against -- either openly and/or through various forms of indirect stratagems in which people become pawns to be used, and if necessary sacrificed, to check the perceived antagonist.

Kohut distinguishes between messianic personalities and charismatic personalities (rather than 'leaders' or 'prophets') within the foregoing context of primary narcissism gone awry. The messianic personality is someone who projects a sense of grandiosity outward in the form of an 'object' and identifies this externalized, "idealized superego", or 'self', as God who is to be served, worshiped and from whom revelation/guidance is received. The charismatic personality, on the other hand, is someone who internalizes the sense of grandiosity and equates one's own being with an idealized sense of the omnipotent 'self' or Godhead which is to serve as an example for others.

Kohut believes a messianic personality is pulled by externalized ideals and the challenge of trying to emulate and live up to those ideals. A charismatic personality, however, is driven by ambitions revolving about her or his need for self-aggrandizement, together with a validation of that sense of grandiosity through the recognition and acknowledgment of others.

Following up on an idea of Kohut's, Oakes advances the theoretical possibility that 'seekers' may hook up with 'prophets' in ways which are mutually accommodating. In other words, individuals who have had their own problems negotiating the transition from primary narcissism to a more 'realistic' way of understanding that the world does not revolve around one's existence, may have 'extraordinary needs' which a messianic or charismatic prophet is perceived to be able to address and/or resolve. By helping a messianic or charismatic prophet to validate his or her sense of reality through the act of following such an individual, a seeker hopes to receive, in return, what may be needed in the way of the satisfaction of the seeker's ultimate concerns that will permit that individual to be happy, transformed, content, at peace, in harmony with one self or the world, or whatever else may be the thrust of the ultimate concerns and 'extraordinary needs' of a psychological/emotional nature inherent in the seeker.

Presumably, those individuals who identified with, or felt resonance in, the coping strategy adopted by a messianic personality, prophet or leader, would gravitate toward, or be attracted by, or feel at home in circumstances where the 'idealized superego' had been projected outward and could be sought in the external world as an 'object' of some kind through which one's world could be ordered, guided, and ethically oriented. On the other hand, those individuals who identified or found resonance with the coping strategy developed by a charismatic personality, prophet or leader, might be inclined toward, attracted by, or feel comfortable in an environment where the 'grandiose self' was sought within and, if located, could lead to a sense of omnipotence, freedom, and primal release.

Although there is a certain degree of coherence and consistency to the foregoing theoretical framework and without wishing to argue that there is no one (either among 'prophets' or followers) who operates in accordance with such psychological dynamics, nonetheless, there are a great many reservations one might have concerning such a theory. For instance, to assume that all people externalize an 'idealized superego' or identify with an internalized 'grandiose self' may be a way of accounting for the observed behavior of some individuals, but such an assumption also tends to prevent one from considering the possibility that truth and reality are not necessarily a function of what we project, create, or identify with but may exist quite independently of what we think, feel, and believe.

Not every search for the truth is necessarily a reflection of unresolved issues of primary narcissism. Not every issue of ethics or morality necessarily reduces down to what we seek to impose on reality or what we internalize in the way of parental values. Not every search for identity is necessarily a function of the nuclear self's agenda which, according to Kohut and Oakes, precipitates out of the transition from primary narcissism to more mature modes of interaction. Not every search for wisdom is necessarily a reflection of the development of coping strategies for psychic survival. Not every search for justice is necessarily a reflection of one's likes and dislikes. Not every search for guidance is necessarily an exercise in finding a match between a 'prophet's' psychological profile and one's own psychological needs.

Not every 'prophet' is necessarily a product of the psycho-dynamics of everyday life. Not every thought of awe or omnipotence is necessarily either self-referential or a matter of what one projects onto the universe. Not every experience of love is necessarily a mirrored reflection of the presence of narcissism. Not all dissatisfactions concerning the limitations, problems, and lacuna of psychoanalytical thought are necessarily evidence that denial and other defense mechanisms are at work to save us from the painful realization of repressed wishes, fantasies, impulses, and thoughts.

What is the truth concerning such matters? Whatever they may be, one shouldn't start out by, in various ways, pre-judging the matter.

One cannot claim to be objective while being predisposed to restrict one's investigation to purely psychological principles in relation to some phenomenon without examining the possible merits of metaphysical or trans-personal explanations with respect to that same issue. One cannot claim to be value-neutral while ignoring possible data, experience, and phenomena which are not necessarily consistent with one's philosophical and/or psychological orientation.

Oakes admits that trying to trace such ideas as messianic and charismatic personalities back to the dynamics of infantile phenomenology is a speculative exercise (e.g., 42). However, at other times he speaks in terms which appear to transpose these speculative exercises into 'likely' explanations of this or that phenomenon, or this or that individual (and, I have already pointed out that almost none of what Oakes or Kohut have to say is 'likely' to be accurately reflective of the lives, teachings and personalities of such individuals as Jesus, the Buddha, or Muhammad -- peace and blessings be upon them all -- not to mention any number of other spiritual luminaries who appear among the ranks of both historical Prophets and the great mystical guides from many different spiritual traditions).

Although it is desirable to want to subsume as large a body of phenomena, behavior, and data, as is possible, under the rubric of one theoretical framework, one also has to be prepared to acknowledge the possibility that reality may be far more complex, rich, nuanced, and problematic than the capabilities of any single theory. Moreover, while certain individuals may exhibit behavior and characteristics which are compatible with, say, the theories of Kohut, nevertheless, this does not automatically preclude the possibility that there may be many individuals who do not demonstrate profiles which easily, if at all, conform to the requirements of such a theory. Indeed, there may be a variety of different currents of human potential which are running through the ocean we call 'reality'.

One might be willing to accept Kohut's psychoanalytical theory concerning the way in which some individuals supposedly deal with the problem of primary narcissism. Nonetheless, even if one were to accept Kohut's tendency to conceive of the difference between messianic personalities from charismatic personalities as being a function of whether, respectively, an 'idealized superego' was externalized or a 'grandiose self' was internalized, one still has difficulty understanding precisely how the ideas of 'prophet', 'narcissism', and charisma fit together.

Oakes does suggest that 'seekers' tend to be attracted to, or inclined toward, those 'leaders', 'guides', and 'prophets' who best reflect the 'extraordinary needs' of such 'seekers. As a result, some people are attracted to, and follow, messianic 'prophets', while others are attracted to, and follow, 'charismatic prophets'.

However, right away there is a problem here. If charisma is, to some extent, a function of the resonance of psychological profiles between, on the one hand, a 'prophet' or 'leader', and, on the other hand, a follower, then why refer to only one of the two classes of 'prophets' or 'teachers' as charismatic?

In both cases, there may be some sort of attraction involved. Yet, apparently, the attraction experienced in the case of so-called 'messianic prophets' is not an expression of charisma.

Of course, Oakes argues, quite explicitly, that charisma is very much rooted in someone – 'prophet', 'teacher' 'leader' 'guide' – being perceived to be the embodiment of another individual's ultimate concerns. Nonetheless, the same kind of question which was raised in the foregoing comments needs to be asked again.

If one assumes, as seems logical to do, that both 'messianic prophets' and 'charismatic prophets' might be perceived to embody someone's ultimate concerns, then why does the adjective, charismatic only refer to one of the two classes of 'prophets'? Someone might counter, in Oakes's defense, by saying something along the lines of: 'Well, there are 'extraordinary needs' present in the case of the followers of 'charismatic prophets' that are not present among the followers of 'messianic prophets' and this phenomenon of 'extraordinary needs' together with the idea of the embodiment of ultimate concerns is what gives rise to the experience of charisma'.

However, such a possible response seems rather weak and not without its own problems. More specifically, if 'extraordinary needs' are a reflection of the unresolved issues of someone's psychological profile with respect to, say, primary narcissism, then why should one suppose that the needs of someone who seeks out and follows a 'messianic prophet' are any less extraordinary than the needs of someone who seeks out and follows a 'charismatic prophet'?

For example, why should one suppose that developmental problems surrounding the issue of an externalized 'idealized superego' are any less extraordinary than the developmental problems swirling about the internalization of a 'grandiose self'? What are the criteria for determining what constitutes "extraordinary needs"?

Furthermore, there are also some questions which ought to be directed to the alleged link between charisma and the perceived embodiment of ultimate concerns. In other words, just because someone is seen to embody the ultimate concerns of another individual, why should one automatically assume that

325

the former person will be considered to be charismatic?

Oakes indicates that the meaning of 'ultimate concerns' will vary with the 'seeker' or 'follower' being considered. Ultimate concerns could be of a political, economic, ecological, philosophical, sexual, social, and/or spiritual nature.

We may consider our children to be expressions of our ultimate concerns, but this doesn't necessarily make those children charismatic. We may treat our careers as an expression of our ultimate concern, but this doesn't make our boss charismatic. We may believe that a given political leader embodies our ultimate concerns concerning a variety of social, legal, and economic issues, but we may not necessarily view the leader as charismatic so much as we may evaluate the 'leader' in terms of competence or incompetence, or in terms of someone who is popular or unpopular. A defendant in a murder trial may see his or her defense attorney, the judge, and the jury to be embodiments of her or his ultimate concerns concerning freedom, but this fact does not necessarily cause the defendant to perceive those other individuals as charismatic. We may believe that doctors, school teachers, police officials, fire fighters, and university professors may embody some of our ultimate concerns, but we don't necessarily consider those individuals to be charismatic. The members of a congregation or parish may perceive their minister, rabbi, priest, or imam to embody their ultimate concerns, but those members do not necessarily consider such 'leaders' to be charismatic — although they may consider them to be knowledgeable, approachable, compassionate, interesting, and committed.

Consequently, one need not feel compelled to automatically agree that charisma is a function of the perception that someone embodies our ultimate concerns. Nor is it necessarily the case that charisma is a function of 'extraordinary needs' per se.

According to Oakes, individuals follow a 'prophet', 'leader', 'guru', or 'guide' for a reason (page 126). They are looking for something and come to believe, rightly or wrongly, that such a 'prophet' may be able to provide what they are looking for, or they need something and, rightly or wrongly, they come to believe that the 'prophet/leader/teacher' may be the key to the fulfillment or satisfaction of that need.

Oakes cautions his readers that trying to fathom the deeper motivations which shape the decisions which people make with respect to whether, or not, to follow a 'prophet', 'teacher' or 'leader' is an exercise in speculation. Oakes goes on to indicate that when the people whom he interviewed were asked why they joined a group or decided to follow a 'prophet/leader/guide' that, quite frequently, they responded in terms of wanting to realize some sort of ideal -- such as enlightenment, salvation, or some similar "great work" which involved a transformation of the 'self' – and, yet, when these same individuals were asked what joining a group had permitted them to accomplish or what leaving such a group would mean to them, Oakes said that very different kinds of responses were given.

When the purpose of the 'great work' of self-transformation is not realized, followers often speak in terms of other kinds of values. For instance, they may speak about the process of having been part of something in which they placed their trust and to which they surrendered and which yielded certain kinds of experiential dividends and life lessons other than total self-transformation.

Some of these individuals may have had many of their illusions, naïve and otherwise, dispelled as physical proximity exposed the feet of clay of this or that 'prophet/guide/leader'. Yet, these same individuals may, nonetheless, feel a sense of gratitude for what they have experienced and learned in conjunction with that 'leader/prophet/teacher'. Other individuals speak in terms of the satisfaction derived through having been able to work hard and achieve or learn things which, prior to joining, they may not have thought possible or expected of themselves.

Oakes mentions four qualities which he claims form the core of a follower's attachment to a 'prophet/teacher/leader'. These qualities are: (1) faith (very vaguely and amorphously defined), (2) trust, (3) courage (in the sense of the courage that a 'prophet' gives to seekers in his or her role of someone who, allegedly, has attained salvation or self-realization, and, therefore, is a living exemplar, supposedly, of what is within the grasp of one and all) , and (4) projection (the placing of one's ultimate concerns onto the figure of the 'prophet/guide/leader').

A charismatic 'prophet/leader/guide' could strengthen faith, or induce trust, or inspire courage, or provide a reason for why one believes that such a 'prophet' actually does embody one's ultimate concerns, and, therefore, represents a worthy recipient of such projection. However, admitting this possibility doesn't really make charisma something which is caused by some combination of faith, trust, courage, and/or projection, as much as this may indicate that charisma could play a causal role in the explanation of why someone becomes attached to a given 'prophet/leader/teacher' through faith, trust, courage and projection.

Similar sorts of comments could be made in relation to Oakes' contention that, for example, 'love' and 'freedom' are characteristic of groups led by 'charismatic prophets', whereas 'truth' and 'ethics' are associated with 'messianic prophets'. To begin with, it is not obvious, in any prima facie manner, that someone who is perceived to be an extraordinarily loving human being would necessarily be any more charismatic than someone who is rigorously devoted to the truth, or that someone who is an extreme individualist will necessarily be perceived as being more charismatic than someone who is devoted to duty with respect to moral and ethical issues.

We may be attracted to all of these kinds of individuals. Yet, such attraction is not necessarily of a charismatic kind. We may be attracted for other reasons such as having respect for such people or wanting to emulate them or wanting to learn from them or feeling comfortable around these kinds of individual.

One is still left wondering why messianic 'prophets/teachers/guides' aren't referred to as 'charismatic'. One also is still wondering why so-called 'charismatic prophets' are considered to be 'charismatic'.

Oakes devotes a whole chapter to the idea of the 'charismatic moment'. This is described as an instant, or relatively brief interval of time, in which a person is willing to open up one's heart, to lay bare one's soul, to trust without reservation, to become totally vulnerable to another and surrender.

The charismatic moment is to experience an exhilarating, intoxicating, powerful, intense, electric blurring of boundaries between oneself and the 'prophet/teacher/guide' and/or the group which is led by such an individual. These moments are said to give expression to a primal, life impulse (which Weber refers to as 'pure charisma') that may be charged with sexual energy and are often steeped in a shroud of mystery, secrecy, tension, the unpredictable, a leap into the unknown, and an exhilarating, edgy sort of riskiness — all of which may intensify one's willingness to throw caution to the wind, abandon normal conventions, and become open to the moment.

According to Oakes' the 'charismatic prophet' is someone who is accomplished in inducing such moments through, among other means, establishing rituals conducive to the generation of charismatic moments. Oakes believes that such rituals are one of the most creative accomplishments of a 'charismatic prophet'.

However, Oakes also indicates (page 148) there often is a dimension of the whole process which is beyond the capacity of the 'prophet/teacher/guide', the group, or a follower, to control. More specifically, no one knows, for sure, whether, on any given occasion, the 'spirit' (or whatever it is that is transpiring at a given instant) will flow and the gathering will be anointed with the presence of a charismatic moment.

Apparently, charismatic moments do not necessarily flow through the teacher to the other participants. 'Prophets/leaders/teachers' cannot always produce these moments on demand. Consequently, while 'prophets/teachers/guides' may, or may not be, necessary conditions for the advent of a 'charismatic moment', they are not always sufficient conditions for such phenomena.

When reading Oakes, one often is puzzled because he sometimes alternates among a variety of expressions which are not necessarily reducible to a single phenomenon. Sometimes he talks about charismatic prophets – and, indeed, the title of his book is Prophetic Charisma – as if they are the source of, or channel for, charisma.

However, sometimes he talks about how charisma is a product of the way followers project their ultimate concerns onto a given 'prophet/leader/guide', and on still other occasions he talks about how charismatic prophets are very adept in creating rituals which can lead to the experience of charismatic moments and, yet, whether, or not, the spirit moves on such occasion seems to depend on something beyond what the 'prophet/teacher/leader' brings to the table in the way of creative rituals.

Oakes states that: people who are narcissistic personalities are often perceived as individuals who project an image of unshakeable confidence and strength concerning their purpose, role, and mission in life. Oakes also describes such individuals as being perceived as courageous, even fearless, with respect to those who oppose her or him. Moreover, the capacity of many narcissists to exhibit an uncanny sensitivity to social and individual psychological dynamics lends them an aura of someone with supernatural powers. Finally, because narcissists have an inflated sense of their own self-importance, they also tend to be perceived as being positive and upbeat about life.

A narcissistic individual may appear strong and self-confident because she or he cannot admit the possibility that he or she may not be whom she or he takes himself or herself to be. Such an admission is an anathema to the narcissist.

A narcissistic personality may appear courageous and fearless because, in a very real sense, their psychic survival depends on being able to oppose anything which would cast doubts upon, or bring into question, or cast aspersions and ridicule upon the narcissist's beliefs about who she or he is and what role they play in the scheme of things. When opponents seek to put them in a corner, they often respond with the ferocity of someone fighting for survival -- a courage and fearlessness which can be camouflaged to appear as being in defense of truth and justice when it is really self-serving.

Oakes describes the charismatic prophet as someone who utilizes some of the strengths of his or her narcissistic condition to attract, influence, and manipulate seekers and followers. When people encounter someone who seems to be strong, self-confident, purposeful, committed, positive, courageous, fearless, and insightful, they may be induced to consider such individuals to be extraordinary personalities and quite different from most other individuals, and depending on how adept the narcissist is in camouflaging the true significance and meaning of such qualities (that is, as expressions of a pathological strategy for coping in life rather than any form of spiritual accomplishment or realization), a narcissistic personality may, on the surface, seem like someone who possesses the 'pure charisma' which is believed to mark the 'anointed ones' of destiny or Divinity.

Oakes points out how the career choices of many people who go on to assume the role of a 'prophet/leader/guide' often have a connection to activities in which communication tends to play a central role. For example, on page 88, Oakes lists such careers as: entertainers, sales people, teachers, clergy, and counselors (especially in conjunction with alternative heath) as having prominence in the backgrounds of many of the people in his research.

People who have the gift of gab, people who are adept in the arts of social influence, people who have experience with using language skills to shape the ideas, opinions, values, and desires of other people – all of these individuals are specialists in framing reality to serve their purposes – which need not mean that all such individuals are pursuing malevolent or exploitive purposes, but, under the right circumstances, this could be the case. Narcissists who enjoy strong skills of communication, persuasion, influence and the framing of reality tend to use such skills in manipulative, controlling, and destructive ways, but if a narcissist can succeed in inducing people to believe that something other than what is actually going on is going on, then this can be an extremely powerful means of altering one's sense of reality, identity, purpose, truth, meaning, right, and wrong.

Finally, if one adds to the foregoing set of qualities an element of what is referred to as love, the package can assume quite a powerful presence in the perception of a seeker. Only much later, if at all, will a seeker discover that such 'love' is really nothing more than a manipulative device devoid of all empathy and compassion for another and solely geared toward priming the pump of narcissistic supply which is the life blood of a narcissistic personality and which is sucked from other human beings like a vampire with an inexhaustible hunger for that which they do not have and which can only be provided by warm bodies and souls.

In the beginning, however, all of this is hidden from view. First, superficial impressions may dominate the perception of a seeker – to the benefit of the narcissist and to the detriment of the seeker.

Presumably, it is the foregoing package of perceived qualities which helps a narcissistic personality to appear, to some, as a charismatic figure and, thereby, enable a 'prophet/leader/guide' to arrange for 'charismatic moments' which induce vulnerability, trust, surrender, and even a sense of complete abandon in some seekers/followers. The creation of such moments is part of the repertoire of tricks and stratagems the narcissist has picked up over the years to help manage his or her world in a way that permits a continuation in the flow of narcissistic supply to come her or his way as followers -- caught up in the rapture, ecstasy, power, and release of such moments – shower the 'prophet/leader/teacher' with adulation, reverence, gratitude, and love (i.e., provide narcissistic supply).

The seeker/follower interprets such moments as a validation of the idea that truth and spiritual transcendence are being channeled through the 'prophet/leader/teacher'. The 'prophet/teacher/guide' interprets such moments as a validation that he or she is who she or he believes himself/herself to be in the cosmic scheme of things and, therefore, that she or he has a right to the adulation and love which is being showered upon him/her.

Notwithstanding the foregoing considerations, one might still ask the question: What is the source of the charisma of a charismatic moment? Alternatively, what makes such moments charismatic?

If one defines charisma as the perceived embodiment of one's ultimate concerns, then seemingly, the charisma of a 'charismatic moment' would appear to be connected with the character of the experience which arises during that period of time. However, just because an experience is intense, powerful, inexplicable, mysterious, ineffable, emotionally moving, and ecstatic, does this necessarily make the experience a manifestation of the embodiment of one's ultimate concerns?

LSD, nitrous oxide, Ecstasy, alcohol, sensory deprivation, marijuana, giving birth, falling in love, and holotrophic breathing can all lead to experiences which bear many of the characteristics of so-called 'charismatic moments'. Many of the aforementioned, powerful, emotional qualities can be experienced when one looks up into the sky on a clear night sky away from the city lights, or when one sees a range of mountains, or watches ocean waves come crashing into shore, or witnesses the power of nature in the form of a tornado, hurricane, lightening, volcanic eruption, or earthquake. The right musical, artistic, cinematic, literary settings or performances have the capacity to induce many of these same kinds of experiential qualities.

Charismatic moments can be manufactured or naturally occurring. These kinds of experience may, or may not, be about ultimate concerns, but, nonetheless, they have the capacity to move us in fundamental ways – often in ways about which we may become uncertain or confused as to exactly why we may feel moved or affected in the way we are.

On several occasions, Oakes refers to the work of Charles Lindholm in relation to the phenomenon of charisma. According to Lindholm, the primary, but hidden, purpose of a charismatic group is not necessarily to help people to discover their essential spiritual identity or to realize ultimate spiritual concerns but, rather, to experience itself again and again as a certain kind of collective. Charismatic moments give expression to these kinds of experience.

In many ways, if the goal of a collection of people is to experience itself not just as a group but as a group which journeys through, or is opened up to, or is, to varying degrees, seeking to be immersed in intense, powerful, moving, primal, mysterious, emotional, joyous, ecstatic experiences, then the phenomenon of charisma -- whether manufactured, illusory, delusional, or real – becomes the raison d'etre underlying the structure, dynamics, and activities of the people in this sort of group. As such, certain kinds of experience become ends in themselves, rather than a possible means for struggling toward a spiritual understanding, knowledge, and insight concerning truths and realities which may transcend those experiences.

In such a context, 'charismatic prophets' are those individuals who serve as facilitators for arranging, manufacturing, and moving people in the direction of experiencing (or believing they are experiencing) charismatic moments. If this sort of facilitator is a narcissistic personality, then the idea of a charismatic moment becomes the bait which is used to lure people to help the 'prophet/leader/teacher' catch what is necessary for his or her own charismatic moments ... namely, to feed off the souls of the people who wander into the vampire's lair. If the aforementioned facilitator is not a narcissistic personality, then one has to carefully study the dynamics and structure of the group with which such a facilitator is affiliated in order to determine whether the group has any constructive, spiritual purpose other than as a venue for generating certain kinds of experiences.

People who troll the waters of life seeking charismatic moments need to understand that there are other beings who are also trolling the waters of life, and these latter beings are trolling such waters in search of people who are trolling the waters seeking charismatic moments. If one is only seeking certain kinds of experiences -- described as charismatic, trans-personal, mystical, or altered states of consciousness — and if one is not interested in gaining knowledge, understanding, and insight in order to become a better person with respect to developing and bringing into harmonious balance such character qualities as: patience, kindness, compassion, honesty, tolerance, love, forgiveness, fairness, generosity, integrity, nobility, peacefulness, altruism, modesty, and moral courage, then one is a very good candidate for winding up on a milk carton as a soul who has become lost or missing somewhere along the way.

Elsewhere in this book (e.g., see the chapter entitled: 'A Fate Worse Than Death'), considerable time was spent describing some of the phenomenological boundary dynamics entailed by spiritual abuse and why disengaging from spiritual abuse, even when one may be aware that spiritual abuse is going on, can be very difficult to do. In addition, something also has been said within this book about how powerfully addictive certain kinds of operant conditioning learning schedules are which exhibit what are referred to as intermittent, variable - interval reinforcement properties.

Charismatic moments naturally lend themselves to becoming part of an intermittent, variable-interval reinforcement learning schedule in which the learned behaviors connected to seeking additional exposures to such moments can be very hard to extinguish once this sort of seeking behavior is set in motion. Once a person has had the experience of some sort of charismatic moment, this moment can be the point out of which emotional and psychological addiction arises.

In a sense, a narcissistic personality who is playing the role of a 'charismatic prophet' is pushing the charismatic moment like someone would push cocaine, heroin, or Ecstasy. The narcissistic personality is someone who, himself or herself, is addicted to a different drug -- namely, the narcissistic supply of adulation and surrender coming from others -- and the narcissistic personality uses this addiction to justify her or his efforts to make charismatic junkies of other human beings in order to preserve his or her own access to a constant source of narcissistic supply.

Irrespective of what one may believe about the existence of God or transcendent, spiritual truths, or the realization of essential identity and potential, a spiritual narcissist knows there are millions of people who believe in such things ... each in his or her own way. This is the belief, this is the holy longing, to which a narcissistic, charismatic 'prophet/leader/guide' seeks to appeal and, subsequently, exploit or manipulate in the service of his or her pathology.

There is one other entry point to the issue of charisma which Oakes explores in an attempt to provide understanding with respect to the phenomenon of charisma. This additional avenue involves the work of Max Weber.

Although Oakes introduces his readers to the ideas of Weber fairly early in his book on Prophetic Charisma, I have left these ideas for the last part of the present essay. I have done this for a number of reasons but, perhaps, the primary one being that what Weber has to say dovetails with the way in which I wish to finish the discussion.

Oakes notes that Weber is the individual who is responsible for many of our modern ideas about the phenomenon of charisma. Weber describes charisma as a particular dimension of the personality of certain, special people which engenders in others a sense of feeling that the latter are in the presence of someone who is extraordinary, or someone who possesses supernatural capabilities, or someone who has some sort of close proximity and elevated status in relation to Divinity.

Weber indicates that charisma may be felt and manifested in non-religious contexts, but, nonetheless, he maintains that charisma is largely a religious or spiritual phenomenon. Furthermore, even though Weber was an advocate for seeking and providing social (rather than, say, psychological) explanations concerning the causes of a variety of individual and cultural dynamics, he also was of the opinion that ideas were capable of altering society and individuals in ways that could not be reduced down to purely social factors ... this was especially the case in conjunction with religious ideas.

According to Weber, the phenomenon of charisma gives expression to a continuum of possibilities. These range from: something that Weber referred to as 'pure charisma', to: relatively mechanical and derivative elements of charisma.

Weber considered instances of 'pure charisma' to be very rare and may only have been present during the very early, originating/creative stages in the formation of a group or movement when people first began to gather around a charismatic leader/personality. For Weber, the more routine manifestations of charisma usually arose after the founding force had passed away and/or when the original charisma had become diluted as that force is dispersed among secondary leaders and communities rather than being focused in one individual or the original group of followers.

On the one hand, Weber seems to believe that charisma was an expression of a fundamental, elemental, primitive life force. Yet, at the same time, Weber also appears to indicate that the source of charisma's capacity to influence resides as much in the power which followers cede to a leader as it does in the qualities of charisma independent of such followers.

While it may be possible for a group of people to create the illusion of charisma being present in a given person when such is not the case (e.g., the manufactured charisma of celebrity status), nevertheless, presumably, there is a certain 'something' present in a charismatic individual which has the capacity to attract people and induce them to become inclined to place trust in that individual or to surrender, to varying degrees, to that individual. So, without wishing to dismiss the idea of manufactured charisma, Weber would seem to have something more in mind when he talks about 'pure charisma' – 'something' which exists prior to, and independently of, group dynamics.

Somewhere between pure charisma and routine charisma lay several possibilities which Weber refers to, respectively, as 'magical' and 'prophetic' charisma. Magical charisma is said to be characteristic of shamans who use charisma to, on the one hand, introduce people to the realm of ecstasy, while, on the other hand, helping to maintain the basic structure of simple or primitive groups, communities, or society. As such, magical charisma is largely a conservative, stabilizing force.

Prophetic charisma is described by Weber as characteristic of more complex communities or societies. Such charisma supposedly is given expression through individuals who announce the sort of mission (often religious, but it could be political in nature) which is intended to lead to social change, if not revolution. Through a charismatic force of personality, and/or through the performance of miracles and wondrous deeds, and/or through a capacity to induce intense, passionate, and ecstatic experiences in others, a person who possesses prophetic charisma is capable of affecting other human beings in ways which run very deep emotionally, psychologically, physically, spiritually, and socially.

According to Weber, some charismatic personalities use charisma to assist others to become explorers of ecstatic mysteries. Some charismatic personalities, referred to as 'ethical prophets', use charisma as an ethical instrument intended to lead people in the direction of developing a life devoid of aggression, hatred, anger, fear, and violence by inducing states of euphoria, enlightenment, as well as what would now be termed 'born again' conversion experiences. Still other charismatic personalities seek to arouse, shape, and channel the passions of people to serve, whether for good or evil, various political, financial, and social ends.

Weber believes that the experience of intense, euphoric, passionate, ecstatic states comes about when charisma is used to put an individual in touch with his or her own inner psychological/emotional primeval, instinctual depths which enables an individual to break away from, or become released from, the inhibiting forces of convention and repression which normally hold people in place within a given society. As such, Weber maintains that charisma is a life force that is inherently antagonistic to the forces of inhibition, constraint, convention, and conservation which normally modulate the dynamics of social interaction. For Weber, the natural inclination of charisma is to seek to overthrow, transform, or cast off all external values of conventional society as it initiates individuals into that which is located beyond the horizons of traditional social structure ... something so 'other' that it is viewed as belonging to a divine realm that transcends normal society and conventions.

Weber considered charisma to be: too irrational, unpredictable, unwieldy -- and, therefore, dangerous -- to be tamed and controlled in any responsible fashion. Although he believed that charisma could serve as the creative spark which ignited the fires of social progress, he also was of the opinion that limiting the influence of charisma – at least in any 'pure' sense -- to the early period of originating or creating would be the prudent thing to do.

The Qur'an speaks about 'alastu bi rabikum' -- the time when, prior to being brought into this plane of existence, God gathered the spirits together and asked them: "Am I not your Lord?" Anything which resonates with that experience has a quality of jazb about it – that is, a euphoric, ecstatic condition as one is drawn back toward that moment, or as one is drawn toward a state which resonates, in some way, with that original, primal time of an aware, felt, intimate, loving, direct connection with the Divine presence.

From a mystical or spiritual perspective, authentic Prophets do not call us back to some biological state of the womb in which one, allegedly, felt one with the universe. Authentic Prophets do not call us back to some mythical state in which all boundaries between the mother and the self were dissolved so that the mother and the individual were felt to be as one, nor do authentic Prophets call us back to a condition of primary narcissism when, supposedly, we feel ourselves to be omnipotent, sacred, god-like creatures around which the universe rotates and in whose service the universe has come into existence, nor do authentic Prophets call us back to some instinctual, primeval, emotional depths that is seeking to release from the conventions and values of society.

Instead, authentic Prophets call us to seek the truth concerning the purpose, meaning, possibilities, dangers, and nature of existence. Authentic Prophets call us to inquire into our essential identities and potentials. Prophets call us to honor the rights of all aspects of creation, as well as to learn how to engage life through justice, integrity, gratitude, love, sincerity, courage, compassion, sacrifice, kindness, honesty, patience, and humility. Authentic Prophets call us to discover the true nature of our relationship with all of Being and to go in search of the essential meaning of worship.

From a mystical or spiritual point of view, authentic Prophets are the individuals chosen by Divinity who are provided with a charismatic authoritativeness (said by traditions to consist of forty-seven different parts, one of which concerns the ability to provide correct interpretation of dreams) as a Divine gift to enable such individuals to carry out their mission, as best their individual capacity and God permit, to call people back on a journey of return to their spiritual origins, nature, identity, purpose, potential, and destiny. In such individuals, charisma is the felt manifestation of the presence of this Divine gift. In such individuals, charisma is a reflection of the Realities being expressed through 'alastu bi rabikum': "Am I not your Lord?" because no one else other than God has provided the gift of charisma which marks this point of resonance with the Divine Presence.

If one accepts the principle that there is no reality but Divinity, then the passion play of Divine Names and Attributes forms the woof, warp, and fabric through which the tapestry of creation and every modality of manifestation is woven. Everything to which we are attracted bears, to one degree or another, the imprint of the underlying Reality.

As such, there are many kinds of charisma. There is a form of charisma associated with every manner in which Divinity discloses something of the Divine Presence. Natural wonders the mysterious, incredible athletic performances, great musical or artistic talent, literary masterpieces, extraordinary heroic deeds, works of great intelligence or profound inventiveness and creativity ... all of these attract according to the degree that they give manifestation to the charisma inherent in the Divine Presence which is peeking through the veils of Creation.

Power carries an aura of charisma because none other than God's will permits someone to ascend to the throne of power. Even Satanic power and capabilities may have a quality of charisma to them because such powers and capabilities are exercised only by God's leave and which serve -- in a way that God understands but Satanic forces do not -- Divine purposes.

The natural inclination inherent in the pure charisma which is given expression through the lives of authentic Prophets is constructive, not destructive. It is benevolent, not malevolent ... it is peaceful, not aggressive and hostile ... it is committed to the distribution of fairness, justice, and the honoring of the rights of all facets of Creation, rather than given to the generation of upheaval, discord, and rebellion ... it is oriented toward the acquisition of essential knowledge, wisdom and understanding through which the constructive potential of life, both individually and collectively, can be released and set free, rather than being oriented toward primitive forms of physical and emotional release associated with the individual desires, whims, and wishes of the nafs or carnal soul.

If God wishes, authentic Prophetic charisma offers spiritual nourishment to both individuals and communities. God willing, people become strengthened and constructively energized through the presence of authentic Prophetic charisma.

The desire to be in the presence of authentic Prophetic charisma is part of the holy longing which seeks to feel re-connected, in an intimate way, with the Divine ... to be returned to the sacredness of the occasion of 'alastu bi rabikum'. Authentic Prophetic charisma is the catalyst provided by Divinity that is intended to help facilitate such a connection and return.

It is unfortunate that Oakes has used the term 'prophetic charisma' to refer primarily to pathological attempts to counterfeit authentic expressions of 'prophetic charisma'. This has happened, I believe, because the sample which Oakes used to develop his notion of a prophet was problematic and skewed in certain, pathological directions.

The 'package' of qualities which is manifested through narcissistic personalities attempting to convince others (and themselves) that they possess the charisma of an authentic Prophet is but a counterfeit of the qualities which are in evidence in an authentic Prophet. This package is an illusory/delusional framework which is intended to create an impression that qualities like: confidence, purpose, strength, courage, fearlessness, meaning, identity, love, social insight, creativity, powers of communication, persuasiveness, transformation, and transcendent experiences of spiritual ecstasy are present in an authentic, sacred way when such is not the case.

Quite frequently, when people encounter spiritual abuse, this experience tends to destroy a person's faith and capacity to trust. Once one has felt betrayed in an essential way – which is at the heart of all forms of spiritual abuse -- regaining a sincere desire to continue on one's quest to realize one's holy longing is very difficult to do.

A mistake which many people make who write about spiritual abuse is to approach the issue from an excessively rational, philosophical, and psychological perspective ... one which seems to tend to preclude the possibility that the phenomenon of Prophetic charisma as an expression of the Presence of Divinity in our midst -- calling us back to a journey of return to our spiritual potential and essential identities -- is not a myth, fantasy, delusion, or mere belief.

Although I believe that Oakes' work on 'Prophetic Charisma' contains much that is interesting, insightful, and useful, I also feel that, ultimately, his study fails to place the phenomenon of charisma in a proper spiritual perspective. One of the reasons why narcissistic personalities can fool people -- and some narcissists are much better at this than are others – is because individuals in the throes of narcissistic personality disorder are able to turn people's natural vulnerabilities concerning issues of holy longing against the latter.

In other words, even when someone seeks the sacred out of a sincere desire for the truth and not out of the 'extraordinary needs' of, say, unresolved, developmental issues involving the alleged infantile stage of primary narcissism, nonetheless, such an individual doesn't really know precisely for what they are longing. There are many kinds of experiences and circumstances which can resonate with the condition of 'alasti bi rabikum (Am I not your Lord)? in a misleading manner.

A narcissistic personality who is trying to pass herself or himself off as a charismatic prophet/leader/teacher knows that seekers don't know -- that is why the latter group of people are seeking answers from others about how to satisfy their sense of holy longing ... because they don't know how to do this on their own. Even in the case of sincere people, what the latter sort of individuals don't know constitutes a source of vulnerability through which such sincerity can be misinformed, led astray, corrupted, or entangled in a variety of ways.

Narcissistic personalities are often masters at re-framing experience to make it appear to be other than what it is. Satan is the prototypic role model for such a narcissistic personality disorder.

At one point, Oakes mentions that in The Heart of Darkness Joseph Conrad, through the character Marlow, suggests that a "fool is always safe". In other words, an individual who doesn't care about the holy longing within, who is not sincere about matters of essential importance to existence, will rarely be fooled by those who – through manufactured or natural charisma of one kind or another -- seek to use the attractiveness of such charisma to mislead people into supposing that something essentially substantial is being offered when such is not the case. Fools are always safe from being misled in this manner because they have no interest in, and feel no attraction for, things that actually matter.

Intelligent, sincere, decent people are vulnerable to the presence of counterfeit spiritual charisma. Mistakes of judgment concerning whether, or not, some individual is capable of helping one fulfill one's holy longing are relatively easy to make, and, unfortunately, once made, not all of these mistakes admit to easy solutions.

Short of God's Grace, there is no fool-proof way to identify or avoid narcissistic personalities who seek to prey on holy longing. However, one point that may well be worth reflecting on in this respect is the following -- any use of charisma which invites one to abandon basic principles of decency, kindness, honesty, integrity, compassion, generosity, fairness, modesty, humility, patience, tolerance, forgiveness, peacefulness, and love toward one's family or other human beings irrespective of their beliefs, should be considered to be a tell-tale sign that spiritual abuse is being perpetrated. This is so no matter how euphoric and ecstatic various 'charismatic moments' may be which are associated with such a use of charisma.

There is a fundamental problem inherent in any use of charisma that does not assist one to become a better human being, with a more fully developed and realized moral character which is encouraged to be actively practiced and not just thought about as an abstract ideal. However, sometimes – depending on the forces at play in a given set of circumstances and depending on the skills of the narcissistic perpetrator who is busy weaving a tapestry of illusions, delusions, and manipulative deceit -- discovering that such a problem exists can be a long difficult process, and, furthermore, disengaging from such circumstances once this problem has been discovered is not necessarily an easy, painless, straightforward thing to accomplish. Indeed, sometimes, long after one has left a narcissistic personality who has been posing as a charismatic prophet, remnants of the toxicity continue to flow through one's system ... not because one wishes this to be the case but because this is often part and parcel of the destructive, insidious nature of the ramifications ensuing from spiritual abuse.

15.) <u>A Story and Its Possible Symbolism</u>

The following story was told to me and a friend of mine by the individual who, at one time, I considered – incorrectly – to be an authentic Sufi shaykh (spiritual guide). The story was told not as a fictional account but as something which had actually happened.

I had never known (at least up to that point) the alleged shaykh to lie. So, the telling of the story – especially, in the light of subsequent events that led to my discovery of the counterfeit nature of this individual who referred to himself as a shaykh – makes me wonder about the significance of the story and why it was told.

Quite independently of whatever the motivations were of the spiritual charlatan for relating the story, there are some elements in the story which lend themselves to some reflections on the issue of spiritual abuse and terrorism. From this perspective, the following story may have some symbolic significance.

****

After supper is over, we linger at the table, talking with Baba (This means 'spiritual father'). He begins to tell an incredible story.

Apparently, two of his mureeds, or followers, from Houston phone one night some time <u>shortly after</u> 9/11, and inquire about visiting Baba as soon as possible. They sound very scared and upset.

They tell Baba they can be at his house late the next day if they drive all night. They don't want to take an airplane, even though one of the two works for an airline.

When they arrive, they begin to tell why they are so upset. A brother or sister of theirs (I was never quite certain whether the brother/sister was from the husband's or wife's side of the family) has been having difficulty getting a job. This is <u>prior to</u> 9/11.

A friend of his tells him about a job possibility in New York City. The friend shows him an employment advertisement.

The brother or brother-in-law calls the number appearing on the ad, and an application is sent to him. He fills out the form and returns it to the company.

A little later, the brother/brother-in-law receives a telephone call indicating that the company would like for him and his wife to come to New York for an interview. All expenses will be paid.

They receive an airplane ticket, together with instructions concerning their hotel accommodations while in New York. They are informed that on such and such a date, the couple will be picked up by a limousine service and driven to the airport in Houston.

On the indicated date, the plans unfold as announced. When they arrive in New York, they are met by another limousine which transports them to the hotel in Manhattan where they are to stay.

They are taken to a very swanky suite. A short time after their arrival, someone knocks on the door and a hospitality basket is delivered.

They eat supper in the hotel restaurant, return to their room, and begin to partake in one of the non-alcoholic beverages which came with the hospitality basket delivered earlier. A half hour, or so, later, there is a knock on the door.

Two people are at the door -- a woman and a man. They are there to give massages to the couple from Houston.

About this time, both the husband and the wife are beginning to feel a little strange ... woozy and light-headed. They don't remember much after answering the door.

The next morning, both husband and wife awake in separate rooms within the suite. They each have a vague sense of having been sexually assaulted the evening before, but they are not exactly sure and, so, they say nothing to one another.

They go to the scheduled interview set for the afternoon. When they eventually find their way to the room, the room turns out to be a huge convention amphitheater-like auditorium, with a raised stage at the front.

There are hundreds of people already gathered. Most of the people look to be from Pakistan, India, and/or the Middle East.

The seats are equipped with head phones, and there also seem to be a set of toggle switches or buttons in the arm rests of the seats. The participants are instructed to put the headset on at a certain point, but before this happens, a white man goes on stage and addresses the audience.

He indicates the interview process will consist of people responding to certain visual images which will be shown on the screen. The participants will do this by using the switches embedded in the arm rests of their chairs.

After a further discussion of the interview process takes place, the speaker opens things up to questions. At a certain point, someone in the audience asks the speaker to say something about the company which is behind all of this.

The man says 'we are the people who make and break governments.' Shortly thereafter, the participants are instructed to put on the headsets, the room darkens, and the lowered screen fills with images, and the headphones fill with voices.

The couple who are related to Baba's mureeds (devotees or followers) say that although they don't remember much of what took place during the interview, they each seem to recall images of planes flying into tall buildings, and, as well, they recall being asked whether they could watch their children die.

After this, things are pretty much a blank. Sometime later, at night, they find themselves in a daze, walking the streets of Manhattan, their clothes disheveled. They have no recollection of how they got to where they are.

The return flight to Houston is not far away. They return to the hotel, pick up their bags and head for the airport.

A few days after the couple returns to Houston, some strange events begin to take place. The wife (who had gone to New York) tries to kill her husband. She keeps calling him the devil or dajjal (imposter).

Things become so bad that she has to be hospitalized for a time. Eventually, she calms down and returns home.

Not too long after this, the husband goes crazy and does the same sort of thing to his wife that his wife earlier had done to him. He threatens her and calls her the devil or dajjal.

| A Story |

Over time, he, too, calms down. But, both he and his wife continue to live with a great deal of trauma, and, eventually, they tell their story to Baba's mureeds who are now relating it to Baba. But, they are doing so after 9/11 already has taken place.

****

The foregoing story raises some very important questions. If the story is not true, then why did the alleged shaykh tell the story as if it were? What was he trying to accomplish? Was it a test in blind acceptance of whatever he said?

Alternatively, if the story is true, then, why weren't the authorities notified about it? Was the idea to create an atmosphere of fear, anxiety, panic, and paranoia in those to whom the story is told so that they would stay away from authorities or government figures -- after all, generally speaking, people who enter into a state of dissociation as a result of such scare tactics, tend to be more vulnerable to suggestion and other forms of social influence?

The story has many, potential symbolic elements. For instance, consider the following points.

To begin with, the victims in the story were not looking to engage in illegal or immoral activity. They were looking for something which was much needed -- namely, a job.

That need was exploited by, and entangled within, an entirely different agenda. This theme has resonance with the manner in which many spiritual frauds operate -- for, false shaykhs, and other charlatans, use the holy longing which is within all of us (that, in and of itself, is entirely God-given and innocent), and they take advantage of our inherent, spiritual vulnerability in order to wed that holy longing to something which is very unholy and evil.

Secondly, the couple in the story were drugged through a hospitality basket and induced into an altered state of consciousness. This, too, is what often happens among fraudulent spiritual teachers -- that is, various techniques of seeming kindness, gift-giving, hospitality, love-bombing, and so on, are used to lower people's defenses and render them more

346

pliable and compliant with respect to an agenda of abuse and exploitation which is to follow. Many people are sexually assaulted or exploited in other ways, while under the influence of the altered states of consciousness which are induced by techniques of 'hospitality'.

Thirdly, just as in the story, people who are found by, or find their way to, fraudulent spiritual guides (without knowing that this is what has happened) are tested again and again. The tests are always re-framed as something other than what they are, and these tests can be very, very subtle, but, the series of tests are themselves a way of inducing a person to enter situations and circumstances which they might not otherwise do if the reality to which the tests are leading were presented clearly in the beginning (for example, becoming a suicide bomber).

Fourthly, the purpose of the tests is to separate off the 'insiders' from the 'outsiders' -- that is, to enable the spiritual fraud to differentiate between those who will do his or her bidding and those who are not with the program. Those who have passed the tests, are, in turn, used by the charlatan to extend his or her sphere of influence over more and more people through the use of this 'proxy' army of committed workers.

Some of the people who are being used in this fashion are not aware of what is going on. Others among those who have passed various tests are aware, to varying degrees, about what is going on and use this awareness to better position themselves within the group's pecking order.

Fifthly, the person in the story who gets up on the stage and announces that 'we are the people who make and break governments' may be an allusion to people -- namely, spiritual charlatans, terrorist leaders, as well as so-called government leaders who lead people into war unnecessarily -- whose business is the making and breaking of souls, and they take great pleasure in this facet of their activity.

They love influencing, controlling, exploiting, duping, manipulating, and abusing people. They derive pleasure from hurting people and destroying the legitimate spiritual and democratic aspirations of those with whom such so-called guides come in contact.

347

Sixthly, the people who do not past the appropriate tests are, like the couple in the story, cast out. Such individuals either get moved to the fringe -- even as they suppose they are still part of things -- or these individuals are disposed of in one way or another, or they are intentionally abused to such an extent that, just as in the story, they find themselves walking about life in a dazed, dissociated state -- not knowing quite what has hit them.

Finally, when such abused people try to return to their 'normal' lives, they often encounter tremendous difficulty in making the transition or adjustment. The poisoning which has taken place at the hands of a spiritual fraud linger in a person's system, long after one has discontinued associating with such abusive people.

Sometimes, as was true in the foregoing story, people end up engaged in recriminations against one another. Sometimes, the people who have exited such groups are left with values, beliefs, behaviors, and ideas which were implanted during the periods of trance which were induced through the spiritual charlatan or terrorist 'leader'.

Oftentimes, when those who exit abusive groups (whether spiritual or political) try to tell their story to others, the nature of the story is so alien to someone who has not, himself or herself, gone through such experiences, that the escapees are not believed. Or, when such people try to help others in the group to escape, the spiritual charlatan already has arranged things so that the ones who have exited are the ones who are perceived, by those who remain as the ones who are being abusive, uncaring, lying, mentally disturbed, under the influence of Satan, or the like – not the fraudulent guide. Consequently, those who managed, through one means or another, to extricate themselves or who are helped to become extricated from an abusive group/teacher, are perceived as being unreliable, without credibility, operating from vested interests, or trying to steal spirituality away from those who are still being held hostage by the abusive group and/or fraudulent teacher.

Sometimes, someone may even say that the people who have managed to escape are merely serving as publicists for, yet, another theory of conspiracy – a conspiracy about spiritual abuse or terrorism or political oppression. Or, such individuals are judged to be individuals who brought on their own misery and deserve whatever happens to them at the hands of unscrupulous people.

People can say whatever they like. However, anyone who has not been raped does not really have any understanding of the horrors of such an experience. The former individuals tend to lack insight into the phenomenology of: betrayal, vulnerability, fragileness, guilt, loss of self-esteem, humiliation, trauma, doubt, anxiety, confusion, stress, conflict, alienation, anger, outrage, violation, and feelings of having been degraded -- physically, emotionally, psychologically, and spiritually -- which are associated with physical rape. To be spiritually raped is to be dragged into the dark spaces of dissociation which are similar to those that are experienced by someone who has been sexually assaulted.

Society has taken a very long time to even begin to learn that no one asks to be raped. In fact, many people are still of the opinion that anyone who gets raped must have been doing something to 'cause' or bring on the sexual assault.

However, no matter what one does, no one wishes to be placed in a situation where their wishes and will count for less than nothing. One's behavior may be careless or imprudent or risky or foolish, but few people do so with the intention of wanting to be abused, degraded, humiliated, lied to, and/or exploited.

Society, in general, is still in denial about the extensive nature of spiritual abuse which is being perpetrated across all strata of society. This abuse is so intimately intertwined with the lives of many people that the vast majority of these individuals do not even recognize they are being abused through lies, misinformation, re-framing, hidden agendas, problematic guidance, manipulation, exploitation, or techniques of social influence, compliance, and obedience.

People suppose they understand the nature of trances and altered states of consciousness. Yet, many of these same individuals fail to appreciate the fact that they live much of their lives in a series of trance states ... there is a reason why the great mystics have said that we are in a state of sleep and when we die, we wake up.

Many people call themselves mystics or Sufis or whatever. Many of these same people live in a state of sleep and get annoyed whenever anyone comes along and says something which may disturb their sleep or which suggests that, perhaps, they are not as aware of the reality of things -- especially with respect to themselves -- as they suppose.

The foregoing story is a wake-up call -- not with respect to a conspiracy theory of some kind, but as a reminder that many of us are being spiritually abused (by fraudulent shaykhs, theologians, imams, group leaders, media outlets, and/or governments) and, yet, we have been induced to believe otherwise. The people who specialize in the making and breaking of souls are circulating amongst us in various guises.

16.) <u>Terrorism, Dissociation, and Spiritual Abuse</u>

You may be asking yourself the question of why you should read something which sounds as academic and 'heavy/intense' as the foregoing chapter title might seem to suggest. The shorter answer to such a question is that ignorance is a weapon which is wielded by many sides of the fundamentalist issue in order to hide the truth about various facets of the phenomenology and dynamics of terrorism and spiritual abuse.

People who are ignorant are that much more vulnerable to being manipulated and exploited by those who use terrorism (irrespective of their 'side' on the matter) to promote tools of violence as the way to solve problems rather than promoting tools of faith as the best way to engage most of the difficulties facing human beings. Ignorance is not bliss but is, in fact, one of the major causes of the perpetuation of the terrorist phenomenon, and those who perpetuate terrorism include not just terrorist groups but those who believe they can conduct a successful war on terrorism, along with those who blindly support either side.

All three of the foregoing elements in the terrorist equation (terrorists; those who conduct violent, oppressive campaigns against terrorists; and those who blindly follow either of these approaches) are steeped in ignorance of one kind or another. The following essay seeks to critically examine some of the phenomenology and dynamics surrounding terrorist activity in the hope that insight rather than ignorance may inform a person's understanding of this matter.

In a previous chapter ('Fate Worse Than Death') some of the dynamics of dissociation were explored in connection with the issue of spiritual abuse. In general, dissociation has to do with a state in which memory, consciousness, perception, identity, and understanding tend to become unconnected with one another.

Usually, one of the prominent causal features of dissociation is the presence of some form of trauma, intense stress, torture, abuse, and/or threat. Experiencing this pushes many individuals in the direction of a phenomenological condition characterized by a combination of one, or more, of the following possibilities: despair, fear, terror, anxiety, alienation, de-realization (reality loses its sense of realness), vulnerability, loss of identity, doubt, insecurity, hopelessness, humiliation, de-personalization (loss of one's sense of being a person), directionlessness (absence of any plan or ideas about how to proceed in life), purposelessness, depression, a sense of rootlessness (not feeling at home anywhere), demoralization, meaninglessness, lack of motivation, loss of control, and/or a sense of chaos and unpredictability concerning events.

The experience of dissociation may be acute (that is, transitory in nature) or chronic. Moreover, the intensity of felt dissociation may vary over a continuum of possibilities -- ranging from that which is relatively low grade (although sufficiently strong to disrupt the way in which memory, identity, consciousness, perception, and understanding are normally connected to provide a relatively functionally coherent and consistent view of the world), to that which is severe and completely debilitating.

All forms of dissociation are experienced as being painful in essential ways -- although some forms may be felt to be more painful and more essential than others. Furthermore, due to factors such as personality, individual history, culture, and so on, different people may be vulnerable, to varying degrees, to the manner in which circumstances are experienced as dissociative in such essential ways

One of the primary reasons for the experience of psychic and somatic pain in conjunction with dissociation is that one's essential sense of being a human is under attack. In other words, we all tend to think of being human in terms of the awareness, meaning, purpose, identity, choice, hopefulness, personhood, understanding, and sense of belonging (family, community, friends, and so on) which normally are woven into our perception of reality.

However, if the force of circumstances, or one's perception of the force of those circumstances, undermines one's existential sense of what it is to be a human being, then one begins to enter into a realm where our ideas about ourselves, others, and reality begin to dissolve. As a result, memory, perception, identity, motivation, and awareness begin to become dysfunctional, and whatever mode of glue (spiritual, emotional, conceptual, social, personal, philosophical, and/ormythological) which was holding things together begins to dissolve and, as a result, one loses one's sense of integration and rootedness.

Clinically speaking, DSM-IV (Diagnostic and Statistical Manual of

Mental Disorders, 4th Edition) identifies five categories which are intended to encompass the sorts of dysfunctional responses which might arise in conjunction with the experience of dissociation. These are: (1) dissociative amnesia (a form of memory lapse which affects one's ability to remember important details about one's personal history); (2) dissociative fugue (often characterized by the assumption of a new identity along with a lapse of memory concerning one's previous identity); (3) dissociative identity disorder (formerly known as multiple personality disorder and a condition in which two or more distinct identities are believed to have arisen within one and the same person); (4) depersonalization disorder (an intense, recurrent sense of having become detached from, and no longer identifying with, one's mental and bodily processes as one's own); (5) dissociative disorder not otherwise specified (a grab bag classification which seeks to cover all other instances in which symptoms of dissociation exist but which do not appear to be subsumable under any of the previous four categories).

Dissociative disorders all constitute responses to the presence of felt dissociation. In one sense, all such responses are dysfunctional because they require one to lose parts of oneself in the form of lost memory, identity, awareness, perception, understanding and integration as the price which is to be paid for being able to function at all. On the other hand, considered from another perspective, however dysfunctional dissociative disorders may be relative to one's normal way of doing things prior to the advent of felt dissociation, nonetheless, such disorders all constitute an attempt by the individual to forge a way of responding to, and dealing with, the intense pain of the dissociative state.

Given the foregoing, I believe that terrorist activities constitute a dysfunctional response to the felt presence of dissociation (in effect, I am proposing a new category for the dissociative conditions listed in DSM-IV). Furthermore, above and beyond the parts of an individual which, to varying degrees, are lost and have become separated from one another (such as identity, awareness, perception, memory, and understanding) through the choice of a dysfunctional response to the felt presence of dissociation, something else has become lost in the dysfunctional responses which are expressed through terrorism -- namely, a terrorist is someone who has lost faith in the non-violent tools which God has provided through revelation and the spiritual teachings of the prophets and saints concerning the nature of Divine guidance.

Dissociation does not just mark an individual's separation from memory, perception, identity, and awareness. The experience of dissociation may also induce one to lose contact with values, morality, faith, and ethical considerations.

One does not have to believe in God in order to appreciate the fact that if another person does believe in God, and then, suddenly, due to the trauma of circumstances, becomes spiritually disoriented, the loss of contact with faith which may be entailed by such disorientation is likely to have a profound impact on the way in which that individual seeks to find ways of warding off the felt presence of dissociation. One does not have to believe in God to understand that if a person lives in a community or culture where religious themes play significant roles in the shaping of perception, identity, memory, and awareness, then if such an individual either loses contact with faith, or, perhaps, never had any faith to begin with, that person is likely to couch one's coping strategy in religious terms even if the underlying motivations are quite remote from any sort of authentic spirituality. And, if one does believe in God, then the foregoing considerations are likely to be appreciated in an even more intimate way.

Similarly, just because someone couches his or her rhetoric in terms such as 'democracy', 'freedom', 'political duty', 'rights', and 'justice', this does not necessarily mean that such a person actually sincerely believes in democracy, freedom, and rights. Different cultures give expression to philosophical, political, mythological, social, and spiritual themes which some people seek to parasitically exploit to serve an agenda other than the purposes and principles actually valued by a given culture while, simultaneously, having the appearance (but only the appearance) of being appropriate uses of those principles and purposes.

Just as the sort of dissociative disorders noted above in conjunction with DSM-IV all can be seen as attempts to fend off the experience of dissociation, however dysfunctional such attempts may be, so too, becoming a terrorist is a dysfunctional attempt to fend off the painful experience of dissociation. Just as the five categories of dissociative

354

disorders noted above all give expression to dysfunctional attempts to establish a new way of trying to integrate being in the face of felt dissociation (a form of integration which can never be functional because essential parts of being have been lost or separated off from that process of integration), so too, terrorist activities are an attempt to fashion a new manner of integrating experience -- and, again, an attempt which can never be successful because essential parts of being have been lost or separated off from such attempts at integration.

None of the foregoing is meant to excuse the acts of a terrorist. Nor, is any of the foregoing (nor what follows) intended to suggest that criminal penalties may not be appropriate responses to terrorist activities -- after all, there are many people who may suffer from a pathological condition, and the existence of such a condition does not render the acts of those people less culpable although these sorts of condition may, or may not, be mitigating factors in the assigning of punishment for such crimes. However, trying to understand the dynamics of terrorist activity should be considered to be an important step toward learning how to treat such a condition in a way that is not, itself, predicated on, and steeped in, the dynamics of dissociation and, therefore, equally dysfunctional.

A terrorist is someone who during her or his encounter with dissociative states has lost contact with important facets of perception, memory, understanding, identity, awareness, and, as well, moral or spiritual values. Furthermore, in the process of responding to the felt presence of dissociation, such an individual has made, or has been induced to make, dysfunctional choices concerning the issue of how to fashion a new sense of integrated being as a way of dealing with, and fending off, the felt presence of dissociation.

As is the case with other individuals who choose dysfunctional, maladaptive coping strategies for dealing with the felt presence of dissociation, a terrorist is someone who has been pushed or pulled into a condition of dissociation through traumatic, stressful, and/or abusive events. When individuals, families, communities, governments, corporations, and/or nations pursue political, economic, social, religious, and militant policies which, intentionally or unintentionally, push people into dissociative states, then the former agencies help sow the seeds for terrorism.

Alternatively, the foregoing comments concerning the issue of dissociation helps to explain -- whether one is dealing with terrorist groups or recruitment into the military -- why the best candidates for induction are people who are in their late teens and early twenties. This is so because, oftentimes, the lives of such people are in transition with respect to issues of purpose, meaning, identity, career, family, alienation, and values.

As a result, such individuals are most at risk when it comes to being vulnerable to being induced to accept a 'solution' for their sense of dissociation which is wedded to the idea of a willingness to commit violence against anything which is painted as a potential means of pulling one (or one's society) back into dissociation.

One can examine almost any set of circumstances existing in the world today, or in the past, where terrorist acts are perpetrated, and one, invariably, will find the forces of dissociation playing a very fundamental role in the etiology of the disorder known as terrorism. Whether one is considering so-called Christians who murder doctors involved with abortion clinics, or: Ian Paisley's Irish Protestant movement, the Aryan Nation, the Irish Republican Army, suicide bombers of Hamas, the Chechnyan Liberation movement, the Japanese group Aum Shinrikyo, Bin Laden's al-Qaeda, the Khalistan movement of militant Sikhs, the independence struggle in Kashmir, the violence of people such as Dr. Baruch Goldstein, Yigal Amir, and the Israeli settlers movement, the Rwandese Patriotic Front-led murderous rampage against Tutsi and moderate Hutu in Rwanda, the genocide in Darfur, Sudan, the Sendero Luminoso (The Shining Path) of Peru, the Contras in Nicaragua, the Balkan wars, the Tamil Tigers in Sri Lanka -- in all of the foregoing sets of circumstance (and many more which could be cited), a variety of historical, cultural, political, religious, ethnic, racial, philosophical, and/or economic forces converged together that pushed or pulled people (both collectively and individually) into dissociative states which threatened them, or were perceived to threaten them, with a loss of control, purpose, meaning, identity, and stature in their lives, and, as well, induced a sense of alienation, anxiety, stress, fear, doubt, chaos, unpredictability, helplessness, vulnerability, insecurity, despair, humiliation, hopelessness, and/or de-realization with respect to events going on around them.

For example, consider the 1967 Israeli defeat of the Arabs. Many Arabs referred to this defeat as *"al-nakba"* – the catastrophe. *Al-nakba,* alludes to something beyond just a military reversal. Indeed, the defeat was, in a sense, a symptomatic expression of something pathological in many facets of Arab affairs at the time -- corruption, tyrannical governments, dysfunctional economies, modernism gone awry, incompetent politicians, failed socialist experiments, chaotic violence, fourth-rate armies, borrowed technologies, as well as fawning, subservient relationships with the major powers. This notion of *al nakba* -- the catastrophe -- is an indication of the forces (intellectual, cultural, political, social, technological, international, spiritual, and historical) which were pulling many Arabs into the currents of dissociation.

The issue was not just a matter of ethnic, national, historical, racial, linguistic, military, and cultural dissolution, but spiritual dissolution as well ... after all, if theirs was the true religion, then how could God permit such things to happen. This led to a lot of unanswered questions about identity, purpose, meaning, truth, character, government, society, and spirituality which, in turn, pulled and pushed many Arabs further into the grip of dissociative states ... states that rendered some of these individuals vulnerable to the spiritual abuse of those who were inclined to acts of violence and used the idea of a religiously-coated terrorism as the solution for reversing *al-nakba* and extricating themselves from the psychic and soul-wrenching pain of their dissociative condition.

Terrorism is the only dissociative disorder which seeks to push others into the same state of dissociation as the one which underlies that dysfunctional response. The purpose of terrorism is to seek, whether directly or indirectly, to induce the lives of others to become: chaotic, de-personalized, de-realized, alienated, fear-laden, stressful, anxious, unpredictable, insecure, meaningless, hopeless, vulnerable, purposeless, lacking in direction, depressed, despairing, filled with humiliation, and demoralized.

On the one hand, the purpose of terrorism is to maximize the collateral damage of dissociation in others -- the ones who the terrorist

357

perceives have been responsible, directly or indirectly, for the presence of dissociation in his or her own lives. On the other hand, the purpose of terrorism is to seek to induce those who are perceived to be the cause of dissociation in the life of the terrorist to cease and desist with respect to those activities which are believed to have led to the presence of dissociation in the life of the terrorist.

Generally speaking, although there are exceptions to this (e.g., Billy Milligan -- if one considers him a true case of dissociative identity disorder), those who suffer from the sort of dissociative disorders listed in DSM-IV do not harm others. The dysfunctional, maladaptive coping strategies which arise out of the dissociative conditions underlying those strategies are primarily geared to help the individual cope with his, or her, own internal sense of dissociation in terms which are self-directed rather than other-directed.

In the case of terrorism, however, one of the primary driving forces being expressed through the dysfunctional, maladaptive coping strategies of a terrorist dissociative disorder is to do violence (emotional, psychological, social, physical, economic, and/or spiritual) to others. The terrorist believes that the cause of his or her felt sense of dissociation has a remedy which revolves around an external locus of control, whereas most dissociative disorders involve remedies which revolve around an internal adjustment (involving memory, awareness, perception, and/or identity) to the felt presence of dissociation.

The terrorist generates, or is induced to generate, delusions (belief systems which tend to be false and detached from actual conditions) concerning the role of the 'other' in the etiology of the felt presence of dissociation. These delusional states are possible because of a loss of contact with the sort of integrated elements of memory, perception, identity, and awareness which are necessary for performing a reality check -- a loss of contact which has been brought on by the presence of dissociative elements in the life of the terrorist.

The presence of felt dissociation does not automatically lead to a dissociative disorder. Furthermore, as indicated previously, although all dissociative disorders constitute dysfunctional, maladaptive coping strategies, terrorism is only one possible response to the felt presence of dissociation.

One of the factors which determines whether, or not, the presence of felt dissociation will lead to a dissociative disorder of the terrorist variety revolves around the issue of faith. More specifically, although the rhetoric of terrorism is often imbued with themes of God, Divine justice/judgment, religious truths, faith, and the like, one of the delusions from which a terrorist suffers is the belief that he or she is still in functional contact with tools of faith or morality.

Despite the religious rhetoric of terrorists, violence is not a tool of faith or morality. In fact, with very limited exceptions, the presence of violence is, usually, a symptom of an absence of faith or morality -- and this is as true for nations which collectively perpetrate violence and terrorism in the name of some delusional theory concerning God, democracy, freedom, and justice as it is for individuals who perpetrate violence in the name of some personal, delusional form of justification.

To be sure, certain acts of violence may be legitimately reconcilable with a spiritual or moral perspective within some limited contexts (at the same time this is not meant to dismiss the possibility of choosing to be non-violent, even at the cost of one's life or the life of one's loved ones, can also be a moral, faith-based response to the same set of circumstances). These contexts of, potentially, justifiable violence are far more limited and constrained than some people may suppose, and such contexts usually involve repelling -- within boundaries which should not be transgressed -- direct, unavoidable, unprovoked or unjustified acts of physical aggression against one's person, one's family, or one's local community.

Notwithstanding the foregoing sorts of special, limited circumstances (and, perhaps, not even then, as necessary as such acts may be), violence toward others cannot be considered to be a tool of faith or morality. Indeed, tools of faith such as: patience, kindness, forgiveness, tolerance, love, compassion, charitableness, humility, nobility, integrity, objectivity, balance, hope, fairness, and honesty form an integral part of Divine guidance across all spiritual traditions due to, among other things, the capacity of such qualities to assist a person to find alternative solutions to problems which are not violent in nature. As such, tools of faith and morality are the direct antithesis of tools of violence as ways of seeking to: resolve conflict, worship Divinity, submit

359

to Divine guidance, or treat others with righteousness and equitability.

In many instances, the delusion that violence toward others is a way of demonstrating one's faith in, or love of, or commitment to, God has been induced through a process of spiritual abuse which is perpetrated by so-called 'leaders' who wish to manipulate, deceive, and exploit people -- people who are vulnerable due to an on-going condition of dissociation -- to serve the non-spiritual ends of the 'leaders'. Such 'leaders' teach a delusional approach to life rather than an approach which is rooted in the aforementioned tools of faith, but, the delusional 'solution' which is taught constitutes a much easier and simpler -- albeit spiritually and morally reprehensible -- way of doing things.

Acquiring tools of faith is very difficult work ... often requiring a lifetime of struggles. Acquiring tools of violence, on the other hand, is relatively effortless, often taking no more than a few hours, days, or weeks of one's time.

Acting in accordance with tools of faith requires considerable thought, reflection, focus, insight, prayer, meditation, and wisdom concerning all sides of a problem. Acting in concert with tools of violence often requires little thought except that which is given to how to perpetrate the act.

One of the primary obstacles to performing terrorist acts is the presence of faith. One of the primary techniques of spiritual charlatans (whether they call themselves shaykhs, ministers, imams, teachers, theologians, government leaders, muftis, preachers, rabbis, gurus, mujtahids, or the like) who are involved in terrorism and wish to entangle others in their violent delusions is to undermine, corrupt, eliminate, distort, or mislead whatever faith exists in a candidate for terrorism ... a candidate being defined as someone whose condition of dissociation makes them vulnerable to the development of dysfunctional, maladaptive coping strategies concerning the handling of such felt dissociation.

Perhaps the best way of illustrating the connection between spiritual abuse and terrorism is to take an in-depth look at the delusional systems which are created by those who wish to induce others to commit acts of terrorism. Although the following discussion focuses on the issue of jihad, the underlying principles and ideas are applicable to virtually any context in which one person ('leader'), institution, group, agency, or government seeks to induce others to commit acts of violence on his/its behalf.

The delusional dimension of the process through which a susceptible individual (e.g., drawn from among people who have been pushed toward dissociation as outlined earlier) buys into, or becomes shaped by, a delusional system (such as terrorism, or some other relationship of undue influence -- as in relation to so-called 'mystical' charlatans) is an extremely important element in bridging the transformation from non-terrorist to terrorist activities. Such delusional systems give expression to three main features which are very enticing to certain people in a state of dissociation: (1) delusional systems help an individual to escape the pain of dissociation by replacing a deep sense of: alienation, fear, stress, feeling scattered, doubt, malaise, anxiety, depression, identity diffusion, and the like, with a sense of purpose, meaning, direction, identity, coherency, direction, focus, motivation, and belonging; (2) delusional systems offer a coping strategy -- maladaptive though it may be -- for resisting the pull of dissociative states which, like vultures waiting for something to die, exist at the horizons of one's life due to prevailing circumstances; (3) delusional systems provide a rationalized system of values which lowers the threshold with respect to a person's willingness to commit violence against those who -- according to the delusional system being touted -- are perceived, rightly or wrongly, as having a major role to play in helping to bring about one's previous condition of dissociation.

Anyone who believes that terrorists are, for the most part, inherently sociopathic monsters -- that is, they are born, not made -- completely misunderstands the phenomenon of terrorism. To be sure, there are certain individuals who gravitate to terrorist activities because of the presence of some form of mental pathology (such as anti-social personality disorder, narcissistic personality disorder, borderline personality disorder, and so on), but these individuals often become "leaders" within terrorist movements, and, consequently, such individuals tend to induce others to sacrifice their lives in the commission of violence rather than sacrificing their own lives.

The foot-soldiers of terrorism tend to be individuals who are "rescued" from a dissociative condition. There are "reasons" -- maladaptive though those 'reasons' may be -- for allowing oneself to come under the influence of a delusional terrorist paradigm concerning the ills of the world and how to 'heal' those maladies.

Individuals from financially and socially well-to-do backgrounds, who are well-educated, are as vulnerable to being pulled or pushed into dissociative states as people from a background of poverty who live amidst the bottom strata of society and are poorly educated. The determining factor is not socio-economic but whether, or not, an individual is grappling with the psychic dogs of dissociation, and, thereby, is vulnerable to the enticements of the sort of delusional systems which appear to offer a way to free himself or herself from the painful, debilitating grip of dissociation.

One should try to keep the foregoing considerations in mind when reading the following discussion about jihad. Jihad -- when construed in the sense of indiscriminate violence -- gives expression to a delusional paradigm which encompasses a variety of pay-offs for susceptible individuals. Some of these payoffs concern myths about the afterlife. Some of these payoffs involve the money which may be paid to one's relatives when one sacrifices one's life for 'the cause'. Some of these payoffs may have to do with the adulation and respect which one believes will accrue to oneself when one has sacrificed one's life.

First and foremost, however, one of the major payoffs of such a delusional system is the way in which individuals in a dissociative condition are provided with a way out of that condition, not fully understanding (again, as a result of the influence of the delusional paradigm in which they are becoming entangled) that there is a huge price to be paid which dwarfs whatever payoffs may come their way. That price is the loss of their soul and any remnants of authentic faith which they may have had prior to becoming entangled in terrorist activities ... a loss which is due to a reliance on the tools of violence to solve problems rather than the tools of faith.

A considerable amount of time is spent in the following pages examining some of the arguments which extremist, fundamentalist jihadists use to try to justify violence, as well as justify their selection of targets against which such violence is to be directed. By deconstructing the delusional character of the paradigm of violence, one is in a better position to develop programs and policies which are based on actual insight into some of the dynamics of the terrorist perspective rather than based on political theologies concerning democracy, capitalism, and freedom which, unfortunately, all too frequently are rooted in the very same kind of delusional phenomenology as the terrorists against which such theologies are aimed.

It is a very seductive argument -- whether this is propagated by would-be terrorists or by those who regulate the activities of military units -- to claim that acts of violence are warranted by goals of 'truth', 'justice', salvation, and 'freedom'. It is a very powerful argument -- whether this is put forth by would-be terrorists or by those who regulate the activities of military units -- to seek to induce people to believe that God, duty, and/or honor sanctions or legitimizes violence against a given people or set of individuals. It is a very compelling argument to assert -- whether this is done by would-be terrorists or by those who regulate the activities of military units -- that one is engaged in a great, cosmic war between the forces of good and evil and that the side for which one is committing violence gives expression to the 'good' rather than the 'evil' and, consequently, this somehow sanitizes indiscriminate violence and rehabilitates it. It is a very alluring argument -- whether this is made by would-be terrorists or by those who regulate the activities of military units -- that all those who are labeled as 'evil-doers', or people of unacceptable spiritual pedigree, or people who will not submit to our way of life, deserve to be oppressed or do not deserve due process or are not worthy of equitable treatment.

Most of the following comments are directed specifically at those who are advocates of indiscriminate violence against people and societies that are considered to be un-Islamic, infidels, unbelievers, apostates, or insufficiently Muslim. However, the horizontal implications of the following comments are intended to extend to anyone who believes that indiscriminate violence against people -- irrespective of who these people may be -- is something which gives expression to civility, common decency, spiritual etiquette, or actually gives the most eloquent expression of what Divinity truly wishes for humanity.

363

Almost any spiritual or humanistic tradition can fabricate arguments justifying violence. However, almost invariably, such arguments totally distort principles by removing issues from their appropriate contexts and, as well, by ignoring the many other principles of such a tradition which come down firmly on the side of tools of faith rather than tools of violence.

The term "jihad" has been bandied about by both Muslims and non-Muslims. Oftentimes, individuals from both of these groups (e.g., fundamentalists of all stripes tend to use words in ways which best express their dogmatic interests) have sought to exploit this word by means of delusional systems which are intended to serve something other than the truth.

In Arabic, jihad is a verbal noun which conveys a sense of striving, struggle, or determined effort. Quite frequently in the Qur'an, the term jihad is followed by the words fi sabil Illah which means: in the way, path, or cause of God.

If the 'way', 'path', or 'cause' of God were meant to be violent, God wasted an awful lot of time with the thousands of other verses of the Qur'an which explore issues that are far removed from matters of armed conflict. If the 'way', 'path' or 'cause' of God were meant to be violent and oppressive (as so many fundamentalists seem to suppose), then one can't help but wonder why the Qur'an spends so much time talking about the importance of qualities such as patience, forgiveness, peace, tolerance, kindness, integrity, equitability, charitableness, honesty, modesty, and love.

Mujahid is the active participle of the underlying root and refers to someone who strives, struggles, or makes a determined effort. A mujahid, therefore, is someone who participates in jihad, broadly construed -- which is to say: activities that encompass a wide variety of modes of struggle, striving, and making a determined effort.

In Arabic there are terms which give expression to the idea of armed conflict much more directly, and less ambiguously, than does the word jihad. For instance, both 'harb' and 'qital' refer to the act of waging war, and, yet, the more ambiguous and nuanced term "jihad" is the word around which discussion revolves.

Those Muslims who are prone to violent solutions to problems don't say: "Let's declare 'harb' or let's declare 'qital'". They say "We are declaring jihad" because the term "jihad" has a noble spiritual currency in Islam which war-mongers frequently wish to leverage for purposes other than the 'cause', or 'path' or 'way' of God.

Under the appropriate circumstances, harb or qital may be subsumed under, or encompassed by, the idea of jihad. However, not all forms of jihad will necessarily be expressed through the waging of armed conflict.

The Prophet (peace be upon him) is reported to have said that 'one performs the best jihad when one stands up and speaks out against injustice in the face of tyranny and oppression'. Moreover, when asked by A'isha (may God be pleased with her) about whether women should be participating in the armed conflict which was taking place, Muhammad (peace be upon him) is reported to have said: 'The best and the most superior jihad is the Hajj (pilgrimage) which is accepted by God'.

Some people claim that the latter saying of the Prophet applies only to women. However, the people who make such an allegation have absolutely no evidential proof concerning what the intention and frame of mind of the Prophet was at the time he is reported to have made the statements about the Hajj which is accepted by God as being the most superior form of jihad. Moreover, those who seek to argue that the foregoing reported words of the Prophet were intended only for women seem to forget that the Prophet accepted the pledge of fidelity, support, and willingness to die in the way of God, which was given at Hudaibiyah in 6 A.H., from both women and men.

At the very least, the Prophet's statement to A'isha demonstrates that jihad can mean something besides armed conflict. In other words, in the foregoing hadith (a saying or tradition which is attributed to the Prophet), Muhammad (peace be upon him) is reportedly using the term jihad to refer to a form of striving and struggle which is other than armed conflict, and, therefore, anyone who wishes to reduce jihad to being nothing more than a synonym for waging war is contradicted by such sayings of the Prophet.

There is also another saying attributed to the Prophet which makes

365

a distinction between the lesser jihad (al-jihad al-asghar) and the greater jihad (al-jihad al-akbar). More specifically, according to this tradition, the Prophet was returning from a physical battle against those who were seeking to oppress, if not destroy, Muslims. The Prophet indicated to those with him that they were going from the lesser jihad to the greater jihad, and when someone asked about what the Prophet meant, the Prophet explained that the physical battle was the lesser jihad and the struggle against one's inner, carnal soul was the greater jihad.

The foregoing tradition does not appear in any of the major compilations of hadith. However, this fact, in and of itself, means little more than that the methods used by those who compiled hadiths did not capture or yield the foregoing saying.

In other words, one needs to understand that any given collection of hadiths does not encompass everything which the Prophet actually said but, rather, includes only those sayings or traditions which are considered to be authentic sayings based on the methodology used to collect such sayings. There may be many things which the Prophet said which do not appear in a given compilation of hadiths simply because such sayings either fell outside the reach of those methods or because those methods did not recognize such sayings as being authentic.

The Prophet (peace be upon him) may, or may not, have said the above tradition about the distinction between the greater and lesser jihad. All that can be said is that none of the major sets of compilations contains the aforementioned hadith, but, nevertheless, the hadith is accepted as authentic by many Sufi shaykhs who are well versed in the methodology of hadith compilation, and, nonetheless, despite knowing that the above tradition does not appear in any of the major collections, the tradition is accepted by them as authentic.

Before proceeding on, there is a point which needs to be made concerning labeling in conjunction with terrorists who come from a Muslim background. Some refer to them as followers of a militant form or strain of Islam.

The concept of a 'militant Islam' is a term which has arisen in order to confuse issues, and this is often done by those who are pushing their own anti-Islamic agenda or by those who are under the influence of those who are seeking to advance such an agenda. In truth, those individuals who come from a Muslim background and pursue terrorism do not give expression to a militant form of Islam because what they are espousing is not Islamic in the least, even though the vocabulary surrounding their acts of violence may have been hijacked from an Islamic lexicon.

Using the mythological loom from which the idea of militant Islam is spun, one could just as easily speak about a militant Christianity because Adolph Hitler arose from a Christian background. Hitler was not giving expression to a militant form of Christianity – indeed, he was not giving expression to any kind of Christianity -- and people from a Muslim background who are terrorists are not giving expression to a militant form of Islam.

Muslim terrorists do not constitute a militant form of Islam. In fact, properly speaking, they cannot even be called Muslims, any more than Satan can be called a Muslim despite the fact that he believes in God.

These individuals are nothing more than dogmatic extremists who preach a delusional system consisting of a wholly invented fundamentalist theology which cannot be reconciled with the actual teachings and principles of Islam. They are fundamentalist, extremist war-mongers who have sought to gain proprietary control over the word 'jihad' in order to mislead people, and in the process, they have reduced the term 'jihad' to a soulless, uni-dimensional distortion of that word's actual spiritual richness.

Such people are fundamentalist, extremist jihadists. They are people who have infested the term "jihad" with their own virulent, delusional system of theology, and one would be far closer to the truth if one kept all mention of Islam and Muslims out of any discussion concerning such violent extremists.

Fundamentalist jihadists like to speak about jihad in terms of its being the most virtuous deed one can perform. They site hadiths such as the following which is narrated by Abu Huraira (may God have mercy on his soul) in Volume One of Bukhari:

"A man came to God's Apostle (peace be upon him) and said "Instruct

367

me as to such a deed as equals jihad (in reward)." The Prophet (peace be upon him) replied, "I do not find such a deed." Then he added, "While the Muslim fighter is in the battlefield, can you enter your place of worship to perform prayers without cease and fast and never break your fast?" The man said, "But who can do that?" Abu Huraira (may God have mercy on his soul) added, "The Mujahid (i.e. the person participating in jihad) is rewarded even for the footsteps of his horse while it wanders about (for grazing) tied on a long rope".

In another hadith which is narrated by Abu Said Khudri (may God be pleased with him), somebody asked:

"O God's Messenger (peace be upon him)! Who is the best among the people?" God's Messenger (peace be upon him) replied, "A believer who performs jihad with his life and wealth."

The latter hadith is more general than the former hadith. More specifically, the latter hadith does not mention battlefields or armed conflict, and, consequently, leaves open the possibility that the Prophet (peace be upon him) may have been speaking about jihad in a more inclusive sense, encompassing an array of different kinds of striving which were not restricted just to armed conflict.

The Qur'an indicates that:

"God has preferred in grades those who strive hard with their wealth and lives above those who sit (at home). Unto each, God has promised salvation, but God has preferred those who strive hard above those who sit (at home) by a huge reward." (4: 95)

In the foregoing verse, the Qur'an is clear that those who strive hard with their wealth and lives are preferred above those who merely sit at home and do not use their wealth and lives to struggle in the way of God. Nevertheless, it is important to note that the Qur'an also indicates that those who do not strive hard with their wealth and lives are not necessarily condemned thereby but, rather, if they seek to submit in other ways, are promised salvation by God.

In addition, once again, the wording of the Qur'an leaves open the possibility that a broader form of striving is being indicated than just armed conflict. Unfortunately, those individuals who are inclined toward violence often like to interpret the Qur'an according to their own violent inclinations, and they use their predilections to mislead (and, therefore, spiritually abuse) people who are vulnerable while in a state of dissociation ... people who are, therefore, desperately trying to seek release from their internal turmoil and pain.

More specifically, if someone feels lost, alone, alienated, scattered, hopeless, and without a sense of purpose or identity (i.e., they are in a state of dissociation), and then, someone comes along and says I know a way for you to have purpose, meaningful identity, hope, a sense of belonging, and focus, then, naturally, the former individual is likely to express some degree of interest in such a 'solution'. If the person in a condition of dissociation hears, as well, that the aforementioned solution to one's problems is also the most virtuous deed in the sight of God, and this claim can be "proved"(?) through verses of the Qur'an as well as through words which the Prophet, himself, has uttered, it is very difficult for a Muslim who is in a dissociated condition not to be very intrigued with such possibilities.

Understanding the foregoing motivational dynamics, 'leaders' who are prone to violence and who are in need of foot-soldiers for the leader's agenda will actively troll the waters of society for those individuals who are in a dissociated state and, therefore, who are very vulnerable to anything which appears to offer an escape from their personal, emotional, and spiritual problems. The elements of doing violence to others and sacrificing one's own life will be introduced at a time, and in a context, when the 'candidate' for terrorist acts is likely to be most receptive to the 'pitch' which is intended to close the deal which converts someone into a once and future terrorist.

It is interesting that none of the foregoing hadiths or verses of the Qur'an which have been mentioned in the last several pages use the words 'harb' or 'qital'(that is, the Arabic words which unambiguously give expression to waging war and armed conflict). No one, apparently, came to the Prophet and asked him: "Show me a deed that is the equal to 'harb' or 'qital'. Furthermore, the Prophet did not say that he knew of no deed which was the equal of 'harb' or 'qital'.

Moreover, the Qur'an did not say that God prefers, by degrees, those who engage in 'harb' and 'qital' over those who sit at home. Striving with one's life and wealth can be done in many different ways other than by engaging in armed conflict, and, yet, fundamentalist extremists who are inclined toward violence wish to restrict the meaning of jihad to being only about armed conflict.

Even with respect to the issue of whether, or not, jihad is the most virtuous deed, there are hadiths which indicate that jihad -- independently of how it is understood -- is not necessarily the most virtuous of deeds which a Muslim can perform. For instance, in Volume 1, Book 10, Number 505 of Bukhari, one finds the following tradition which is narrated by 'Abdullah:

"I asked the Prophet "Which deed is the dearest to God?" He replied, "To offer the prayers at their early stated fixed times." I asked, "What is the next (in goodness)?" He replied, "To be good and dutiful to your parents". I again asked, "What is the next (in goodness)?" He replied, 'To participate in Jihad (spiritual struggle) in God's cause."

A variation of the foregoing hadith is reported by Abu Huraira (may God have mercy on his soul) in Volume 1, Book 2, Number 25 of Bukhari:

"God's Apostle (peace be upon him) was asked, "What is the best deed?" He replied, "To believe in God and His Apostle (Muhammad). The questioner then asked, "What is the next (in goodness)? The Prophet (peace be upon him) replied, "To participate in Jihad (religious fighting) in God's Cause." The questioner again asked, "What is the next (in goodness)?" He replied, "To perform Hajj Mubrur, (that pilgrimage which is accepted by God and which is performed with the intention of seeking only God's pleasure)."

370

In Volume 2, Book 15, Number 86 of Bukhari collection of hadiths, Ibn Abbas (may God be pleased with him) narrates the following:

"The Prophet said, "No good deeds done on other days are superior to those done on these (first ten days of Dhul Hijja)." Then some companions of the Prophet said, "Not even Jihad?" He replied, "Not even Jihad, except that of a man who does it by putting himself and his property in danger (for God's sake) and does not return with any of those things."

Finally, in another hadith, the Prophet Muhammad (peace be upon him) is reported to have said:

"There is a polish for everything which takes away the rust of that which is polished, and the polish for the heart is the remembrance of God (zikr). One of the Companions said: "Is not repelling the infidel like this?" Muhammad (peace be upon him) said: "No! Even if one fights until one's sword is broken.""

In each of the aforementioned hadiths, there are deeds that are being described which, contrary to the proclamation of modern-day jihadists, are better or superior to that of jihad. Moreover, the one exception to the foregoing statement concerns the sort of jihad in which a person places his or her own life and wealth at risk and, then, both dies and loses one's wealth in the process.

Nonetheless, even in the latter instance, the emphasis is on risking and losing one's life and wealth rather than on killing others. Modern-day extremist jihadists seek to conflate and confuse the two (that is, willingness to give one's life and killing others), but the two are not the same.

Indeed, there is another reported hadith which underlies the foregoing emphasis of sacrificing one's life rather than on the taking of the lives of others. More specifically: (Book 21, Number 21.14.33)

"Yahya related to me from Malik that Yahya ibn Said said, "The

371

Messenger of God (may God bless him and grant him peace) was sitting by a grave which was being dug at Medina. A man looked into the grave and said, 'A terrible bed for a believer. 'The Messenger of God (may God bless him and grant him peace) said, 'Terrible? What you have said is absolutely wrong.' The man said to the Prophet, 'I didn't mean that, Messenger of God. I meant being killed in the way of God.' The Messenger of God (may God bless him and grant him peace) said, 'Being killed in the way of God has no like!"

The Prophet (peace be upon him) did not say that killing in the way of God has no like. He said being killed in the way of God has no like. If one speaks out against tyranny (and speaking out in this way is a form of jihad) and dies in the process, then, according to the foregoing hadith, this is an act which has no like. If one goes on a Hajj that is accepted by God (another form of jihad) and dies along the way, then this kind of action is one of the things for which there are no other non-jihad oriented activities that can compare. If one strives with all one's life and wealth against one's own carnal soul (a further form of jihad -- the greater jihad according to authentic Sufi shaykhs), then this is a form of activity with which non-jihad activities cannot compare.

As indicated previously, on certain occasions, the Prophet (peace be upon him) said that such and such was superior to jihad, while, on other occasions, he seemed to indicate that jihad was superior to all other kinds of activities. When juxtaposed next to one another, some people may be inclined to consider such traditions to be contradictory.

However, the Prophet is reported to have counseled people to speak with others according to the level of understanding of those with whom one was speaking. Consequently, quite plausibly, depending on circumstances, audience, and the Prophet's own spiritual state at the time of a given discussion, the Prophet may have emphasized certain actions at some junctures to certain people, while emphasizing other actions at certain junctures to people of a different level of understanding or who had a different set of needs to be addressed which took priority under a different set of circumstances.

All of the guidance was valid, and all of the teachings, when properly delineated, could be reconciled with one another. However,

372

how that spiritual material was presented, as well as what kind of emphasis would be given to such material, might vary from situation to situation and from person to person.

For example, during Hajj, different people came to the Prophet and indicated they had performed the various rites of pilgrimage in a certain sequence. They were seeking assurances from the Prophet that what they had done was correct.

The sequence of steps observed by these individuals was different in a number of instances. Yet, the Prophet is reported to have indicated that all such sequences were acceptable.

Similarly, there was a time when one of the Companions heard someone reciting the Qur'an in a way which was different from the way in which the former individual recited the Qur'an. Since that person had learned to recite from the Prophet, he took exception with a manner of reciting the Qur'an which differed from the one he had learned.

They both went to the Prophet in order to discuss the situation. After providing demonstrations of their respective modes of reciting the Qur'an, they were informed that both styles of Quranic recitation were correct, and, in fact, there were seven different major modes of reciting the Qur'an, along with a larger number of minor variations, all of which were acceptable.

Consequently, just because different people may understand something in a variety of ways does not necessarily mean, in and of itself, that all such understandings can't simultaneously be true. Truth may admit to a variety of degrees of freedom, and unfortunately, God's truth tends to be far more expansive than is the willingness of people who insist on making truth conform to their narrow, inflexible, dogmatic, limited, and, quite frequently, error-riddled conceptions of that truth.

Notwithstanding all of the foregoing considerations, one should try to keep certain factors in mind when thinking about hadiths of any kind. First of all, and quite ironically, there are hadiths which indicate that the Prophet did not approve of people making compilations of his sayings, and, as well, there are hadiths which indicate that on a number of different occasions the Prophet had such collections brought to him and destroyed.

Ibn Saeed Al-Khudry reported that Prophet Muhammad said:

"Do not write anything from me except Qur'an. Anyone who wrote anything other than the Quran shall erase it."

In another tradition, some thirty years after the Prophet had passed away, Zayd Ibn Thabit (may God be pleased with him), a close companion of the Prophet, visited the Khalifa Mu'aawiyah and related a story about the Prophet which Mu'aawiyah liked. Mu'aawiyah ordered someone to write the story down. But Zayd said: "the messenger of God ordered us never to write down anything of his hadith,"

In another tradition narrated by Abu Huraira (may God have mercy on his soul), the messenger of God was informed that some people are writing his hadiths. The Prophet took to the pulpit of the mosque and said, "What are these books that I heard you wrote? I am just a human being. Anyone who has any of these writings should bring it here." Abu Huraira said we collected all these writings and burned them."

Abu Bakr Siddiq (may God be pleased with) had a collection of some 500 hadiths of the Prophet. However, after hearing from the Prophet (peace be upon him) about the dire consequences which might befall anyone who perpetrated untruths concerning what the Prophet said, this close Companion of the Prophet burned his collection of sayings after spending the night struggling over the issue of whether, or not, to retain his set of traditions.

Hazrat 'Umar and Bibi A'isha (may God be pleased with them both) each had disagreements over the accuracy and authenticity of a variety of hadiths which had been collected and related by Abu Huraira (may God have mercy on him). Abu Huraira (may God have mercy on him) was among the first to begin compiling a collection of alleged Prophetic sayings and who, despite only being in the company of the Prophet for a few years had, apparently, collected thousands of hadiths

374

more than people who had spent decades in the company of the Prophet.

During the time when Hazrat 'Umar (may God be pleased with him) was Caliph, he directed Abu Huraira (may God have mercy on his soul) to stop reporting hadiths to others as a result of the aforementioned disagreements concerning the extent of the authenticity and accuracy of some of the traditions being reported by the latter individual. Abu Huraira (may God have mercy on his soul) complied with this directive until after Hazrat 'Umar (may God be pleased with him) was assassinated, at which point Abu Huraira (may God have mercy on his soul) began, again, to promulgate his collection of hadiths

In another context, Caliph, Hazrat 'Umar (may God be pleased with him) appointed Abu Huraira (may God have mercy on his soul) to be governor of a certain region. However, after a time, the Caliph recalled his governor and asked him to explain how someone who had assumed such a position with no money had accumulated so much money in such a short period of time and required his governor to turn over a substantial portion of the money which the governor had accumulated during his tenure.

One of the conditions or requirements devised by later traditionalists, such as Bukhari and his student, Muslim, for determining which hadiths were to be accepted as authentic and which ones were to be rejected revolved about the moral character of the individuals who were part of the isnad, or chain of transmission, for a given saying. Without wishing to pass any final judgment about the quality of the character of Abu Huraira (may God have mercy upon his soul), nonetheless, the foregoing discussion concerning disagreements about whether, or not, Abu Huraira (may God have mercy on his soul) was reporting Prophetic sayings accurately and whether, or not, he had conducted himself with integrity when a governor during the Caliphacy of Hazrat 'Umar (may God be pleased with him) tend to raise the sorts of question which might have disqualified Abu Huraira (may God have mercy on his soul) as a reliable source of hadiths. However, many people seem to disregard such considerations, and, as a result, one finds many sayings among the major collections of hadith that are attributed to the Prophet, yet which are traced back to Abu Huraira (may God have mercy upon his soul) as the primary narrator.

In addition to the foregoing considerations, one might also reflect upon the following facts. Muslim, who was a student of Bukhari and who became a prominent compiler of hadiths in his own right (and both of these compilers of traditions began their work several hundred years after the Prophet had passed away), rejected more than four hundred of the hadiths which his mentor considered to be authentic, while Bukhari rejected some 4-500 hadiths which his student, Muslim, considered to be authentic.

None of the compilers of hadith are the Prophet (peace be upon him), and none of the compilers of hadith are the Qur'an. Even when what is reported by compilers of tradition are authentic and accurate, these compilers do not necessarily provide any clues about the intention with which the Prophet said such things, or toward what kind of an audience (whether restricted or general) instruction was being directed by the Prophet, or what the meaning was of what the Prophet may have said.

The foregoing comments are not intended to demonstrate that there is no such thing as an authentic hadith of the Prophet. Rather, the previous discussion is meant to induce a certain amount of caution when thinking about reported hadiths and whether, or not, and the extent to which, one believes that such hadiths ought to govern one's life -- this is especially the case in situations where one is being told that killing other people or doing violence to other people is the greatest virtue a Muslim can perform -- which many fundamentalist, extremist, jihadist leaders attempt to claim.

Whatever one's views may be with respect to the authenticity of this or that hadith, the foregoing demonstrates that would-be terrorist leaders can cite the Prophet Muhammad (peace be upon him) as a authority for terrorist activities only by either completely ignoring hadiths which contradict their point of view, and/or selectively interpreting the traditions of the Prophet, and/or failing to consider individual hadiths against a far larger backdrop of teachings from the hadith and Qur'an which are intended to place limits on, as well as modulate in various ways, traditions which are being removed from, or considered independently of, a much larger context of spiritual guidance.

As a result, vulnerable people -- that is, those who often are in dissociative states and are seeking solutions for the pain, stress, doubt, anxiety, fear and so on of felt dissociation -- are not permitted by terrorist 'leaders' to explore all sides of a spiritual issue. Instead, these spiritually abusive 'leaders' present only that information which usually has been re-framed, or deliberately distorted, or taken out of context and, therefore, removed from the limiting influence of other kinds of spiritual values and teachings which also should be taken into consideration before any decision is reached in a given matter ... for example, whether to commit violence against others.

In addition to the foregoing sorts of consideration, there are some individuals who -- lacking in tools of faith and, as a result, become inclined to resort to tools of violence as a way of 'settling' matters -- seek to frame the situation in ways that 'help' identify those people who should be the 'rightful' objects of their violence. For instance, there are some Muslims who have divided up the world into Dar al-Islam (the Abode of Islam) and Dar al-Harb (the Abode of War). Some of these same Muslims have further subdivided Dar al-Harb into People of the Book and polytheists.

Although both the Prophet and the Qur'an do speak about Muslims, people of the Book, and polytheists, neither the Prophet nor the Qur'an speaks in terms of Dar al-Islam and Dar al-Harb. These are concepts developed by theologians, jurists, philosophers, and others who arose after the Prophet passed away and who were advancing their own theoretical hermeneutics concerning their understanding of things.

The fact of the matter is there are parts of the Muslim world which are engaged in harb, while there are parts of the non-Muslim world which are not so engaged. If Dar al-Harb is meant to refer to those parts of the world which are at war with faith, then there are times when some Muslims should, themselves, be included in Dar al-Harb, just as there are times when the peace and submission to God which prevails in some non-Muslim communities would render them to be part of Dar al-Islam.

Furthermore, there is prima facie evidence from the Qur'an that placing People of the Book within Dar al-Harb is actually a mistake. For

377

example, in the Qur'an, one finds the following verses:

[2:62] "Surely, those who believe, those who are Jewish, the Christians, and the converts; anyone who (1) believes in God, and (2) believes in the Last Day, and (3) leads a righteous life, will receive their recompense from their Lord. They have nothing to fear, nor will they grieve."

[5:69] "Surely, those who believe, those who are Jewish, the converts, and the Christians; any of them who (1) believe in God and (2) believe in the Last Day, and (3) lead a righteous life, have nothing to fear, nor will they grieve."

(The parenthetical numbers -- 1, 2 and 3 -- in the foregoing have been added for the purpose of emphasis ... they are not part of the original Quranic text).

In addition, one also finds the following verses in different parts of the Qur'an:

[2:136] "Say, "We believe in God, and in what was sent down to us, and in what was sent down to Abraham, Ismail, Isaac, Jacob, and the Patriarchs; and in what was given to Moses and Jesus, and all the prophets from their Lord. We make no distinction among any of them. To Him alone we are submitters."

[2:285] "The messenger has believed in what was sent down to him from his Lord, and so did the believers. They believe in God, His angels, His scripture, and His messengers: "We make no distinction among any of His messengers." They say, "We hear, and we obey. Forgive us, our Lord. To You is the ultimate destiny."

[3:84] Say, "We believe in God, and in what was sent down to us, and in what was sent down to Abraham, Ismail, Isaac, Jacob, and the Patriarchs, and in what was given to Moses, Jesus, and the prophets from their Lord. We make no distinction among any of them. To Him alone we are submitters."

[4:150] Those who disbelieve in God and His messengers, and seek to make distinction among God and His messengers, and say, "We believe in some and reject some," and wish to follow a path in between;

[4:151] these are the real disbelievers. We have prepared for the disbelievers a shameful retribution."

To claim that People of the Book, Jews, Christians, converts, or anyone who believes in God, and in the Last Day, and seeks to do righteous works are not members of Dar al-Islam seems, at the very least, a problematic notion. Moreover, to try to claim that distinctions should be made among the Prophets in the sense that the followers of some should be assigned to Dar al-Islam and the followers of others should be assigned to Dar al-Harb is inconsistent with what the foregoing verses of the Qur'an are directing Muslims to do and, in fact, is precisely the sort of thing about which the Qur'an is seeking to warn believers to avoid in 4: 150-151, noted above. Finally, to use such terms as 'harbis' with respect to people who do believe in God and the Last Day, and who seek to do righteous works -- and, therefore, actually are, from the perspective of the Qur'an, among those who, according to their understanding, submit to God -- seems arbitrary, arrogant, presumptuous, lacking in humility, and unjustifiably discriminatory.

The creation of categories such as Dar al-Islam and Dar al-Harb is exploited by radical, violence-prone extremist leaders in a number of ways. For instance, once one has constructed a category of people who are described as being beyond the pale of Islam (i.e., Dar al-Harb), then it becomes a quick hop, skip and a jump to begin referring to everyone in such a category as infidels, unbelievers, apostates, idol-worshipers, and people of jahili [that is, those who supposedly exemplify the qualities of spiritual ignorance -- jahiliyyah -- which existed in Arabia prior to the advent of the Prophetic mission of Muhammad (peace be upon him)].

Thus, consider the following verse of the Qur'an:

379

"You shall fight back against those who do not believe in God, nor in the Last Day, nor do they prohibit what God and His messenger have prohibited, nor do they abide by the religion of truth -- among those who received the scripture -- until they pay the due tax, willingly or unwillingly." (9: 29)

Some individuals attempt to use the foregoing as justification for waging war against Christians and Jews because they claim that the latter groups do not "abide by the religion of truth" They claim that this verse gives Muslims permission to fight and wage war against such groups.

Such an understanding is problematic in a number of ways. First of all, individuals who argue in this manner cannot convincingly demonstrate -- via the complete set of teachings given expression through the Qur'an and hadith ... not just partial, distorted, and selectively edited versions of these texts -- that God intends for the foregoing verse to apply for all times and to all Muslims, rather than to just the Prophet and the circumstances of that period of history.

There appears to be a general belief among many Muslims that because the Qur'an is a book of Divine guidance, then this means that whatever occurs, or is said, in relation to the Prophet is applicable to everyone else. However, the fact of the matter is there are differences between the Prophet and other Muslims.

For more than thirteen years -- a time encompassing the period of time in Mecca and the first several years after hijra, or migration, from Mecca to Yathrib (later Medina) -- God did not permit Muslims to defend themselves through armed conflict. This was the case despite the many forms of abuse -- including a two year period of siege in which the Prophet, members of his family, and followers were nearly starved to death -- which were directed against Muslims, in general, and the Prophet, in particular.

At a certain juncture following hijra – the move to Medina from Mecca -- and prior to the Battle of Badr, permission came for the Prophet to organize the defense of Muslims against aggression. Over the next five or six years, there were a number of armed battles which took place, and, yet, through all these conflicts, no more than 250 non-Muslims were killed and an even smaller number of Muslims lost their lives.

Following the conquest of Mecca by Muslims, there were various minor conflicts with several regions near Mecca and Medina, but these were handled largely through the tactic of siege rather than armed battles. Toward the last few years of the Prophet's life, there was peace in the land.

Why do modern-day, fanatical, fundamentalist extremist jihadists automatically assume that the part of the Prophet's life which should be used as a model for conduct is armed conflict rather than the non-violent approach -- despite substantial provocation -- which characterized the vast majority of the Prophet's life? Why do these modern-day jihadists automatically assume that the Divine permission which was given to the Prophet with respect to the waging of war under certain circumstances necessarily accrues to all ensuing generations of Muslims? Why do modern-day jihadists only treat those portions of the Qur'an which mention armed conflict (and there are about 164 verses, out of some 6,000, or so, total verses in the Qur'an which deal with these matters) in terms of the permissions to fight which is given rather than the many prohibitions which place due limits on such permission, and rather than on the many other non-violent spiritual lessons which are woven into the Quranic text surrounding, as well as within, such verses? Why do modern-day jihadists accrue to themselves the same spiritual authority and stature of the Prophet and, therefore, arrogantly presume that God necessarily will extend to them the same permissions concerning armed conflict that was accorded to the Prophet Muhammad (peace be upon him) or that the Prophet approves of what they are doing?

Secondly, with respect to the earlier Quranic verse (9:29) which extremist jihadists try to use to justify violence against Christians and Jews, the fact of the matter is that Christians and Jews do believe in God as well as the Last Day, and they prohibit many, if not most, of the same things which God and the Prophet prohibit -- such as: killing, stealing, dishonesty, corruption, injustice, adultery, not respecting one's parents, and so on. Even the dietary prohibitions given through the

Qur'an are observed by Jewish people and should be observed by Christians because such prohibitions are in the Old Testament, and, yet, many Christians have been misled by their so-called church leaders into supposing that such dietary permissions and prohibitions do not apply to them even though many of these Christians accept what is in the Bible as the Word of God.

Thirdly, the foregoing Quranic verse refers to those who do not abide by the "religion of truth among those who received the scripture". This raises a variety of questions.

For instance, with respect to the identity of those individuals who are alluded to as those who do not abide by the religion of truth, there is some ambiguity -- at least on the surface of the Quranic text -- both with respect to who these individuals are and the precise way in which such people are not abiding by that 'religion of truth'. In addition, one wonders who, beside God and the Prophet, is qualified to make such a judgment?

Whose conception of the "religion of truth" is to serve as the standard against which all other understandings are to be measured? -- that of the Wahhabis? that of the philosophers? that of the fundamentalist theologians? that of jurists? that of the jihadists who treat everyone as an apostate and infidel except those who believe and act as they do (and, maybe, not even them)? What proofs can be offered that such interpretations are acceptable to God? Why should only the opinions of theologians and jurists be considered in such matters, and why doesn't the quality of such theological and juridical opinions seem to manner so much as the fact they are willing to give their blessings to violence and armed conflict against anyone who disagrees with them? Moreover, to what extent must someone not abide by the religion of truth before one can wage war against them?

After all, none of us is perfect. We all make mistakes for which we are in need of God's forgiveness, if not, as well, the forgiveness of our fellow human beings. Consequently, to one extent or another, there are few, if any, of us who do not, in one way or another, fail to abide by the religion of truth. If this were not so, we would not be encouraged to seek God's forgiveness. If this were not so, the Qur'an would not have indicated:

"If God were to take humankind to task for their wrong-doing, God would not leave on Earth a living creature, but God reprieves human beings until an appointed time. (16: 61)

Is one to assume that in the earlier Quranic verse (i.e., 9: 29), God is instructing human beings to make constant war on one another no matter how trifling the manner may be in which someone does not abide by the religion of truth and despite the fact that, notwithstanding the mistakes which someone may make, that, nonetheless, such people still do believe in God, the Last Day, and the things which have been prohibited by God and the Messenger? And, just how does God's directive that there is to be no compulsion in matters of deen (spiritual way) fit into the alleged directive that Muslims are supposed to fight anyone who does not abide by the religion of truth?

God is not saying things in a contradictory way. Human beings -- such as would-be terrorist leaders -- are imposing contradictions upon the sacred texts by failing to take into consideration the entire body of teachings and how those teachings can modulate one another in ways which give human beings a lot more degrees of freedom concerning the manner in which one abides by 'the religion of truth' than do fanatical, fundamentalist, violence-prone, extremist jihadists who are trying to induce people to adopt a delusional framework through spiritually abusive techniques of misrepresenting the teachings of the Qur'an and the Prophet.

In addition to the foregoing considerations, the Quranic verse (9: 29) noted previously indicates there is still a remedy which permits Muslims to avoid having to fight back even if those other individuals do not believe in God, nor the Last Day, nor prohibit what God and the Prophet forbid, nor abide by the 'religion of truth' -- even if they are among the people who have been given scripture. More specifically, if those who satisfy the foregoing conditions pay jizya (a tax on non-Muslims), then not only is no fighting required, but the paying of the jizya tax is the end of the matter and there are no further requirements which need to be imposed on such people with respect to matters of belief or abiding by the 'religion of truth'.

In the time of the Prophet, there was a legitimate source of

383

authority through which reasonable judgments about such matters could be made. Furthermore, the requirement for paying jizya extended only to those who lived within territory controlled by that legitimate source of authority. In other words, jizya was not a tax which could be levied on just anyone by just anyone.

For hundreds of years, now, there are serious questions which can, and should, be raised about whether most of the people who currently govern in the Muslims world -- or who, in the past, have governed in the Muslim world -- constitute legitimate sources of authority. In fact the very issue of what it means for someone to be said to possess a legitimate source of authority (and on what grounds and in whose opinion) or whether such individuals are spiritually competent to make judgments about various social and individual matters (such as jizya or collecting it) -- all of these matters are still very much unsettled within the Muslim world. Consequently, there also are serious questions which need to be asked today about who, if anyone, in the Muslims world has the legitimate, God-given spiritual authority to even ask for Divine permission to fight back against those who do not believe in God, nor the Last Day, nor prohibit what God and the Messenger prohibit or who do not abide by 'the religion of truth' -- and such matters are quite apart from the issue of defending oneself, or one's immediate family, or one's local community against unjust, unprovoked aggression.

Just because someone issues a fatwa (theological decree concerning legal issues), or just because someone speaks Arabic, or just because someone has attended this or that madrassa (school), or just because some people recognize someone as a spiritual authority, or just because someone has certain degrees or a certain educational pedigree -- none of this necessarily means anything in and of itself. Unfortunately, these days, there are a lot of irresponsible, spiritually ignorant, abusive 'leaders' (among both alleged Sufis as well as their exoteric namesakes) who call themselves shaykh or sheik and who seem to believe they are Divinely qualified to tell other people how to live their lives.

There are many individuals who are claiming that all manner of spiritual permissions has been given to them. However, claiming this, and actually being given such permission, are not necessarily the same thing -- especially when there are many questions which those people need to answer with respect to the fact that they seem more interested in inventing their own religion than following the full guidance given by God through the Qur'an and through the quality of character of the Prophet Muhammad (peace be upon him).

Above and beyond the many questions which have been raised in the foregoing discussion, there is the question of why anyone would prefer the tools of violence over the tools of faith? Why, in other words, should fighting back -- even when permission is given -- always have to be understood to mean violent, armed conflict? Why can't fighting back mean employing the tools of faith? Wasn't the Prophet Muhammad (peace be upon him) reported to have said: "If someone treats you with nafs (the lower soul), then, treat them with ruh (spirit)?"

Yes, there are times when fighting back, in the sense of armed conflict, may be unavoidable. But, surely, discretion is the better part of valor.

The Qur'an indicates that "oppression is worse than murder" (2: 217). Yet, many of those who claim to be conducting jihad, in the sense of armed conflict, against the infidels are, themselves, guilty of much oppression, including against themselves, in relation to matters of truth.

In Volume 3, Book 43, Number 624, one finds the following hadith which is narrated by Anas:

"God's Apostle said, "Help your brother, whether he is an oppressor or he is an oppressed one. People asked, "O God's Apostle! It is all right to help him if he is oppressed, but how should we help him if he is an oppressor?" The Prophet said, "By preventing him from oppressing others."

Almost all those who have committed themselves to armed conflict against those whom they consider to be infidels, apostates, unbelievers, and jihilist are guilty of oppressing others because they indiscriminately use tools of violence and oppressive compulsion. In the process, many innocent lives are destroyed.

Those who are inclined toward violence seem bereft of the tools of faith which, God willing, might open up the possibility of peaceful

385

means for resolving difficulties. Unfortunately, most of these violence-prone individuals appear to have lost faith in the tools of faith -- the very tools for which they claim to be fighting and which they claim people are not practicing and the absence of which they cite as the cause of all the problems which face the Muslim community.

Fanatical, extremist, fundamentalist jihadists need to be restrained from oppressing others. However, using violence to restrain these individuals is neither, necessarily, the only option or the best option. Preferably, such individuals need to be shown that what they believe and what they are being taught and what they are teaching and what they are trying to bring about is delusional in character and an expression of spiritual abuse (which is always oppressive), and as such, is not, at all, an accurate reflection of God's guidance in the Qur'an or the example provided by the Prophet Muhammad (peace be upon him).

Once an individual jettisons considerations of discernment in such matters -- as extremists frequently are intent on doing -- then, one will begin to see certain verses of the Qur'an, along with various hadiths selectively and inappropriately used in conjunction with the members of such artificially constructed groups.

For example, verses such as:

"And say not of those who are killed in the Way of God, "They are dead," Nay, they are living, but you perceive (it) not." (2: 154)

or,

"And if you are killed or die in the Way of God, forgiveness and mercy from God are far better than all that they amass (of worldly wealths, etc.)." (3:157)

or,

"Think not of those who are killed in the Way of God as dead, Nay they are alive, with their Lord, and they have provision. They rejoice in what

386

God has bestowed upon them of His Bounty ..." (3:169-170)

or,

"But those who are killed in the Way of God, He will never let their deeds be lost." (47:4)

are cited, and potential converts to the terrorist cause are told that being killed in the way of God (Shaheed) is just the flip side of the coin of killing others in the way of God. Furthermore, the way of God is equated with performing jihad, and, then, jihad is restrictively interpreted to mean engaging in armed conflict against whoever is labeled and demonized as being infidels, apostates, unbelievers, and jihilia by the extremist leaders. In truth, all of the Quranic verses concerning armed conflict specifically focused on the permission to engage in defensive wars which was given to Prophet Muhammad (peace be upon him) by God. At a certain juncture, a pledge (sometimes referred to as the Pledge of Ridhwan) was taken by those who were traveling with the Prophet at a place called Hudaibiyah, near Mecca. The nature of this pledge, which was taken by both men and women, was to give support to the Prophet and to be willing to engage in armed conflict whenever called upon to do so by the Prophet.

The pledge was directly accepted by the Prophet. However, as the Qur'an indicates:

"Surely, those who pledge allegiance to you, are pledging allegiance to God. God approves their pledge; He places His hand above their hands." (48:10)

The Pledge of Ridhwan took place in the month of Dhul Qadah, 6. A.H. No fighting ensued immediately following the taking of this pledge, but, rather, a peace treaty was negotiated.

When the aforementioned treaty had been drawn up, it began with "In the Name of God, the Beneficent, the Merciful." The Quraish objected to this and wanted it struck from the accord. The Prophet had those words struck from the agreement.

Next, the Quraish objected to the fact that the document was signed with the name of Muhammad (peace be upon him), Messenger of God. They indicated that this was the very issue with which they most disagreed and wanted this removed from the agreement as well. The Prophet complied.

The treaty contained provisions and conditions which a number of the Muslims, who were accompanying the Prophet, felt placed Muslims at a tremendous disadvantage and which they believed were almost entirely favorable to the Meccan forces opposed to the Prophet. Some of the Muslims grumbled about, and were unhappy with, the terms of the accord.

The Prophet noticed the visible lack of pleasure with the accord and addressed the matter, asking the Muslims with him why they were upset with the treaty. After informing him of their concerns, the Prophet indicated that, in point of fact, the treaty was a great victory because it gave them the opportunity, free from hostilities and in an atmosphere of peace, to invite people to Islam.

Indeed, many people accepted Islam during this period of negotiated peace. And, the peace ended when the non-Muslims broke the conditions of the treaty, and it was the breaking of the treaty by the non-Muslims which led to subsequent armed conflict over the next several years.

The Qur'an mentions the pledge taken by the Muslims at Hudaibiya in the following way:

"Indeed God was pleased with the believers when they gave their Bai`at (pledge) to you, (O Muhammad) under the tree, He knew what was in their hearts, and He sent down 'As Sakinah (calmness and tranquillity)' upon them, and He rewarded them with a near victory." (48: 18)

How many of modern-day radical, fundamentalist terrorists who call themselves Muslim understand that the reference to the "near victory" mentioned in the foregoing Quranic ayat may have been an allusion to the establishing of peace through non-violent means which followed soon after the collective making of the pledge of allegiance? Many so-called modern-day "jihadists" mention the Pledge of Ridhwan -- albeit in a distorted way which, through misdirection, seeks to transform a willingness to die into a willingness to kill -- and, yet, these same "leaders" fail to mention that such a pledge was immediately followed not by war but by a peace accord.

In the treaty of Hudaibiyah, the Prophet permitted, among other things, one of the most basic, recurring themes of the Qur'an -- namely, 'in the Name of God, the Beneficent, the Merciful' -- to be removed from the document, and, as well, he permitted his own role as a Prophet to be denied and struck down. Where is the battle cry of the 'jihadists' in these actions of the Prophet ... a battle cry which supposedly demands that the duty of all Muslims is to wage war against the pagans, unbeievers, infidels or people who are under the influence of the times of jahiliyyah and force these individuals to submit to Islam.

Presumably, modern-day jihadists would assassinate the Prophet as an apostate because he abdicated his responsibility -- according to them -- of observing the alleged duty to participate in violent, armed conflict against anyone who would not submit to Islam. Presumably, modern day jihadists would consider the Prophet to be a leader of insufficient and inadequate faith because he was inclined to use tools of faith first and foremost and would only sanction armed conflict under very specific and narrow set of conditions, as a last resort after other, peaceful, avenues had been met with rejection and hostility.

Modern-day, fundamentalist jihadists are spiritual charlatans who selectively distort the Qur'an, the hadiths, along with Islamic history, in order to re-frame matters in a way that can be used to induce those who are in a state of dissociation to commit violence and feel as if they (those in a dissociative state) are serving the wishes of God and the Prophet when nothing could be further from the truth. This is spiritual abuse of the worse kind.

Extremist, terrorist leaders attempt to argue that the permission for armed conflict spoken of in the Qur'an, along with the Prophetic/Divine acceptance of pledges concerning participation in armed conflict are

389

both in perpetuity and universal in character. In other words, they are claiming that such verses of the Qur'an give carte blanche permission to anyone and everyone to engage in armed conflict against whomever is labeled as unbelievers, apostates, or infidels, and, moreover, such extremists are alleging that the pledge of anyone -- regardless of circumstances, time, and intentions -- concerning his or her willingness to engage in armed conflict against whomever will automatically be accepted by the Prophet and God.

All such arguments are nothing but theological speculation and presumption. In fact, consider the following from Bukhari which is narrated by Nafi':

"During the affliction of Ibn Az-Zubair, two men came to Ibn 'Umar and said, "The people are lost, and you are the son of 'Umar and a companion of the Prophet, so what stops you from coming out and joining the conflict?" He said, "What stops me is that God has prohibited the shedding of my brother's blood." They both said, "Didn't God say, 'And fight then until there is no more affliction?' Ibn 'Umar said "We fought until there was no more affliction and so that worship would be for God Alone, while you want to fight until there is affliction and until the worship becomes for other than God." (Volume 6, Book 60, Number 40)

Through another group of sub-narrators, Nafi narrated the following hadith:

"A man came to Ibn 'Umar and said, "O Abu Abdur Rahman! What made you perform Hajj in one year and Umra in another year and leave the jihad for God's Cause though you know how much God recommends jihad?"

"Ibn 'Umar replied, "O son of my brother! Islam is founded on five principles, i.e. believe in God and His Apostle, the five compulsory prayers, the fasting of the month of Ramadan, the payment of Zakat, and the Hajj to the House (of God).

"The man said, "O Abu Abdur Rahman! Won't you listen to why

God has mentioned in His Book: 'If two groups of believers fight each other, then make peace between them, but if one of them transgresses beyond bounds against the other, then you all fight against the one that transgresses. and:--"And fight them till there is no more affliction. (49.9)"

Ibn 'Umar said, "We did this, during the lifetime of God's Apostle when Islam had only a few followers. A man would be put to trial because of his religion; he would either be killed or tortured. But when the Muslims increased, there were no more afflictions or oppressions."

Interestingly enough, and perhaps related to the foregoing comments of ibn 'Umar (may God be pleased with him) -- who was the son of Hazrat 'Umar (may God be pleased with him) -- is the following tradition. More specifically, there is a long hadith narrated by Hazrat 'Umar (may God be pleased with him) in which a stranger, who showed no signs of travel upon his clothes, came to the Prophet one day while the latter was seated with a number of Companions. The stranger proceeded to question the Prophet about the nature of Islam, Iman (faith), and Ihsan (spiritual excellence). Nowhere in the answers given by the Prophet to these queries by the stranger was there any mention of jihad as being one of the five duties of a Muslim, or of jihad being one of the six basic articles of faith, or of jihad being the essence of spiritual excellence. And, yet, when the Prophet asked Hazrat 'Umar (may God be pleased with him) if he knew who the stranger was and Hazrat 'Umar (may God be pleased with him) replied in the negative, the Prophet is reported to have said: "That was Gabriel (peace be upon him) and he has come today to teach you your deen."

When the assassination of Hazrat Hassan (may God be pleased with him) was being plotted and plans were set in motion to trick his wife into poisoning him, Hazrat Hassan (may God be pleased with him) did not declare jihad against those who were plotting against him even though he knew about the plot and knew that his wife was involved. Instead, when he was dying from the poisoning, he warned his wife about the dangers which lay in wait for her at the hands of those who had induced her to poison him (her conspirators were going to assassinate her after she completed her mission).

When Hazrat Hussein (may God be pleased with him) traveled a great distance to stand up to, and resist, the oppression of Yezid, Hazrat Hussein (may God be pleased with him) did not compel his companions and family to engage in armed conflict. Rather, he gave them all the opportunity to withdraw from the situation and save their lives -- which they chose not to do and, as a result, almost all of them were slaughtered.

Whenever the Prophet Muhammad (peace be upon him) participated in armed conflict, it is reported that he never raised a weapon against those who were opposed to him. The extent of his physical resistance was that, from time to time, he would pick up the arrows which had been shot at the Prophet, as well as the Muslim warriors surrounding him, and, then, hand the arrows to the Muslim archers.

The Prophet was always in the thick of battle because taking his life was the primary focus of his adversaries. Yet, he did not wield a weapon or try to kill anyone even though he was constantly under attack during such battles.

His jihad was of the very highest order of striving. He was willing to sacrifice his own life and all that he possessed for the sake of God, and, yet, he did not take the life of others.

At the battle of Badr, which is the first, major armed confrontation between Muslims and non-Muslims, the Prophet picked up some pebbles from the ground and threw them in the direction of the opposing forces. After this happened, the far superior and better equipped army of those who sought to exterminate the Prophet, Muslims and Islam all scattered, apparently perceiving themselves to be under attack by strange beings who filled the hearts of the Muslim opposition with tremendous fear. The Qur'an informed the Prophet about this occasion with "it was not you who threw when you threw. God is the one Who threw." (8: 17)

God had given the permission for Muslims to defend themselves in the battle of Badr. The Prophet complied with the Divine directive in a relatively non-violent manner.

Contrary to the claims of modern-day, extremist 'jihadists', the

392

Prophet did not pursue a policy in which polytheists must accept Islam or die. For example, Muhammad (peace be upon him) is reported to have said:

"When you meet your enemies who are polytheists, invite them to three courses of action. . . . Invite them to (accept) Islam; if they respond to you, accept it from them and desist from fighting against them. . . . If they refuse to accept Islam, demand from them the Jizya [the tax on non-Muslims which is fairly nominal]. If they agree to pay, accept it from them and hold off your hands. If they refuse to pay the tax, seek God's help and fight them". (*Sahih Muslim,* book 19, no. 4294)

First, one should understand that the foregoing counsel was given in relation to a situation in which a Muslim ambassador was assassinated in Byzantium territory. Secondly, the foregoing hadith refers to polytheists and not to people of the Book – that is, people who believe in God, or people who believe in the Last Day, or to converts. Thirdly, the polytheists are to be invited -- not compelled -- to accept Islam, for, indeed, as the Qur'an stipulates -- and as modern-day, extremist 'jihadists' are averse to remembering: "There shall be no compulsion in religion: the right way is now distinct from the wrong way." (2:256) Fourthly, as long as such polytheists pay the jizya tax (and Muslims, themselves, are required to pay zakat, so something is not being imposed on non-Muslims for which Muslims do not have a counterpart in financial responsibility in relation to the community), then, no further action is indicated, and they should be left alone. Fifthly, there is absolutely no indication about whether, or not, the foregoing hadith was meant to be a universal principle applicable across all time or was intended only for the circumstances which existed at that time. Finally, if polytheists refuse to pay the jizya tax, it does not necessarily follow that the only way of fighting with them is to kill them or do violence against them.

One could apply economic sanctions against them. Or, one could interact with them in non-cooperative, but non-violent ways. One could keep one's social distance from them and not take them as allies or friends. Or, one could refuse to help defend them against other people

393

who aggress against them.

With respect to anyone who was seeking to oppress the Prophet and the Muslim community, the Qur'an says:

"If they resort to peace, so shall you, and put your trust in God. He is the Hearer, the Omniscient." (8: 61)

The Qur'an did not say that the Prophet shall resort to peace only if the antagonists surrender to Islam. The guidance was unconditional and revolved only around the issue of whether, or not, those who were being hostile sought peace.

One of the favorite Quranic verses of modern-day, extremist jihadists is sometimes referred to as the 'Sword Verse'. This verse says:

"Once the Sacred Months are past, (and they refuse to make peace) you may kill the idol worshipers when you encounter them, punish them, and resist every move they make. If they repent and observe the obligatory prayers and give the obligatory charity, you shall let them go. God is Forgiver, Most Merciful." (9: 5)

Just prior to the foregoing verse is a Divine reminder that:

"If the idol worshipers sign a peace treaty with you, and do not violate it, nor band together with others against you, you shall fulfill your treaty with them until the expiration date. God loves the righteous." (9: 4)

Just after the so-called 'Sword Verse' there is guidance (9: 6) about how the Muslims should provide safe passage to any of the idol worshipers who request it so that such a person can hear the word of God and, then the individual should be permitted to return to her or his people.

Furthermore, when one considers the 'Sword Verse', itself, in the context of the Quranic guidance which comes both before and after that verse, there are a number of factors which should be taken into consideration. First, the permission to fight is being given only if the idol-worshipers refuse to make peace. Secondly, Muslims are not being given permission to actively seek out such idol worshipers but, rather, Muslims are being told that 'if' the idol-worshipers should be encountered, and if they refuse to make peace, and if one is not bound by any treaties with them, and if they are not seeking safe-passage, and if they do not repent for their aggression, then one has a variety of options -- namely, one may, if necessary, kill them, or one may punish them in some non-lethal and, possibly, non-violent way, or one may seek to resist (again, possibly, in non-violent ways) every non-peaceful move they make, or one may accept their becoming Muslim. Thirdly, one needs to emphasize that Muslims are not being specifically ordered to kill idol-worshipers but, rather, this is just one possibility among a number of options -- although, not surprisingly, those who are inclined to violence always wish to indulge their predilection for violence and conveniently forget that God is providing an array of alternatives. Fourthly, and, perhaps, most importantly, there is nothing to indicate that the Divine guidance expressed through the 'Sword Verse' is intended to serve as carte blanche permission for all Muslims who come after the Prophet to be able to kill idol-worshipers or to engage the latter in armed conflict.

Finally, and once again, attention needs to be drawn to the fact that the 'Sword Verse' refers to idol worshipers or polytheists -- not to people of the Book, not to Jews, not to Christians, not to those who believe in God, or the Last Day, or who seek to do deeds of righteousness for the sake of God. Although modern-day, extremist jihadists seek to try to expand the category of 'idol worshipers' to include everyone with whom they disagree or who disagrees with them, or whom they consider to be 'insufficiently Muslim', or whom they consider to be apostates, or whom belongs to another faith tradition, or are secular leaders, or whom they consider to be infidels, nonetheless, the so-called 'Sword verse' applies only to idol worshipers/polytheists, and the mental gymnastics of fanatical, extremist jihadists are just part of the package of techniques they have to spiritually abuse those who are vulnerable as a result of the latter's condition of dissociation due to a variety of personal, social, political, economic, historical, and spiritual circumstances.

Some of these modern-day extremist jihadists refer to the Quranic verse:

"For this reason did We prescribe to the children of Israel that whoever slays a soul, unless it be for manslaughter or for mischief in the land, it is as though he slew all men; and whoever keeps a soul alive, it is as though he kept alive all men; and certainly Our apostles came to them with clear arguments, but even after that many of them certainly act extravagantly in the land." (5: 32)

They use the foregoing verse as justification for committing free-wheeling aggression against other than idol worshipers, claiming that those whom the terrorists oppose are precisely those individuals who are spreading mischief and corruption in the land. How convenient!

The Qur'an verse above does not specify what constitutes mischief. Consequently, the arguments of extremist jihadists concerning the meaning of the foregoing Quranic verse are rather presumptuous and self-serving.

However, if one reflects upon the rest of the Qur'an, then one might suppose that the real mischief makers are those who continue to commit aggression and resist overtures to peace, or those who seek to oppress and tyrannize believers (of all stripes), or those who are polytheists and are seeking to destroy believers (of all stripes), or those who are driving believers (of all stripes) from their homes or who are actively preventing believers (of all stripes) from worshiping Divinity. Somewhat ironically, the activities of modern-day, extremist jihadists tend to qualify such jihadists as being the very sort of mischief makers to whom they claim to be opposed.

One might also note in passing that it is interesting that the 'Sword Verse' only mentions prayer and zakat in reference to the conditions which the idol-worshipers are to observe if they are to be let go. Nothing is said about the first pillar of Islam concerning the bearing witness that 'there is no reality but Divinity and that Muhammad is the Messenger of God'. Furthermore, there is nothing said in the verse about those who repent having to observe either fasting or Hajj.

When -- for their own self-serving, non-spiritual goals -- fanatical, extremist 'jihadists' seek to broaden the notion of who is to be considered to be an infidel, or a corrupter of the earth, or a polytheist, or an unbeliever, or an apostate, or one who is under the influence of jahiliyyah (ignorance), or one who is 'insufficiently Muslim' -- that is, all of the categories of human beings with respect to whom the 'jihadists' claim that a 'real' Muslim is not only justified in killing in the 'way of God', but, nay, has a religious duty to do so -- some of these fundamentalist fanatics wish to make women, children, the elderly, and non-combatants as legitimate targets for violence. In truth, there is no Quranic support for such delusional ideas, nor is there any justification for this in the traditions of the Prophet Muhammad (peace be upon him).

In Book 21, Number 21.3.9 of Muslim, one finds the following tradition:

"Yahya related to me from Malik from Nafi from Ibn Umar that the Messenger of God, may God bless him and grant him peace, saw the corpse of a woman who had been slain in one of the raids, and he disapproved of it and forbade the killing of women and children."

In another tradition, the following is reported:

"Yahya related to me from Malik that he had heard that Umar ibn Abd al-Aziz wrote to one of his governors, "It has been passed down to us that when the Messenger of God, may God bless him and grant him peace, sent out a raiding party, he would say to them, 'Make your raids in the name of God and in the way of God. Fight whoever denies God. Do not steal from the booty, and do not act treacherously. Do not mutilate and do not kill children.' Say the same to your armies and raiding parties, God willing. Peace be upon you."

Book 21, Number 21.3.10 of Muslim reports the counsel of Hazrat

Abu Bakr as-Siddiq (may God be pleased with him) – the first Caliph, father in-law and close companion of the Prophet – namely:

"I advise you ten things: Do not kill women or children or an aged, infirm person. Do not cut down fruit-bearing trees. Do not destroy an inhabited place. Do not slaughter sheep or camels except for food. Do not burn bees and do not scatter them. Do not steal from the booty, and do not be cowardly."

In addition, as noted previously, the Quranic verse 5: 32 indicates that whoever kills another human being for "other than manslaughter or corruption in the Earth" it is as if such an individual killed the whole of humanity. How is it that women, just because they are women, or children, just because they are children, or the elderly, just because they are elderly, or a Muslim who one considers to be 'insufficiently Muslim' have – according to some fanatical 'jihadists' -- suddenly become perpetrators of corruption in the Earth and, therefore are worthy of being killed ... despite the fact that the Qur'an, the Prophet (peace be upon him), and Abu Bakr Siddiq (may God be pleased with him) all teach something quite different?

Some extremist 'jihadists' refer to Quranic verses such as:

"True believers are only those who have faith in God and the Messenger of God and have left doubt behind, and who strive hard in God's cause with their possessions and their lives. They are the ones who are sincere." (49: 15)

These terrorist leaders use verses such as the foregoing to manipulate those who are already vulnerable to dissociative states brought about a variety of political, economic, social, physical, and spiritual trauma and push the latter further into dissociation. Such so-called leaders -- who, in reality, are nothing but spiritual abusers of others -- argue that if anyone has doubts about the violence which is being advocated, or if they are not willing to kill themselves while striking out at, and slaying, the enemies (including women and children)

398

of God, then such individuals are not true believers, and they are not sincere, and they have no faith in God and the Messenger.

Unfortunately, people who already are in a state of dissociation due to other circumstances in their life usually do not have a lot of emotional, intellectual, and spiritual tools to counter arguments like the foregoing ones of the extremist jihadists. The former individuals do not want to be pulled further into the pain of dissociation that is encompassed by such charges, and, consequently, it is often easier for them to comply with the manipulation of spiritual charlatans who are inclined to violence than to have to try to ward off questions about their alleged lack of faith and sincerity in relation to God and the Messenger.

Similar things could be said about individuals in the U. S. who, out of trauma concerning the destruction of the World Trade Towers, do not wish to be pulled or pushed further into dissociation by having, as well, to defend against the charges of those among their fellow Americans who claim that those who are not willing to join in and kill whomever (including women, children, the elderly, and non-combatants) is indicated by government leaders with respect to the Twin Tower tragedy, are not true patriots or are traitors to democracy, or are not lovers and defenders of freedom. Like their counterparts among Muslims elsewhere in the world, there are many people in the United States who do not have the emotional, intellectual, and spiritual tools which are necessary to resist such attempts to manipulate those who are in a state of dissociation and, as a result, are vulnerable to becoming victims of the spiritual abuse which is being perpetrated by government "leaders". After all, Jesus (peace be upon him) never killed anyone, and he did not advocate the killing of anyone, but this little fact of inconvenience does not seem to deter those who consider themselves Christians [which, supposedly, means those who follow the teachings of Jesus (peace be upon him), the Christ] from being willing to commit acts of violence or terrorism ... neither of which would have met with the approval of Jesus (peace be upon him).

There was, and is, another stratagem adopted by many fundamentalist and fanatically oriented jihadists. These jihadists include: (1) the kharijis, a sect which arose during the Caliphacy of

399

Hazrat 'Ali (may God be pleased with him) -- which ended in 661 A.D. -- and who (i.e., the kharijis) considered all Muslims who did not accept their interpretation of Islam to be infidels who should be killed and who, as well, developed the idea of a continuous armed conflict against all people who disagreed with them; (2) Shiekh ul-Islaam Taqi-ud-deen Ahmad ibn Taymiyyah (1268-1328) who wrote extensively about jihad and who glorified the idea of jihad as being superior to Islamic obligations of fasting, the hajj (greater pilgrimage) and the umrah (lesser pilgrimage); (3) Muhammad al-Wahhab (1703 – 1792), founder of the radical, puritanical, and dogmatic theology which, today, is known as Wahhabism and which calls for a return to medieval Islam as the only solution to the problems facing the Muslim community); (4) Rashid Rida (1865-1935), who founded the salafiyyah movement which has the goal of seeking to bring about a return among Muslims to what was claimed to be the pure Islam of the pious forbearers (the salaf) of early days; (5) Hassan al-Banna (1906 – 1949), founder of the Islamic Brotherhood in Egypt which rejected all western approaches to government and advocated violence to establish governments that would rule according to Shari'ah; (6) Sayyid Qutb (1906-1956), who expanded upon the teachings of Hassan al-Banna and called for, among other things, the assassination of any government leaders who were considered to be standing in the way of a return to Islamic rule ; (7) Muhammad Abdus Salam Faraj (1952 – 1982), implicated in the assassination of Anwar Sadat and author of the booklet, _Al-Faridah alGha 'ibah_ (The Neglected Duty), which sought to argue that all problems facing Muslims were due to a failure of the Muslim world to consider jihad -- in the sense of armed, violent conflict -- to be a mandatory duty of Islam for every Muslim in relation to all non-Muslims and anyone who was considered to be 'insufficiently Muslim'; (8) Abdullah Azzam (1941-1989), a Palestinian whose most well-known works – In Defense of Muslim Lands, and Join the Caravan -- sought to make jihad an armed, global tool of violence and after he was assassinated in 1989, the group which he founded, Makhtab al Khadimat, was taken over by bin Laden; and, (9) Shiekh Omar Abdul Rahman, who is now serving time in a U.S. prison for his part in the pre-9/11 bombing of the World Trade Center.

The stratagem being referred to in the opening sentence of the previous paragraph concerns the claim that God demands the establishment of an Islamic state which will rigorously and meticulously apply shari'ah to all facets of the lives of people living in such a state and require that all people within the state observe Islam. This idea is directly contradicted by the aforementioned Quranic verse (2: 256) which indicates that there can be no compulsion in matters of deen (that is, the sphere of faith-oriented activities).

However, if one is not satisfied that the foregoing limitation which is being placed on the relation between the state and its citizens is authentic, then, consider the following verses from the Qur'an:

"Whatever benefit comes to you (O man), it is from God, and whatever misfortune befalls you it is from your own self; and We have sent you (O Prophet) to mankind as an apostle; and God is sufficient as a witness.

"Whoever obeys the Apostle, he indeed obeys God; and whosoever turns back, then, We have not sent you as a keeper over them." (4: 79-80)

Or:

"Say (O Muhammad): "This is the truth from your Lord," then, whoever wills let him believe, and whoever wills let him disbelieve." (Qur'an, 18: 29)

And, again:

"You shall remind; you are entrusted to remind. You have no power over them." (88: 21-22)

And, finally:

"Say, "Obey God, and obey the Messenger." If they refuse, then he is responsible for his obligations, and you are responsible for your obligations. If you obey him, you will be guided." (24: 54)

In the foregoing Quranic verses, the Prophet is being told that neither is it his responsibility to be an enforcer with respect to whether, or not, people turn back from deen, nor does the Prophet have any power over such individuals. The Prophet also is being informed that each person is responsible for his or her own choices concerning matters of deen, and if a person chooses to disbelieve, then, leave that individual free to do so, but those who obey the Prophet will be rightly guided.

The Prophet is reported to have encouraged people to repent of their sins to God rather than report them to him. However, if a Muslim did insist on confessing sins to him -- a sin for which a penalty, of some kind, was associated -- then, as a matter of acting in accordance with Divine guidance concerning applying the penalty which God had indicated for such actions (and not as a result of any requirement to compel people in matters of deen) -- a judgment would be made, and, where indicated, a punishment would be enacted.

Once, during the time when Hazrat 'Umar (may God be pleased with him) was Caliph, he was walking about the city and was accompanied by someone. When the two passed a walled compound behind which could be heard a great deal of revelry, the person walking with the Caliph turned to him and in a manner which suggested that sinful things were happening on the other side of the wall, he asked if Hazrat 'Umar knew what was going on in that compound. Hazrat 'Umar (may God be pleased with him) is reported to have said: "It is not my task to sniff out the sins of other people."

The task of a Muslim ruler is neither to establish an Islamic state nor to enforce shari'ah in the sense of compelling people to observe deen in a particular way. The task of a Muslim ruler is to act with equitability and righteousness. The task of a Muslim leader is not to impose shari'ah on others ('there can be no compulsion in matters of deen' – Qur'an 2: 256) but to impose the real shari'ah on himself or herself so that she or he will be able to act with equitability and righteousness and not oppress others.

When the Prophet Muhammad (peace be upon him), by the Grace

of God, defeated the Meccans and their allies for the final time, he forgave them, placed one of the local people in charge, and returned to Medina. He did not charge this person with the task of establishing an Islamic state.

In Volume 4, Book 53, Number 387 of Muslim, Abu Humaid As-Saidi narrates that:

"We accompanied the Prophet in the Ghazwa of Tabuk and the king of 'Aila presented a white mule and a cloak as a gift to the Prophet. And the Prophet wrote to him a peace treaty allowing him to keep authority over his country."

The King of 'Aila was not charged with the task of establishing an Islamic state. This same sort of arrangement prevailed, as well, in other instances where the Prophet signed peace treaties. In other words, those with whom the Prophet negotiated peace treaties were not charged with the task of establishing an Islamic state but were only required to observe the conditions of the peace treaty.

Prior to the time when the Prophet passed away, he had not instructed people to establish an Islamic state. In fact, no particular form of government was indicated, but whoever governed was expected to govern in accordance with principles of equitability and righteousness.

In the Qur'an one finds the following verses concerning the issue of equitability:

"O you who believe, equivalence is the law decreed for you when dealing with murder -- the free for the free, the slave for the slave, the female for the female. If one is pardoned by the victim's kin, an appreciative response is in order, and an equitable compensation shall be paid. This is an alleviation from your Lord and mercy. Anyone who transgresses beyond this incurs a painful retribution." (2:178)

"O you who believe, you shall be absolutely equitable, and observe God, when you serve as witnesses, even against yourselves, or your

403

parents, or your relatives. Whether the accused is rich or poor, God takes care of both. Therefore, do not be biased by your personal wishes. If you deviate or disregard (this commandment), then God is fully aware of everything you do." (4:135)

"During the Sacred Months, aggression may be met by an equivalent response. If they attack you, you may retaliate by inflicting an equitable retribution. You shall observe God and know that God is with the righteous." (2:194)

"O ye who believe. Be steadfast witnesses for God in equity and let not hatred of any people seduce you so that you do not deal justly (with them). Deal justly, that is nearer to your duty." (5: 8)

"They are upholders of lies, and eaters of illicit earnings. If they come to you to judge among them, you may judge among them, or you may disregard them. If you choose to disregard them, they cannot harm you in the least. But if you judge among them, you shall judge equitably. God loves those who are equitable." (5:42)

"God does not enjoin you from befriending those who do not fight you because of religion and do not evict you from your homes. You may befriend them and be equitable towards them. God loves the equitable." (60:8)

Elsewhere in the Qur'an believers are warned to be equitable in matters of commercial transactions, the conducting of loans, as well as in the treatment of orphans, adopted children, spouses, and slaves (and as with many other issues such as consumption of alcohol and the rights of women, the trend of reformation in the Qur'an was toward encouraging Muslims to free slaves, not keep them or take them, but if slaves were maintained, then, these individuals had the right to be fed, clothed, and treated in the same way as other members of the family). Equitability is a re-current theme throughout the Qur'an.

Righteousness is also a theme which is reiterated and emphasized throughout the Qur'an. Being pious, just, grateful, patient, kind, charitable, compassionate, honest, sincere, loving, tolerant, forgiving, repentant, humble, modest, and one who does not transgress due boundaries, are qualities which are advocated throughout the Qur'an.

The Prophet Muhammad (peace be upon him) is reported to have said:

"Muslims are brothers and sisters in deen, and they must not oppress one another, nor abandon assisting each other, nor hold one another in contempt. The seat of righteousness is the heart; therefore, that heart which is righteous does not hold a Muslim in contempt."

A Muslim is anyone who submits to God, and who believes in the Last Day, and who tries to act in accordance with the qualities of righteousness, and who seeks to abide by the deen (spiritual way or method) of God. One should not be too quick to jump to conclusions about who is, and who is not, a Muslim ... and, therefore, one should not be too quick to jump to conclusions concerning whom one must not oppress, nor whom one should avoid abandoning in assistance, nor whom one should treat with righteousness.

The Prophet Muhammad (peace be upon him) is reported to have said: "I have been given all the Names and have been sent to perfect good character."

Principles of equitability and righteousness are at the heart of good character. If one has lost confidence in the capacity of the tools of faith -- such as equitability and righteousness -- to assist others and to help one refrain from oppressing them, and if one believes that violent, armed conflict is the only solution to problems, one fails to understand that is not possible to violently impose good character on others and, therefore, the purpose for which fundamentalist, extremist jihadists claim to be fighting -- the establishment of Islam -- will always be doomed to failure. Good character can only arise through struggle within oneself, not through imposition from without.

There are some advocates of violent, armed conflict -- such as Muhammad 'Abd al-Salam Faraj (author of the Neglected Duty) -- who believe that it is not necessary to make any plans for what should be done after the time of jihad (in the sense of armed conflict), but, rather, one should just pursue jihad and, then, God will provide what is needed later on. How foolish, ill-considered, and illogical!

405

If one is prepared to trust in God to look after things following jihad -- in the sense of armed conflict -- then why not trust in God to look after things prior to, if not independently of, armed conflict? If one is prepared to use tools of violence in the way of God because one believes that such a tool has been sanctioned by God, then why not be equally prepared, if not more so, to use the tools of faith which have clearly been sanctioned by God in the Qur'an and in the teachings of the Prophet Muhammad (peace be upon him)?

Why are fanatic, fundamentalist, extremist jihadists so intent on reducing the tools of Islam down to nothing but violence when such a reduction cannot be justified either by the full array of teachings of the Qur'an or by the traditions of the Prophet? These are individuals who have lost their faith in the tools of faith, and, yet, they are promoting themselves as the defenders of faith.

The tendency of people who have lost their faith in the tools of faith is to spiritually abuse others and to oppress them. People who have lost their faith in the tools of faith must resort to delusional systems of thought because they have lost contact with the only thing which is capable of putting them in touch with spiritual truth -- namely, real, authentic, sincere faith that God's guidance concerning principles such as equitability and righteousness have a far greater capacity for transforming individuals and society than tools of violence and oppression could ever have.

Tools of violence are limited, stop-gap measures for extreme sets of circumstances which rarely exist. Tools of faith encompass an unlimited array of opportunities for pursuing principles of equitability and righteousness which are intended to provide the primary means through which one engages struggle within oneself, in relation to others (both believers and unbelievers), and with all of life.

The Prophet Muhammad (peace be upon him) understood this truth (as did all Prophets). The Qur'an bears witness to this truth (as do all Books of revelation). Unfortunately, those who are inclined to making violence the solution to everything neither understand the foregoing truth, nor do they bear witness to it in their lives.

Those who have lost faith in the tools of faith and who advocate violence and oppression as the solution to all problems create delusional belief systems concerning the teachings of God and the Prophet Muhammad (peace be upon him). The truth will not permit them to advocate what they are advocating in the way they are advocating it, and, as a result, the only recourse they have -- if they are not prepared, spiritually speaking, to acknowledge the truth of things -- is to create delusional belief systems which seek to justify what they are doing as being in accordance with the wishes of, and by permission of, God ... neither of which is true.

Those who are in a state of dissociation (due to political, social, economic, international, historical, and/or personal trauma) are vulnerable to the delusional teachings of those who worship violence like an idol. The reason why those who are in a state of dissociation are vulnerable is because the psychic, emotional, psychological and spiritual pain of dissociation is very intense and eats away at the fabric of the soul.

For such a person, meaning, purpose, identity, motivation, and truth are very elusive, whereas, doubt, anxiety, fear, alienation, depression, hopelessness, helplessness, directionless, loss of identity, and de-personalization are all too real, prevalent, and intense. A person in such a condition of dissociation will grab onto almost anything if they are led to believe that what is being acquired will permit them to escape the pain of dissociation.

Terrorist leaders are individuals who understand the condition of dissociation and the kind of vulnerability to which that state opens people up. Terrorist leaders -- as well as the theologians, imams, government leaders, and jurists who support them -- are spiritually abusive individuals who exploit that vulnerability by (1) locating individuals who are in a state of dissociation, (2) initiating the latter individuals into a delusional framework which undermines whatever remnants of faith are present in the person who is in a dissociated state and, thereby, (3) inducing such a person to abandon the tools of faith and to pick up the tools of violence as a way of solving problems -- both personal and collective.

Terrorist 'leaders' -- whether of the state-sponsored or small group, variety -- are very clever in the techniques used to manipulate and exploit people who are in a state of dissociation. For instance, such leaders often get individuals to sign contracts and/or make videos about their coming exploits and, by doing this, those leaders have a means of pushing the individual back into a dissociative state by labeling anyone who does not follow through on a terrorist act to be: cowardly, a traitor, an unbeliever, one who lacks faith in God, someone who has betrayed the community, or a person lacking in character.

The foregoing technique has an unsettling resonance with something, unfortunately, which also happens in so-called democratic, free societies in relation to people who object to the use of violence and oppression as a means of solving problems (whether domestic or international in nature). People in the United States who advocate using the tools of faith rather than tools of violence to solve problems are often threatened with a barrage of accusations concerning their loyalty, patriotism, rationality, and/or commitment to democracy, and such labeling is intended to push people into the pain of dissociation and, thereby, either punish them for speaking out, or silence them through the specter of being pushed further toward the condition of dissociation.

In Muslim's collection of hadith, one finds the following narration of Bibi A'isha:

"God's Apostle said, "If somebody innovates something which is not in harmony with the principles of our religion, that thing is rejected." (Volume 3, Book 49, Number 861)

To insist on using the tools of violence as the primary and best, if not only, way of dealing with the problems which face the Muslim community, is an innovation which is not in harmony with the principles of deen when such deen is considered in its entirety and issues are not removed from their proper context. Consequently, in accordance with the teachings of both the Qur'an and the Prophet Muhammad (peace be upon him) the approach of the people who prefer tools of violence over tools of faith should be rejected.

The delusional teaching of various fundamentalist jihadists gives expression to shirk -- that is, the associating of partners with God. This is so because, in reality, such individuals are inventing a religion of their own and they have declared themselves lords of such a religion and, as well, they not only consider themselves to be the 'prophets' of this new religion, but they consider the words which issue forth from their mouths to be the word of God. As the Qur'an indicates:

"Shall we tell you who will be the greatest losers in their works? Those whose striving goes astray in the present life while they think they are working good deeds." (18: 104)

The spiritual abusers who constitute the terrorist leaders, together with those vulnerable individuals whom become infected with the delusional teachings of those so-called 'leaders' concerning the nature of jihad and Islam, both pursue strivings of the foregoing sort. These are individuals who have forgotten, or who never knew, that the Prophet Muhammad (peace be upon him) is reported to have said:

"Shall I not inform you about a better act than fasting, charity, and prayer? – making peace between one another. Enmity and malice tear up heavenly rewards by the roots."

When those who govern -- whether Muslim or non-Muslim -- do not observe the principles of equitability and righteousness (principles with which all spiritual and humanist traditions tend to be in agreement) and, as a result, oppress those whom they govern, then, people have the right to resist such oppression, injustice, and unrighteousness through whatever combination of the tools of faith that may, God willing, help the oppressed to overcome oppression, and in the process, serve the best interests of the oppressor as well. The purpose of such resistance is not to establish an Islamic state, nor to impose shari'ah on the community, but, rather, to reinstate principles of equitability and righteousness as the proper tools of governance.

A state should be governed neither by secular nor religious principles. A state should be governed by those principles of equitability and righteousness which help create, God willing, a safe and protected environment through which people will have the opportunity, without being compelled in either a secular or a religious direction, to strive and struggle toward realizing one's essential potential and identity.

Anyone who believes that the terrorist phenomenon is going to be defeated by waging a war on terrorism in which indiscriminate violence is used as the antidote to the indiscriminate violence of terrorism has just handed terrorists a major victory. Using indiscriminate violence and oppression to combat the oppression of terrorist violence does nothing but pour oil onto a raging fire, both spreading the fire and making it more intense.

Every violation of human rights, every curtailment of freedom, every subterfuge concerning constitutional principles, every show of force which results in "collateral damage", every imprisonment of innocent people, every expression of contempt for the international community, every penny which is spent benefitting government contractors more than it does people who are being oppressed, every form of oppression which is brought about by occupying forces, every opportunity for real democracy which is undermined by the imposition of sham democracy, every denial of the real causes which help push people into dissociative conditions -- all of the foregoing mistakes of the "war on terrorism" can be woven into the fabric of the delusional paradigm of terrorists in the most problematic way. More specifically, it is not the delusion which can be shown to be completely false that constitutes the most difficult problem facing those who wish to try to realistically address the issue of terrorism ... rather, one of the biggest obstacles facing the search for peace involves those terrorist-oriented delusional systems which are laced with actual exemplars of inhumanity, cruelty, and oppression that have been committed by the other side and, thereby, lend a ring of truth and authenticity to the other false claims by the propagandists of terrorism (whether in the form of theologians, jurists, government leaders, self-styled revolutionaries, or imams).

Every time indiscriminate violence and oppression are used in an attempt to quell the tide of terrorism, one has difficulty differentiating the so-called 'good' (because it comes from us not them) forms of terrorism from those 'evil' forms of such activity which are perpetrated by

410

those whom we condemn -- and, in truth, both varieties of terrorism and oppression are equally reprehensible. Once one resorts to using the same tools of violence as extremist, fundamentalist jihadists, then, the tools of faith which are the only tools that, God willing, have the chance to solve the problems which underlie terrorism, become lost in the shuffle and with this loss, so, too, are opportunities lost for making real, lasting progress with respect to the many problems and forces which play key roles in the etiology of the dissociative states that render people vulnerable to the delusional systems of the proponents of terrorism.

Terrorism (whether state sponsored or that of a small group or set of terrorist cells) is an expression of spiritual abuse. The spiritual abuse is perpetrated through the intention of so-called 'leaders' to exploit and manipulate someone who is in a state of dissociation and to assist the latter out of that condition through a delusional system which undermines faith and is intended to induce people to replace the tools of faith with tools of violence.

As such, the intention of terrorist leaders is very similar to the intention of spiritual charlatans. Each seeks to undermine faith through initiating vulnerable people into a delusional perspective that helps lower the threshold against committing acts (violent or otherwise ... with respect to one's self or in relation to others) that are contrary to the actual requirements of spiritual etiquette.

There are legitimate forms of jihad and there are illegitimate forms of jihad. The legitimate forms of jihad have nothing to do with indiscriminate violence and, with the exception of very special and limited circumstances, have nothing to do with violence. Rather, all forms of legitimate jihad -- whether in the form of speaking the truth in the face of tyranny, or the performance of a Hajj which is accepted by God, or struggling and striving against the problematic urgings of the desires and motivations of the nafs (the seat of rebellion against Divinity in a human being) -- have to do with refining moral character through sacrifice, and not with sacrificing moral character (as well as the concomitant tools of faith which are associated with such character) through committing violence against others.

There are legitimate forms of mysticism, and there are illegitimate forms of mysticism. The legitimate forms of mysticism require the assistance of someone who is not a spiritual charlatan, just as the pursuit of authentic jihad (which only very rarely requires armed conflict and when this is truly necessary must be pursued within strict guidelines) requires assistance from those who are well ensconced in the tools of faith rather than the tools of violence.

Lightning Source UK Ltd.
Milton Keynes UK
24 October 2010

161837UK00006B/8/P